The Modern Presidency and Economic Policy

The Modern Presidency and Economic Policy

JOHN P. FRENDREIS
Department of Political Science
Loyola University of Chicago

RAYMOND TATALOVICH
Department of Political Science
Loyola University of Chicago

F.E. PEACOCK PUBLISHERS, INC.
ITASCA, ILLINOIS

Cover photo by The Image Bank/Anthony Johnson

423.93
1-87740211

To our parents, Genevieve C. and John J. Frendreis and
Mildred Tatalovich

CONTENTS

List of Figures   ix
List of Tables   xi
Preface   xiii

PART I   Economic Policy and American Politics

CHAPTER 1   *Managing the Economy*   3

CHAPTER 2   *Origins of Economic Policymaking*   19

PART II   The Development of Economic Policy

CHAPTER 3   *Economic Policymaking in the Executive Branch*   45

CHAPTER 4   *Presidential Power and Congressional Budgeting*   77

CHAPTER 5   *The Federal Reserve Board and Monetary Policy*   113

CHAPTER 6   *International Economic Policy*   139

PART III   The Politics of Economic Policy

CHAPTER 7   *Business Cycles and Postwar Macroeconomic Policy*   169

CHAPTER 8   *The Politics of Countercyclical Policy*   197

CHAPTER 9   *Public Opinion and Economic Policy*   221

PART IV   Economic Policy and Economic Performance

CHAPTER 10   *Presidential Styles of Economic Management*   255

viii   CHAPTER 11   *Responding to Fiscal Crisis: Gramm-Rudman-Hollings, the Balanced Budget Amendment, and Federal Deficits*   287

CHAPTER 12   *A Presidential Economic Scorecard*   307

Appendix: Recruitment Profiles for Key Economic Policymakers   317

Index   325

LIST OF FIGURES

Figure 1.1   Comparison of Carter's Presidency and Reagan's First Term, Selected Economic Indicators, 14

Figure 2.1   Average Monthly Deficit per Year, 1932–1941, 31

Figure 3.1   Organization of the President's Economic Advisers, 67

Figure 4.1   Deficits and Surpluses Measured in Constant (FY87) Dollars, 93

Figure 4.2   Federal Debt at End of Fiscal Year as a Percentage of GDP, FY40–FY92, 94

Figure 5.1   Organization of the Federal Reserve System, 118

Figure 6.1   U.S. Exports and Imports as a Percentage of GDP, 1959–1992, 141

Figure 6.2   Exports as a Percentage of GDP for Selected Countries, 1990, 143

Figure 7.1   Percent of Civilian Labor Force Employed, 1946–1992, 173

Figure 7.2   Unemployment and Inflation During the Truman Presidency, 1946–1952, 175

Figure 7.3   Unemployment and Inflation During the Eisenhower Presidency, 1953–1960, 178

Figure 7.4   Unemployment and Inflation During the Kennedy-Johnson Presidencies, 1961–1968, 180

Figure 7.5   Unemployment and Inflation During the Nixon-Ford Presidencies, 1969–1976, 184

Figure 7.6   Unemployment and Inflation During the Carter Presidency, 1977–1980, 187

Figure 7.7   Unemployment and Inflation During the Reagan-Bush Presidencies, 1981–1992, 189

Figure 8.1   Civilian Unemployment Rate, 1955–1969, 202

Figure 8.2   Changes in Federal Spending, FY62–FY69, Measured in Constant (FY82) Dollars, 203

Figure 8.3   Annual Rate of Inflation Before, During, and After Imposition of Nixon Administration Prices and Incomes Policy, 210

x

Figure 9.1   Monthly Unemployment Rate and Presidential Approval
                Ratings, Jan. 1989–Nov. 1992, 239
Figure 9.2   Gallup Poll Trend on Political Party Better for Prosperity,
                240
Figure 10.1   Short-Term Phillips Curve, 270
Figure 10.2   The Laffer Curve, 275

LIST OF TABLES

Table 4.1   Forecasts of Macroeconomic Conditions in Presidential Budgets, 1981–1989, 88

Table 4.2   Growth in Federal Revenues and Expenditures by Presidential Term, 1953–1992, 91

Table 4.3   Fiscal Components of Budget Deficits, 1970–1986, 95

Table 4.4   Differences Between Presidential and Congressional Budgets by Function, Fiscal Years 1983–1988, 98

Table 4.5   Federal Budget Growth vs. Population and GDP, 1929–1990, 100

Table 4.6   Federal Budget Outlays by Function, 1980 and 1990, 103

Table 5.1   Indicators of Macroeconomic Performance, 124

Table 6.1   U.S. International Transactions, 1966–68, 1970–72, 1984–86, 155

Table 6.2   Net U.S. Trade, 1984–1992, 161

Table 7.1   Business Cycle Expansions and Contractions in the U.S., 1854–1991, 171

Table 9.1   Gallup Poll Trend on "Most Important Problem," 230

Table 9.2   Public Attitudes Towards Government Spending, Selected Years 1973–1990, 233

Table 11.1   Actual vs. Full-Employment Deficits Under Reagan, 289

Table 12.1   Presidential Economic Scorecard, 308

Table A.1   Recruitment Profiles for Chairmen, Council of Economic Advisers, 1946–1993, 318

Table A.2   Recruitment Profiles for Secretaries of the Treasury, 1946–1993, 320

Table A.3   Recruitment Profiles for Director, Bureau of the Budget and Office of Management and Budget, 1946–1993, 322

Table A.4   Recruitment Profiles for Chairmen, Federal Reserve Board, 1934–1993, 324

PREFACE

The economy, it is sometimes said, is like the weather: people talk a lot about it, but nobody does anything about it. A corollary to this might be: people talk a lot about the economy, but they do not actually know much about it. A major reason for this is that the study of the economy falls mainly to economists, and modern economics can be a daunting subject, filled with mathematical formulae, complicated graphs, and specialized terms. Moreover, most people are less concerned with the functioning of the economy as it pertains to economic theory than they are to the functioning of the economy as it pertains to their lives. Thus, they are only partially concerned with how the economy works and more interested in how the economy might be made to work better.

Concern for making the economy work better is a central element of political debate and a subject that thus attracts the attention of many political scientists. Yet, despite the fact that managing economic policy is a standard topic in introductory American government classes, there are almost no books on the subject that are written in such a way as to be accessible to a general audience. As teachers and researchers, we have felt a need for such a book. This volume is the result.

The Modern Presidency and Economic Policy examines the management of the American economy. This has been a particular object of the national government—and particularly of U.S. presidents—since World War II, and we cover in detail the experiences of postwar presidents from Truman through Clinton. The book is written for several audiences. Its primary audience, we hope, will be students enrolled in classes studying the presidency, American public policy, and American economic policy. In teaching the first two types of classes, we have found that the treatments of economic policymaking in presidency and public-policy texts are much too brief to give students an adequate understanding of this vital and complex subject. We also hope the book will be read by others—students and nonstudents—who wish to learn more about economic policymaking. Finally, the book contains much information (including tables and figures) that represents original research of interest to scholars, particularly those whose previous research has dealt only indirectly with presidential economic policymaking.

xiv   The book is divided into four parts. Part I describes the goals and historical foundations of modern macroeconomic policymaking in the United States. Part II describes the mechanics of macroeconomic policymaking, including fiscal policy, monetary policy, and international economic policymaking. Part III turns to the politics of economic policymaking, describing the actions taken by the various postwar presidents to influence the economy, considered against the backdrop of the actual performance of the economy during each of their terms. Later in Part III we focus on one of the most important elements of the politics of this area, the relationship between public opinion and economic policymaking. Finally, in Part IV, we consider how well modern presidents have coped with the challenges of managing the economy, concluding the book with a "presidential economic scorecard" that assesses economic performance during each of the modern presidents' terms.

We wish to thank a number of people. Ted Peacock has provided us with constant encouragement, much more than we deserved. Norman Mysliwiec was a meticulous copy editor; his work has improved the book in many ways, large and small. A number of friends and colleagues gave us assistance and support at various stages of this project: Leo Wiegman, John McCarthy, Vince Mahler, and Robert Aduddell deserve particular mention. John W. Sloan (Department of Political Science, University of Houston), Steven Shull (Department of Political Science, University of New Orleans), and Michael Genovese (Department of Political Science, Loyola Marymount University) provided careful reviews of the entire manuscript, which greatly strengthened the final version. Finally, Laura L. Vertz and Anne K. Tatalovich provided much encouragement and assistance throughout the writing of this book, beginning with the earlier data collection and continuing through the final copy editing; Scott Frendreis provided one of the authors with the kind of necessary distractions that only a four-year-old (eventually a five-year-old, then a six-year-old) can. We hope these simple words can convey the real gratitude we feel to all of these people.

PART I

Economic Policy and American Politics

CHAPTER 1

Managing the Economy

On March 1, 1991, George Bush's presidential approval rating stood at 91 percent, the highest level recorded in more than a half century of systematic public-opinion polling. One year later, his approval had dropped to 39 percent.[1] In the process, President Bush's image had gone from that of the victor of the Persian Gulf War, viewed as virtually unbeatable for reelection to a second presidential term, to a beleaguered president whose reelection was very much in doubt and who faced powerful challenges, first from within his own party, and later from a formidable Democratic opponent.

What happened during this time that produced such a dramatic change in presidential fortunes? A number of factors contributed to the decline in President Bush's popularity (e.g., the unclear aftermath of the Gulf War and the onset of the presidential election), but the overwhelming cause of this decline was the poor performance of the U.S. economy. A lengthy downturn in the economy had begun during the summer of 1990. Although this downturn had been underway for over six months before the peak of the president's popularity in March of 1991, the approaching hostilities in the Persian Gulf had limited the degree to which the public had translated their concern over the economy into negative evaluations of presidential leadership. The public euphoria following the swift victory of allied ground forces in the spring of 1991 led, however, to public expectations that the economy would shortly begin to improve. Although some improvements were seen during the summer, by fall the performance of the economy was again faltering. As unemployment con-

4   tinued to rise, public discontent with the president's performance increased. Although George Bush was able to withstand the opposition within his own party to his renomination, he eventually was defeated in his bid for reelection in what was widely viewed as a referendum on the performance of the economy during his term in office. In effect, George Bush's political fate became inextricably linked to the public's perception of his performance as the "manager of prosperity."

PUBLIC EXPECTATIONS CONCERNING THE ECONOMY

This brief account of the changing popular fortunes of former President Bush illustrates three important facts concerning the performance of the U.S. economy and U.S. politics. First, economic performance is of great—sometimes paramount—interest to the U.S. public. It is easy to see why this is the case. Behind the mass of economic statistics that are collected and disseminated to the public are the basic realities of a person's everyday life: Do I have a job? Is my rent going up? Do groceries, children's clothes, and textbooks cost more than they did last year? Are interest rates low enough that I can afford to buy a new car or finance a home mortgage?

This is not to say that economic questions are the only ones that engage people's attention. During a war, Americans have traditionally viewed economic issues as being of less importance than questions of war and peace. At other times, other issues—crime, drugs, political scandals—may also compete for the public's attention. However, in normal times, the performance of the economy, particularly the performance of a few key indicators such as the unemployment and inflation rates, is regarded by the public as the most important issue in the political arena.

Second, the American public expects the government—and especially the president—to take actions that will improve the performance of the U.S. economy. Put somewhat differently, the American public sees the U.S. economy as something that can be manipulated by governmental policy, and it expects governmental leaders to enact public policies that lead to the achievement of beneficial economic goals, in effect, to *manage the economy*. As we shall see in Chapter 2, this is a fairly recent expectation in historical terms. Although the public has always looked to presidents and political parties for leadership during times of economic difficulty, it is only in the twentieth century that a generalized expectation has taken hold that the government, and particularly the president, should continually monitor the economy and take steps to influence its performance.

Third, there is a clear linkage between economic performance and **5** the political fortunes of our governmental leaders. Once again, this is particularly true for the president, whose popularity often waxes and wanes with major changes in such politically significant statistics as the rate of inflation and the number of unemployed persons. Indeed, the president has become so uniquely associated in the public mind with economic management that downturns in the economy are associated with losses in congressional elections by the president's party rather than with losses by the party that actually controls Congress (when Congress is controlled by the president's opposition).[2] In some ways, national elections—even for offices other than the presidency—are at least partially referenda on the performance of the economy.

MANAGING THE U.S. ECONOMY

Policy Goals in Managing the Economy

As B. Guy Peters notes, "Economic policy has a number of goals, all socially desirable but not always mutually compatible."[3] He goes on to identify the four traditional goals of economic policy, sometimes labeled the **golden quadrangle**, as "economic growth, full employment, stable prices, and a positive balance of payments from international trade."[4] Each of these goals deserves some elaboration.

Economic Growth. Economic growth essentially means an increase in the amount of goods and services produced by the economy. The value of all of the goods and services produced in a country is known as the **gross national product (GNP),** and an increase in the GNP may come about in any one of three ways:

1. More of the productive capabilities of the society are employed to produce goods and services (e.g., when more people are hired).

2. The productive capacity of the society is increased (e.g., when new factories are constructed).

3. The productivity of the existing resources is increased (e.g., workers' productivity rises due to new training or changes in production techniques).

Although undesirable costs may be incurred to achieve this economic growth, the economic growth itself is essentially beneficial, since it means that more goods and services are available to be distributed among the

6   population. Since in most societies population is generally increasing, a rising GNP (economic growth) is essential if the average person's economic position is going to be improved over time. If economic growth does not keep pace with population increases, economic gains for some must come at the expense of others, a situation that generally leads to social conflict.[5] On the other hand, if the rate of economic growth exceeds the rate of population increase, it is at least *possible* that some may gain without anyone losing, although this is not necessarily the only distribution of the additional goods and services that might result.

Another commonly reported measure of the size of the economy is the **gross domestic product (GDP).** The GNP and GDP are closely related, differing only in how they treat the goods and services produced in the U.S. by labor and property supplied by non-U.S. residents and the goods and services produced outside of the U.S. by labor and property supplied by U.S. residents. The GNP includes the latter but not the former, while the GDP includes the former but not the latter. While the distinction between GDP and GNP is important for national income calculations for some nations, in the United States they are very close—less than 1 percent apart in 1990. (Because the U.S. government reports some data series in terms of GNP and others in terms of GDP, we utilize both of these measures throughout this book.)[6]

Full Employment.   Achievement of the second broad goal of economic policy, **full employment**, means that all those willing and able to work are employed. Put somewhat differently, all of the productive human resources of a society are being employed in the production of goods and services. Note that this does not mean that all people are employed. A society may decide that some people should not or may not be employed, children for example. Alternatively, some people may not wish to be employed in the economy, for example, students or adults caring for children or other dependents. Full employment also does not mean that the unemployment rate is zero. In the United States, the **unemployment rate** is calculated as the number of unemployed persons who wish to be employed divided by that number plus the total number of employed persons.

$$\text{unemployment rate} = \frac{\text{number of unemployed}}{(\text{number of unemployed} + \text{number of employed})} \times 100$$

Experts on the labor market generally believe that it is not possible to reduce the number of unemployed persons to zero. First, at any given time, a certain number of people will be between jobs, if only temporarily. Far from being unfortunate, this is in fact desirable, since for the labor market to function efficiently employment should be constantly in a process of adjustment across geographic labor markets and different firms in order to meet new demands and to incorporate technological innovations. Second, a certain number of people may not possess the necessary skills to be productively employed within the economy. For example, there is a limit to the number of jobs that can be filled by people who are illiterate. If the number of people wishing to work who possess this limitation exceeds the number of available jobs, unemployment must result. Note that this source of unemployment is a function of two things, the skill level of the workers (what is sometimes called their human capital) and the demands of the labor market. Changes in either can cause the degree of this sort of unemployment to rise or fall.[7] This latter source of unemployment is not considered desirable, although it may result from otherwise desirable events, such as productivity-enhancing technological innovations. An obvious response to this problem, however, is to alter the workers' human capital (skill level) so that they may be productively employed, and demands are often directed toward the government to promote this sort of worker retraining.

Collectively, these two sources of unemployment produce the rate of **structural unemployment**, the level of unemployment that exists when the country is actually at the full employment level. What is this level in the United States? A traditional answer has been 3 percent unemployment, although some economists (and political leaders) would claim that the actual level is higher, perhaps as high as 5 or 6 percent. Whatever answer is given is clearly a mixture of both technical and political considerations, since it rests in part upon an assessment of how many people our society feels can or should be left in the category of unemployed workers with inadequate human capital to be productively employed.

Stable Prices. The third broad goal of economic policy is stable prices. Over time, the prices for various goods and services fluctuate. A period of generally rising prices for goods and services is described as a period of **inflation**; the opposite condition, generally falling prices, is referred to as **deflation**.[8] In the United States, price stability is measured by the government with a number of statistics, the best known of which is the **consumer price index (CPI)** (often referred to as the cost-of-living index), which calculates the current prices of a predetermined (and fixed over time) set of goods and services. The current value of the CPI is simply the ratio of the current price to the price of the same set of goods and services in the base period of 1982–84, multiplied by 100. Thus, the CPI had an average value of 100 during the period 1982–84; periods with higher prices have a CPI of more than 100, while periods with lower prices have a CPI of

8   less than 100. In August 1992, the value of the CPI was 140.9, which means that the same set of goods and services that cost $100.20 in August 1983 cost $140.90 in August 1992.[9] The CPI is calculated monthly, and a rising value indicates price inflation, while a falling value indicates price deflation.

Although in recent years the periods of inflation have far exceeded those of deflation, historically both of these patterns have been seen with regularity; and, when severe, both are highly disruptive. In general, changes in prices in either direction will produce both winners and losers. Since during inflationary periods both wages and prices tend to rise,[10] the losers tend be those for whom price increases exceed increases in wages, or more precisely, income. Thus, people on fixed incomes, such as retired people and people relying on income from long-term, fixed-interest investments, will suffer. Similarly, individuals and corporations that have made long-term loans (e.g., 30-year fixed-rate mortgages) will see these assets decline in value, since the future value of the principal (loan amount) and interest will be less than the current value of the principal. (This was one major problem faced by the savings and loan industry during the period of high inflation in the U.S. during the 1970s.) On the other side of the coin, those who have borrowed money at lower interest rates will generally gain from inflation, since their rising wages will make it easier to repay these loans. During deflationary periods, the winners and losers are reversed: people with fixed incomes and lenders are winners, while borrowers are losers. In fact, though, prolonged or severe inflation or deflation are bad in a general sense for the economy, since they make it difficult to confidently make long-term economic decisions.

Positive Balance of Payments.   The final element of the "golden quadrangle" is a positive **balance of payments** from international trade. The balance of international payments is actually made up of three components, the current account (essentially trade in goods and services), the capital account (long and short-term movement of capital), and movement of gold-and-reserve assets.[11] The most visible of these components is the current account, which is largely made up of the trade in merchandise and the so-called "invisibles," such as travel, shipping fees, and insurance fees. The current account is sometimes called the balance of trade. A situation in which the total value of all exports exceeds the total value of all imports is referred to as a positive, or "favorable," balance of trade. The reverse is a negative, or "unfavorable," balance of trade. Actually, the terms *favorable* and *unfavorable*—in fact the overall goal of a "positive balance of international payments"—are unfortunate, since there are periods in a nation's development when a negative balance is more beneficial than a positive balance. In the public mind, and in the public statements of many political leaders, a negative balance of trade or international payments appears to represent a situation where the U.S. is becoming poorer at the expense of our trading partners, but this is not necessarily the case. As we discuss more fully in Chapter 6, the merits of positive or negative international payments balances depend more on the reasons the surpluses or deficits are run rather than on the simple fact that there is a positive or negative balance. Although the public often focuses its attention on a few summary statistics such as the balance of trade, the actual goal of economic policy in the area of international economics is that the nation's economy interact with the international economy in such a way that other economic goals—stable prices, full employment, productive capital investment—are achieved. Over a very long period of time (e.g., a century) this will probably be manifested in small or moderate (but not excessively large) positive balances in international payments, although during particular periods, more benefit may come from negative balances than from positive ones.

Structural Change.   Economic policy is directed toward the achievement of goals other than the four components of the "golden quadrangle." Two are particularly worthy of mention: structural change and the distribution of wealth. The first of these has both a domestic[12] and an international dimension. On the domestic side, the U.S. economy is always in a process of change, wherein some industries are expanding while others are declining; the nature of production is being altered; and the regional (in fact, global) concentration of production is changing. A general goal of economic policy is to promote structural changes that will support the other goals, like economic growth or price stability. Historically, the major activities of the U.S. government in this regard have been one step removed from actual decisions on where and how to produce goods and services. Two examples of this less-direct form of promoting structural change are government support for infrastructure development (e.g., canals, railroads, roads) and support for education, particularly in such areas as agricultural and scientific research. A developing debate in the United States, however, is whether the government should take an even more active role in promoting structural change through the creation of a **national industrial policy**. The clearest model for such a policy is Japan, where the national government organizes and subsidizes the activities of private corporations directed at developing new industries that have significant prospects for growth, often through expanded global exports. According to some proponents of such a policy in the United States, the U.S. government should play a similar role in targeting key areas for research and new product

10   development. Opponents respond that such a policy is not necessary, since private actors will themselves identify such opportunities; in their view, government intervention simply acts to distort what they see as the more efficient decision-making processes of private corporations. Whether indirect or direct, intrusive or reactive, a portion of economic policy is directed toward the management of domestic structural change—even if only to leave it largely to the decisions of private actors.

The international dimension of the management of structural change relates to efforts to bring about structural changes in the economies of other nations or in features of the international economic system. Examples of policies directed toward this goal are actions directed toward stimulating consumer spending in certain U.S. trade partners (e.g., Japan) and toward reducing government deficits in debtor nations. The domestic and international dimensions of structural change may even converge: much of the U.S. policy debate over a national industrial policy is double-edged, dealing not only with the extent to which the U.S. government should promote such a policy domestically, but also to what extent the U.S. will be comfortable with the use of such policies by its economic competitors.

Distribution of Wealth.   A final goal of economic policy concerns the distribution of wealth. To some in the United States, the distribution of wealth is not a question addressed by economic policy; it is a given: wealth accrues to those who acquire it within the normal operation of the free-market, capitalist system. Indeed there are few people in the United States who would not broadly support some version of this statement. At the same time, the U.S. government makes few significant decisions in connection with taxing and spending that do not raise distributional questions. For example, because the portion of earnings saved (known as the marginal propensity to save) increases as personal income rises, a government interested in cutting taxes in order to increase private savings would get the greatest result by targeting the tax cut only to the wealthiest people. Because such a policy would have the added effect of literally "making the rich richer," it would in all likelihood not be adopted—not because it would not promote economic growth or stabilize prices or promote the balance of payments, but because it would alter the distribution of wealth in a way the society does not wish to see it altered. Unlike the first three goals discussed (but similar to the last one), there is no clear, consensual goal for U.S. economic policy regarding the distribution of wealth. At the same time, influencing this distribution (or not influencing it, for some) remains one of the ends against which various economic actions are measured.

The Philosophical Foundation of U.S. Economic Policy

How wealth will be generated and distributed is not only a basic issue in economics, it is one of the fundamental issues of politics. Indeed, among the most basic questions answered in each society is the one that addresses how the goods and services produced by that society will be allocated. Over the last 150 years, a fundamental debate has occurred between two theories of how this should be done: **capitalism** and **socialism.** For a number of reasons, capitalism has been the dominant economic ideology within the United States. Much of the basic debate over how to structure and manage the U.S. economy has dealt with different views of how to improve a capitalist economy rather than whether a capitalist system is itself desirable.

In very simple terms, a capitalist economic system is one in which ownership and control over the basic means of economic production—land, labor, and capital (e.g., machinery)—rests with individuals. The types, quantities, and prices of the goods and services produced by the economy are determined by a myriad of individual transactions occurring in free markets. In addition to leading to the most efficient[13] use of available resources, such a system of production and distribution maximizes individual choice and the individual pursuit of self-interest, two attributes also highly prized by the American political culture.

Rather than arguing over whether individuals or the state should own the factors of production, a basic debate within the U.S. economic context has focused on how well the U.S. capitalist system operates and whether there are circumstances in which government intervention in private markets is desirable. As we show in the next chapter, this debate commenced in earnest during the Great Depression of the 1930s, leading to fundamental changes in public expectations concerning what the government can and should do to secure economic prosperity—in effect, to the view that government action should be directed toward the achievement of the economic goals detailed above.

Policy Tools for Managing the Economy

To achieve the diverse, and sometimes conflicting, goals of economic policy, the government has three basic tools: fiscal policy, monetary policy, and regulatory policy. Since these are discussed in much greater detail in later chapters, we discuss them only briefly at this point.

Fiscal policy refers to the taxing and spending policies of the government. Since the 1930s, this has been the chief weapon in the government's economic arsenal. Fiscal policy is important in a number of ways. First,

12   the overall level of taxation and governmental spending has a powerful effect on the aggregate demand for goods and services in the country, which in turn exerts a strong influence on such things as inflation and unemployment. Since the end of World War II, and particularly during the 1960s and 1970s, the federal government has attempted to influence the economy by adjusting taxing and spending levels (and thus, the federal budget surpluses or deficits), often following an economic doctrine known as Keynesian economics, which is described in detail in the next chapter. In addition to the overall effect of fiscal policy on aggregate demand, specific elements of taxing and spending policy may also be directed at achieving the various goals of economic policy. For example, changes to the tax code may be written in such a way as to alter the distribution of income or stimulate particular kinds of economic activity. Similarly, spending decisions may be taken with an eye toward creating structural changes in the U.S. economy. A significant example of this is represented by postwar decisions on the location of major federal facilities and defense contractors, which are thought to have been influential in the transformation of the South from a relatively underdeveloped, poor region to an area of strong economic growth in the last decades of the twentieth century.[14]

Monetary policy involves the regulation of the money supply. Unlike fiscal policy, which is under the control of elected officials like the Congress and the president, control of monetary policy rests with the Federal Reserve Board, an independent body relatively insulated from the public. Through the variety of mechanisms described in Chapter 5, the Federal Reserve Board regulates the amount of money in circulation. Since money includes bank deposits and other financial instruments as well as currency, much of the Federal Reserve Board's activity is directed at financial institutions, which it also plays a role in regulating. Monetary policy is considered of great importance in regards to price stability, and, according to an economic theory known as monetarism (an alternative to Keynesian theory), may even be a more effective vehicle than fiscal policy for influencing overall economic performance.

The final major tool of economic policy, **regulatory policy**, is really a variety of devices, the common element of which is that the government attempts to control or influence the behavior of individuals and corporations,[15] in effect altering the existing operation of the marketplace. Important forms of economic regulation include the supervision of the securities markets, regulation of financial institutions, requirements concerning labeling and the disclosure of information necessary for informed behavior by consumers, establishment of procedures affecting labor relations, and the prohibition of activities regarded as anti-competitive (e.g., price-fixing). In general, regulatory policy has two basic purposes, which are not always complementary. The first is the promotion of conditions deemed necessary for the efficient functioning of the marketplace. The second is the prevention of outcomes that, while they may be the normal product of market interactions, are deemed socially undesirable. While regulatory policy is, like all political questions, the subject of much debate, it is those aspects of regulation related to the latter purpose that are the subjects of the most intense political conflict. During the Reagan and Bush presidencies there was very serious conflict over the costs and benefits of regulation, particularly over regulations—such as environmental and health and safety regulations—that are not directly concerned with the production of goods and services but that are viewed by some as having important (negative) economic effects.

Control of Economic Policy.   Control over the various tools of economic policy is not concentrated in the hands of any one political authority; rather, it is dispersed among many actors, a common feature of much of U.S. governmental policy, particularly domestic policies. (These actors and their various powers and functions are the subject of Part II of this book.) Despite this dispersion of power, from a political perspective much of the credit or blame concerning the performance of the U.S. economy goes to the president. There are at least three reasons for this. First, the president is the most visible of all governmental officials, and, particularly during the twentieth century, has come to be viewed by the public as the **"manager of prosperity."**[16] Second, the president has more direct and indirect influence over economic policy than any other actor. Through such things as the preparation of the annual budget, the exercise of influence within the legislative process, appointment of heads of regulatory bodies and executive agencies, and the statutory presidential responsibility for collecting economic statistics and describing the nation's economic health, the president plays some role in virtually every action relating to the management of the economy. Third, the quadrennial presidential election process firmly connects the performance of the economy to the political fortunes of the president in a way that is not true for any other governmental official. Whether the voters use the election as a referendum of past performance or a chance to choose among alternative futures, a significant issue in all recent presidential elections has been the performance of the economy. As a result, from a political perspective (the perspective from which this book is written), it is useful to consider the historical record of economic performance as being divided into periods defined by the terms of the various presidents. This produces, in effect, a "presidential economic scorecard."

14   RATING PRESIDENTS ON ECONOMIC PERFORMANCE

In 1984 President Reagan asked the electorate a rhetorical question, "Are you better off today than you were four years ago?" In effect, he asked them to make a comparison between economic performance during his first term in office and economic performance during the term of his predecessor, President Carter. Part of the reason for President Reagan's overwhelming reelection that year was that most of the electorate felt they could answer "yes" to his question. It is instructive to see exactly what the difference in economic performance was between the Carter and first-term Reagan presidencies.

As Figure 1.1 indicates, a comparison of the performance of the economy during Carter's presidency and Reagan's first term yields mixed results. During Reagan's first four years, the inflation rate dropped dramatically—in fact, it was even lower than the figure shows when Reagan posed his question in 1984. On the other hand, employment and economic growth

Figure 1.1   Comparison of Carter's Presidency and Reagan's First Term, Selected Economic Indicators

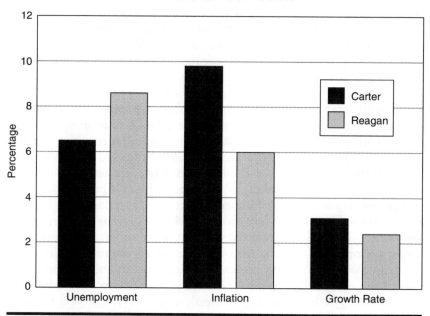

Source: Calculated by authors from data in 1992 *Economic Report of the President.* Macroeconomic indicators are four-year average unemployment rate, average yearly change in CPI over four years, and average yearly change in real GNP over four years.

were much better during the Carter years. Fortunately for Reagan, how-ever, not all economic statistics are equal in the eyes of the voters. In 1984 public satisfaction with the falling rate of inflation—coupled with an ap-parent belief that the economy was performing much better in general and the expectation that Reagan would keep taxes low—outweighed any dis-satisfaction flowing from the higher unemployment and lower growth, and Reagan was returned to office.

This suggests that popular perceptions and economic realities are not always the same. To better understand the performance of the U.S. econ-omy and assess the efforts of postwar presidents to manage it, in the last chapter of this book we will present and discuss a presidential economic scorecard. This economic scorecard is based on five macroeconomic in-dicators: GNP, unemployment, inflation, balance on the current account (i.e., balance of trade), and productivity. The first four of these relate to the four elements of the "golden quadrangle," while the fifth is considered a key element in the continued health of the economy.

The scorecard reports figures for all postwar presidential terms, begin-ning with the second Truman term, the first full term after the war's end. We begin at this point because it marks the onset of the period in which the U.S. public has had the expectation that the government, especially the president, will *manage* the economy. As we see in the next chapter, passage of the Employment Act of 1946 marks the point at which this function—previously viewed as being best left outside of the realm of government activity—was formally declared to be a responsibility of the U.S. government.

Since the postwar period includes a variety of presidents drawn from both political parties, it opens up discussion of a number of questions. Who had the best and the worst economic performance? Does political party have any relationship to macroeconomic conditions? In some ways the scorecard is as much an indication of the economic challenges faced by each president as a report on the president's performance.

To fully understand what these economic indicators suggest about presidential performance in managing the economy, we need to have a better understanding of the mechanics and politics of economic policy-making. Our purpose in describing the scorecard at this point is to set the stage for the sections that follow. In the next chapter we complete our initial overview by describing the historical origins of modern American economic policymaking. Following this, in Part II of the book we describe the important actors in economic policymaking and the mechanics of fiscal, monetary, and international economic policymaking. In Part III we focus on economic policymaking as an issue in American politics. Finally, in light of what has been learned in the intervening chapters, in Part IV

16 we consider the question of how economic policy may influence economic performance, concluding with a detailed consideration of the presidential economic scorecard.

KEY TERMS

golden quadrangle, gross national product (GNP), gross domestic product (GDP), full employment, unemployment rate, structural unemployment, inflation, deflation, consumer price index (CPI), balance of payments, national industrial policy, capitalism, socialism, fiscal policy, monetary policy, regulatory policy, manager of prosperity

ADDITIONAL READING

Dolbeare, Kenneth and Patricia Dolbeare. *American Ideologies*, 3rd ed. Chicago: Rand McNally, 1976. A brief and readable discussion of competing political ideologies within American politics.

Lieberman, Carl. *Making Economic Policy*. Englewood Cliffs, NJ: Prentice-Hall, 1991. Very short primer on the policy tools in U.S. economic policy.

Samuelson, Paul A. and William D. Nordhaus. *Economics*, 14th ed. New York: McGraw-Hill, 1992. Popular and understandable economics text, covering both microeconomics and macroeconomics.

NOTES

1. The March 1, 1991, *USA Today* poll reported a 91 percent approval rating; the March 6, 1991, *Washington Post* poll reported a 90 percent approval rating; and the February 28–March 3, 1991, Gallup Poll reported an 89 percent approval rating, the highest in Gallup's fifty-year measurement of presidential approval. The February 19–20, 1992, CNN/*USA Today* poll measured President Bush's approval at 39 percent.

2. Much has been written on this and related questions, beginning with Edward R. Tufte, "Determinants of the Outcomes of Midterm Congressional Elections," *American Political Science Review* 69 (September 1975): 812–826. This is discussed in more detail in Chapter 9.

3. B. Guy Peters, *American Public Policy: Promise and Performance*, 3rd ed. (Chatham, NJ: Chatham House, 1993), p. 174.

4. Ibid., pp. 174–175.

5. Lester Thurow, *Zero Sum Society* (New York: Basic Books, 1980).

6. A clear discussion of GNP and GDP may be found in "Gross Domestic **17** Product as a Measure of U.S. Production," *Survey of Current Business* 71 (August 1991), p. 8.

7. For example, in 1900 a large percentage of the U.S. population resided in rural areas and were employed in the agricultural sector, where skills such as literacy are less relevant. As agricultural productivity has increased during the twentieth century due to the mechanization of agriculture, the demand for un-skilled agricultural workers has decreased. If no other changes had occurred in the U.S. labor market (e.g., if the demand for urban industrial workers had not risen during the same period), this would have led to an increase in unemployment.

8. These definitions and the following discussion of price stability are taken from the discussion in Paul A. Samuelson and William D. Nordhaus, *Economics*, 14th ed. (New York: McGraw-Hill, 1992), pp. 587–594.

9. CPI figures are for CPI-U, the Consumer Price Index for all urban con-sumers, which covers approximately 80 percent of the population. Although the average CPI-U over the entire base period of 1982–84 was 100, the closest monthly figures to 100 were 99.9 in July 1983 and 100.2 in August 1983. The CPI is calculated for particular components of goods and services, such as energy, food and housing costs, and overall, that is, for all of the goods and services considered together. The overall index is the most commonly cited statistic. A new series was begun in 1987 with a 1987 base equal to 100; monthly CPI statistics continue to be reported using the 1982–84 base, although some statistics are also reported with the 1987 and 1967 bases.

10. Increases in prices and wages are obviously interrelated, since wages are an element in the cost of producing goods and services, and hence in the prices charged for these goods and services.

11. This discussion of the balance of international payments is based on Sa-muelson and Nordhaus, *Economics*, pp. 671–674.

12. This is identified as a fifth basic goal, along with the four elements of the "golden quadrangle," in Peters, *American Public Policy*, pp. 180–181.

13. It should be noted that in economic terms, efficiency means that the factors of production are employed in such a way as to obtain the greatest return, regardless of what is actually produced. It may be more efficient, in these terms, for a society to produce luxury speedboats for the wealthy than enough food for the poor—if these goods compete for the same factors of production and the wealthy are willing to pay more for speedboats than the poor are willing (or able) to pay for food.

14. See Kirkpatrick Sale, *Power Shift* (New York: Random House, 1975); and David C. Perry and Alfred J. Watkins (eds.), *The Rise of the Sunbelt Cities* (Beverly Hills: Sage, 1977).

15. Kenneth J. Meier, *Regulation: Politics, Bureaucracy, and Economics* (New York: St. Martin's Press, 1985), p.1.

16. Clinton Rossiter, *The American Presidency* (New York: Harcourt Brace and World, 1960), p. 37.

CHAPTER 2

Origins of Economic Policymaking

To many people *economics* is a technical term for, as L. M. Fraser stated fifty years ago, "a system of theoretical and positive knowledge," whereas the older term *political economy* embraces institutional arrangements and public policy and carries a strong normative connotation that the government *ought* to guide the workings of the economic system.[1] The concept of **political economy** is that the government and the economy are never entirely separate institutions, although the degree of integration can vary widely according to time and place. A wide range is possible in this degree of integration; the political economy under eighteenth century laissez faire principles allowed only a small role for government, whereas "democratic socialism" in modern European nations signifies that government owns the means of production in sectors like banking, heavy industry, and mining.

In the United States, popular support for an activist federal role in the macroeconomy was the political legacy of the Great Depression and the election of President Franklin D. Roosevelt in 1932. Roosevelt's victory was the culmination of an emerging political coalition of "have-nots" that began in 1928 (but whose presidential candidate, Democrat Alfred E. Smith, was defeated). The working classes, Catholic immigrant groups, rural southern blacks, intellectuals, and union organizers who voted for FDR made demands for social justice and progressive reforms.

The 1932 presidential election not only established the political hegemony of the Democratic party for a generation but, more importantly, set the political stage for FDR's New Deal, Keynesianism, and ultimately

20   the Employment Act of 1946. Together these episodes defined a new political economy for the modern United States, one in which the laissez faire policies that dominated the period before the 1930s were replaced by an expectation that government should and would intervene in the economy in order to bring about improved economic performance. Before considering how this policy shift came about, we need to better understand the intellectual arguments concerning the proper role of government in regulating the economy, in particular, the competing arguments of classical laissez faire economics and Keynesian economics. Following this discussion, we will turn to an examination of the historical developments that resulted in the U.S. government's assumption of the role of macroeconomic manager.

THEORIES OF POLITICAL ECONOMY

As we noted in Chapter 1, throughout U.S. history there has been broad, consensual support for a capitalist economic order. A capitalist economic system is one in which there is private ownership of the means of production and in which a large portion of economic decisions are made by private, self-interested actors. Even in such a system, however, government has a role to play. This role may range from a fairly minimal one—a neutral referee for private economic interactions, basically limited to protecting private property rights and enforcing contracts—to a much more activist one—where government action is viewed as an essential supplement to private actions in bringing about socially desirable economic outcomes.

Laissez Faire

After the Civil War the federal government's role in the economy was fairly limited, the chief policies being tariffs designed to promote industrialization, support for land-grant colleges to encourage agricultural research and development, and land-grant subsidies to encourage western development. Later, political agitation by small farmers and rural interests led to the first regulation of railroads when the Interstate Commerce Commission was established in 1887. But macroeconomic policymaking was an alien concept; the **business cycle**—the fact that economic performance alternated between good and bad times—was an accepted fact of life for most Americans. As President Warren G. Harding declared in 1921: "There has been vast unemployment before and there will be again. There will be depression and inflation just as surely as the tides ebb and flow."[2]

This sentiment reflected the influence of **classical** or **laissez faire ec-** **21** **onomics**. Coined by Gournay, a French physiocrat, the term is derived from the phrase, *"laisser faire, laissez passer, le monde va de lui-meme"* (let do, let go, and the world goes on by itself). Laissez faire doctrine was popularized in 1776 by the Scotsman Adam Smith in his famous *Inquiry into the Nature and Causes of the Wealth of Nations*. That treatise argued that labor, capital, and land are the resources of production that generate a nation's wealth, which then is distributed among the suppliers of those resources as wages, profits, and rent.

According to this theory, a nation's wealth is increased by free private enterprise, unrestrained by government regulations so that individuals can pursue their own economic self-interest. When someone maximizes the product of his labor, Smith wrote, "he intends only his gain, and he is in this . . . led by an invisible hand to promote an end which is no part of his intention. . . . By pursuing his own interest he frequently promotes that of society more effectively than when he really intends to promote it."

The keystone to Smith's political economy was the "obvious and simple system of natural liberty" under which self-seeking individuals influenced by automatic ("invisible hand") market forces provide for the nation's collective economic well-being. Competition among entrepreneurs would give consumers the best products at the lowest prices; therefore government had only a few duties to perform: provide for the common defense, administer justice, subsidize public works, safeguard foreign commerce, support elementary schools, and maintain "the Sovereign or Commonwealth."

Over the next 150 years the primary concern of economists schooled in the classical tradition was what is now known as *microeconomics*. It sought to understand how prices allocate scarce resources among competing markets, but the critical question—will those resources find any employment at all—was not asked because it was assumed. Their microeconomic framework assumed that as each individual market reaches an "equilibrium" stage then the sum of all markets would give rise to full employment. Whatever resources did not find employment through the market mechanism were either not employable or voluntarily held off the market.

Since 1830 there had been periodic interest in the business cycle, but economic contractions were essentially neglected in the study of microeconomics. If markets tend toward equilibrium, then the business cycle is merely a temporary imbalance between supply and demand in one or several markets, and the economy would be self-correcting in the long run. Simply give the free market enough time, and everyone seeking work will find employment. Any firms producing goods that were not being pur-

22   chased had only to adjust both wages and the prices of the goods based on market signals in order to clear their inventories.

Classical economists believed that competition among self-interested consumers, businesses, and resource suppliers, operating through markets that cleared due to supply and demand, would correct downturns and yield economic growth. This wisdom of laissez faire economics was always at odds with the reality of the business cycle, but its theoretical position held sway until 1936, when the English economist John Maynard Keynes introduced a revolutionary new understanding of economic processes.

Keynes and Macroeconomics

Keynes's theories gained acceptance, however, because the political underpinnings of laissez faire orthodoxy were shattered by the economic collapse of the 1930s. As columnist Walter Lippmann observed in 1935, the "acceptance by the government of responsibility for recovery . . . mark great changes in a political system that until 1929 was committed to the general doctrine of *laissez faire*."[3]

Not until the 1948 publication of Paul Samuelson's *Economics: An Introductory Analysis* was the discipline of economics separated into "micro" and "macro" economics. And like his text (now in its fourteenth edition), this distinction has endured because Samuelson formally recognized the importance of macroeconomics in our lives. But its intellectual legacy began with the publication by John Maynard Keynes of *The General Theory of Employment, Interest, and Money* in 1936. This is the book that founded a "Keynesian revolution" and forced economists to ask questions previously ignored or assumed away.[4]

Macroeconomics analyzes four broad sectors of the economy—business, households, the foreign sector, and government. Businesses buy resources (raw materials) and sell goods and services. Households sell resources and buy goods and services. The foreign sector makes purchases and sells goods, services, and resources. Government buys goods and services but also derives revenue from businesses, households, and foreign concerns through taxes. Businesses and households, on the other hand, receive income from government as "transfer payments" that are unrelated to the buying or selling of resources or goods and services. Examples are Social Security benefits, welfare checks, and grants to aid research and development.

The four sectors interact in resources and goods/services markets to generate the flow of income received and the flow of product (or expenditures) produced. It was Keynes who first explained these methods by which national income is determined. **National income** equals the total expenditures for goods and services by those who buy them for consumption or investment. This is the flow of expenditures definition. National income is also the total money paid by producers as income through wages, interest, profits, and rent. Income is received by individuals who then either spend the money on the consumption of goods and services or save it. National income equals consumption plus savings.

The key macroeconomic question is, will the level of income (from total output) be enough to generate full employment of resources? Once an equilibrium (or stable) level of national income is achieved, Keynes argued, it will not change unless the determinants of national income—consumption or investment—are changed. Keynes's unique insight was that *any* level of national income could be an equilibrium level, although that amount may not be sufficient to yield full employment. Keynes concluded that depressions may not be temporary departures from full employment but rather a permanent condition. This was a radical break from laissez faire orthodoxy, which had held that the natural working of the marketplace (the "invisible hand") would lead to a natural equilibrium point that was at the full-employment level.

In both the Keynesian and classical views, the quantity of goods and services produced (output) and the prices of these goods and services are determined by the aggregate demand for goods and services by society and the aggregate supply of goods and services by society, i.e., the equilibrium point is the intersection of aggregate demand and aggregate supply curves.[5] The two views differed in terms of how they saw changes in aggregate demand influencing output and prices. For classical economists, changes in aggregate demand could only affect prices, since natural adjustments of wages and prices would always insure that the equilibrium point was at the full-employment level. In contrast, Keynes viewed depressions and severe recessions as being produced by an inadequate level of aggregate demand. By boosting aggregate demand, output (and hence employment) could be increased, often with little effect on prices.

But what could increase aggregate demand? With some simplifications, aggregate demand may be seen as being composed of three elements: private consumption, investment by businesses, and government spending for goods and services. Keynes's revolutionary insight was to argue that government could be the agent for increasing aggregate demand, either directly through an increase in its own spending or indirectly through reductions in taxes, which would stimulate private consumption and investment (because of increased savings).

In a depression, only the government can act to increase aggregate demand, because high unemployment will result in a decline in consumer spending and—since inventories of goods are increasing—in business in-

24   vestment as well. Keynes argued that fiscal policy—cutting taxes and raising expenditures—is a much more effective strategy to generate economic
recovery than monetary policy (cutting interest rates to increase the supply
of money and credit).[6] He debunked the value of balanced budgets and
alleged, to the contrary, that deficit spending was essential during times
of economic contraction.

With monetary policy neutralized, Keynes concluded that *only* fiscal
stimulus could be effective when interest rates were low relative to historic
levels. Either an increase in government spending (with taxes held constant) or a reduction in taxes (with government spending held constant)
was needed to increase aggregate demand and shift the equilibrium point
toward the full employment level. This means *deficit* financing.

Although during the 1930s interest was essentially focused on
Keynes's prescriptions for an economy operating at a level below full employment, his theory also had applicability to combating inflation in an
economy operating at the full employment level. Under conditions of full
employment, inflation was seen as being created by excess demand—in
effect, by a level of demand that was seeking more goods than the economy
could produce, thereby bidding up the price of the goods being produced.
The Keynesian remedy for this condition is precisely the opposite of the
recessionary prescription: an increase in taxes or a reduction in governmental spending, either or both of which should lead to a governmental
surplus. Thus, in the long run, the government budget should basically be
in balance, alternating between surpluses to combat inflation and deficits
to combat recessions and depressions.

The political implications flowing from the growing acceptance of
Keynes's view that monetary policy had to be relegated to a secondary
role are great. **Keynesian economics** stresses an activist fiscal policy by the
national government, assigning a continuous and large role to the public
sector in the macroeconomy, and thereby sounding the death knell for
pure laissez faire economics. Before turning to our detailed examination
of the economic and political events through which Keynes's views came
to dominate economic policymaking in the U.S., we need to briefly discuss
a later challenge to the Keynesian view, supply-side economics.

A Challenge to Keynesianism: Supply-Side Economics

By the 1960s, Keynesian economics had become the dominant
theory of the political economy in the United States, at least in governmental circles, if not in academe. In recent decades, the orthodoxy of the
Keynesian "new economics" (as it became known in the 1960s) has been
challenged several times—first by monetarism, then by rational expecta-

tions theory, and most recently by supply-side economics.[7] Of these, the latter has been the most important politically, representing one of the major intellectual underpinnings for the economic policies of Presidents Reagan and Bush. The economic policies of these two presidents are discussed in later sections; here we wish to focus on the theoretical challenge represented by the supply-side view.[8]

In many ways, **supply-side economics** represents a return to the themes of classical economics, drawing on the views of such classical figures as Adam Smith, J. B. Say, and James Mill.[9] Like other challenges to Keynesianism, it argues that Keynesian economics, particularly as applied to the contemporary U.S. economy, places too much emphasis on management of aggregate demand. In particular, this is seen as a short-term view, of greatest applicability in combating a temporary severe economic downturn like the Great Depression, but of little use in changing the long-term potential of the economy or in combating inflation. The centerpiece of supply-side economics is the argument that economic production will be enhanced, both in the short run and, more importantly, in the long run, by increasing the incentives of producers to invest in new production. This not only will lead to enhanced productivity through new investment, but will also address the problem of inadequate demand through the operation of Say's Law, which states that supply generates its own demand (e.g., newly employed workers will purchase more goods). The key macroeconomic tool for supply-side theorists is the reduction of tax rates, with a secondary emphasis on the elimination of a substantial amount of existing governmental regulations that affect economic decision making. Together with monetary policies aimed at making credit available while holding down the inflation rate, these prescriptions are advanced by supply-side advocates as being more effective than the Keynesian demand-side policies discussed above.

Contemporary Mainstream Economics

As it evident from this discussion, economists do not speak with one voice in their analyses of macroeconomic processes or preferred macroeconomic public policies. Throughout this book, we will speak of a **mainstream economic** view. What does this mean? According to Samuelson and Nordhaus, mainstream economics is an amalgamation of the Keynesian new economics of the 1960s with the neoclassical economic views of late nineteenth century economists like Leon Walrus, a viewpoint they term "neo-Keynesian."[10] Put somewhat differently, the mainstream economic viewpoint is one that accepts the Keynesian ideas that aggregate demand strongly affects the level of short-term economic activity and that

151, 520

26   government fiscal policies can alter the aggregate level of demand. At the same time, the mainstream viewpoint also partially accepts the insights of alternative schools, such as the monetarists' emphasis on monetary supply and the rational expectationists' and supply-side view that microeconomic incentives to suppliers can significantly affect macroeconomic performance.

Gabriel Almond has described the field of political science as being characterized by several distinct sects or schools of thought seated at "separate tables," speaking mainly to themselves. However, he sees most political scientists as being in a "cafeteria of the center," in which they accept some of the insights of these separate tables, yet decline to follow strictly the views of any one sect.[11] In some sense this is also true of economics, although there is a much greater area of commonality amongst economists, principally over the operation of microeconomics. In the realm of macroeconomics, however, there are clear divisions between the nearly libertarian Chicago School, rational expectationists, supply siders, Marxian radical economists, and 1960s-style Keynesians. Some of these schools, such as the Chicago School, whose members have won several Nobel prizes in economics, have achieved great prominence. Yet most economists—those we term the mainstream economists—are not adherents of any one school but are rather located in their own cafeteria of the center, incorporating elements from each of the schools but beginning with a neo-Keynesian view of the macroeconomy.

GOVERNMENT MANAGEMENT OF THE MACROECONOMY

The Great Depression

On October 28, 1929—"Black Monday"—over 9 million shares of stock were sold at a lossed value of $14 million. The next day 16 million more shares were traded. By today's standards (for example the record 604 million shares traded on October 19, 1987) this activity seems inconsequential, but during the 1920s that volume was enormous. Although stock prices had in fact been slowly falling since the late summer, this massive collapse of investor confidence in late October has come to represent in the public mind the onset of the massive economic downturn that followed.

The stock market collapse did not cause the **Great Depression**, though it undermined business confidence, and thus discouraged capital investment. As a result, employment, production, and prices all fell dramatically from 1929 through March 1933, the low point of the economic cycle (what economists call the "trough" of the business cycle). There was **27** modest economic improvement during the early years of the New Deal, but in 1937–38, another recession within the Great Depression occurred. This monumental collapse of America's economy lasted twelve years, from 1929 until 1941, and not until America entered World War II as the "arsenal of democracy" did the nation reach full employment again.[12]

Gross National Product in real terms (after dollar amounts are adjusted for increases or decreases in prices) dropped by one-third, reflecting a massive loss of industrial production, and staggering numbers of Americans were thrown out of work. Only 3.2 percent of the work force was unemployed in 1929, but this rose steadily to 24.9 percent—one-fourth of the work force—in 1933. Although prices fell during this period of deflation, the decrease was less than the drop in incomes, so real per capita disposable (after tax) personal income fell from $1,236 in 1929 to $893 in 1933. Because people could no longer afford to purchase consumption goods, corporate profits plummeted so much that, by 1932–33, the cost of production exceeded business revenue. Since there was excess industrial capacity in the nation, businesses had no incentive to expand or upgrade plants and equipment.

The Government Responds to the Depression

Although federal spending almost tripled as a percentage of GNP during the period from 1929 to 1933, the infusion of public funds was inadequate to reverse the economy's sharp downward trend. The spending increase was not part of an effort to increase federal expenditures to counteract the depression, however, because President Hoover viewed government frugality as essential to economic recovery. Since he believed that a balanced budget was essential to economic recovery, in the spring of 1932 Hoover urged economy measures on Congress and increases in personal, corporate, and estate taxes. In the end, a steadily deteriorating economy defeated his strenuous efforts to bring expenditures and revenues into balance.

At this time the Democratic party also subscribed to the then orthodox view of the necessity of balancing the budget, and the deficits were exploited by candidate Roosevelt in the 1932 presidential campaign. FDR called the 1933 deficit of over $1.6 billion "so great that it makes us catch our breath," and he declared: "The budget is not balanced, and the whole job must be done over again in the next session of Congress."[13] One week after his inauguration, President Roosevelt again spoke at length about the evils of the deficit: "It has contributed to the recent collapse of our banking structure. It has added to the ranks of the unemployed." And he

28   warned: "Too often in recent history liberal governments have been wrecked on the roots of loose fiscal policy. We must avoid this danger."[14] To put government's finances in order, FDR acted to fulfill the 1932 Democratic party plank calling for a balanced budget. At his urging, Congress adopted the Economy Act on March 20, 1933, which reduced the pay of federal employees and benefits paid to veterans in order to save $450 million.

Roosevelt's policy of retrenchment was only temporary, as he came to appreciate that government could not provide work-relief to the unemployed within the limits of a balanced budget. After a brief period of initial caution, FDR moved boldly to confront the economic crisis by using a three-pronged strategy: *relief* for the jobless, *reform* of capitalism, and *recovery* from the economic contraction. The policies enacted toward this end are the heart of the Roosevelt program known as the **New Deal**.

Federal deficits resulted because Roosevelt wanted to spend money on these relief, reform, and recovery programs. FDR's approach was essentially pragmatic rather than philosophical, being guided throughout the Great Depression by economic realities. The fact that deficit financing might increase aggregate demand and have an expansionary impact on the economy was not the driving motivation behind the New Deal programs. Government at all levels provided direct relief to the unemployed, and the federal government first became involved when the Federal Emergency Relief Act of 1933 was enacted. But the huge numbers of jobless and the slowness of direct relief efforts caused FDR to turn to public works and work-relief as more effective ways to reach the needy. The Public Works Administration (PWA) was created in 1933 to employ laborers on huge construction projects. Later the Civil Works Administration (CWA) and the Works Progress Administration (WPA) hired the able-bodied to build public works; the Civilian Conservation Corps (CCC) gave unemployed youth training while upgrading the nation's forests and parks; and the National Youth Administration (NYA) provided work to help high school and college students earn income to pay their expenses. At the height of this effort in early 1934 about 7,900,000 households with 28,000,000 members were getting some kind of aid.[15]

Other programs were enacted to use federal regulatory authority to reform business practices, labor-management relations, and social welfare. The Federal Deposit Insurance Corporation (FDIC) guaranteed deposits should banks fail; the Securities and Exchange Commission (SEC) regulated stock and bond markets; and the National Labor Relations Board (NLRB) monitored the efforts of workers who wished to organize unions. The Social Security Act of 1935 created the modern system of social-welfare through pensions for the retired, welfare for the blind, disabled, and needy, and a federal-state cooperative program of unemployment compensation for people temporarily out of work. The Fair Labor Standards Act of 1938 required minimum wages and maximum hours for workers engaged in interstate commerce.

Although the New Dealers viewed work-relief and reform as aiding the cause of economic recovery, their main assault on the Great Depression called for, as FDR told Congress, "the machinery necessary for a great cooperative movement throughout all industry in order to obtain wide reemployment, to shorten the working week, to pay a decent wage for the shorter week, and to prevent unfair competition and disastrous overproduction."[16] On June 16, 1933 the National Industrial Recovery Act (NIRA) was enacted, to be administered by the National Recovery Administration (NRA). Each industry was urged to formulate a "code of fair competition," which established fair practices regarding wages, hours, working conditions, and collective bargaining. The NRA approved these codes, after which they were binding on all companies within the industry whether or not they voluntarily joined the NRA. The first was the Cotton Textile Code of July 9, 1933. By May 1935, there were 557 basic and 189 supplemental codes affecting about 95 percent of all industrial workers.[17]

The New Deal's counterpart for the farm sector was the Agricultural Adjustment Act of May 12, 1933. Farmers had not enjoyed the prosperity of the 1920s, and things only worsened when the depression hit. Since commodity prices were falling, farmers tried increasing output in order to maintain their income, but this action only further depressed farm prices. The fundamental cause of low farm income, Roosevelt believed, was the crop surpluses. The purpose of the AAA was to guarantee that farm producers would obtain the same purchasing power relative to the value of nonfarm goods that existed during the "base period" of 1910–1914, a time of general farm prosperity. Local associations of farmers and allotment committees would assign production quotas to each farm and monitor compliance. The farmers who entered into these agreements kept production within the allotments set and received payments from the federal government, funded by a tax levied on the food processors.

The NRA and AAA were essentially public cartels aimed at restricting the operation of the free market in the interest of achieving a socially desirable outcome through government planning. But they were short-lived experiments. The NIRA was nullified by the Supreme Court in 1935 in the case of *Schechter Poultry Corp. v. United States*, while the AAA was held to be unconstitutional one year later in the case of *United States v. Butler*. In both cases the Supreme Court felt the exercise of such power exceeded the authority of the federal government.

30   After the AAA and the NIRA were declared unconstitutional Roosevelt had to think about alternatives to generate economic recovery. Historians call the period that followed the Second New Deal, with a shift away from regulation and planning and toward the use of fiscal policy to stimulate economic growth. This development parallels the rise of the new economics as taught by Keynes and his growing numbers of disciples.

Countercyclical Policy in the 1930s

A deep recession during 1937–1938 stalled the recovery, and Roosevelt reacted by using increased public works spending through the WPA. This new downturn prompted New Dealers to reconsider their position on budgets and fiscal policy. Some of FDR's advisers had long argued against efforts to balance the budget, and as early as 1933 Rexford G. Tugwell stated: "We cheerfully and without criticism raised some 20 billions of dollars in two years to fight a war in 1917–1918, and no one ever questioned its repayment."[18] But a more powerful rationale had surfaced when professional economists began to challenge the wisdom of balanced budgets.

Even before Keynes, some economists in Great Britain and the United States understood that planned countercyclical public spending has an expansionary effect on the economy whether financed by tax increases or by government borrowing and deficits.[19] In the 1920s, such thinkers as William T. Foster, Waddill Catchings, and Sumner Slichter tried to re-educate Herbert Hoover on the subject, but he remained unconvinced. Economists began to advance the so-called "pump-priming" theory. As economist Alvin H. Hansen explained, pump-priming meant that "a certain volume of public spending, varying under different conditions, will have the effect of setting the economy going on the way toward full utilization of resources on its own power, without further aid from government spending."[20] This view argued that federal deficit spending was needed as a *temporary* stimulation for the economy, which afterwards would recover and expand towards full employment. As we know from above, Keynes extended this reasoning even further by arguing that government intervention in the economy must be *permanent* to assure a condition of full employment. In modern economics this strategy is called **countercyclical fiscal policy**, wherein the government acts to directly stimulate the economy through job training, public employment, and unemployment insurance programs whenever the economy enters a trough in the business cycle and employment falls.

Despite the changing views among scholars, there still was no conscious embrace of Keynes's views among policymakers. In June 1934

Keynes had recommended that federal deficit spending needed to reach **31** $400 million per month in order to bring about economic recovery. That year he also met with President Roosevelt, but he later told Frances Perkins that he had "supposed the President was more literate, economically speaking"; to Alvin Johnson he reiterated, "I don't think your President Roosevelt knows anything about economics."[21] But he was not alone in this respect. With the exception of Marriner Eccles (chairman of the Federal Reserve Board) and Lauchlin Currie (an Eccles aide who became the first economic specialist in the White House under FDR), no leading figure in the Roosevelt administration understood how to use fiscal policy to bring about economic recovery.[22]

In fact, the United States did not reach Keynes's target of deficit spending until 1941, when the nation prepared for World War II. Figure 2.1 shows the average monthly deficit incurred each year during 1932–

Figure 2.1   Average Monthly Deficit per Year, 1932–1941

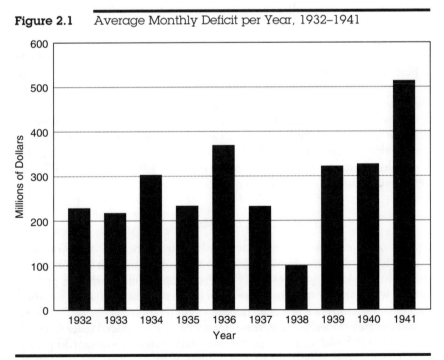

Source: U.S. Department of Commerce, Bureau of the Census, *Historical Statistics of the United States: Colonial Times to 1957* (Washington, DC: U.S. Government Printing Office, 1957), p. 711.

32   1941. It is noteworthy that the sharp decline in deficit spending between 1936 and 1938 coincided with a new recession.

From the technical perspective of fiscal policy, the New Deal was no success story. As E. Cary Brown observes, fiscal policy "seems to have been an unsuccessful recovery device in the thirties—not because it did not work, but because it was not tried."[23] Brown estimated the net contribution of government spending and tax policy toward moving the GNP to the full-employment level, and he determined that the federal impact never exceeded 2.5 percent of the needed full-employment level. The significant drop from 1936 to 1937 meant that in the latter year the federal government deficit had a negligible 0.1 percent stimulative impact on the GNP, which served to trigger the recession that followed. By 1940, Keynes was distressed by the failure of countercyclical spending in the United States. "It seems politically impossible," he wrote, "for a capitalistic democracy to organize expenditures on the scale necessary to make the grand experiment which would prove my case—except in war conditions."[24] That insight very shortly proved to be prophetic.

In the end, World War II ended the Great Depression—thanks to a massive dose of deficit spending. In 1941 the federal government spent $13.2 billion and ran a $6.1 billion deficit. But during 1942–45 total spending was nearly $307 billion, and the federal deficit exceeded $184 billion, as revenues accounted for only 40 percent of expenditures. At the end of the war, the federal debt stood at more than $250 billion, six times the figure of 1940. These huge expenditures coupled with the war's manpower requirements (12 million men under arms) caused the economy to achieve full employment. As late as 1941 the jobless rate was 9.9 percent, almost three times the 1929 level. Over the next four years, however, the unemployment rate fell steadily to 4.7 percent, 1.9 percent, and 1.2 percent, rising slightly to 1.9 percent in 1945.

The Employment Act of 1946

An economic contraction had followed the end of World War I, and the Roosevelt administration wanted to prevent that from happening again. On January 5, 1942, FDR stated: "I am confident that by prompt action we shall control the price development now and that we shall prevent the recurrence of a deep depression in the postwar period."[25] Three years later he pondered the adverse impact of much reduced federal spending in his 1945 budget message. He said that "full employment in peacetime can be assured only when the reduction in war demand is approximately offset by additional peacetime demand from millions of consumers, businesses, and farmers, and by federal, state, and local governments."[26]

The rising intellectual influence of Keynesian economics, the experience with full employment during World War II, and vivid memories of the Great Depression (coupled with concerns that a postwar recession might occur) led Congress to enact the **Employment Act of 1946** (Public Law 79-304). This statute put the national government on record as being responsible for the health of America's economy. This conscious decision to redefine the government's responsibility—rather than the temporary (if sometimes massive) employment initiatives of the 1930s—represents the clear turning point toward Keynesian economics in U.S. policymaking.

The legislative battle over passage of this act showed that classical economics was by no means a dead issue, however. The proposal caused tremendous hostility in the business community, among Republicans, and among political conservatives who feared giving the chief executive direct authority over the economy. As a result, the 1946 act is a milestone not only for its symbolism, but also for what it failed to achieve.

This statute was approved by the House of Representatives by a lopsided 320–84 vote on February 6, 1946, and passed by the Senate without opposition two days later. When final enactment is this easy, either the bill is very consensual or (as in this case) its most controversial provisions have been removed prior to final consideration. In particular, PL 79-304 sets economic goals for the national government, but it stops short of giving the president any mandate to implement Keynesian economics. The declaration of policy in Section 2 seems substantial:

> The Congress hereby declares that it is the continuing policy and responsibility of the federal Government to use all practicable means consistent with its needs and obligations and other essential considerations of national policy with the assistance and cooperation of industry, agriculture, labor, and state and local governments, to coordinate and utilize all its plans, functions, and resources for the purpose of creating and maintaining, in a manner calculated to foster and promote free competitive enterprise and the general welfare, conditions under which there will be afforded useful employment, for those able, willing, and seeking to work, and to promote maximum employment, production, and purchasing power.

It is politically significant that this language does *not* mandate a full-employment policy; the only thing stipulated is that government create the conditions under which persons willing and able to work can find jobs. Its commitment is to "maximum" (not full) employment along with maximum production and purchasing power. And these goals are supposed to be attained in a manner designed "to foster and promote free competitive enterprise," an affirmation of laissez faire principles. These compromises—

34   and the significant omission of policy tools to carry out the act's broad
goals—are a reflection of the act's tortured legislative history.

The Employment Act was authored by Senator James E. Murray (D-
MT), a progressive reformer and opponent of big business.[27] Initially his
efforts were backed by only a few lobbyists from liberal groups and organized labor, but Murray sensed a political opportunity to promote this legislation. In the 1943 State of the Union Message, Roosevelt remarked that
"[war veterans] will have the right to expect full employment—full employment for themselves and for all able-bodied men and women in America who want to work."[28] That goal was also endorsed by his party's 1944
platform that stated: "The Democratic party stands on its record in peace
and in war. To speed victory, establish and maintain peace, guarantee full
employment and provide prosperity. . . ."[29] Even the Republicans echoed
this sentiment, with their party's 1944 platform calling for "the fullest
stable employment through private enterprise," and their presidential candidate, New York Governor Thomas E. Dewey, even declaring at one
campaign stop:

> Government's first job in the peacetime years ahead will be to see that
> conditions exist which promote widespread job opportunities in private
> enterprise. . . . If at any time there are not sufficient jobs in private en-
> terprise to go around, the government can and must create job oppor-
> tunities. . . .[30]

Senator Murray dramatized the problem when the War Contracts
Subcommittee, which he chaired, drafted the report "Legislation for Re-
conversion and Full Employment" to outline his proposal. It declared that
every "American able to work and willing to work has the right to a useful
and remunerative job in the industries or shops or offices or farms or mines
of the nation." The federal role was explicit: "It is the responsibility of
the government to guarantee that right by assuring continuing full employment." The report embraced the Keynesian model for generating full
employment through public spending by proposing a "National Employment and Production Budget" to estimate how many jobs were needed to
assure full employment and the projected GNP necessary to generate that
number of jobs. Congress would be authorized to appropriate whatever
funds were necessary to eliminate any "deficiency" in the national budget
to achieve the full-employment level of GNP.

These far-reaching recommendations did not, however, appear in the
draft legislation Murray introduced in the Senate. Murray and his allies
correctly sensed the mood of the opposition: veterans groups, trade associations, wealthy farmers, the Republican party, and political conservatives. They opposed the wording "full employment" and any government

"guarantee" of the right to work as well as the reliance on federal spending as the policy instrument to achieve a full-employment level of GNP. The conservatives were not unsympathetic to the notion of full employment but attacked the philosophy underlying Murray's bill as being un-American and smacking of totalitarianism.

Nor was the opposition impressed with John Maynard Keynes. Because he frontally attacked laissez faire economics and justified massive government intervention in the macroeconomy, the critics branded Keynes a radical and a socialist. However, Robert Heilbroner argues that "it would be a grave error in judgment to place this man, whose aim was to rescue capitalism, in the camp of those who want to submerge it."[31] Keynes was an economic conservative in the same sense as Roosevelt. Both sought to safeguard capitalistic institutions and economic freedom. As he concluded in *The General Theory*:

> [While] the enlargement of the functions of government, involved in the task of adjusting to one another the propensity to consume and the inducement to invest, would seem to a nineteenth-century publicist or to a contemporary American financier to be a terrific encroachment on individualism, I defend it, on the contrary, both as the only practicable means of avoiding the destruction of existing economic forms in their entirety and as the condition of the successful functioning of individual initiative.[32]

Advocates of full employment controlled the deliberations in the Senate, but Murray's bill still had to be weakened to secure its passage. In the words of one participant, what emerged from the Senate was a law that "promised anyone needing a job the right to go out and look for one."[33] The Senate bill articulated a full-employment goal but refused to authorize the federal government to spend whatever moneys were needed to assure a full-employment level of GNP. A conservative coalition of Republicans and southern Democrats dominated the outcome in the House; the House deliberations were also influenced by President Truman's lukewarm support for the bill.

A House-Senate stalemate led to a conference committee to resolve the differences, and President Truman actively joined the struggle to promote the Senate version. However, more compromises had to be made, for example, "maximum" replacing "full" employment in the policy declaration. The result was a much watered-down employment bill that easily obtained overwhelming majorities in both chambers. What was salvaged in this new law?

First, the Employment Act required the president sixty days after the beginning of Congress to submit to the legislature an "Economic Report" detailing

(1) the levels of employment, production, and purchasing power obtaining in the United States and such levels needed to carry out the policy declared in Section 2; (2) current and foreseeable trends in the levels of employment, production, and purchasing power; (3) a review of the economic program of the federal government and a review of economic conditions affecting employment in the United States or any considerable portion thereof during the preceding year and of their effect upon employment, production, and purchasing power; and (4) a program for carrying out the policy declared in Section 2, together with such recommendations for legislation as he may deem necessary or desirable.

Second, it established a **Council of Economic Advisers (CEA)** within the Executive Office of the President. Composed of three members appointed by the president with the advice and consent of the Senate, the council was supposed to analyze and interpret economic developments, evaluate programs and government activities, and formulate and recommend national economic policy. The CEA was also directed to give the president an annual report each December.

Third, the Employment Act created a Joint Committee on the Economic Report in Congress, consisting of seven Senators and seven Representatives. Renamed the **Joint Economic Committee** in 1954, its three functions were (1) to study the Economic Report, (2) "to study means of coordinating programs in order to further the policy of this Act," and (3) to issue, no later than May 1 of each year, a report to guide the House and Senate standing committees. Unfortunately, the Joint Economic Committee has failed to exert much leadership over fiscal policy, and budgetary reforms enacted in 1974 delegated more authority over these matters to newly created Budget Committees. As one commentator has observed, the Joint Economic Committee acts more like "the world's largest economics class" than a powerful committee of Congress.[34]

The 1946 act actually limited White House leadership over macroeconomic policy nearly as much as it enhanced it. The bill's sponsors had wanted to institutionalize economic planning within the Executive Office of the President, ideally through the budget process, but that proposal was attacked by a vocal minority of conservatives who simply would not entrust economic planning based upon Keynesianism to the executive branch. The result was an amendment in the House that provided for an Economic Report and a Council of Economic Advisers but no National Employment and Production Budget.

Despite its limitations, from the vantage point of history the Employment Act of 1946 is a watershed in the development of America's political economy. Intellectual opinion was changed as "hundreds of economists and government policy planners had come by the end of the thirties to accept the Keynesian analysis as the new orthodoxy."[35] Thinkers now **37** disparaged the view that a balanced budget was a moral imperative, and they accepted deficits as necessary during economic downturns. Although the Employment Act failed to create all of the policy tools necessary to achieve its ambitious goals, the nature of the political debate over management of the macroeconomy had clearly undergone a dramatic change. The question was no longer one of laissez faire versus economic management, but instead a debate over the extent and precise nature of government management of the macroeconomy.

The direct political consequence of Keynesianism was that the 1946 Employment Act, according to political scientist Clinton Rossiter, established the presidential role as the "manager of prosperity."[36] However, the law did not require policymakers to achieve full employment, or even to define the meaning of a fully employed economy. This deficiency has led to periodic debates between Republicans and Democrats, liberal and conservative economists, and the White House and Congress about how vigorously the federal government ought to wage a full-employment macroeconomic policy. It has also meant that the goal of full employment is simply one of many economic goals pursued by policymakers, goals whose achievement may, as we noted in Chapter 1, conflict with the goal of full employment.

A Modern Postscript: The Humphrey-Hawkins Act

Thirty-two years later, to strengthen the policy mandate in the 1946 law, Congress enacted the Full Employment and Balanced Growth Act (PL 95-523), commonly known as the **Humphrey-Hawkins Act**. The original version of that legislation proposed that the federal government be the "employer of last resort" in order to achieve a 3 percent unemployment rate, but like the battle over the 1946 act, the legislative process yielded a final bill that does little more than raise public expectations. The stated purpose of the Humphrey-Hawkins Act is "the fulfillment of the right to full opportunities for useful paid employment at fair rates of compensation of all individuals able, willing, and seeking to work." However, other concerns are also noted, such as reasonable price stability, the desirability of balanced budgets, an improved balance of trade, and a stable international monetary system.

The Humphrey-Hawkins Act is the direct progeny of the 1946 Employment Act as Democrats in Congress sought to reaffirm their party's historic commitment to full employment. But times had changed. There was a policy consensus in 1946; there was no such agreement in 1978. In 1946 this policy consensus led Congress to clearly commit the national

38   government to macroeconomic management, although it stopped short of giving the president broad powers to pursue this goal. The 1978 act was equally limited in terms of policy initiatives, but it also lacked the clearer sense of purpose and goals contained in the 1946 act.

The key economic fear that prompted the enactment of the Employment Act was vast unemployment from the depression, but by 1978 inflation had displaced joblessness as the most important economic problem. And as public concern turned to the dangers of higher prices, Keynes's policy prescriptions and macroeconomic theories became subject to major theoretical attack within the economics profession. Indeed, Keynesian economics offered little guidance in how to combat a persistent problem of the 1970s, **stagflation**, the simultaneous occurrence of both rising unemployment and rising inflation.

The Humphrey-Hawkins Act required that the first Economic Report pursuant to the law (1979) establish the goals of a 4 percent unemployment rate and a 3 percent increase in the CPI for the year 1983. The timetable for those goals could be altered by the president beginning with the 1980 Economic Report, in which case the executive has to specify the year when he expects to reach the designated unemployment target. (These dual goals have, in fact, never been attained since the law's passage.)

The act also requires the president each year to set numerical goals for such key indicators as unemployment and employment, real income, prices, and productivity over a five-year period. The president must also provide, with the budget, projections of federal spending and revenues that are consistent with achieving those economic goals. The president is armed with no programs or authority with which to carry out these ambitious objectives, although the act seeks to improve coordination among economic policymakers through revised procedures.

Following the passage of the Humphrey-Hawkins Act, President Jimmy Carter—although a Democrat—faced the problem of having to define a macroeconomic policy that increased employment while not rekindling inflation. Carter made the decision to disregard the Humphrey-Hawkins mandate and postpone its full-employment timetable. Subsequent presidents have also ignored the act's mandate. As we shall see in later chapters, other concerns have come to dominate the economic policymaking stage—regulation of the financial markets, foreign trade balances, and, finally, persistent large federal budget deficits and an ever-increasing national debt.

KEY TERMS

political economy, business cycle, classical economics, laissez faire economics, national income, Keynesian economics, supply-side econom-

ics, mainstream economics, Great Depression, New Deal, countercyclical **39**
fiscal policy, Employment Act of 1946, Council of Economic Advisers
(CEA), Joint Economic Committee, Humphrey-Hawkins Act, stagflation

ADDITIONAL READING

Bailey, Stephen K. *Congress Makes a Law*. New York: Columbia University
Press, 1950. An interesting case study by a political scientist of the enactment
of the Employment Act of 1946.

Campagna, Anthony S. *U.S. National Economic Policy—1917–1985*. New York:
Praeger, 1987. Surveys the economic problems of World Wars I and II, the
Great Depression, and the postwar era, the macroeconomic policies used, and
the degree of success achieved.

Chandler, Lester V. *America's Greatest Depression, 1929–1941*. New York:
Harper and Row, 1970. A thorough examination of the causes and impact of
the economic collapse of the 1930s and the effects of New Deal programs in
aiding economic recovery.

Galbraith, John Kenneth. *The Great Crash 1929*. Boston: Houghton Mifflin,
1954. A very readable account by a prominent economist of the conditions
underlying the 1929 stock market crash.

Harrod, Roy F. *The Life of John Maynard Keynes*. London: Macmillan, 1951. A
biography of the founder of modern macroeconomic theory, his upbringing, and
professional career.

Schlesinger, Arthur M., Jr. *The Crisis of the Old Order, 1919–1933*. Boston:
Houghton Mifflin, 1957. Volume I in The Age of Roosevelt series discusses the
failed political leadership of the 1920s and the causes of the Great Depression.

Schlesinger, Arthur M., Jr. *The Coming of the New Deal*. Boston: Houghton
Mifflin, 1958. Volume II in The Age of Roosevelt series focuses on
antidepression policy during 1933 and 1934, including the National Industrial
Recovery Act.

Terkel, Studs. *Hard Times: An Oral History of the Great Depression*. New York:
Avon Books, 1971. Interviews of ordinary people who recall their economic
hardships during the 1930s.

Van Vleck, George W. *The Panic of 1857*. New York: AMS Press, 1967. A brief
account of the causes and consequences of what is called "the first modern crisis
in American history" to show how little the federal government did to
counteract this depression.

NOTES

1. Cited in John Eatwell, Murray Milgate, and Peter Newman, eds., *The
New Palgrave: A Dictionary of Economics*, Vol. 1 (New York: The Stockton Press,

40   1987), p. 906. The complex history behind the terms *economy* and *political economy* is summarized on pp. 904–907.

2.   Quoted in Stephen K. Bailey, *Congress Makes a Law* (New York: Columbia University Press, 1950), p. 6.

3.   Walter Lippmann, "The Permanent New Deal," *Yale Review*, New Series 24 (1935), p. 661.

4.   Lawrence R. Klein, *The Keynesian Revolution* (New York: Macmillan, 1950), p. vii.

5.   See Paul A. Samuelson and William D. Nordhaus, *Economics*, 14th ed. (New York: McGraw-Hill, 1992), especially Chapters 4 and 26, for a fuller discussion of the role of aggregate supply and aggregate demand in the macroeconomy.

6.   Keynes argued that during an economic contraction a "liquidity trap" occurs. Under this condition the interest rate would be so low that it could not be driven down further by policymakers. However much the money supply is increased, dollars would be held idle because people have no financial incentive to purchase bonds. Altering the money supply would thus have no significant effect on aggregate demand.

7.   James Tobin, "Supply-Side Economics: What Is It? Will it Work?" pp. 132–138 in Thomas Hailstones (ed.), *Viewpoints on Supply-Side Economics* (Reston, VA: Reston Publishing, 1982).

8.   Relatively accessible discussions of supply-side economics from both economic and political perspectives can be found in two edited volumes, Richard Fink (ed.), *Supply-Side Economics: A Critical Appraisal* (Frederick, MD: Aletheia Books, 1982); and Thomas Swartz, Frank Bonello, and Andrew Kozak, eds., *The Supply Side: Debating Current Economic Policies* (Guilford, CT: Dushkin Publishing Group, 1983).

9.   Robert E. Keleher and William P. Orzechowski, "Supply-Side Fiscal Policy: An Historical Analysis of a Rejuvenated Idea," pp. 121–159 in Richard Fink, ed., *Supply-Side Economics: A Critical Appraisal*.

10.   See their discussion of the "Evolution of Economic Thought" in Chapter 22 of Samuelson and Nordhaus, *Economics*.

11.   Gabriel A. Almond, "Separate Tables: Schools and Sects in Political Science," *PS: Political Science and Politics* 21: 828–842.

12.   See Lester V. Chandler, *America's Greatest Depression, 1929–1941* (New York: Harper and Row, 1970). This excellent study guides the discussion in this section.

13.   Quoted in Lewis H. Kimmel, *Federal Budget and Fiscal Policy, 1789–1958* (Washington, DC: The Brookings Institution, 1959), p. 166.

14.   Quoted in Ibid., p. 176.

15.   Chandler, *America's Greatest Depression, 1929–1941*, p. 194.

16.   Quoted in Lippmann, "The Permanent New Deal," p. 223.

17.   Ibid., pp. 229–230.   **41**

18.   Rexford G. Tugwell, "How Shall We Pay for All This, *American Magazine* 116 (1933), p. 87.

19.   In England "The Minority Report of The Poor Law Commission" (1905–1909) had recommended that public works expenditures be undertaken when unemployment reached 4 percent of the labor force. For an extensive discussion of "The Minority Report" see: Sidney and Beatrice Webb, *English Local Government: English Poor Law History, Part II, The Last Hundred Years* (London and New York: Longmans, Green and Company, 1929), Chapter VII, pp. 631–715.

20.   Alvin H. Hansen, *Fiscal Policy and Business Cycles* (New York: W. W. Norton, 1941), p. 262.

21.   Quotes found in Arthur M. Schlesinger, Jr., *The Politics of Upheaval* (Boston: Houghton Mifflin Company, 1960), p. 406.

22.   See, for example, the discussion of Eccles in ibid., p. 407.

23.   E. Cary Brown, "Fiscal Policy in the Thirties: A Reappraisal," *American Economic Review* 46 (December 1956), 857–879. Quote found on pp. 863, 866.

24.   John Maynard Keynes, "The United States and the Keynes Plan," *New Republic* 103 (1940), p. 158.

25.   Quoted in Kimmel, *Federal Budget and Fiscal Policy, 1789–1958*, p. 233.

26.   Quoted in ibid., p. 234.

27.   Stephen K. Bailey, *Congress Makes a Law* , p. 20.

28.   *New York Times* (January 8, 1943), p. 12.

29.   *New York Times* (July 21, 1944), p. 12.

30.   *New York Times* (September 22, 1944), p. 13.

31.   Robert L. Heilbroner, *The Worldly Philosophers* (New York: Simon and Schuster, 1961), p. 244.

32.   John Maynard Keynes, *The General Theory of Employment, Interest, and Money* (New York: Harcourt, Brace and Company, 1936), p. 380.

33.   Senator Alben Barkley (D-KY), quoted in Bailey, *Congress Makes a Law*, p. 128.

34.   John W. Lehrman, "Administration of the Employment Act," *Twentieth Anniversary Symposium, Joint Economic Committee*, U.S. Congress, February 23, 1966, p. 89. A summary of its meager role in fiscal policymaking is found in: Lance T. LeLoup, "Congress and the Dilemma of Economic Policy," in Allen Schick, ed., *Making Economic Policy in Congress* (Washington, DC: American Enterprise Institute for Public Policy Research, 1983), pp. 24–25.

35.   Bailey, *Congress Makes a Law*, p. 20.

36.   Clinton Rossiter, *The American Presidency* (New York: Harcourt Brace and World, 1960), p. 37. The first edition of this work was published in 1956.

PART II

The Development of Economic Policy

CHAPTER 3

Economic Policymaking in the Executive Branch

Up to this point, much of our discussion has seemed to imply that there is a single, coherent thing called economic policy that is determined in accordance with a clear underlying theory such as classical or Keynesian economics. It is time for this impression to be dispelled. In reality, there is no single economic policy, but rather a myriad of separate policy decisions that individually and collectively influence the U.S. (and increasingly, the global) economy. Far from being coherent, in many ways these policy decisions are *disjointed*, that is, they are directed at separate ends and interact in ways that are generally unplanned.

Moreover, there is no single institutional actor that possesses either the authority or the policy tools to develop and implement a single coherent economic policy. In the public's mind—perhaps more importantly, in the *voting* public's mind—the president has this authority and power. Indeed, the president does comes closest to fulfilling this role, although much of the president's ability to influence the economy is indirect, via the appointment power or the ability to influence legislation. Nor does Congress, which in the original constitutional vision was viewed as the preeminent policymaking institution in our government, exercise such power. In economic policy, as in other policy areas, statutory directives are generally blunt instruments, which are translated into specific policy decisions by actors other than the legislators who pass the legislation.

46   Although authority is fragmented and the policy vision is frequently disjointed, most economic policy is formulated and implemented within the executive branch of our national government. Within this branch, one actor—the president—exercises disproportionate influence. As we will see in this and later chapters, the president's ability to create a more coherent economic policy—indeed, to be an effective "manager of prosperity"—is dependent on many factors, not the least of which is the president's own approach to the job of being president.

In this chapter we will begin the process of understanding how the president goes about doing this. We first present a brief model of the economic policymaking process. Following this, we describe the president's role as an economic policymaker, and then we examine the major actors who directly assist the president in policymaking. Next we turn to a discussion of the aspect of economic policymaking least under the president's control, the work of independent regulatory bodies. Finally, we close the chapter by considering the question of who, if anyone, controls and coordinates economic policymaking within the executive branch.

THE PROCESS OF ECONOMIC POLICYMAKING

The process of policy development can be analyzed from a variety of perspectives. Our discussion will approach the development of economic policy as a sequence of stages. The crucial first stage is known as **agenda setting.** In this stage, decision makers first become aware of a problem's existence and begin to consider potential approaches to addressing the problem.[1] Agenda setting is followed by the stage of **policy formulation**, where various alternative solutions to the policy problem are proposed and compared, and then by **policy adoption**, where the authoritative decision-making body determines that a particular alternative will be the policy that is pursued. Adoption is then followed by the stage of **policy implementation**, in which the adopted policy directives are translated into specific actions by governmental officials. The final stage in the policy cycle is the process of **policy evaluation and reformulation**, in which the policymakers consider what actual policy activities have been undertaken, their effects on the original problem, and what modification, if any, should be made in the policy in light of this analysis.

A variety of actors are active in the various stages. The first are actors from the national government, such as the president, heads of executive branch agencies, members of Congress, the courts, and the bureaucracy. In addition to these federal officials, state and local government officials may also be active, depending on the aspect of economic policy in question (e.g., state governments are active in the regulation of financial institutions). Beyond these governmental actors, private sector actors may also be involved. These may include private individuals, but they are more likely to be representatives of interest groups. These interest groups may range from groups with fairly broad policy interests, such as the AFL-CIO and the Business Roundtable, to groups with very specific goals, such as a particular industry's trade association or the National Taxpayer's Union.

Some actors are more important in some stages than in others. Nongovernmental actors play their greatest role in the first two stages, agenda setting and policy formulation. Indeed, an issue or policy proposal is generally put on the policy agenda through the work of some particular individual or group, and while members of Congress and the president possess a clear advantage in their ability to raise issues for public consideration, nongovernmental actors often play a key role in this as well.

Nongovernmental actors, especially interest groups, continue to be important in the policy formulation stage in that they frequently develop policy proposals of their own as well as react to the proposals of others. In economic policy, a traditional advantage of the executive branch—and of a particular part of the executive branch, the Council of Economic Advisors—in the development of economic policy proposals rested on the fact that it contained a group of staff economists not found elsewhere, and hence it was able to argue effectively that its proposals were more sound technically.[2] Executive branch agencies still possess great strength in knowledge and technical expertise that gives them great influence in policy formulation, but other actors—such as Congress and interest groups—have developed similar strength and, as a result, increased influence in this area.

Governmental actors dominate in the next two stages of the process, policy adoption and policy implementation. In the most general sense, Congress is the crucial agent for policy adoption in that it establishes the statutory basis for economic policy. However, it is increasingly the case that many authoritative decisions concerning economic policy are made by other governmental actors, such as regulatory agencies, offices in cabinet departments such as Treasury and Commerce, and the courts.[3] Moreover, it is increasingly difficult to separate the adoption of a policy from its implementation, an activity that even more clearly falls within the province of the bureaucracy.[4] Of course, in both of these stages, other actors continue to play a role, even though Congress or a bureaucratic agency may dominate. Finally, the policy evaluation and reformulation stage once again involves a broader array of actors. Formal evaluations may be undertaken by governmental bodies such as oversight subcommit-

48   tees or the GAO or by outside groups, while reformulation often resembles the initial stages of the policy process.

THE PRESIDENT AND ECONOMIC POLICY

The economic policymaking system is fragmented and does not produce a clear, coherent policy based upon a sound theoretical framework. At the same time, the president is the chief economic policymaker, viewed by the public and other political leaders as the "manager of prosperity." While seemingly contradictory, both of these statements are nevertheless true. The truth of the first statement will become increasingly evident as we proceed through succeeding chapters. The truth of the second statement lies in recognizing that the president is the "solution" to a policy detective story: only the president possesses the three elements necessary for acting in this area—the motive, the opportunity, and the means.

We begin with the motive. At an obvious level, the president wishes to influence the economy because a strong economy is good for the nation. More important from a political perspective, however, is that the president needs to influence the economy because the voting public expects the president to do so. The president's popularity rises and falls with improvements and declines in the nation's economic performance. More to the point, a president's reelection chances may also be affected by changing economic fortunes.[5] Even for presidents who are not seeking reelection, the political fortunes of the other members of their party usually remain significant to them, and these, too, may be harmed by adverse economic changes.

Second, the president possesses the opportunity to play a dominant role in determining economic policy. As we noted in the previous chapter, the Employment Act of 1946 gave the president the responsibility for preparing an annual Economic Report. Just as with the annual State of the Union message and the preparation of the annual budget, this gives the president the formal responsibility for identifying problems and proposing solutions for them—in effect, to place economic issues on the public agenda and begin the process of policy formulation.

Finally, the president possesses the means to influence economic policy. There are several "weapons" at the president's disposal. First, the president has the statutory responsibility for preparation and submission of the annual budget to Congress. This is highly significant, since the budget is (or at least, should be) the chief vehicle for employing fiscal policy to affect the economy. Second, the president's veto power gives the president a significant role in the passage of legislation, including not only the

budget, but all other legislation affecting economic policy as well. Third,   **49**
the president, as head of the executive branch, is in command (at least in
theory) of many bureaucratic offices with significant responsibilities for
formulating and implementing economic policy. Finally, through the appointment power, the president selects the heads of all executive branch
agencies, including the otherwise independent bodies such as the Federal
Reserve Board and the various regulatory commissions.

THE ECONOMIC ADVISORY SYSTEM

President Roosevelt relied upon a highly personalized, informal,
and ad hoc advisory system to cope with the Great Depression and implement his New Deal. He recruited experts in public administration, finance
and economics, and corporate law from universities and business, a group
that became known as his Brain Trust. At that time the chief executive
was not given a full-time professional staff, so most of these aides were
"loaned" to FDR by various agencies where they were formally employed.
The use of academic thinkers was an innovation unique to FDR, and it
began a new tradition within the executive branch. As Hugh S. Norton
observes: "No present-day candidate would dream of entering the [presi-
dential] race on a serious basis or preparing to take office without position
papers on various topics. Both prior to the nomination and in the inter-
regnum after an election, his advisers remain active, drawing up programs
and proposals designed to solve 'the economic problem.' "[6]

Franklin Roosevelt was a transitional figure; his impromptu advisory
network could not survive the growing and more complex demands of the
contemporary federal government. Once the New Deal was established,
FDR understood how much government had grown, and he appointed a
Committee on Administrative Management to study this development.
Its 1937 report concluded: "The President needs help. His immediate staff
assistance is entirely inadequate. He should be given a small number of
executive assistants who would be his direct aides in dealing with the
managerial agencies and administrative departments."[7] With this advice,
in 1939 Roosevelt created the **Executive Office of the President (EOP)**.
This marked the beginning of the "institutionalized presidency," where
agencies are added as advisory bodies to the chief executive. The White
House Office was the first agency in the EOP, but it was quickly joined by
the Bureau of the Budget (BOB), which President Roosevelt transferred
from the Department of the Treasury. The Employment Act of 1946 created the **Council of Economic Advisers (CEA)**, which also was housed
in the EOP. The BOB (today called **Office of Management and Budget,**

50   or **OMB**), the CEA, and the Department of the Treasury became known as the "**Troika**" during the 1960s, when they came to dominate economic policymaking within the executive branch.

Other agencies are also involved in economic policymaking. The most important is the Federal Reserve Board ("the Fed"), established by the Federal Reserve Act of 1913 as an independent agency not under the direct control of the president. The term "Quadriad" was also coined in the 1960s to describe collaboration between the Fed and the Troika members. (The policy activities of the Federal Reserve Board are discussed in detail in Chapter 5.)

Anderson terms these executive branch actors "the **economic subpresidency**," which he describes as acting "to assist the president, at his level, by providing him with assistance in defining problems and alternatives, in making and communicating decisions, and in securing acceptance and compliance with them."[8] Each president structures an advisory system according to his personal needs and style of governance. In no arrangement do all advisers enjoy equal access to the White House or carry equal influence. Every president recruits staff members and agency heads who share his general priorities and philosophy, but personal rivalries and jurisdictional squabbles always characterize the arena of bureaucratic politics. Who are recruited to staff these agencies? What values do they bring to the task of managing the macroeconomy? Does cooperation or conflict typify the relationships among these decision makers? These are some of the questions we hope to answer in this section.

Council of Economic Advisers

The CEA is somewhat unique among federal agencies because it has not experienced the degree of empire building that afflicts so many bureaus. Its three members are appointed by the president with Senate confirmation. At first they acted as a collegial body, but under Reorganization Plan No. 9 of 1953, President Eisenhower elevated the chairman to be the operating head of the CEA. The chairman appoints the staff, hires consultants, and advises the president. The size of the CEA has not changed, and past chairmen are unanimous in the opinion that no enlargement should occur. The CEA is supposed to be an advisory body without operational duties, but periodically the CEA has been given operational responsibilities, such as overseeing wage-price guidelines during the Kennedy-Johnson administrations. Its professional staff numbers between fifteen and twenty-five, which is small enough to assure their loyalty to the chairman but still allow some division of labor.

The Council of Economic Advisers has been the preserve of academic economists. This is illustrated by the recruitment pattern of CEA chairmen. Between 1946 and 1993 all CEA chairman were economists, and all but three had previous experience at universities or research institutions. (See Table A.1 in the Appendix for more detailed profiles of the sixteen CEA chairmen between 1946 and 1993.) There is high turnover among its membership as well as by the professional staff, and wholesale changes in membership usually accompany each new incumbent in the White House. A disadvantage of the "in-and-out" recruitment pattern is that, unlike other agencies with permanent staffs, the CEA lacks an "institutional memory" about the workings of the federal government. Its members lack experience in dealing with other agencies or the time needed to develop personal networks with key decision makers. This deficiency is ameliorated somewhat when the CEA chairman has some previous experience on the council. Of the sixteen chairmen, six had been CEA members and two more (Schultze and Weidenbaum) had served as CEA professional staffers.

A small number of elite universities are the educators for the CEA members. Curiously, half of the Ph.D. degrees held by members were conferred by the University of Chicago, Harvard, and MIT, which hold opposing economic philosophies. Harvard and MIT, like most economics departments, have subscribed to Keynesian economics for most of the postwar period, while the University of Chicago has been a stronghold of monetarist (and rational expectationist) thinking, a partial legacy of economist Milton Friedman's long tenure there. It is less surprising to find that nine Chicago graduates were appointed to the CEA by Republican presidents, with five serving under Ronald Reagan.

Keynesians dominated the CEA during the terms of John Kennedy and Lyndon Johnson, when Ivy League schools were over-represented; of the ten economists who served from 1961 to 1968, Harvard produced four and Columbia one. More recently, President Clinton's CEA appointments appear to represent a return to a more Keynesian approach; all three of his initial CEA appointments are graduates of MIT, the economics program which has continued to accept the more interventionist view "that government has a powerful role to play in building a strong economy."[10] These recruitment patterns indicate that CEA members reflect the partisan orientation of those presidents who appointed them.

The Council of Economic Advisers serves the president in four capacities, according to JFK's chairman, Walter Heller.[11] First, the CEA is supposed to provide the best data, analysis, and forecasts state-of-the-art economics will allow. This is accomplished by a daily stream of memoranda to the president and meetings, when needed, to keep him abreast

52   of the latest economic developments. Second, the CEA advises the president on how best to achieve his macroeconomic goals. There is no assurance that the president will heed that advice, but efforts at persuasion are better than not trying at all. As Gardner Ackley, CEA chairman under Johnson, noted: "If his economic adviser refrains from advice on the gut questions of policy, the president should and will get another one."[12] Third, the council also tries to "educate" the president about macroeconomic theory. On this score both Heller and Ackley had modest success. Heller finally convinced JFK that tax cuts were needed to avoid recession, and Ackley prevailed upon LBJ to seek an income tax surcharge to curb inflationary pressures. Finally, the CEA must translate the jargon of economics into a language the president understands and can use. There is no place on the CEA for a purely abstract thinker.

In exercising these four goals, a delicate political balance must be achieved. The CEA must be an adviser without being a political advocate. It must share the president's economic values, but without jeopardizing its professional standing and objectivity. The council must provide a candid appraisal of the economy, but not become a constant critic. From time to time this fragile relationship has broken down, but those examples are few and far between.

The CEA's essential function is to provide economic advice to the president, and for the CEA knowledge is power. Its influence depends entirely upon the technical expertise possessed by its professional membership; its advice can be forthright, because the CEA is beholden to nobody except the chief executive. As Walter Heller put it: "The President knows that the Council's expertise is fully at his command, undiluted by the commitments to particular programs and particular interest groups that . . . tend to build up in the various line agencies of government."[13] The CEA also focuses on the macroeconomy, and thus, unlike federal agencies that mostly deal with specific problems, it shares with the president a "national" perspective on policymaking.

There is more agreement by economists on microeconomic questions than on macroeconomic problems,[14] and this bias affects the CEA as well. One study found "virtual agreement among these Democratic and Republican [CEA] chairmen that economists of all persuasions examine micro issues with similar theoretical and ideological perspectives that favor markets and competition and oppose subsidies and restraints on free economic activity."[15] Thus, the CEA can be expected to oppose minimum wage increases and farm price supports as costly interferences with the marketplace, and its hostility to wage-price controls reflects the belief that they distort the market without dealing with the underlying causes of inflation.

This perspective is illustrated by the CEA's position on the major revision of immigration law passed during the 1980s. In 1986 Congress enacted legislation to curb the flow of illegal immigrants to the United States. The bill was supported by the Immigration and Naturalization Service as well as by President Reagan, but the Council of Economic Advisers disapproved. It argued that penalties on employers who hire illegals would be a "labor market tax" and thus might reduce the nation's output of goods and services. Though economic issues were not paramount in the congressional debate, the council nonetheless addressed this public policy from its vantage point of economic theory.[16]

On macroeconomic policy the CEA bias is towards economic expansion. Unlike the Fed, the CEA is less obsessed with the problem of inflation, and, unlike Treasury, the CEA is more inclined to utilize fiscal policy to achieve macroeconomic objectives. Within this general orientation, however, are partisan differences regarding the trade-off between unemployment and inflation. Basically, the views of the CEA under presidents of different parties reflect the Democratic emphasis on fighting unemployment and the Republican emphasis on fighting inflation. After interviewing ten CEA Chairmen, Hargrove and Morley conclude that

> Except for Truman, the Democrats tried too hard to fine-tune remedies
> for inflation. Understandably they wanted the smallest possible reces-
> sion. As a result, they opted for the least restraint that their models told
> them would slow down the economy. . . . The Republicans, on the other
> hand, because they seem to abhor inflation more and unemployment
> somewhat less, tended to adopt stabilization strategies which, if anything,
> erred on the side of overkill. Under all three Republican administrations
> [Eisenhower, Nixon, Ford], they tended to hit the economy hard with
> restraint and then bring the patient back to life with stimulus if that was
> needed, as it always was.[17]

The tension between advice and advocacy was apparent from the council's inception. The CEA's first chairman was Edwin G. Nourse, who headed the American Economic Association in 1942. As a nonpartisan professional (who was not enamored with the New Deal), Nourse saw his role as advising President Truman on various economic options and their consequences. He would not endorse any one policy and refused to testify before Congress. The story is told that, after reading a report where Nourse pondered the alternatives "on the one hand" and "on the other hand," President Truman expressed an anguished cry for a one-armed economist.[18] When Nourse resigned in 1949, CEA member Leon H. Keyserling, a fervent supporter of the New Deal, was elevated to the chairmanship, giving Truman an economic adviser more to his liking.

54   Presidents want economic advisers who share their views. Truman
preferred the liberal Keyserling to the more conservative Nourse, and President Eisenhower was comfortable with Arthur Burns's cautious approach
to countercyclical policy. Alan Greenspan reinforced Gerald Ford's orthodox views on economics. As John Sloan notes: "Greenspan attained a
prominent role in economic policymaking because much of what he was
advocating was compatible with Ford's beliefs. Ford was a moderately conservative Republican who, as a member of the House Appropriations Committee, had warned his fellow legislators for many years that the federal
government had become too active and expensive."[19]

This match between a CEA chairman and the president was virtually
perfect under President Kennedy. The zenith of CEA political influence
came during this period because the council reflected Keynesian economics, which dominated the profession at that time. Its espousal of countercyclical policy supported the liberal agenda of JFK and the Democratic
party, and so, more than usual, politicians and economists walked hand in
hand.

Many commentators believe, on the other hand, that the CEA's reputation declined substantially during the Reagan administration. The first
two CEA chairman during that administration, Murray Weidenbaum and
Martin Feldstein (both academics), resigned their CEA chairmanships.
The friction between Martin Feldstein and other White House staffers
illustrates the tension between acting as both an economic adviser and an
economist providing the expertise of the economics profession. Feldstein
began to lose influence when he went public and expressed to Congress
his contrary views about supply-side economics. He was alarmed about the
triple-digit deficits and counseled the need for a tax increase, views not in
line with the rest of Reagan's economic advisors. Feldstein lost repeated
battles over taxes to Donald Regan (who was then treasury secretary) and
eventually resigned.

The Reagan administration appeared anxious to avoid further criticism from academic economists and thus turned next to a business economist they felt would be more supportive of Reagan administration policies, Beryl Sprinkel (who was affiliated with the Harris Trust and Savings
Bank of Chicago). With the Sprinkel appointment, supply-side economists
and monetarists solidified their position within the administration. Since
Chairman Sprinkel and both his colleagues on the CEA were University
of Chicago Ph.D.s, the degree of commonality of outlook on the CEA
became extremely high, a condition made more significant since the Chicago School represents a minority opinion among economists. The desire
to have economic advisers who are loyal team players was not unique to
President Reagan. What was unusual was that Reagan's CEA was selected

in such a way that they would defend macroeconomic policies that were often questioned by mainstream economists.

President Bush returned to the pre-Reagan pattern of appointment by choosing Michael Boskin of Stanford University to be his CEA chairman. While there were no real departures in macroeconomic policy during the first several years of the Bush administration, initial reports suggested that Boskin's reputation and operating style improved the image of the council. However, as the Bush presidency went on, Boskin's influence waned in comparison to that of other Bush advisers, notably OMB Director Darman and Treasury Secretary Brady.[20]

President Clinton's appointment of three MIT graduates to the CEA, including CEA Chairperson Laura D'Andrea Tyson, who had no substantial reputation as a specialist in macroeconomics, indicates that the recent pattern of emphasizing policy orientation over professional reputation in CEA appointments is continuing.[21] Of course, to some extent this is a function of the decline in consensus among economists themselves over the most effective way to manage the macroeconomy. The increasing diversity over macroeconomic theory seen among economists during the 1970s and 1980s means that presidents are increasingly able to select economic advisers whose theoretical predictions are likely to coincide with the practical political desires of the president.

Secretary of the Treasury

This office dates back to the first cabinet. George Washington relied heavily on his treasury secretary, Alexander Hamilton, who acted decisively to regularize the nation's finances and credit structure. Ever since, the **secretary of the treasury** has been among the most influential economic advisers to the president. Between 1946 and 1993, sixteen men have served as secretary of the treasury. The majority were business executives, bankers, or financiers, and six were recruited directly from private business. The obvious exceptions are James A. Baker III, an attorney; John Connally, who held previous elective office; and Lloyd Bentsen, who left the chairmanship of the Senate Finance Committee to become Clinton's treasury secretary. Only two earned a Ph.D., and eight had law degrees; four others had only a B.A. degree. It would be accurate to characterize these men as successful entrepreneurs, and some (like Humphrey, Regan, and Bentsen) were very wealthy. (See Table A.2 in the Appendix for more detailed profiles of the postwar secretaries of the treasury.)

Recent secretaries of the treasury have often vied with CEA chairmen for influence over economic policy. Under President Eisenhower the strongest rival to CEA Chairman Arthur Burns was George M. Humphrey,

56   treasury secretary until 1957. Humphrey's brand of fiscal conservatism dominated over this period, sometimes to Ike's embarrassment. In a much publicized incident, Humphrey disavowed the executive budget for FY58 on the very day it went to Congress, and he warned of a "depression that will curl your hair" if cuts were not made in the amounts proposed by Eisenhower. President Kennedy's treasury secretary was Douglas Dillon, and his view that budget deficits would hurt JFK's popularity and business confidence held sway as late as January 1963. When Kennedy finally acceded to demands by the CEA that a tax cut be recommended, the final shape of that tax package reflected Dillon's view against one large tax cut. When President Nixon appointed John Connally secretary of the treasury in 1972, he became the administration's spokesman for macroeconomic policy. It was Connally who persuaded Nixon, despite the opposition of the CEA, to impose wage-price controls. More recently, Bush's treasury secretary, Nicholas Brady, maintained a dominance over the CEA that had begun under the two powerful Reagan treasury secretaries (Donald Regan and James Baker).

On the other hand, during the Ford and Carter administrations the treasury secretaries were eclipsed by especially strong CEA chairmen. For example, Ford's CEA chairman, Alan Greenspan, enjoyed the president's total confidence, while treasury secretary William E. Simon acted more as a public spokesman for business and a defender of the free enterprise system. Ford's deep concern about "uncontrollable" federal spending reflects Greenspan's influence. A determined, skillful, and dynamic CEA chairman can hold extraordinary influence with the president whenever the treasury secretary assumes a more passive role.

At a symbolic level the secretary of the treasury can be said to represent American capitalism, which explains why a well-known figure in business or banking is often chosen. Presidents make appointments to this office to reassure Wall Street and corporate America that a responsible individual is the guardian of the nation's finances. This political requirement is undoubtedly more important for Democratic administrations. Corporate leaders assume that the GOP is pro-business but may fear that liberal Democrats harbor anti-business attitudes. The appointment of Douglas Dillon, a Republican, by President Kennedy was done partly to reassure the business community. More recently, President Clinton's appointment of Lloyd Bentsen, a moderate Democrat with business experience, was widely seen in the same light.[22]

Although Treasury usually exerts a "conservative" influence over macroeconomic policymaking, this bias results more from its institutional responsibilities than from how its secretary is recruited. There is a general division of labor among the Troika agencies. The CEA provides forecasts of economic performance. The OMB estimates federal expenditures. Treasury (which includes the Internal Revenue Service) collects the revenue generated by the tax system and also has the duty of funding the national debt. Efforts to tamper with the internal revenue code arouse the Department of the Treasury because "reform" might cost the federal government money, and reduced revenues in the face of growing expenditures means larger deficits.

Selling government securities to borrow private money to service the deficit brings Treasury into contact with influential members of the financial community. The borrowing requirements of government can be substantial. Since FY88 over 14 percent of total federal outlays each year have gone to pay *interest* on the nation debt. When federal borrowing is this large (about $200 billion per year in recent years), debt management becomes complicated. High deficits exert upward pressure on interest rates, which act to "crowd out" private borrowing for investment, and high interest also raises the cost to the Treasury of funding the national debt. Two ways of alleviating the costs of debt management are to keep the deficit small by maximizing revenue and to stabilize interest rates. Such concerns make Treasury a counterweight to other advisers, mainly the CEA, who might encourage tax cuts to stimulate the economy.

The advisory role of the treasury secretary is also bolstered by the department's involvement in international monetary policy. In some areas of international finance, the Department of the Treasury has substantial control over the policymaking apparatus.[23] Financial assets are transferred by Treasury between the U.S. and foreign countries in order to satisfy the balance on current account. Technically this is done through the Federal Reserve Bank of New York, acting as an arm of the Treasury Department. An obvious consideration is the exchange rate of the U.S. dollar on world markets. Asset flows are facilitated when the rate of exchange is fixed (as it was prior to 1971) or when the value of the U.S. dollar as determined in world financial markets is relatively stable. Although influenced by many diverse factors, exchange rates are stabilized by lower rates of inflation in the domestic economy. These concerns encourage Treasury to adopt a cautious outlook on macroeconomic policy, especially whenever the threat of inflation exists.

Office of Management and Budget

The Bureau of the Budget (BOB) was established by the Budget and Accounting Act of 1921, and it became part of the Executive Office of the President when the EOP was created in 1939. Its successor agency, the Office of Management and Budget (OMB), was created by President

58   Nixon in 1970. The OMB is crucial due to its ongoing budgetary function and extensive institutional memory. By virtue of its expertise, accumulated experience, and contacts throughout the federal government, the OMB can utilize much historical knowledge to serve the president. The professionalism of the OMB staff, therefore, adds a dimension to the economic advisory system that newcomers, like the CEA chairman and even the treasury secretary, cannot provide. Since 1974, the presidential appointments of both the director and deputy director of the OMB must be confirmed by the Senate.

The basic function of the OMB is to assist the president in preparing and executing the federal budget. The budget covers spending for a **fiscal year**, which runs from October 1 to September 30.[24] At any one point in time, the OMB is at work on three successive budgets. First, the OMB is involved in the preparation of the budget for the next fiscal year. Second, the OMB monitors the execution of the budget of the current fiscal year. This means that the OMB monitors spending from numerous accounts by all executive branch agencies reporting to the president, making certain that disbursements do not proceed at a pace that will exhaust the accounts before the close of the fiscal year. Third, the OMB audits the budget from the previous fiscal year to determine whether that year's funds were properly expended.

The OMB's importance as an element of the economic subpresidency rests mainly upon its involvement in the preparation of the annual budget. (In the mid-1980s the OMB was also given responsibility for considering the economic impact of regulations proposed by executive branch agencies, making it a key actor in the Reagan administration's efforts at deregulation.) The budgetary cycle begins with the development of assumptions regarding the future course of the economy and predicted expenditures and revenues over the next fiscal year. This results in a target deficit or surplus figure, from which the basic budgetary guidelines are drawn up following consultation with the president. The OMB then prepares instructions for executive branch agencies concerning how they should prepare their budget requests. These requests are reviewed through several iterations by the OMB; only at the last stage are appeals made to the president. The result is then submitted to Congress as the president's budget. During subsequent budgetary hearings in Congress, the director of the OMB becomes the chief spokesperson for the administration before Congress.

Twenty-two men have served as BOB or OMB director since 1946, with most having either a law or doctoral degree. By occupation there have been six economists, four lawyers, eight businessmen or bankers, two federal careerists, and two ex-members of Congress. (See Table A.3 in the

Appendix for more detailed profiles.) The one distinctive characteristic is **59** that most (sixteen) had some previous experience in the federal government, and specifically with the BOB or the OMB. Nine became the director after serving as assistant or deputy director of the agency.

This pattern of inside recruitment was most common during the 1940s and 1950s, the period when BOB achieved its greatest reputation. During the Truman and Eisenhower terms the budgetary process had become routinized and was monopolized by the BOB. With Kennedy, however, its role in screening legislative requests by agencies (the "central clearance" function) was limited to routine matters. New Frontier programs were initiated by the White House, and this approach was used even more so when President Johnson promoted his Great Society.

The fundamental problem confronting the BOB/OMB is elaborated upon by Kermit Gordon, its head during Kennedy's tenure:

> As one moves down through the officials in the executive hierarchy, the Presidential perspective fades rapidly, and parochial conceptions take its place. Consider the official who directs the day-to-day operations of even a broadly defined program. . . . He directs the work of large numbers of people, he disposes of large sums of money, he deals every day with weighty, intricate, and delicate problems. He has probably spent most of his adult years in the highly specialized activity over which he now presides. He lives at the center of a special world inhabited by persons and groups in the private sector who stand to gain or lose by what he does, certain members of Congress who have a special interest in his actions, and a specialized press to which he is a figure of central importance. . . . The rest of the federal government may seem vague and remote, and the President will loom as a distant and shadowy figure who will, in any event, be succeeded by someone else in a few years.[25]

Given this perspective, budget officers generally question whether all funds requested by agencies are necessary. Each budget request must be viewed in terms of presidential priorities and spending targets. The BOB gained the reputation of being a budget-cutter—even during the growth years of the 1960s, when economic prosperity generated more revenues for government. Later, when the economy grew less robustly, government indebtedness grew, and the White House became occupied by Republicans, the long-standing skepticism of the BOB hardened into strenuous opposition to higher levels of federal spending.

President Nixon politicized the operations of the Office of Management and Budget. As a result, staff turnover increased, the OMB became involved in controversial and illegal actions like Nixon's impoundments, and professionals were replaced with political operatives. In 1960 the BOB had only five appointed officials, but the 1970 reorganization (creating

60   OMB) added a new layer of program associate directors who were White House political appointees. Three OMB directors who served under Nixon—Shultz, Weinberger, and Ash—became presidential spokesmen. Their activities meant that OMB was identified "more as a member of the President's own political family and less a broker supplying an independent analytic service to every President,"[26] a situation that alarmed some scholars. A contrary view, though, is that modern presidents must achieve deep political penetration into the bureaucracy in order to exert meaningful control over the policymaking process.[27]

Under President Reagan the OMB was at the forefront of the political battle over domestic spending cuts. David Stockman, who headed the OMB until July 1985, was considered by many to be the agency's most effective director. The 1981 legislative enactment of budget cuts and tax overhaul was engineered by Stockman, whose expertise overwhelmed the opposition. He dominated the congressional hearings with detailed statistical trends, economic projections, and budgetary estimates. But eventually Stockman's public criticism of supply-side economics damaged his credibility within the Reagan administration. He had to resign because the White House objected to his view that taxes had to be increased substantially to reduce the soaring deficits.

Politics continues to overwhelm professionalism at the OMB, and it seems unlikely that this development will be reversed by the White House any time soon. With budgets tight, as spending continues to outstrip revenues, current and future presidents, regardless of their party or ideology, must have a loyalist as head of the OMB in order to shape the budget according to their own priorities. In addition, presidents need an OMB director who can effectively interact with Congress. Both of these desires were apparent in President Clinton's 1993 appointment of Leon Panetta, the chair of the House Budget Committee, as OMB director.

INDEPENDENT REGULATORY AGENCIES

In addition to the executive branch agencies directly under the president's control, several other agencies within the executive branch also play a role in the formulation and implementation of economic policy. These are the **independent regulatory agencies**, the most important of which is the Federal Reserve Board. These bodies are termed independent because they are given broad legislative mandates to make policy and are headed by officials who are appointed by the president (subject to Senate confirmation) for long, fixed terms of office. The latter means that, unlike other presidential appointees in the executive branch who serve at the

president's pleasure, the heads of these regulatory bodies may not be re-   **61**
moved from office before the end of their statutory terms.

In general, these bodies have been made independent so that their
operations are insulated from constant political pressures, under the theory
that the activities being regulated are ones in which the public interest is
better served by decision making that is less immediately responsive to
normal political pressures. This is not to say that these agencies are totally
independent. The appointment power is an important source of presidential influence; while every president has been surprised by the subsequent
behavior of some of his appointees, careful selection procedures mean that
a president is normally able to appoint individuals who share the president's views on important policy questions. In addition, both the president
and Congress can exert continuing influence over these agencies through
their control over the annual agency budgets and by altering the statutes
that govern the agencies' behavior.

Federal Reserve Board

The Federal Reserve Act of 1913 created a **Federal Reserve
Board** in Washington and twelve regional banks. That law did not specify
where ultimate authority rested, so there was a period when the regional
banks, notably the Federal Reserve Bank of New York, dominated the
relationship. By enactment of the Banking Act of 1935 the Federal Reserve Board was renamed the Board of Governors of the Federal Reserve
System (known generally as the Fed), and the appointment of regional
bank presidents was made subject to approval by the Board of Governors.
To further strengthen its control over the Federal Reserve Banks, the
makeup of the important **Federal Open Market Committee (FOMC),**
which buys and sells government securities, was changed. It now includes
the seven members of the Fed's Board of Governors, the president of the
Federal Reserve Bank of New York, and four other presidents of regional
banks who rotate annually. Although the regional banks are not without
influence, power is generally concentrated in the Board of Governors.

The seven members of the Board of Governors are appointed by the
president to fourteen-year terms, subject to Senate confirmation. The president designates one member as chairman, another as vice-chairman; both
serve four-year terms in these roles. Through 1993, there have been fourteen chairmen of the Fed, seven since 1934. (See Table A.4 in the Appendix for more detailed profiles.) Of these seven, nearly all had experience in banking or finance. With the exception of Thomas B. McCabe,
who served only three years under Truman, and G. William Miller, who
resigned to become secretary of the treasury under Carter, these men en-

62   joyed long tenure in office. Marriner S. Eccles chaired the Fed for fourteen years under Roosevelt and Truman. The almost nineteen-year tenure of William McChesney Martin, Jr., spanned the presidencies of Eisenhower, Kennedy, Johnson, and Nixon. Arthur Burns's eight years paralleled the terms of Nixon, Ford, and Carter. Paul A. Volcker was appointed by President Carter and continued into Reagan's second term before he was succeeded by Alan Greenspan, who has continued to serve under Presidents Bush and Clinton. This longevity signals one political advantage when the Fed deals with other economic advisers to the president.

The chairman of the Fed stands as a powerful symbol of financial integrity and prudence in monetary policy. The appointee must have the confidence of the business community, and this standard weighed heavily in Kennedy's decision to reappoint the conservative William McChesney Martin: "In mid-1961 . . . until fairly late in 1961, Kennedy was still thinking of replacing Martin, but as the date for reappointment or new appointment came up, Martin's standing in the domestic and international financial community kept rising, . . . and by the time the date arrived, Kennedy had decided to reappoint Martin."[28] Similarly, the rising concern among business executives and financiers that had followed the departure of Arthur Burns in 1978 was only ended with the choice of Paul Volcker in 1979. As *Business Week* observed: "Shattered confidence in the Carter administration left the president no choice but to select a man who would be instantly hailed as the savior of the dollar, even though that meant bringing in a Fed chairman far more conservative than Carter would have preferred."[29] Continued business confidence in Volcker helped bring about his reappointment by President Reagan in 1983.

The chairman dominates the Federal Reserve System due to his formal powers and force of personality. He is the spokesperson for the Fed, and outsiders listen to his every word as some indication of future policy. The chair represents the Fed to other agencies and thus can make decisions without formal review by the entire Board of Governors. The Board of Governors has delegated to the chairman supervisory authority over the professional staff. Perhaps most importantly, through personal lobbying and appeals, the chairman generally can sway votes at meetings of the Board of Governors and the FOMC.

The function of the Fed within the U.S. economy has evolved over time. The agency was originally created to maintain liquidity in the banking system and thereby reduce bank failures during panics. Through time its major function had become to stabilize the macroeconomy through monetary policy.[30] The Fed also has responsibility for regulating the operations of member banks.[31] Beyond these monetary and regulatory activities, the twelve regional Reserve Banks serve as clearinghouses for checks and loan money to both member and nonmember banks.

The members of the Board of Governors are essentially a policy elite largely acceptable to the financial community and the economics profession. Three-fifths had previous experience within the Federal Reserve System before they were appointed to the Board of Governors.[32] The individuals who control monetary policy are a very homogeneous group, according to John Woolley: "The Federal Reserve continues a long history of administration by white, male, upper-middle-class technicians."[33] The obvious result is that Fed decision making is consensual. In a sixteen-year period studied, 86 percent of the decisions made by the Federal Open Market Committee were unanimous, and three-fifths of the split decisions involved only one dissenting vote.[34]

But the Fed must delicately balance political relationships to safeguard its independence. Although bankers have access to the Board of Governors, and generally applaud its anti-inflation stance, the Fed has not been "captured" by the banking industry. And though its economic analysis is thoroughly mainstream, no one school of thought dominates. When Keynesian economics lost some credibility during the 1970s, for example, the Fed began to integrate new approaches. Monetarism is now reflected in the Fed's use of monetary aggregates, in addition to the discount rate, to regulate the flow of credit.

Despite its independence, the record of performance suggests that we should not exaggerate the importance of short-term political squabbles between the Fed and the White House. Informal and formal contacts with the executive occur at regular intervals, and an understanding emerges between both parties on how the economy is working and what corrective steps are needed. Fed policy rarely catches the White House off guard because, as Woolley observed,

> both the president and the Federal Reserve are solidly in the mainstream. There usually *is* a mainstream consensus on the nature of the economic problem. . . . One consequence of the process of recruiting and selecting both presidents and Federal Reserve officials is that they will rarely be far apart, and when differences occur they will not be profound. . . . as far as president and Federal Reserve are concerned, monetary and fiscal policy move together.[35]

Despite this general record of cooperation between the Fed and the executive branch, the Reagan administration wanted more assurances that monetary policy would aid supply-side economics. In October, 1985 President Reagan nominated Manuel H. Johnson, Jr., and Wayne D. Angell to the Federal Reserve Board. Both Johnson (who had been assistant sec-

64   retary of the treasury for economic policy) and Angell were sympathetic to supply-side arguments. The appointment of Johnson especially upset some economists; Alan Blinder, then of the Brookings Institution and later a Clinton CEA member, remarked: "I'm very disappointed to see someone so personally associated with supply-side economics on the Federal Reserve Board."[36] After being confirmed by the Senate, Johnson and Angell joined two existing Reagan appointees (Preston Martin and Martha R. Seger) as the so-called "Gang of Four" who subsequently lobbied Fed Chairman Volcker to accept two reductions in the discount rate in early 1986 to its lowest (6.5 percent) level in eight years.

In addition, the Fed must be wary of Congress, but there are serious obstacles to legislative oversight of monetary policy. Few members of Congress have the requisite knowledge or the political incentives to give much attention to the task. Usually Congress threatens to intervene in monetary policymaking in the wake of public reactions following hikes in interest rates or slumps in housing construction (since mortgages are interest sensitive). These conditions occurred in the mid-1970s, so the opportunity was ripe for legislative sanctions against the Fed.[37] New legislation requiring lower interest or credit expansion was successfully opposed by then-Fed Chairman Burns, but Congress did enact House Concurrent Resolution 133, which obliges the chairman of the Fed to appear at congressional committee hearings to explain the Fed's monetary objectives. Another congressional tradition is for populist representatives to complain about high interest rates and demand that the Fed pursue an "easy money" policy. In the 1950s and 1960s the Federal Reserve Board was a favorite political target for Wright Patman (D-TX), while during the 1982 recession a congressional outcry was led by Henry S. Reuss (D-WI). The most recent attempt to bring monetary policy more under the control of Congress and the president occurred in 1989, amidst concern that the economy was beginning to slow; once again enactment failed. While Congress from time to time may express its displeasure with monetary policy, so far no structural reforms have undercut the formal autonomy of the Federal Reserve Board.

Other Regulatory Bodies

A number of other regulatory bodies have policy responsibilities that affect the operation of the economy. Some of the most important include the Securities and Exchange Commission, which regulates the equity market (e.g., stock market activities), the Interstate Commerce Commission, which regulates interstate transport by truck and rail, and the Federal Trade Commission, which (along with the Justice Depart-

ment) oversees the enforcement of antitrust legislation. Additional agen-   **65**
cies that make or implement policy with important economic effects include the National Labor Relations Board, the Federal Energy Regulatory
Commission, and the Federal Deposit Insurance Corporation.

Most, if not all, of these regulatory efforts are directed at the microe-
conomy, that is, at altering the behavior of individual people or firms, in
order to achieve outcomes seen as socially desirable. Of course, the lines
between microeconomic and macroeconomic effects are not always clear-
cut. For example, in antitrust policy the general goal is to prevent the
creation of a firm or a group of firms acting together (a cartel) that will
dominate a particular market and thereby be able to set prices that are
not the result of competition among suppliers. The targets of this policy
are individual firms, but the goal is one with a collective effect—the prices
society must pay for the products produced in the noncompetitive market.
Moreover, the specific antitrust actions taken, like the breakup of the Bell
System in 1983, may have implications for macroeconomic concerns such
as the rate of productivity improvement in the macroeconomy. In fact, a
major contention of the supply-side theorists who influenced the Reagan
administration was that the aggregate effect of the various regulatory activities of the agencies described above (plus others, such as the Environmental Protection Agency and the Occupational Health and Safety Administration) was to lower incentives for producers throughout the
economy and thereby reduce the overall level of economic activity.

As a general rule, these other regulatory bodies do not possess the
independence that the Fed has in developing monetary policy. Several of
the agencies (e.g., EPA and OSHA) are either part of cabinet departments
or are noncabinet agencies whose heads report directly to the president.
The independent regulatory bodies are somewhat more independent, but
they are generally headed by fewer commissioners than the Fed, who serve
shorter terms.[38] In addition, it is far more likely for Congress to modify
the statutes governing these agencies' activities than has been true for the
Fed, whose basic statutory responsibility has not been altered since 1935.
Indeed, the exceptional efforts of the Reagan administration to create a
Fed Board of Governors supportive of Reagan policy were noteworthy
because they were unusual—and they were only partially successful. Reagan's efforts to influence the other regulatory bodies were both less controversial (with some exceptions, such as the EPA) and more successful.

WHO COORDINATES POLICY?

Given their differing recruitment patterns, values, and institutional responsibilities, the major executive branch economic actors—the

66   CEA, the OMB, the Fed, and Treasury—hold dissimilar macroeconomic viewpoints. The problem is compounded by the often conflicting goals of macroeconomic policy: price stability and high employment, economic growth and productivity, and a healthy trade balance. Furthermore, to achieve an optimal mix of these macroeconomic goals, policymakers must utilize both fiscal and monetary policies as they interrelate with both the domestic *and* the international economies.

The task of coordinating the activities of these bodies rests with the president, but this is clearly a Herculean task. To begin with, no one policy apparatus exists within the federal government for this purpose—until 1993 there has been no counterpart to the National Security Council, whose purpose is to advise "the President with respect to the integration of domestic, foreign, and military policies relating to the national security" of the United States. The organization of economic policymaking in the White House has been ad hoc and informal, changing according to each president's governing style, and influenced by whatever economic problem gets priority at a given time.

Formal Mechanisms for Coordination

Modern presidents have experimented widely with various methods of organizing their economic advisory team (Figure 3.1). One of the most important constraints is size, because when a president includes other advisers in addition to the OMB director, treasury secretary, CEA chairman, and Fed chairman, he has to formalize those relationships through some kind of institutional arrangement. President Reagan initially utilized a system of cabinet councils, seeking advice from the largest number of officials whose responsibility touched on economic affairs. On the other hand, President Nixon preferred dealing one-on-one with Treasury Secretary John Connally, his chief economic adviser.

The advantages and disadvantages of alternative types of economic advisory systems have been described by Roger Porter.[39] Using the Council of Economic Advisers to coordinate macroeconomic policymaking would be an obvious solution except that the CEA is too small and resists taking on any operational duties. One alternative is to appoint a White House assistant to oversee economic policy, as was done when President Nixon gave Treasury Secretary George Shultz a "double-hat" by designating him assistant to the president for economic affairs. Shultz had succeeded John Connally as treasury secretary, who, although he did not have a similar White House double appointment, had also served as the informal "czar" of Nixon administration economic policy.[40]

Figure 3.1   Organization of the President's Economic Advisers

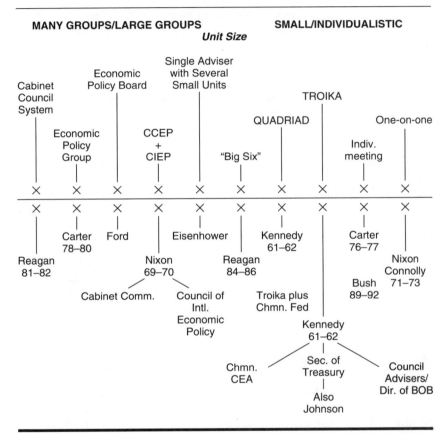

MANY GROUPS/LARGE GROUPS   SMALL/INDIVIDUALISTIC

Unit Size

Source: Reprinted with permission from Michael A. Genovese, "The Presidency and Styles of Economic Management," *Congress and the Presidency*, vol. 14, no. 2 (Autumn 1987), p. 157, Table 2. Adapted by the authors.

Later, under President Ford, L. William Seidman was designated assistant to the president for economic affairs, although he did not retain the overall control exercised by the Nixon "czars." However, Jimmy Carter ended the practice of employing a White House assistant as his chief economic spokesperson, relying instead on his CEA chairman to guide economic policy. This uneven record led Porter to conclude that "presidents have generally not relied heavily on White House economic policy assistants to organize the pattern of economic advice and decision making

68   to the same degree that they have for national security affairs or domestic affairs."[41]

A more common vehicle of coordination has been the creation of interagency committees, working groups, or councils, but such groups lack institutional continuity since they have rarely survived the administration that created them. Under President Eisenhower, CEA chairman Arthur Burns created an Advisory Board on Economic Growth and Stability and a Council on Foreign Economic Policy. The most successful coordinating mechanism was the Troika operation of the Kennedy and Johnson administrations, which involved regular discussions between OMB, CEA, and Treasury, not only at the agency head level, but at two lower levels, a middle-range level (called T2) and a technician level (T3). This regular Troika activity did not, however, survive into the Nixon administration.[42] President Nixon preferred the naming of a single powerful economic "czar," although originally he created a large body of department and agency heads called the Cabinet Committee of Economic Policy.

The Watergate scandal drove Nixon from office amid charges that he had created an "imperial" presidency, and Gerald Ford moved to democratize the White House decision-making processes. One change was the creation of the **Economic Policy Board (EPB),** which Ford considered to be "the most important institutional innovation of my administration."[43] A somewhat large body like the Cabinet Committee of Economic Policy of the early Nixon years, it differed in that it had a more formal structure (an executive director and an executive committee that met regularly) and clearer support from the president. It lasted 27 months, during which the EPB met 520 times and considered 1,539 agenda items ranging from macroeconomic policy, taxes, energy, and trade relations, to Third World economics and international monetary policy. While presidents often adapt a crisis mentality when dealing with economic issues—putting out one brush fire before a new one erupts—the EPB allowed some degree of long-term planning by anticipating problems before they became too serious.

The EPB institutionalized a "multiple advocacy" approach to decision making so that the president was exposed to different views, and President Ford helped that process by probing the analyses offered by his advisers. The EPB's executive director, L. William Seidman, guaranteed all participants full access to President Ford, so individuals did not usually try to circumvent the EPB and approach the president directly for special consideration. Nor was there any attempt to force policy agreement. Says Porter: "Whatever the final outcome, the process was designed first and foremost to provide alternatives and arguments for the President's judgment—not to reach a consensus."[44]

The EPB was not without its flaws. The collegial process was slow-moving, trivial issues were not always separated from important problems, and prolonged debate wasted the president's valuable time. All in all, however, "the EPB not only had the reputation of being the most effective policy council in the Ford period, but also the most sustained, comprehensive, and successful collegial attempt ever to advise a president on economic policy matters."[45]

As has become typical, this coordinating mechanism did not survive the presidential transition. Although similar in name, President Carter's Economic Policy Group (EPG) had neither the regularity of interaction nor the confidence of the president. As a result, its deliberations degenerated into a forum for "turf fights" between the participating departments and officials.

Perhaps in response to the reputed disarray of executive branch decision making during the Carter years, Ronald Reagan "employed during his first term cabinet-level 'councils' in the economic policy sector much more extensively than had any of his predecessors."[46] President Reagan used this device to make sure that his administration acted together in key policy areas. Most important was the Cabinet Council on Economic Affairs (CCEA), which controlled the domestic economic policy agenda. Its members were the secretaries of treasury, state, commerce, labor, and transportation, the OMB director, the CEA chairman, the U.S. trade representative, other cabinet members when appropriate, and President Reagan, who chaired the proceedings. It met two to three times each week to deliberate on policy problems and to solicit research by subcabinet working groups. However, President Reagan did not regularly attend the CCEA sessions, which led other members to skip the meetings as well. In addition, the heads of Treasury, OMB, and CEA, along with the secretary of state and the assistant to the president for policy development sometimes agreed beforehand not to bring specific issues before the CCEA. Another problem was that other councils—the Cabinet Council on Commerce and Trade, the Trade Policy Committee, and the National Security Council Senior Interagency Group on International Economic Policy—fought for control of international economics.

After 1985, President Reagan moved away from the cabinet council arrangement and delegated responsibility over economic policy to a few key individuals. His successor employed a similar system. Although an Economic Policy Council (chaired by Treasury Secretary Brady) formally existed for the first three years of the Bush administration, it was never a significant vehicle for economic policymaking; President Bush preferred to meet directly with key advisers, especially with Treasury Secretary Brady and OMB Director Darman.

70   The National Economic Council

Even before taking office, President Clinton announced that he would create a **National Economic Council**, which he hoped would serve to coordinate domestic and international policymaking in a manner similar to the workings of the National Security Council in military and foreign policymaking. The president would chair the council, while its daily operations would be overseen by the senior economic adviser, a new position carrying the same rank as the national security adviser. Clinton's initial appointment to this post was Robert Rubin, a longtime Democratic fund raiser and investment banker who headed the New York firm of Goldman, Sachs & Company.

The membership of the Economic Council will likely evolve over time, but at the outset, it contained the traditional actors—OMB director, CEA chair, and treasury secretary—as well as additional cabinet department heads, such as the secretaries of labor and commerce. The extended membership reflected President Clinton's view that economic policy must be coordinated over a broad front, with special emphasis placed on coordinating domestic and international economic policies. The creation of this council was also intended to reflect the fundamental importance President Clinton believed should be attached to economic policy.

Whether this structural innovation can be effective and eventually become institutionalized remains an open question. Some prominent economists have questioned the need for such a council, preferring that the president rely upon traditional bodies such as the CEA instead.[47] In addition, there will clearly be problems of coordination among so many significant actors. Indeed, one question that remains to be answered is who is in charge of economic policymaking in the Clinton administration. President Clinton has indicated that he will be the chief economic policymaker for his administration; at the same time, others—such as Labor Secretary Robert Reich and Senior Economic Adviser Rubin—have been described as playing major roles. The traditional major actors such as OMB director and treasury secretary are also certain to seek significant influence over economic policymaking. The early experience with the National Economic Council has been mixed, with "high marks for 'process,' " but less success at producing new legislation capable of being enacted by Congress.[48] In the end, two factors will determine the success of the new Economic Council as a policymaking institution: the extent of regular subcouncil interaction (a high degree of which was seen in previous successful coordinating mechanisms like the 1960s' Troika and Ford's Economic Policy Board) and the commitment and attention of every administration's "economist-in-chief"—the president.

Presidential Coordination of Economic Policy

In the end, the degree of coordination of economic policy within the executive branch depends upon the president. Clearly, the experiences of most recent presidents suggests that total coordination is not really possible—there are simply too many units with diverse missions and outlooks for policy development to be either smooth or single-minded. The specific structural mechanisms employed to coordinate economic policy have alternated between centralizing control in a single, major figure and constructing interagency economic councils, but in any case, the most successful attempts at coordination have occurred when the president has had a strong interest in economic policy and was able to assemble a group of economic policymakers with a similar outlook on economic problems and policy.

This, in turn, rests upon the president's willingness and ability to use his appointment powers to create a more coherent vision of economic policy. During periods of greater consensus, such as during the heyday of Keynesian economics in the 1960s, the major emphasis in appointments was on professional standing, prior experience, and ability to work with other actors. As the theoretical consensus has fractured since the late 1970s, presidents have been more anxious to employ ideological criteria in selecting their key appointees. This may have reached its zenith during the Reagan administration, when conscious attempts were made by the president and his closest advisers to appoint supply-side and neo-classical economists to most key policy positions, even though these economic viewpoints represented a minority in the economics profession. Until a new consensus on economic issues appears, however, this pattern is likely to continue.

In the economic sphere, the president has heavy responsibilities but limited power. The public has high expectations, but the president often has limited room to lead and act. He clearly has greatest control when dealing with policy that is formulated and implemented by officials directly under his control, namely, elements of the Executive Office of the President (OMB and CEA), cabinet departments, and other executive agencies reporting directly to the president. The president is also able to exert substantial control over most of the independent regulatory agencies through such means as appointments, the budget, and influence over legislative mandates.[49] The president has the least control over policies that involve dealing with other institutions that are relatively independent. The first of these, monetary policy, which is the special province of the Federal Reserve Board, we have begun to examine in this chapter; we will return to consider the mechanism by which monetary policy is formulated

72 and implemented in Chapter 5. The other major policy tool only partially under the president's control is fiscal policy, which is ultimately the result of legislative action over taxation and the budget. This legislative action, which involves both the president and Congress, is the subject of our next chapter.

KEY TERMS

agenda setting, policy formulation, policy adoption, policy implementation, policy evaluation and reformulation, Executive Office of the President, Council of Economic Advisors (CEA), Office of Management and Budget (OMB), Troika, economic subpresidency, secretary of the treasury, fiscal year, independent regulatory agencies, Federal Reserve Board (Fed), Federal Open Market Committee, Economic Policy Board (EPB), National Economic Council

ADDITIONAL READING

Anderson, James E. and Jared E. Hazelton, *Managing Macroeconomic Policy: The Johnson Presidency*. Austin, TX: University of Texas Press, 1986. In-depth examination of economic policymaking during the Johnson administration, with special attention to the development of the economic subpresidency.

Campbell, Colin. *Managing the Presidency: Carter, Reagan, and the Search for Executive Harmony*. Pittsburgh: University of Pittsburgh Press, 1986. Two chapters detail the economic advisory system of Presidents Carter and Reagan.

Hargrove, Erwin C. and Samuel A. Morley, eds., *The President and the Council of Economic Advisers*. Boulder, CO: Westview Press, 1984. Oral history of CEA chairmen who served during 1949–1980, focusing on their relationship with the president and the impact of economic knowledge on decision making.

Kettl, Donald F. *Leadership at the Fed*. New Haven: Yale University Press, 1986. Excellent study of the leadership styles of four powerful Fed chairmen: Marriner S. Eccles, William McChesney Martin, Arthur F. Burns, and Paul Volcker.

McDonald, Forrest. *Alexander Hamilton: A Biography*. New York: W. W. Norton, 1979. Excellent study of the first secretary of the treasury and architect of the nation's financial system.

Norton, Hugh S. *The Employment Act and the Council of Economic Advisers, 1946–1976*. Columbia, SC: University of South Carolina Press, 1977. A study of the CEA from Truman to Nixon, with added coverage of Congress' Joint Economic Committee.

Nourse, Edwin G. *Economics in the Public Service*. New York: Harcourt, Brace, and World, 1953. The first CEA chairman explains the events leading to the

Employment Act of 1946 and the role of the CEA and the Joint Economic **73**
Committee under Truman.

Porter, Roger B. *Presidential Decision Making: The Economic Policy Board.*
Cambridge, England: Cambridge University Press, 1980. Superb analysis of the
advisory group organized by President Ford to integrate both domestic and
international economic policy.

Shultz, George P. and Kenneth W. Dam. *Economic Policy Behind the Headlines.*
New York: W. W. Norton, 1977. Informative discussion of the "workaday
world" of policymaking during 1969–1974, including such issues as wage-price
controls, budgets, and taxes.

Stein, Herbert. *The Fiscal Revolution in America.* Chicago: The University of
Chicago Press, 1969. Easy-to-read discussion of the impact of Keynesian
economics on fiscal policymaking by modern presidents through the Johnson
administration.

Stein, Herbert. *Presidential Economics: The Making of Economic Policy from
Roosevelt to Reagan and Beyond.* New York: Simon and Schuster, 1984. The
author, who became CEA chairman under Nixon, elaborates upon and updates
his account of fiscal policymaking through the Nixon, Carter, and early Reagan
administrations.

NOTES

1.   This type of stage model of policy development is a familiar framework
for understanding public policy; e.g., see James E. Anderson, *Public Policy-Making:
An Introduction* (Boston: Houghton-Mifflin, 1990), and Charles Jones, *An Introduction to Public Policy.* For a discussion of a variety of alternative approaches, see
Thomas R. Dye, *Understanding Public Policy,* 6th ed. (Englewood Cliffs, NJ: Prentice-Hall, 1987), Chapter 2.

2.   James E. Anderson, "The President and Economic Policy: A Comparative
View of Advisory Arrangements," paper presented at the 1991 annual meeting of
the American Political Science Association, Washington, DC.

3.   For example, on the role of the Supreme Court, see James E. Anderson,
Politics and the Economy (Boston: Little, Brown, 1966), pp. 45–49.

4.   Randall Ripley and Grace Franklin, *Policy Implementation and Bureaucracy,* 2nd ed. (Chicago: Dorsey, 1986).

5.   Robert S. Erikson, "Economic Conditions and the Presidential Vote,"
American Political Science Review 83 (June 1989), 567–573.

6.   Hugh S. Norton, *The Employment Act and the Council of Economic Advisers, 1946–1976* (Columbia, SC: University of South Carolina Press, 1977), p. 65.

7.   Quoted in Raymond Tatalovich and Byron W. Daynes, *Presidential Power
in the United States* (Monterey, CA: Brooks/Cole Publishing Company, 1984),
p. 217.

74   8.   James E. Anderson, "The President and Economic Policy: A Comparative View of Advisory Arrangements," paper presented at the 1991 Annual Meeting of the American Political Science Association, p. 2; see also, James E. Anderson and Jared E. Hazelton, *Managing Macroeconomic Policy: The Johnson Presidency* (Austin, TX: University of Texas Press, 1986), Chapter 2.

9.   Three CEA members did not have the Ph.D., and four obtained their Ph.D. degree or equivalent from a European university. Kermit Gordon had a B.A. degree; Alan Greenspan had an M.A. degree at the time of his CEA service (he later received a Ph.D.); and Leon H. Keyserling had an LL.B. degree. The four others were: Karl Brandt and William J. Fellner from the University of Berlin, Henrik S. Houthakker from the University of Amsterdam, and Martin Feldstein from Oxford University. Walter Stewart is counted as receiving a Ph.D., although he actually received the degree Doctor of Letters from Princeton University. Paul McCracken is counted only once, although he served on two different occasions (1956–59 and 1969–71).

10.   Steven Greenhouse, "Cambridge Pushes Chicago Aside," *New York Times* (February 2, 1993), p. C1.

11.   This discussion is based upon Heller, *New Dimensions of Political Economy*, pp. 14–18.

12.   Gardner Ackley, "The Contribution of Economics to Policy Formation," *The Journal of Finance* 21 (May 1966), 169–177. Quote on page 176.

13.   Walter W. Heller, *New Dimensions of Political Economy* (Cambridge, MA: Harvard University Press, 1966), p. 52.

14.   An excellent analysis and critique of the microeconomic views are provided in: Steven E. Rhoads, *The Economist's View of the World* (Cambridge, England: Cambridge University Press, 1985).

15.   Erwin C. Hargrove and Samuel A. Morley, eds., *The President and the Council of Economic Advisers* (Boulder, CO: Westview Press, 1984), p. 15.

16.   Reported in Robert Pear, "Reagan Advisors Say Bill on Aliens Can Hurt Economy," *New York Times* (January 23, 1986), pp. 1, 12. Also see Robert Pear, "Aide Says Reagan Backs Aliens Bill," *New York Times* (January 24, 1986), pp. 1, 7.

17.   Hargrove and Morley, eds., *The President and the Council of Economic Advisers*, p. 33.

18.   Reported in Craufurd D. Goodwin and R. Stanley Herren, "The Truman Administration: Problems and Policies Unfold," in Craufurd D. Goodwin, ed., *Exhortation and Controls: The Search for a Wage-Price Policy 1945–1971* (Washington, DC: The Brookings Institution, 1975), p. 37.

19.   John W. Sloan, "Economic Policymaking in the Johnson and Ford Administrations," *Presidential Studies Quarterly* 20 (Winter 1990), p. 116.

20.   Steven Greenhouse, "Bush's Economic Aides Defending Reputations," *New York Times* (November 14, 1992), p. A7.

21.   This is not meant to imply that recent CEA members lack significant **75** professional reputations, but only that presidents choose economists with significant reputations from within the macroeconomic "camp" that they favor. For example, each of Clinton's CEA nominees are considered to have solid academic credentials. While CEA Chair Tyson's recent reputation is based on work on international trade, Clinton's second CEA nominee, Alan Blinder of Princeton University, has a significant reputation as a macroeconomist.

22.   See, for example, "Reports of Clinton Nominees Ease Fears of Bond Traders," *New York Times* (December 8, 1992), p. C1.

23.   Control is actually shared to a significant degree with the Fed, acting as the U.S.'s central bank. The treasury secretary plays a very public role in periodic formal meetings among finance ministers, while central bankers consult and coordinate with one another on a relatively continuous basis.

24.   The fiscal year takes its number from the year in which it ends. Thus FY93 covers the period 10/1/92–9/30/93.

25.   Kermit Gordon, "Reflections on Spending," in J. D. Montgomery and A. Smithies, eds., *Public Policy* 15 (1966), 11–22. Reprinted in Thomas E. Cronin and Sanford D. Greenberg, eds., *The Presidential Advisory System* (New York: Harper and Row, 1969), pp. 58–67. The quote appears on p. 60 of Cronin and Greenberg.

26.   Hugh Heclo, "OMB and the Presidency—The Problem of 'Neutral Competence,'" *The Public Interest* 38 (Winter 1975), 87.

27.   See Richard P. Nathan, *The Administrative Presidency* (New York: Wiley, 1983).

28.   Quoted in Hargrove and Morley, *The President and the Council of Economic Advisers*, p. 191.

29.   "The Dollar Chooses a Chairman," *Business Week* (August 6, 1979), p. 20.

30.   Michael D. Reagan, "The Political Structure of the Federal Reserve System," *American Political Science Review* 55 (1961): 64–76.

31.   All federally chartered commercial banks, plus some state-chartered banks, are members of the Federal Reserve System. While a minority of all U.S. banks, these banks collectively represent well over half of the bank assets in the U.S.

32.   John T. Woolley, *Monetary Politics: The Federal Reserve and the Politics of Monetary Policy* (Cambridge, England: Cambridge University Press, 1984), pp. 56–57.

33.   Ibid., p. 67.

34.   Ibid., p. 61.

35.   Ibid., p. 130.

36.   See Peter T. Kilborn, "New Fed Nominees: Manuel H. Johnson," *New York Times* (October 15, 1985), pp. 1, 34. Quote is on p. 34.

76   37.   The following discussion is based upon Woolley, *Monetary Politics*, pp. 144–147.

38.   As Keech and Morris demonstrate, the large number of appointees and long terms of the Fed greatly inhibit a president's ability to quickly influence the Fed, and have helped to maintain the Fed's independence; see William R. Keech and Irwin L. Morris, "Institutional Limitations on Presidential Influence over the Federal Reserve," paper presented at the 1991 Annual Meeting of the Southern Political Science Association.

39.   Roger B. Porter, "Economic Advice to the President: From Eisenhower to Reagan," *Political Science Quarterly* 98 (Fall 1983), 403–426.

40.   Anderson, "The President and Economic Policy."

41.   Porter, "Economic Advice to the President," p. 417.

42.   Anderson, "The President and Economic Policy."

43.   Quoted in Roger B. Porter, *Presidential Decision Making: The Economic Policy Board* (Cambridge, England: Cambridge University Press, 1980), p. 212.

44.   Ibid., p. 177.

45.   Ibid., p. 212.

46.   See Colin Campbell, *Managing the Presidency: Carter, Reagan, and the Search for Executive Harmony* (Pittsburgh: University of Pittsburgh Press, 1986), pp. 140–147.

47.   This was the view expressed by two Nobel laureates, James Tobin and Robert M. Solow, in "Clintonomics Doesn't Need A Czar," *New York Times* (December 10, 1992), p. A19.

48.   Steven Mufson, "The Eye of the Economic Whirlwind," *Washington Post National Weekly Edition* 10:34 (June 21–27, 1993), p. 8.

49.   For example, see Joseph Stewart, Jr., James E. Anderson, and Zona Taylor, "Presidential and Congressional Support for Independent Regulatory Commissions: Implications of the Budgetary Process," *Western Political Quarterly* 35: 318–326; and Terry M. Moe, "Control and Feedback in Economic Regulation: The Case of the NLRB," *American Political Science Review* 79: 1094–1116. For a somewhat different view, stressing the role of professionalism in administrative change, see Marc Allen Eisner and Kenneth J. Meier, "Presidential Control versus Bureaucratic Power: Explaining the Reagan Revolution in Antitrust," *American Journal of Political Science* 34: 269–287.

CHAPTER 4

Presidential Power and Congressional Budgeting

The federal budget is an ordering of our national priorities, or, as Aaron Wildavsky puts it, a "series of goals with price tags attached."[1] Since the advent of Keynesian thought in the 1930s, the budget is also the focal point for debate over fiscal policy. Apart from essential political questions like "How will the costs and benefits of government action be distributed across the population?" the budget is also the vehicle for determining the role the federal government will play in increasing or decreasing the aggregate demand for goods and services. Since 1970, total outlays (spending) in the federal budget have ranged between 19 and 25 percent of the gross domestic product. Given its vast size (projected FY93 outlays of $1.47 trillion), alterations in federal spending decisions clearly have the potential to influence aggregate demand.

Unfortunately, over the same period a series of large **budget deficits** (when outlays exceed revenues) have rendered the budget a blunt instrument with regard to fiscal policy. Beyond the stark fact that the continuing large deficits have refocused attention on the issue of deficit reduction rather than the role of fiscal policy in macroeconomic management, additional factors, such as the rise of entitlement programs and resistance to increasing revenues through general tax increases, have reduced the range of fiscal options. As a result, there has been a harmony between fiscal policy and budgetary politics only during recessions, when more spending is needed for economic stimulation. In nonrecessionary times, however, the political calculus underlying budgeting precludes spending reductions or tax increases that are large enough to have a real disinflationary impact.

The relationship between federal budgeting and fiscal policy and the contemporary crisis in the federal budgetary process are two of the principal topics discussed in this chapter. To begin, however, we describe the mechanics of the federal budgetary process and, in particular, how it has evolved over time. A discussion of the development of the budgetary process is in reality an account of the battle for political control over taxing and spending, both within Congress and, more importantly, between Congress and the president. This battle began as early as the administration of George Washington, and it continues to this day.

THE BUDGETARY PROCESS

We begin by briefly describing the operation of the U.S. Congress as it relates to budgeting. In both the Senate and the House of Representatives, much of the careful work involved in legislating (enacting laws) is done in committees and subcommittees. These committees are called standing committees, since the committee structure continues from year to year, with each committee having a specific area of responsibility.

In order for the federal government to spend money on some activity, two related, but different, pieces of legislation must be passed. **Authorizing legislation**, which is considered by the standing committee responsible for the functional area being covered (e.g., the Armed Services Committee for defense issues), establishes the legal authority for the federal government to engage in a specific activity and often sets upper limits for spending on this activity. **Appropriations legislation**, which is considered by the Appropriations Committees, sets aside the actual funds that are to be spent.[2] At present, the budget is actually a set of thirteen appropriations bills, each of which is considered by one of the thirteen subcommittees of the House and Senate **Appropriations Committees**. Revenue-raising legislation is presently considered by the **House Ways and Means Committee** and the **Senate Finance Committee**. As we shall see, these current practices are only the latest version of a process that has undergone considerable evolution in the two hundred years of our constitutional history. This evolution has been punctuated by the passage of two significant pieces of legislation, in 1921 and 1974. This legislation restructured the federal budgetary process and shifted the balance between presidential and congressional control over budgeting and, hence, fiscal policy.

Budgeting, 1789–1921

$\mathbf{A}$rticle I of the Constitution gives Congress the power "To lay and collect Taxes, Duties, Imposts and Excises, to pay the Debts and provide for the common Defense and general Welfare of the United States, . . . To borrow Money on the credit of the United States, . . . To coin Money [and] regulate the Value thereof." Later in the same article, the Constitution declares "No Money shall be drawn from the Treasury, but in Consequence of Appropriations made by Law." Collectively, these clauses define Congressional control over both taxing and spending. James Madison predicted, in *Federalist* 58, that this "power of the purse" would be "the most complete and effectual weapon with which any constitution can arm the immediate representatives of the people, for obtaining a redress of every grievance, and for carrying into effect every just and salutary measure." At first, Secretary of the Treasury Alexander Hamilton dominated the budgetary process by lobbying the Congress to enact his financial program. But criticism of Hamilton by the Jeffersonians led to his resignation in 1794, whereupon the House of Representatives asserted its control over budgeting.[3]

The House began reviewing appropriations bills through its Committee on Ways and Means, which was established in 1802 as the first standing committee of the House. In the Senate, appropriations bills continued to be referred to select (i.e., special) committees until a standing committee, the Committee on Finance, was created in 1816. At this juncture, both the House Ways and Means Committee and the Senate Finance Committee had jurisdiction over *both* revenue and appropriation bills in their respective houses. However, this unified control over finances was jeopardized by a new development, the use of separate funding bills for special purposes. Two appropriations bills were enacted as early as 1794, one funding government administration and another for military spending. This practice escalated during the early 1800s, when separate appropriations were used for such purposes as the Navy, the Post Office, and a Military Academy.

The Civil War fragmented budgetary authority further, because no single committee was able to cope with the complexities of wartime finances. In 1865 the House limited the jurisdiction of Ways and Means to revenue bills only and shifted spending bills to new committees on appropriations and on banking and currency. But soon complaints surfaced that the Appropriations Committee had assumed too much power. By 1876, for example, Appropriations was empowered to *reduce* the amounts in spending bills, which effectively undermined the power of standing legislative committees. To curb the Appropriations Committee, the House

80   authorized certain standing committees to also report money bills to the floor. It is not coincidental that the House moved first against the Appropriations Committee (in 1877) to assure that expenditures for rivers and harbors projects, a classic example of "pork barrel" legislation, would not be trimmed. This assault on Appropriations, says Louis Fisher,[4] occurred because many legislators believed that its preoccupation with economy in government prevented them from delivering benefits to their districts. The Senate also decentralized its appropriations process beginning with rivers and harbors legislation. In 1877 the funding bill for those projects was reassigned from the Appropriations Committee to the Commerce Committee. The complete dismantling of the Committee on Appropriations in the Senate came in 1899, when six other funding bills were assigned to those standing committees with legislative jurisdiction.

What began in the early nineteenth century as a coherent procedure, with the Ways and Means and Finance Committees controlling both taxes and spending, had given way by 1900 to a highly fragmented system. Nobody reviewed finances as a whole. Tax bills went to the Ways and Means Committee and the Committee on Finance. General appropriations were assigned to the House and Senate Committees on Appropriations, but funding bills for specific projects like rivers and harbors were given to the standing committees charged with legislating in these areas. Despite many reforms, this tension between legislative and appropriations committees has persisted. Even though Appropriations Committees in both houses regained control over all spending bills during the twentieth century, standing committees are now allowed to authorize a given level of funding for programs under their jurisdiction.[5]

Budgeting 1921–1974

A movement towards budget reform was encouraged by the string of deficits incurred during 1894–99, 1904–05, and 1910–11. President Taft urged Congress to fund a five-member Commission on Economy and Efficiency to upgrade the budgetary process. Its final report in June 1912 recommended that the president review agency spending estimates and coordinate them into one budget for Congress' approval. But the legislature refused, and Taft directed his agency heads to prepare, in addition to the customary "Book of Estimates" for Congress, a national budget along the lines proposed by the commission. In reaction, Congress ordered the agencies *not* to formulate any budget document, fearing that Taft might cut funding programs targeting their districts.

President Taft's successor, Woodrow Wilson, had been interested in budgetary reform since his days as a professor of political science in the

1890s, but the issue was sidetracked by World War I. During this period various states and localities adopted the executive budget concept, and bipartisan support for that reform was developing in Congress. An **executive budget** is a budget in which all spending requests are combined into a single budget document, which is prepared by some central budgeting authority (usually the chief executive). A principal benefit of an executive budget is that it permits a clearer idea of overall spending and of how the individual components relate to the overall picture. In 1917 President Wilson asked Congress to move toward that goal by assigning all funding bills in each chamber to one committee. By the end of 1919 Wilson threw his support behind the concept of a national budget.

The Budget and Accounting Act was finally signed into law by President Harding in 1921. It established a Bureau of the Budget (BOB) in the Department of the Treasury and created an executive budget wherein the BOB was empowered to "assemble, correlate, revise, reduce, or increase the estimates of the several departments or establishments," with the exceptions of Congress and the Supreme Court.[6] In 1920 the House also consolidated jurisdiction over its spending bills within the Appropriations Committee, and the Senate took similar action in 1922. The hope was that each Appropriations Committee would bring a unified budget to the floor, but this reform came too late to alter the congressional balance of power. Instead the House began the practice of reviewing subcommittee reports (of the Appropriations Committee) individually rather than as a package.

Subcommittees developed autonomy from the whole Appropriations Committee, as well as close working relationships with the standing committees having programmatic jurisdiction over their sections of the budget. These relationships were facilitated by the norm of "reciprocity" whereby subcommittees would defer to one another, and the Appropriations Committee simply ratified their spending decisions.[7] The key standing committees in the Senate had access to the Appropriations Committee by a 1922 rule giving them three *ex officio* members whenever relevant legislative business was conducted, a practice not ended until 1977.[8]

Each agency sent its budget estimate directly to Congress, so in the nineteenth century presidential impact on the budgetary process was not systematic and depended upon the resolve of each incumbent. Following passage of the 1921 act, President Harding moved decisively by appointing Charles G. Dawes the first BOB director, and he issued Budget Circular No. 40 declaring that all agencies must submit their budgets to the bureau *beforehand* so they could be forwarded to Congress as the executive budget. Under Harding, Coolidge, and Hoover, the BOB was mainly concerned about economy in government. This narrow focus prompted Roosevelt to

82   rely on his "Brain Trust" to develop a budget strategy during the depression. The BOB reached its zenith under Harry Truman and Dwight Eisenhower, when the Bureau, rather than just reviewing agency estimates, determined if new program requests by the agencies fit into the president's legislative program. This became known as the **legislative clearance** function.[9]

Until the mid-1960s, preparation and enactment of the federal budget followed a predictable pattern, guided by acceptance of certain general principles by most participants. According to Wildavsky, these included a commitment to balanced (or nearly balanced) budgets, a belief that government spending was basically beneficial, and a preference for "hidden" taxes (such as bracket creep) or selective tax changes rather than across-the-board changes in the tax code.[10] In addition, the participants played well-understood roles: the OMB supervised the preparation of the executive budget but developed a reputation for non-partisan mastery of budgetary details. The House Appropriations Committee served as "guardian of the federal treasury," trimming presidential requests, while the Senate Appropriations Committee played the role of "court of appeals," restoring a portion of the House cuts.[11] Although spending authority rested with the Appropriations Committees and taxing authority rested with the Ways and Means and Finance Committees, the general acceptance of the value of small deficits helped to coordinate their separate activities.

This consensus began to dissolve during the 1960s, when Lyndon Johnson pushed for an expansion of federal programs as he declared a War on Poverty at the same time that defense spending soared due to the costs of fighting the Vietnam War. Using Keynesian economic theory as a justification, liberals argued that budget deficits were not inherently undesirable. The 1960s represented a period of economic expansion, and the Keynesian "new economics" of this period argued that a series of deficits was not bad so long as the economy was growing (particularly if the deficits were partially responsible for continued economic expansion). It should be noted that this is a substantial modification of the views of Keynes himself, who had argued that the function of deficit spending was to stimulate aggregate demand and move the macroeconomy from a point below the full-employment level to the full-employment level. Deficit spending during a period of full employment, like the period 1965–68, is fundamentally dangerous according to the original Keynesian theory, since it risks raising demand over the full-employment level, hence producing price inflation. (Which, in fact, is what occurred.) The only valid reason for deficits during such a period, according to the original Keynesian principles, would be if these deficits were necessary to bring about a basic transformation in the economy that would allow the deficits to be eliminated through subsequent economic expansion. Such an argument was made, but the temporary deficits justified by this argument have actually become permanent; since 1961 the budget has been balanced only once, in FY69.

Other changes also contributed to the collapse of the old budgeting system. The vast expansion of federal programs created a rapidly changing and much more complex federal budget, and Congress found itself increasingly reliant upon the OMB for expert information on the budget. After 1969, when a Democratic Congress faced a Republican Nixon administration, this reliance upon the OMB became increasingly difficult. Nixon accelerated the trend toward politicizing the OMB, and the expertise of the OMB and the CEA (both located in the Executive Office of the President) became a weapon that tilted power toward the president in budgetary disputes with Congress.

The increasing disputes over budgeting, termed a "Seven-Year Budget War" by one expert,[12] culminated in the passage of the **Congressional Budget and Impoundment Control Act of 1974**. The specific trigger for passage of this act was a constitutional crisis associated with abuses of presidential power by President Nixon.[13] The president asserted that he had a power to impound funds—refuse to spend funds appropriated by Congress—as well as the authority to spend funds not appropriated by Congress (specifically, funds to prosecute a war in Cambodia). In response to this assertion of enhanced presidential control over the budget, Congress passed the 1974 act, which is actually composed of two separate acts, an Impoundment Control Act, which severely restricted presidential power to impound funds, and a Congressional Budget Act, which modified the basic budgetary procedure in an attempt to address the problems associated with the collapse of the budgetary consensus since the mid-1960s. As Shuman puts it, "The Congress passed the 'Impoundment Control Act' to discipline the president. It passed the 'Congressional Budget Act' to discipline itself."[14]

Budgeting Since 1974

The reformers had great hopes when the 1974 act was enacted; among its purposes were to assure effective Congressional control over the budgetary process; to provide for the Congressional determination each year of the appropriate level of federal revenues and expenditures; to provide a system of impoundment control; to establish national budget priorities; and to provide for the furnishing of information by the Executive Branch in a manner that will assist the Congress in discharging its duties.[15]

84   A **Congressional Budget Office (CBO)** was created in order to provide Congress with independent economic forecasts and budgetary projections and a level of expert staff assistance similar to what the CEA and
the OMB provide for the president. The act also created a Budget Committee in each house to coordinate spending and revenue-raising through
the establishment of overall budgetary targets, to be determined in accordance with a new budget timetable.

To allow more time to study the budget, the law changed the fiscal
year. From 1844 until 1976 the fiscal year extended from July 1 to June
30. Since the executive budget is submitted each January, the old starting
date of the fiscal year gave Congress about six months to study the proposed budget and enact all the appropriations bills before the start of the
new fiscal year. That rarely happened. From 1964 until 1974 only six
money bills were passed before the July 1 deadline.[16] The 1974 act changed
the start of the fiscal year to October 1, allowing Congress nine months
to study and pass the budget. The 1974 act also created a new timetable
for presidential submission and congressional consideration of the budget.
Over time, Congress still found it difficult to pass appropriations legislation
before the October 1 start of the fiscal year, and the 1974 timetable was
further revised (while retaining the October 1 starting point for the fiscal
year) by the Balanced Budget and Emergency Deficit Control Act of 1985
(known as Gramm-Rudman-Hollings).

The heart of the new budgetary process is the requirement that Congress pass two **concurrent resolutions** on the budget, one in the early
stages of the annual consideration of the budget and one at the close of
the process. The concurrent resolutions link revenue-raising and spending
activity in that the resolutions contain overall revenue and spending targets. Although not laws, the concurrent resolutions are supposed to be
binding agreements by the members of Congress that constrain the separate deliberations of the standing committees, the Appropriations Committees and subcommittees, and the revenue-raising committees. In theory, the first resolution represents an original budgetary agreement and the
second resolution allows revisions to that agreement once the various committees have completed their work on the specific elements of the budget
contained in authorizations, appropriations, and revenue bills. If there is
a difference between the second concurrent resolution and the separately
passed pieces of legislation, Congress is supposed to pass a piece of legislation, a reconciliation bill, that overrides the individual budgetary bills
approved since the passage of the first concurrent resolution.

The key task of the new process, the preparation of the concurrent
resolutions, was delegated by the 1974 act to newly created **Budget Committees** in each house. The initial stages of the new budgetary process

involves the collection of information to be used in preparing this initial resolution. As originally designed, the OMB was to submit to Congress by November 10 a **current services budget** that projected the cost of all existing programs through the upcoming fiscal year, given the assumption that no changes would be made to existing laws. The proposed executive budget for the upcoming fiscal year is submitted in January. Following its submission to Congress, the Congressional Budget Office (CBO)—the congressional staff agency created by the 1974 act—studies the budget's economic assumptions and develops fiscal options, and the Budget Committees collect preliminary estimates from the standing committees on budget authority, spending, and revenues for programs under their jurisdiction. The Joint Economic Committee also sends the Budget Committees its own assessment of the economic impact of the current services budget. Following these preliminary assessments, the Budget Committees hold public hearings.

Under the original 1974 act, all standing committees were supposed to give expenditure estimates to the Budget Committees by March 15, the CBO report was due by April 1, and each Budget Committee was required to introduce its concurrent resolution on the budget to its respective house no later than April 15. (If the House and Senate approved differing versions of the first budget resolution, then a conference committee had to resolve the differences.) The 1974 act mandated that this latter action be completed by May 15, but the 1985 Gramm-Rudman-Hollings Act accelerated the timetable one month, so the deadline for congressional passage of the first concurrent budget resolution is now April 15. The 1985 revisions also accelerated each of the other preliminary steps and eliminated the fall submission of the current services budget (which is now included as part of the January executive budget submission).

The first concurrent resolution lays out less binding targets to guide Congress until the second concurrent resolution (which sets ceilings) is enacted. The targets included amounts for (1) total budget authority, (2) total budget outlays, (3) total budget revenues, (4) total budget surplus or deficit, and (5) total public debt; budget authority and outlays are also earmarked by functional areas. There were sixteen functional areas in the 1974 act, but since then others have been added. There were twenty spending categories in the FY93 budget.[17]

In these broad functional areas the targets for budgetary authority must be allocated to over one thousand specific appropriations accounts by the thirteen appropriations bills considered by the Appropriations Committees. Following passage of the first concurrent resolution, the budget is reviewed in much the traditional way. Tax bills are reported by

86 the Ways and Means and Finance Committees; spending bills are handled by the two Appropriations Committees.

Budget Committees keep track of the decisions made in the House and Senate, and the 1985 revision stipulates that Congress must finish all appropriations bills by June 30. The 1974 act stipulated that two separate actions would follow, a second concurrent resolution and a reconciliation bill (if necessary). The **reconciliation bill** directs the standing committees to make whatever spending and revenue changes are necessary to conform with the agreed-upon ceilings. It implements the budget resolution, and after it is enacted no bill that cuts revenue below or increases spending above the statutory ceilings will be considered. Under the revised Gramm-Rudman-Hollings procedure, the two steps (the second concurrent resolution and reconciliation) are combined—a reconciliation bill must now be adopted by June 15 (two weeks before the final date for appropriations legislation).[18]

The 1974 and 1985 acts divided responsibility between the two branches of government—the president prepares an executive budget and the Congress enacts the budget—but they did not fundamentally transform the politics of budgeting. An early assessment by Allen Schick remains true today. "Congress will not allow itself to be deadlocked by the new process. Procedural roadblocks will be brushed aside if they threaten legislative paralysis or thwart a determined majority. Congress will sooner change its budget process than permit itself to be stalled by the rigors of budgeting."[19] As we will see in Chapter 11, the overriding problem of contemporary federal budgeting—large, continuing budget deficits—persists despite these and other changes to the formal mechanisms of the budgetary process.

Preparing the Executive Budget

Although the president sends Congress his budget in January of the calendar year in which the new fiscal year begins, the preparation of his budget starts almost a year earlier. The combined executive and legislative budgetary processes thus begin almost two years prior to the new fiscal year. For example, the FY93 budget (covering the fiscal year from October 1, 1992, through September 30, 1993) was submitted to Congress by the president in January of 1992, based upon preliminary estimates the agencies began gathering in February–March of 1991.

During February–March of the previous calendar year, agencies begin evaluating their current programs and any prospective changes to estimate their budgetary needs for the next fiscal year. The president confers with the CEA about economic trends and with the OMB regarding total budget estimates. In May and June the president and the OMB make tentative decisions on spending levels, which are communicated to the departments through a set of budgeting instructions prepared by the OMB, and the various agencies submit their formal budget requests to the OMB by September.

Throughout September the OMB examines agency budgets so that by October and early November the OMB director and other White House aides can meet in their budget review sessions. At this time the president consults again with the CEA, Treasury, and the OMB about last-minute changes in fiscal policy or economic conditions that may force adjustments in the budget.

As the OMB reviews the agency requests, various interest groups and local government officials begin lobbying the White House to defend various programs from cuts. In the negotiations between OMB and the agencies, unresolved disputes about spending may be appealed to the president in late November and early December. Once the president makes the final budget decisions, the agencies must revise their budgets accordingly. In December the budget document and Budget Message are prepared for their January submission to Congress.

Beginning with John Kennedy, preparation of the executive budget has been anything but routine, as domestic and foreign crises upset the best laid plans of the OMB. As Schick notes, "the calm, stable budget process managed by Eisenhower gave way to frenetic budgeting by later presidents who were forced to frequently adjust their spending and revenue targets in order to accommodate last-minute policy decisions and changing economic conditions."[20] It does not take long for a president to realize that the budget is shaped by political and economic forces largely beyond the executive's immediate control.

Budget Forecasts

One source of uncertainty in contemporary budgeting is the difficulty of making accurate **forecasts** of economic activity. This is important, since changes in such factors as the level of unemployment and the rate of inflation may alter the projected revenues or outlays by billions of dollars. The difficulties of forecasting economic activity are reflected in Table 4.1, which shows the disparity between administration forecasts of future economic activity and the actual economic conditions for the years 1981–1989. For each year shown, the actual performance can be compared against two separate forecasts, one made in the budget submitted to Congress a year earlier and another in the budget submitted to Congress as the calendar year began. For example, for calendar year 1981, the first

88 **TABLE 4.1** Forecasts of Macroeconomic Conditions in Presidential Budgets, 1981–1989

Year	Budget	President	Macroeconomic Conditions[a]			
			Current GNP[b]	Real GNP[c]	Consumer Price Index[d]	Unemployment Rate[e]
1981 Forecast	FY81	Carter	10.7%	1.7%	9.2%	7.4%
1981 Forecast	FY82	Carter	11.4	0.9	12.5	7.8
1981 ACTUAL			11.6	1.9	10.3	7.5
1982 Forecast	FY82	Carter	13.1	3.5	10.3	7.5
1982 Forecast	FY83	Reagan	8.1	0.2	7.3	8.9
1982 ACTUAL			4.0	−1.9	6.0	9.5
1983 Forecast	FY83	Reagan	11.5	5.2	6.0	7.9
1983 Forecast	FY84	Reagan	6.7	1.4	4.9	10.7
1983 ACTUAL			7.7	3.7	3.0	9.5
1984 Forecast	FY84	Reagan	9.3	3.9	4.6	9.9
1984 Forecast	FY85	Reagan	10.1	5.3	4.4	7.8
1984 ACTUAL			11.0	6.6	3.4	7.4
1985 Forecast	FY85	Reagan	9.1	4.1	4.6	7.6
1985 Forecast	FY86	Reagan	7.8	3.9	4.1	7.0
1985 ACTUAL			6.2	2.7	3.5	7.1
1986 Forecast	FY86	Reagan	8.5	4.0	4.3	6.9
1986 Forecast	FY87	Reagan	7.0	3.4	3.5	6.7
1986 ACTUAL			5.6	2.9	1.6	6.9
1987 Forecast	FY87	Reagan	8.3	4.0	4.1	6.5
1987 Forecast	FY88	Reagan	6.5	3.1	3.0	6.7
1987 ACTUAL			6.8	3.4	3.6	6.1
1988 Forecast	FY88	Reagan	7.2	3.5	3.6	6.3
1988 Forecast	FY89	Reagan	6.5	2.9	4.3	5.8
1988 ACTUAL			7.9	4.4	4.0	5.4

forecast is from the FY81 budget submitted in January of 1980 and the second is from the FY82 budget submitted in January of 1981.

For each year, there are significant differences between the forecasts and actual economic conditions. Usually the second forecasts are better predictions than the first, but in some years (e.g., 1981 and 1987) the earlier forecasts are actually better. There is a tendency to make counter-

TABLE 4.1   Continued

Year	Budget	President	Macroeconomic Conditions[a]			
			Current GNP[b]	Real GNP[c]	Consumer Price Index[d]	Unemployment Rate[e]
1989 Forecast	FY89	Reagan	7.0	3.1	4.1	5.6
1989 Forecast	FY90	Reagan	7.3	3.2	3.8	5.2
1989 ACTUAL			6.7	2.5	4.8	5.2

[a]Macroeconomic conditions are for the calendar year.

[b]Percent change year over year in current dollars GNP.

[c]Percent change year over year in constant dollars.

[d]Percent change year over year in CPI.

[e]Annual average percent of total labor force unemployed, including armed forces residing in the U.S.

Source: Derived from *Congressional Quarterly Almanac* (Washington, DC: Congressional Quarterly, Inc., various years), vol. 36 (1980) p. 134; vol. 37 (1981) p. 272; vol. 38 (1982) p. 178; vol. 39 (1983) p. 428; vol. 40 (1984) p. 132; vol. 41 (1985) p. 438; vol. 42 (1986) p. 541; vol. 43 (1987) p. 582; vol. 44 (1988) p. 188; vol. 45 (1989) p. 72; vol. 46 (1990) p. 119; vol. 47 (1991) p. 60.

vailing errors with regard to unemployment and inflation. Thus, for 1982, both Carter and Reagan overestimated the inflation rate, while underestimating unemployment; the reverse is true for the two Reagan forecasts for 1987.

These errors in forecasting can be of substantial importance. First, they may seriously undermine the projected spending and revenue estimates, which are the starting points for the preparation of the executive budget. Second, even if the overall revenue and spending projections are not seriously affected, these estimates of macroeconomic conditions strongly influence the policy priorities of the president and Congress. During the 1990–91 recession, for example, both private and government economists predicted more than once that the recession would be mild and that a recovery would occur relatively soon without the enactment of a fiscal stimulus package. This caused President Bush to delay seeking any economic stimulus until his 1992 State of the Union Message, leading to a public perception that he was an ineffective economic manager—a perception that contributed strongly to his defeat by Bill Clinton later that year.

90   CONTEMPORARY BUDGETING AND FISCAL TRENDS

Postwar Budgetary Trends

The Great Depression, New Deal programs, and World War II created unusual demands which led to sudden shifts in spending and to federal deficits every year from 1931 to 1946. Afterwards the budget process settled into a routine called **incrementalism**. Each year's budget became the baseline from which to assess how much more money to give each agency for the approaching fiscal year. One study of 37 agencies over a twelve-year period found that their spending requests were within 5 percent of the previous year's budget in one-third of the cases, and a majority did not differ by more than 10 percent.[21] Each requested more funds than needed on the assumption that cuts would be made by the BOB. The House Appropriations Committee also acted as the "guardian of the treasury" by closely scrutinizing the budget; during 1947–1958 it reduced agency requests 77.2 percent of the time. Just as routinely, those agencies would appeal any funding cuts to the Senate Appropriations Committee, which made some restorations. The recommendations of these spending committees were very important, and this research found no difference between the funding level recommended by the Appropriations Committees and subsequent appropriations enacted by the House or Senate in almost 90 percent of the cases.[22]

Budgeting during this period can be termed a "non-zero-sum game" as compared to the "zero-sum" dilemma existing today. A growing economy generates increased tax revenues (called a fiscal dividend), so existing programs can be funded more generously and new programs undertaken. Conflict is moderated, since all agencies can expect to get a larger budget. In contrast, a zero-sum game means that any increase given to one program must be balanced by an equal decrease from another, which aggravates conflict.

The basis for today's zero-sum budget game is revealed by Table 4.2. When revenues grow at a slower rate than the rate of increases in federal spending, the resulting deficits make it more difficult for politicians to divide up the fiscal pie among competing programs, let alone promise the voters new benefits. This disparity caused a small deficit during 1957–60 and in the Kennedy-Johnson term. The four-year deficit of 1965–68 was almost double the previous term, though still modest by today's standards, because over Johnson's term the increase in federal revenues nearly paralleled the increase in federal spending. The growing economy and modest inflation rate allowed LBJ to launch his War on Poverty, because middle-class Americans were enjoying a higher standard of living, even though a larger share of federal funds was being diverted to helping the poor.

TABLE 4.2   Growth in Federal Revenues and Expenditures by
Presidential Term, 1953–1992

Administration	Total 4-year revenues ($ billions)	Total 4-Year expenditures ($ billions)	Total 4-year deficit ($ billions)	Percentage Change in total revenues from previous administration*	Percentage Change in total expenditures from previous administration*
Eisenhower 1953–1956	$ 279.4	$ 286.0	− $6.8		
Eisenhower 1957–1960	331.1	343.3	− 11.9	18.6%	20.0%
Kennedy/Johnson 1961–1964	413.3	434.3	− 21.1	24.8	26.5
Johnson 1965–1968	549.4	588.3	− 38.9	32.9	35.5
Nixon 1969–1972	774.1	820.1	− 46.0	40.9	39.4
Nixon/Ford 1973–1976	1,071.2	1,219.2	− 147.9	38.4	48.7
Carter 1977–1980	1,735.6	1,962.3	− 226.8	62.0	61.0
Reagan 1981–1984	2,484.2	3,084.0	− 599.9	43.1	57.2
Reagan 1985–1988	3,266.3	4,004.7	− 738.5	31.5	29.9
Bush 1989–1992	4,167.0	5,101.5	− 933.6	27.6	27.4

*The percentage change in the incumbents four-year total compared to the four-year total of the previous administration.

Source: Derived from data in *Economic Report of the President, 1993,* p. 435.

The deficit grew slightly over Nixon's first term, although the growth in federal revenues exceeded the growth in federal expenditures. The gap between revenues and expenditures widened during the Nixon-Ford term due to the impact of "entitlement" programs, but the record of 1977–80 shows that Jimmy Carter retarded the growth of federal spending. Nominal expenditures grew at a rate almost equal to that of federal revenues. The worst scenario occurred under President Reagan when his massive income

92   tax cut produced the largest gap between spending and revenues during 1981–84.

The deep 1981–82 recession helped to undercut federal revenues even further, although expenditures continued upwards. The result was enormous budget deficits. The Nixon-Ford deficits totaled $193.9 billion over eight years; the Carter four years added $226.8 billion more; but the Reagan deficits totaled more than $1,338 billion over his two terms. Although increases in revenue outpaced spending increases during the second Reagan term, the deficits continued to grow.

This pattern of large deficits continued under President Bush. Overall, the Bush term witnessed a staggering aggregate deficit of more than $930 billion, a nominal amount greater than the total aggregate debt incurred between 1789 and 1980. The problem of deficit spending has been persistent and steadily worsening over the last twenty years: While the average yearly deficit for the eight Nixon-Ford years was $24 billion, the average yearly deficit grew to $57 billion during the Carter years, $167 billion during the Reagan years, and $233 billion during the Bush years.

The vast increase in the size of the deficits is partly a function of inflation, but even with the effects of inflation removed, recent deficits have reached historically high peacetime levels. Measured in constant dollars, the ten highest deficits recorded since World War II occurred between 1981 and 1992 (see Figure 4.1); the FY92 deficit was the fourth largest since the 1930s, exceeded only by the three World War II budgets (FY43, FY44, and FY45).

The cumulative effect of these deficits can be seen in the size of the national debt. Figure 4.2 shows the national debt as a percentage of the GDP. The cost of fighting World War II and rebuilding after the war are clearly seen in the relative increase in the size of the national debt during that period. However, during most of the postwar period, the relative size of the debt slowly fell, from a high of 127.5 percent of the GDP at the end of FY46 to a low of 33.5 percent of the GDP at the end of FY81. The latter marked a turning point, however; beginning the next year, the national debt doubled over the next decade, reaching 70 percent of the GDP in FY93. The turning point was clearly the first Reagan administration.

At the Crossroads: Budgeting in the First Reagan Term

Reagan's victory over Jimmy Carter also carried the Republicans into the Senate as the majority party for the first time in three decades. Liberals in the House of Representatives had no alternative to Reaganomics (as Reagan's economic programs became known), and many southern Democrats deserted their party to give Reagan the margin of victory

Figure 4.1   Deficits and Surpluses Measured in
Constant (FY87) Dollars

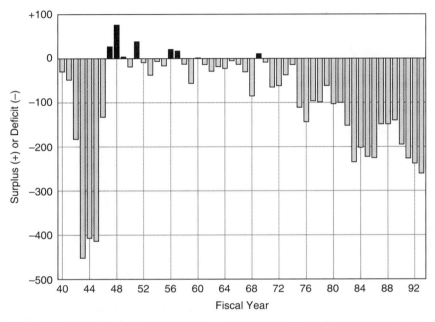

Source: *Budget Baselines, Historical Data, and Alternatives for the Future, January 1993*
(Washington, DC: U.S. Government Printing Office, 1993). Figure for FY93 is an estimate.

on key votes on the budget and taxes. Reagan proposed multiple, and
sometimes conflicting, goals: a balanced federal budget, substantial tax
cuts, greatly increased defense spending, and a reduction in nondefense
spending.

One of the cornerstones of the "Reagan Revolution" was the **Economic Recovery Tax Act of 1981** (ERTA), which cut personal income
marginal tax rates by 23 percent over 3 years and indexed the income tax
rates to inflation beginning in 1985. Reagan's supporters argued that a
massive tax cut would generate so much economic growth that federal
revenues would increase and the budget would be balanced in a few years.
In 1981 the FY83 deficit was projected to be only $23 billion (it was
actually $208 billion), and this overly optimistic economic projection gave
President Reagan tremendous leverage with Congress. "This forecast permitted the administration to claim that if the [economic] program were
adopted in its totality, the country's economic problems would be cured,

Figure 4.2 Federal Debt at End of Fiscal Year as a Percentage of GDP, FY40–FY92

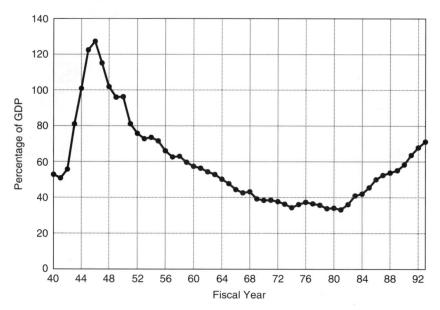

Source: *Budget Baselines, Historical Data, and Alternatives for the Future, January 1993* "Federal Debt at the End of the Year: 1940–1993" (Washington, DC: U.S. Government Printing Office, 1993). Figure for FY93 is an estimate.

and that many who might suffer from the . . . cuts in social programs would benefit from the economic renaissance that would follow. . . ."[23]

In the 1950s and early 1960s, when prices were relatively stable and federal expenditures grew slowly, major fluctuations in the budget were caused primarily by economic conditions. This is not true today. Changes in revenue and expenditures now result from three factors: (1) automatic cyclical effects due to the economy, (2) automatic inflation effects, and (3) policy changes from legislation.

When the economy moves toward full employment, the major effect of economic growth is to generate more revenue for government, just as a recession cuts federal income. Recent history shows that inflation also generates more federal receipts through the "**bracket creep**" effect of income taxes. With rising inflation, people earn more nominal income (though not necessarily more real income), which pushes them into higher income tax brackets, resulting in more tax payments to the federal government. To remove the effect of bracket creep, the 1981 ERTA tax-cut legislation required the upper and lower limits of tax brackets to be annually adjusted for inflation.

However, the most important component of change in the federal budget is the effect of new laws or other policy changes, which in recent years have dramatically unbalanced the budget by increasing expenditures and decreasing revenues. This budget effect is documented by Holloway and Wakefield, who measured the year-to-year changes in these three variables during the Nixon-Ford, Carter, and Reagan presidencies (Table 4.3). The collective impact of the business cycle, inflation, and policy changes worked to increase the federal deficit over the entire period, by the smallest amount under Carter, then Nixon-Ford, and the largest deficit under Reagan. Why? Huge deficits were fueled mainly by *policy changes.* The inflationary effect produced less income for the federal government (due to lower inflation), while new legislation lowered the tax liabilities of many Americans while increasing spending on defense. The rate of increase in nondefense spending was partly slowed, but the overall rate of increase in spending did not change. Coupled with massive revenue losses from ERTA,[24] this led to substantially unbalanced budgets. The anticipated economic growth was not sufficient to generate enough additional revenue to close the deficit gap.

When a short-lived economic recovery peaked in July 1981, a sixteen-month recession took hold. At that point, the conservative coalition that enacted the landmark Reagan tax and budget programs began to unravel, and in 1982 Reagan was forced to make concessions in his economic game plan. Moderate Republicans facing reelection were worried about the cutbacks in domestic programs, and Democrats, sensing a turnabout in public opinion, increased their attacks on Reaganomics. The growing deficits also led Congress to consider new revenue sources. With President Reagan's

TABLE 4.3   Fiscal Components of Budget Deficits, 1970–1986

Period	Total Change: Surplus (+) Deficit (−)	Due to Cyclical Effects	Due to Inflation Effects	Due to Policy Change
1970–1971	− 36.3	− 6.7	+ 78.2	− 107.8
1977–1981	− 8.9	+ 9.6	+ 100.4	− 118.9
1981–1986	− 110.6	+ 22.3	+ 61.3	− 194.2

Source: Thomas M. Holloway and Joseph C. Wakefield, "Sources of Change in the Federal Deficit, 1970–86," *Survey of Current Business* (May 1985), table 4, p. 29.

agreement, Congress enacted a $30 billion (excise) tax hike in 1982, and, with the jobless rate reaching 10 percent in September, there was bipartisan clamor for new jobs legislation.

The key spokesperson for Reaganomics before Congress was OMB Director David Stockman, whose command of budget details and economic forecasts overwhelmed the administration's critics during the early congressional debates over Reagan's programs. Stockman's policy advocacy gave way to second thoughts as revised forecasts showed huge deficits looming ahead. As early as December 1981, in a highly publicized interview, Stockman commented, "I've never believed that just cutting taxes alone will cause output and employment to expand," and "Kemp-Roth [the basis for ERTA] was always a Trojan horse to bring down the top [income tax] rates."[25] He disparaged the supply-side economic theory on which the Reagan economic program was based as being little more than old-fashioned "trickle-down" economics,[26] thus confirming the worst suspicions of the Democrats. These statements proved to be a political bombshell and speculation mounted that Stockman would be forced to resign. He survived, but began to argue that there were limits to how much more domestic social welfare programs could be cut. Studies done midway through the first Reagan term showed that affluent people benefited from income tax cuts, whereas the needy bore the brunt of the budget cutbacks.[27]

In the end, Stockman reverted to more traditional Republican and fiscal conservative arguments, but he made little headway against the hardened opposition of other elements of the Reagan administration, who subscribed to more radical supply-side economic theories. In July 1985 Stockman resigned. When later interviewed on ABC-TV's "This Week With David Brinkley," his comments seemed to have come full circle: He said that a tax hike of at least $100 billion was necessary to reduce the deficit, declaring: "We just can't live with these massive deficits without traumatic economic dislocations."[28]

Budget Priorities

Since 1982 the budgetary pressures caused by the mounting deficits have provoked heightened executive-legislative conflict, and the terms of this political debate continued throughout Reagan's second term. The administration demanded "real" increases in defense expenditures at the expense of social welfare programs. The Democrats in the House maneuvered to restore funding to domestic programs while trying to hold down military spending. The Republican majority in the Senate (which lasted until the Democrats regained control in 1987) took bold, politically risky (but unsuccessful) steps to make cuts in middle-class entitlement programs like Social Security.

97

Table 4.4 illustrates the executive-legislative conflict over spending priorities beginning with the first budget (FY83) to be entirely formulated by the Reagan administration. Congress consistently made cuts in President Reagan's budget requests for science/space/technology, international affairs, and (especially) national defense. The next fifteen functional areas relate to domestic spending, where spending was increased by Congress over what the Reagan administration proposed, the largest increments being earmarked for income security and for education/training/employment/social services.

While the Reagan budgets slowed the growth in some domestic programs, there was no net reduction in federal spending. This predicament was mainly due to the entitlement programs, where President Reagan was unable (and unwilling) to achieve substantial retrenchment. Reagan wanted to reduce federal deficits solely through spending cuts. Nobody in his administration objected to that strategy by advocating a tax hike to solve the deficit problem, and this option was foreclosed once the 1984 election was over.

Walter Mondale told the 1984 Democratic national convention that he would raise taxes and cut spending in order to reduce the projected deficit by two-thirds. "Let's tell the truth," Mondale declared, "Mr. Reagan will raise taxes, and so will I. He won't tell you. I just did."[29] Although a number of factors led to the landslide Reagan victory that fall, the election results reduced both parties' willingness to address the deficits through increased taxation. Following the election, President Reagan remained steadfast in opposing new taxes. Seeing the electoral damage to Mondale, Democrats in Congress avoided for many years risking their political careers on the question of any tax increase.

Various commentators allege that the huge deficits under Ronald Reagan were a "hidden agenda" designed to prevent any expansion of New Deal or Great Society domestic programs. In the face of triple-digit deficits, even liberals think twice before sponsoring new legislation with large price tags. That was certainly the consequence during the Bush presidency. President Bush provided almost no new money to redeem his various campaign pledges, such as improved education, and virtually no new domestic undertakings were launched by the Democratic-controlled Congress.

BUDGETS AND FISCAL POLICY

The Influence of Budgeting on Fiscal Policy

With regard to macroeconomic policy, the most important consequence of the recent budgetary trends is that fiscal policy has been se-

TABLE 4.4 Difference Between Presidential and Congressional Budgets by Function, Fiscal Years 1983–1988 (billions of dollars in budget authority)*

Function	FY1983	FY1984	FY1985	FY1986	FY1987	FY1988
National Defense	−$9.4	−$11.9	−$20.5	−$19.7	−$28.1	−$15.8
International Affairs	−2.2	+1.9	−1.5	+0.7	−5.1	−3.3
Science/Space/Technology	same	+0.2	−0.3	−0.4	−0.4	−0.2
SUBTOTAL	**−11.6**	**−9.8**	**−22.3**	**−19.4**	**−33.6**	**−10.3**
Energy	+0.5	+1.3	+1.1	+0.8	+0.5	+2.0
Natural Resources/Environment	+1.1	+3.2	+1.1	+2.2	+1.5	+1.7
Agriculture	−0.2	−0.5	+5.0	+5.3	+4.2	+3.8
Commerce/Housing/Credit	+3.7	+0.4	+1.4	−0.1	+0.1	+0.8
Transportation	+2.4	+0.2	+0.6	+1.3	+2.8	+4.3
Community/Regional Development	+0.2	+0.8	+0.5	+1.8	+2.4	+1.9
Education/Training/Employment/Social Services	+8.0	+8.4	+3.3	+4.6	+6.5	+7.4
Health	+1.8	−59.6	+1.4	+1.3	+3.3	+2.1
Medicare	a	a	+0.1	−0.2	+0.7	−1.1
Income Security	+17.2	a	+4.4	+11.0	+10.2	+6.5
Social Security	a	a	+1.0	+0.2	+4.9	−0.5
Veterans Benefits/Services	−1.1	−0.5	−0.4	same	+0.3	+0.2
Administration of Justice	same	+0.3	+0.1	+0.4	+0.1	+0.6
General Government	−0.5	−0.5	−0.1	+0.5	−0.7	−0.1
General Fiscal Assistance	−0.2	−1.4	−0.2	+4.9	+0.3	+0.3
SUBTOTAL	**+32.9**	**−47.9**	**+19.3**	**+34.0**	**+37.1**	**+29.9**

*A negative is the amount reduced by Congress; a positive is the amount added by Congress.

riously weakened as a useful policy instrument. Recall that from the perspective of macroeconomic policymaking, the basic purpose of fiscal policy is to use government taxing and spending to influence the level of aggregate demand, stimulating the economy during recessions and slowing it down during periods of inflation. Three separate, but interrelated, factors have rendered this difficult to do. First, the continuing large deficits have taken over nearly all discussions of budgeting, crowding out most other considerations. With the starting point of a $100–250 billion deficit in each year's current services budget, it is difficult to think of moving the expenditure and spending levels in any direction other than toward smaller deficits. Second, the growth of uncontrollable expenditures (discussed in the next section) has meant that a progressively smaller portion of the budget is subject to short-term manipulation for purposes of influencing the macroeconomy. Third, one of the political lessons of the 1984 presidential election—that the public will vote against a candidate who argues for increased levels of taxation—means that a major fiscal policy option was largely ignored, at least during the Reagan and Bush presidencies.

The result has been a situation of essential paralysis with regard to fiscal policy. Throughout the late 1980s and early 1990s, political leaders have roundly denounced budget deficits, but have done little to actually reduce them. At the same time, deficits have been allowed to gradually grow, so that any attempt to reduce them substantially would have a major deflationary effect upon the economy. Moreover, the growth of uncontrollable expenditures and continued public support for many expensive programs (such as Medicare), coupled with resistance to tax increases, has meant that there are few ways to substantially reduce deficits on the expenditure side and no real way on the revenue side. Changes in public attitudes toward defense spending in the wake of the collapse of the Soviet Union have only moderately expanded the available policy options, since the projected FY93 deficit is larger than the *entire* budget for national defense. At the same time, public support for radical structural changes such as a balanced budget amendment to the constitution have grown, a change that, if adopted, would further remove fiscal policy as a policy option for influencing the macroeconomy.

Why Budgets Continue to Grow

By any standard the federal budget has grown by a staggering amount over the past six decades. Table 4.5 compares the increase in federal spending during 1929–1985 to growth rates in the U.S. population and GDP. During this period, the U.S. population doubled, while the total

TABLE 4.5 Federal Budget Growth vs. Population and GDP, 1929–1990

	1929	1990	Percent Increase
Population	121.8 million	249.6 million	105%
Real GDP (1987 dollars)	$821.8 billion	$4,877.5 billion	493%
Real Federal Spending (1987 dollars)	$24.8 billion	$1,110.1 billion	4,376%

size of the U.S. economy increased nearly fivefold. During the same period, however, total federal spending—adjusted for inflation—increased nearly nine times as fast as the growth in the economy and over forty times faster than the increase in population. Since federal spending grew faster than nominal GDP, over time the national budget has come to represent a larger *share* of the nation's total output.

During recession years (e.g., 1949, 1953, 1958, 1961, 1975, and 1982), the federal share of GNP typically rose, due to more federal spending triggered by automatic stabilizers (anti-cyclical spending like unemployment compensation and AFDC). Beyond these temporary fluctuations, though, there were more lasting increases in federal spending as a percent of GNP following the New Deal and the Great Society of the 1960s.

Prior to 1956 there was no steady year-by-year increase in expenditures; the pattern was quite erratic. Since then we have seen increasing federal expenditures *every* year except for 1965. This upward trajectory continued after the Vietnam War, when programmatic expansions of various New Deal and Great Society initiatives obligated the federal government to fund a variety of increasingly costly programs. Since revenues have not kept pace with these spending commitments, deficits have resulted in 33 of the 37 years during the period from 1956 through 1992. Why do budgets continue to grow?

A first reason is simply *bureaucratic survival*. Agencies provide jobs to thousands of employees, give their chiefs political power and status, and distribute benefits to clientele groups. Few programs are ever abolished. One study found that 85 percent of the 175 agencies existing in 1923 still operated fifty years later.[30] In 1976 Common Cause reported that during the previous 15 years 236 new agencies were created, but only 21 had been abolished.[31]

A second reason is incrementalism. Nobody in Congress has enough time or staff to study the whole budget, and prior to 1974 no committee was given that responsibility. The members are usually concerned about whether pet programs targeted to their states and districts are getting enough money as compared to the previous year. The presumption is that existing programs should be continued; the only question is at what rate of spending. This incremental approach does not always involve huge sums of money, but they add up. As Senator Everett Dirksen (R-IL) is alleged to have said, "a billion dollars here, a billion dollars there, and pretty soon you're talking about real money."

A third reason is **pork barrel legislation.** Classic examples of this type of legislation are public works, water resources development, and highway construction. These projects can be targeted to a large number of states and districts, and the president is rarely able to stop them. In 1977, for example, President Carter wanted to cut funding for water projects in the West. He had to retreat in the face of political pressure from Senators on the Interior Committee, the Department of the Interior, and the ranchers, farmers, and small towns that benefited from those projects.

The most important contemporary reason for growing budgets, however, is *uncontrollable spending.* For most of our history the budget was used to fund federal agencies; now a major share is distributed as transfer payments to individuals in the form of Social Security benefits, Medicare and Medicaid reimbursements, welfare grants, federal pensions, veterans benefits, and unemployment compensation. The "payments to individuals" category of the budget represented 28 percent of federal spending in FY65 but passed the 40 percent mark in FY72. From FY74 through FY92 these payments ranged between 46 and 53 percent of federal expenditures, with the highs associated with the recessions of 1975, 1982, and 1992.

These are called **entitlement programs** because the law mandates that benefits be given to whomever meets the eligibility requirements. Since they have permanent appropriations, with the Congress obligated to spend whatever moneys are needed, these outlays are **uncontrollable** (or non-discretionary) **expenditures.** To reduce them, Congress would have to legislate cuts in those benefits. Uncontrollable spending, at least in the short-term, also includes salaries and fringe benefits for the 3 million civilian federal employees, 2 million members of the armed forces, certain other operating costs of government, and interest on the national debt. The latter is no longer a small item; due to the huge deficits, net interest charges rose from 7 to 9 percent of total spending in the 1965–1980 period to 14.4 percent in FY92 (or $199 billion). As a result, uncontrollable expenditures climbed from being 59 percent of total federal expenditures in FY67 to 70 percent in FY73 and 76 percent in the FY81 budget.[32]

102   Only one-fourth of the budget involves spending that is considered controllable. Income security programs, health care, and veterans benefits are mainly uncontrollable, but two-thirds of defense spending *is* considered controllable.[33] Since defense spending represented between 22 and 40 percent of the budget during the period 1970–1990, this has been a tempting area to target for spending cuts. This strategy was pursued, for example, by Jimmy Carter at the start of his term. In contrast, President Reagan wanted real increases in defense spending (i.e., percentage increases in spending that exceeded the inflation rate), so any reduction in federal expenditures would have required very deep cuts in domestic programs. The basis of this dilemma—which prompted renewed conflict between Congress and the White House—is illustrated by the expenditure trends in Table 4.6.

Total spending rose by 112 percent from 1980 to 1990; most functional categories had a lower rate of increase. However, the rate of spending was *higher* for defense, Social Security, Medicare, and interest payments, and these four categories equaled 66.3 percent of total expenditures in 1990. Beginning in 1980, the Reagan administration reversed the five-year trend towards less defense spending by redirecting to the military the largest expenditure increase of any functional area other than interest. Partly as a result, President Reagan had only modest success in curbing the growth of controllable expenditures.

Fiscal Policy and Budgetary Reforms

Louis Fisher argues that "the overwhelming sentiment behind the 1974 Congressional Budget and Impoundment Control Act was to create a procedure capable of restraining the growth of federal spending."[34] When the Joint Study Committee on Budget Control reported to the Congress, it said:

> The constant continuation of deficits plus their increasing size illustrates the need for Congress to obtain better control over the budget. . . . The present institutional arrangements in many cases appear to make it impossible to decide between competing priorities with the result that spending is made available for many programs where the preference might have been to make choices among the programs rather than providing for spending in all cases.[35]

However, new procedures have proven unable to overcome partisan differences during an era of slow economic growth and mounting deficits.

Congress approved the first concurrent resolution by the May 15 deadline only twice from 1977 through 1986. And while 35.6 percent of the

TABLE 4.6 Federal Budget Outlays by Function, 1980 and 1990

Function	1980 Outlay ($ billions)	1980 Percent	1990 Outlay ($ billions)	1990 Percent	Percent Increase 1980–1990
National Defense	$134.0	22.7%	$299.3	23.9%	+123%
International Affairs	12.7	2.0	13.8	1.1	+9%
General Science, Space, and Technology	5.8	1.0	14.4	1.2	+148%
Energy	10.2	1.7	3.3	0.3	−68%
Natural Resources and Environment	13.9	2.4	17.1	1.4	+23%
Agriculture	8.8	1.5	12.0	1.0	+36%
Commerce and Housing Credit	9.4	1.6	67.1	5.4	+614%
Transportation	21.3	3.6	29.5	2.4	+38%
Community and Regional Development	11.3	1.9	8.5	0.7	−25%
Training, Employment, and Social Services	31.8	5.4	38.5	3.1	+21%
Health	23.2	3.9	57.7	4.6	+149%
Social Security	118.5	20.1	248.6	19.9	+110%
Medicare	32.1	5.4	98.1	7.8	+206%
Income Security	86.5	14.6	147.0	11.8	+70%
Veterans Benefits and Services	21.2	3.6	29.1	2.3	+37%
Administration of Justice	4.6	0.8	10.0	0.8	+117%
General Government	13.0	2.2	10.7	0.9	−18%
Net Interest	52.5	8.9	184.2	14.7	+251%
Undistributed Offsetting Receipts	−20.0	—	−36.6	—	—
Total Budget Outlays	**591.0**	—	**1,252.7**	—	**+112%**

Source: Office of Management and Budget, *Budget Baselines, Historical Data, and Alternatives for the Future, January 1993* (Washington, DC: U.S. Government Printing Office, 1993), Part 7, Table 3.2, "Outlays by Function and Subfunction: 1946–1993." Percentages calculated from these raw data; percentages will not total 100% due to rounding.

104 regular appropriations bills were enacted prior to the fiscal year during 1977–1984 (a four-fold improvement compared to the previous eight-year period), two-thirds of these funding bills were enacted during the first two years under the law.[36] Since 1979 most appropriations have been passed after the fiscal year began. John Ellwood counted how many days were needed to finish action on all thirteen regular appropriations bills.[37] The 282-day average during the 1968–1975 period rose to 364 days in the period 1976–1983, a clear signal that conflict over the budget has intensified.

It is obvious that the reforms were no panacea for the modern budget dilemma. Between 1968 and 1975 the deficits totaled $135.9 billion, whereas the eight years of 1976–1983 generated a total deficit of $624.3 billion. Since 1983, the annual deficits (measured as a percentage of the GDP) have remained at the high levels seen in the early 1980s. In nominal dollars, of course, they have continued to grow at a rapid rate. As we noted earlier, even in constant dollars (adjusted for inflation), recent deficits have been enormous.

Many people are worried about the failure of the political branches to take charge of the nation's finances, and there is continuing interest in additional budgetary reform. Four budgetary devices have been particularly discussed: expenditure ceilings, impoundment, a line item veto, and a balanced-budget amendment.

Congress approved weakly designed *expenditure ceilings* in 1967, 1968, 1969, 1970, and 1972.[38] All failed to curb spending, and the 1972 debacle led to the 1974 reforms. Fearing that Nixon would use any expenditure ceiling to justify his impoundments of appropriated funds, the Congress in 1971 decided not to try this approach. But it only delayed a confrontation until the next year, when the president demanded a $250 billion limit on FY73 spending. Nixon was refused any authority to cut expenditures, and ultimately the Congress enacted a law containing two clauses that directly contradicted each other. As Allen Schick explains:

> On October 18, 1972, the last day of the 92nd Congress, the House and the Senate approved a bill raising the statutory limit on the public debt. . . . Section 201(a) of the legislation (PL 92-599) established a $250 billion ceiling on federal outlays for fiscal 1973. . . . Section 201(b), however, provided that the spending limitation would cease to have effect one day after the bill became law and that any action taken pursuant to the limitation would be null and void. . . .[39]

The 1974 Congressional Budget and Impoundment Control Act also established a legislative veto over **presidential impoundments.** An impoundment occurs when the executive refuses to spend money appropri-

ated by the legislature. Impoundments date to the early years of the Re- **105**
public (most likely to Thomas Jefferson) and since then have been justified
by presidents by citing various statutes. The Antideficiency Act of 1950,
for example, permits budgetary reserves "to provide for contingencies, or
to effect savings whenever savings are made possible by or through changes
in requirements, greater efficiency of operations, or other developments
subsequent to the date on which such appropriation was made available."

After Congress failed to enact a spending ceiling for FY73, President
Nixon reacted by vetoing the Federal Water Pollution Control Act
Amendments of 1972. When his veto was overridden, he then impounded
$9 billion earmarked for FY73, FY74, and FY75. In a January 1973 news
conference, Nixon defended his impoundments as an implied power under
the Constitution, but his action was challenged in court. In *Train v. City
of New York*, 420 U.S. 35 (1975), a unanimous Supreme Court ruled
against the Nixon administration, because the law committed those federal funds to states and localities within a definite time period. However,
this opinion did not deal with the basic question of whether impoundment
is an executive power under the Constitution.

The 1974 act sought to clarify this question by statutory means. Title
X of the law distinguishes between temporary ("deferrals") and permanent
("rescissions") impoundments. For a rescission, the president must give
Congress a special message explaining how much budget authority is cut,
the programs affected, reasons why, and its impact on the budget, the
economy, and the affected programs. A rescission is automatically rejected
unless *both* House and Senate approve the impoundment within forty-five
days. A deferral becomes automatic unless *either* House or Senate disap-
proves the action. Congress generally will tolerate the use of deferral authority much more than rescissions.[40]

When President Nixon had taken these steps, Democrats in Congress
angrily charged that Nixon was using impoundments as an item veto to
reorder spending priorities. A **line item veto** grants to an executive the
power to veto a portion of a bill while accepting the remainder of it. As
with other vetoes, item vetoes can be overridden by the legislature, but
this happens rarely given the large majorities needed for veto overrides.
An item veto shifts power from the legislature to the executive, since the
executive is not forced to accept unpalatable policies that have been
linked to actions the executive wants or needs by placing the desirable
and undesirable policies within the same piece of legislation. At least six
presidents, including Franklin Roosevelt and Ronald Reagan, have requested the item veto, and more than 140 bills since 1876 have included
this device.[41] Forty-three governors have this authority, and many argue
that this power ought to be given to the chief executive. (According to a

106   1975 Gallup poll, 69 percent of Americans favor the item veto.[42]) President Reagan included calls for an item veto in several State of the Union Messages, as did President Bush.

It is not obvious that the item veto will lead to spending curbs or balanced budgets, since presidents are not necessarily more tight-fisted with money than Congress. An analysis by Paul Peterson of the period 1947–1984 found that, on average, slightly more funds ($0.8 billion) were recommended by the White House than what Congress appropriated. But which party controlled the presidency made a real difference insofar as "Congress spent more than the president requested when a Republican held the presidency—appropriations exceeded requests by an average of $1.9 billion during these years, compared with $3.4 billion less than requested during Democratic administrations."[43]

Robert Spitzer blames the triple-digit deficits of the 1980s on the executive branch and casts doubt on the assumption that presidential control over spending ought to be strengthened. He observes that

> The item veto is no panacea for the problem of unwise or extravagant legislation. It is a quick fix for a problem whose resolution lies in political accountability for the consequences of political decisions made mostly by the executive. . . . the basic budgetary imbalances of the last few years are attributable principally to marked increases in defense spending, a sweeping tax cut program, and entitlement programs that lock in spending increases. These are all White House–inspired priorities.[44]

Finally, the most radical mechanism proposed to counter the persistent deficits is a *balanced-budget amendment* to the Constitution. Since thirty (of the required thirty-four) states have passed resolutions asking that a constitutional convention be convened for the purpose of proposing such an amendment, the possibility is strong that such an amendment will be seriously considered. Partly to avoid being forced to call such a convention, Congress has also been considering such proposals since 1982, and a proposed amendment was nearly passed during the summer of 1992. Another stimulus to congressional action is the failure of a statute requiring the Congress to move towards a balanced budget—the Gramm-Rudman-Hollings Act—to actually bring about lower deficits. Several versions of a balanced budget constitutional amendment are being considered by Congress. All would basically require a balanced budget unless three-fifths of the House and Senate vote to unbalance it. Different plans offer other provisions, such as temporary waivers of the balancing requirement during wartime or economic recessions.

The latter provision may prove particularly important, since there remain sound reasons for deficit spending during recessions.

There is general agreement among economists that a balanced-budget amendment would straitjacket the use of discretionary fiscal policy and neutralize the automatic stabilizers during a recession. Since federal spending always rises during an economic downturn, an amendment without this waiver would mean that three-fifths of the Congress must voluntarily unbalance the budget; otherwise, taxes must be raised or expenditures cut. Either action is *pro-cyclical* and would make the recession worse. Charles L. Schultze, who was Carter's CEA chairman, gave this dire scenario had that amendment been in effect during the 1975 recession:

> In fiscal 1974, the federal budget was almost in balance; there would have been a $4.5 billion deficit. Then we had a major recession; the unemployment rate rose to 9 percent, GNP fell by 2.5 percent, and in 1976 the federal budget deficit was up to $66 billion. It would not have been enough to slash $66 billion out of expenditures or add $66 billion to taxes—that would have driven the economy down further. . . . It turns out that expenditures would have had to be cut by about $50 billion in 1975 and $100 billion in 1976 in order, ultimately, to get a balanced budget. The unemployment rate would have been about 12 percent, GNP would have fallen not by 2 percent but by near 10 or 11 percent, and we would have had the first true, full-fledged, major depression since the 1920s. Thus, the consequences of trying to have an annually balanced budget can turn out to be horrendous.[45]

KEY TERMS

budget deficits, authorizing legislation, appropriations legislation, Appropriations Committees, House Ways and Means Committee, Senate Finance Committee, executive budget, legislative clearance, Congressional Budget and Impoundment Control Act of 1974, concurrent resolutions, Budget Committees, current services budget, reconciliation bill, forecasts, incrementalism, Economic Recovery Tax Act of 1981, bracket creep, pork barrel legislation, entitlement programs, uncontrollable expenditures, presidential impoundments, line item veto

ADDITIONAL READING

Berman, Larry. *The Office of Management and Budget*. Princeton: Princeton University Press, 1979. Case study of the OMB with an historical treatment of its predecessor, the Bureau of the Budget.

108   Fisher, Louis. *Presidential Spending Power*. Princeton: Princeton University Press, 1975. This pioneering study traces the development of budget making within the executive branch.

Hansen, Susan B. *The Politics of Taxation: Revenue Without Representation*. New York: Praeger Special Studies, 1983. Overviews U.S. tax policy, including its historical development, state taxes, public opinion, and the "tax revolt" of 1978.

Ippolito, Dennis S. *Congressional Spending*. Ithaca: Cornell University Press, 1981. Gives the history behind the 1974 budget law, its impact on spending, and recommendations for reform, including a constitutional amendment to curb expenditures.

LeLoup, Lance T. *Budgetary Politics*, 3rd ed. Brunswick, Ohio: King's Court Communications, 1986. Discusses the budget process including tax policy, spending, and procedural reforms.

Moore, W. S. and Rudolph G. Penner, eds. *The Constitution and the Budget*. Washington, DC: American Enterprise Institute for Public Policy Research, 1980. Twenty-one essays by well-known authorities on the question "Are constitutional limits on tax, spending, and budget powers desirable at the federal level?"

Schick, Allen. *Congress and Money: Budgeting, Spending and Taxing*. Washington, DC: The Urban Institute, 1981. Definitive study of the congressional budget process in the post-1974 era.

Schick, Allen, ed. *Making Economic Policy in Congress*. Washington, DC: American Enterprise Institute for Public Policy Research, 1983. Essays on how the congressional budget process impacts such areas as regulation, taxes, and trade policy.

Shuman, Howard E. *Politics and the Budget: The Struggle Between the President and the Congress*, 3rd ed. Englewood Cliffs, NJ: Prentice-Hall, 1992. An overview of executive-legislative budgetary relations with some coverage of fiscal policy, money and credit, the Nixon and Reagan eras, and the Gramm-Rudman-Hollings law.

Wildavsky, Aaron. *The New Politics of the Budgetary Process*. Glenview, IL: Scott Foresman, 1988. This updated version of the influential study assesses the various strategies used by the participants in the federal budgetary process.

NOTES

1.   Aaron Wildavsky, *The Politics of the Budgetary Process*, 4th ed. (Boston: Little, Brown and Company, 1984), p. 2.

2.   See Louis Fisher, "The Authorization-Appropriation Process in Congress: Formal Rules and Informal Practices," *Catholic University Law Review* 29:5 (1979), pp. 52–105.

3. This discussion of budgeting during the 1789–1921 period is based upon **109** Louis Fisher, *Presidential Spending Power* (Princeton: Princeton University Press, 1975), Chapter 1.

4. Ibid., p. 23.

5. In addition, the boundaries between authorizing and appropriating are often blurred. For example, floor amendments are sometimes attached to budget bills that have the effect of prohibiting certain activities, an activity that traditionally would be part of authorizing legislation. See Aaron Wildavsky, *The New Politics of the Budgetary Process* (Glenview, IL: Scott, Foresman, 1988), pp. 18–19.

6. Reported in Fisher, *Presidential Spending Power*, p. 35.

7. Richard F. Fenno, Jr., *The Power of the Purse* (Boston: Little, Brown and Company, 1966), pp. 162–163.

8. Howard E. Shuman, *Politics and the Budget: The Struggle Between the President and Congress*, 3rd ed. (Englewood Cliffs, NJ: Prentice Hall, 1992), p. 77.

9. See Richard E. Neustadt, "President and Legislation: The Growth of Central Clearance," *American Political Science Review* 48 (September 1954), pp. 641–647.

10. Wildavsky, *The New Politics of the Budgetary Process*, pp. 136–138.

11. See, for example, Fenno, *The Power of the Purse*.

12. Alan Schick, *Congress and Money* (Washington, DC: The Urban Institute, 1980), p. 17.

13. See Shuman, *Politics and the Budget*, pp. 212–214.

14. Ibid., p. 214.

15. Public Law 93-344, "Congressional Budget and Impoundment Control Act of 1974," Section 2.

16. James W. Davis and Delbert Ringquist, *The President and Congress: Toward a New Power Balance* (Woodbury, NY: Barron's Educational Series, 1975), p. 111.

17. The twenty functional areas in the FY93 budget are: national defense; international affairs; general science, space, and technology; energy; natural resources and environment; agriculture; commerce and housing credit; transportation; community and regional development; education, training, employment, and social services; health; Medicare; income security; Social Security; veterans benefits and services; administration of justice; general government; net interest; allowances; and undistributed offsetting receipts.

18. The main purpose of Gramm-Rudman-Hollings is deficit reduction, and the revised procedure requires adoption of a reconciliation bill by June 15 to meet the deficit ceilings contained in the (first) concurrent budget resolution.

19. Allen Schick, "The Battle of the Budget," in Harvey C. Mansfield, ed., *Congress Against the President* (New York: Praeger, 1975), p. 70.

20. Allen Schick, "The Problem of Presidential Budgeting," in Hugh Heclo and Lester M. Salamon, eds., *The Illusion of Presidential Government* (Boulder, CO: Westview Press, 1981), p. 92.

110   21. Wildavsky, *The Politics of the Budgetary Process*, p. 14.

22. Ibid., pp. 48–55.

23. Sheldon Danziger, Robert Haveman, Donald Nichols, Barbara Wolfe, "Reviewing Reagan's Economic Program," *Challenge* 27 (January/February, 1984), p. 42.

24. The Joint Committee on Taxation of Congress estimated the expected reductions in revenue due to ERTA during the first six years as follows: FY81, $1.6 billion; FY82, $37.7 billion; FY83, $92.7 billion, FY84, $150.0 billion; FY85, $199.2 billion; FY86, $267.7 billion. See Joint Economic Committee on Taxation, *General Explanation of the Economic Recovery Act of 1981* (Washington, DC: Government Printing Office, 1981).

25. William Greider, "The Education of David Stockman," *Atlantic Monthly* (December 1981), pp. 27–54. Quotes on p. 46.

26. The so-called "trickle down" theory is the argument that if economic benefits are initially conferred on the wealthier segments of society, some benefits will eventually trickle down to the less well-off strata.

27. See John L. Palmer and Isabel V. Sawhill, eds., *The Reagan Experiment: An Examination of Economic and Social Policies Under the Reagan Administration* (Washington, DC: The Urban Institute Press, 1982); W. Craig Stubblebine and Thomas D. Willett, eds., *Reaganomics: A Midterm Report* (San Francisco: ICS Press, 1983).

28. Quoted in Warren Weaver, Jr., "$100 Billion Tax Rise Is Urged by Stockman," *New York Times* (September 30, 1985), p. 27.

29. Quoted in Rich Jaroslovsky and Jeanne Saddler, "Mondale Accepts the Nomination, Vows to Raise Taxes, Shrink Deficit," *Wall Street Journal* (July 20, 1984), p. 36.

30. Herbert Kaufman, *Are Government Organizations Immortal?* (Washington, DC: The Brookings Institution, 1976), p. 34.

31. *Sunset: A Common Cause Proposal for Accountable Government* (Washington, DC: Common Cause, 1976). Reported in David V. Edwards, *The American Political Experience* (Englewood Cliffs, NJ: Prentice-Hall, 1979), p. 223.

32. Schick, "The Problem of Presidential Budgeting," in Heclo and Salamon, eds., *The Illusion of Presidential Government*, p. 97. Also see Schick, *Congress and Money*, pp. 26–29.

33. Lance T. LeLoup, *Budgetary Politics* (Brunswick, OH: King's Court Communications, 1977), p. 65. Also see 3rd ed. (1986), pp. 51–56.

34. Reported in John W. Ellwood, "Budget Control in a Redistributive Environment," in Allen Schick, ed., *Making Economic Policy in Congress* (Washington, DC: American Enterprise Institute for Public Policy Research, 1983), p. 73.

35. Cited in Allen Schick, "The Three-Ring Budget Process: The Appropriations, Tax, and Budget Committees in Congress," in Thomas E. Mann and Norman J. Ornstein, eds., *The New Congress* (Washington, DC: American Enterprise Institute for Public Policy Research, 1981), p. 304.

36. LeLoup, *Budgetary Politics*, 3rd ed., pp. 182–186.   **111**

37. Ellwood, "Budget Control in a Redistributive Environment," in Schick, ed., *Making Economic Policy in Congress*, pp. 74–81.

38. This discussion is based upon Schick, *Congress and Money*, pp. 30–43.

39. Ibid., p. 17.

40. Ibid., p. 404. During the period from 1975 to June, 1979, whereas only 10 percent of the 470 deferrals requested by Ford and Carter were denied, nearly two-thirds of the 180 rescissions they proposed were disallowed.

41. This discussion is based upon Russell M. Ross and Fred Schwengel, "An Item Veto for the President?" *Presidential Studies Quarterly* 12 (Winter 1982), 66–79.

42. American Institute of Public Opinion, *The Gallup Poll, Public Opinion 1972–1977* (Wilmington, DE: Scholarly Resources, Inc., 1978), p. 527. Also see American Institute of Public Opinion, *The Gallup Poll, Public Opinion 1935–1971* (New York: Random House, 1972), pp. 1172–1173 and 1499–1500.

43. Paul E. Peterson, "The New Politics of Deficits," in John E. Chubb and Paul E. Peterson, eds., *The New Direction in American Politics* (Washington, DC: The Brookings Institution, 1985), p. 375.

44. Robert J. Spitzer, "The Item Veto Reconsidered," *Presidential Studies Quarterly* 15 (Summer 1985), p. 616.

45. Charles L. Schultze, "Politics and Economics of a Balanced Budget Amendment," in W. S. Moore and Rudolph G. Penner, eds., *The Constitution and the Budget* (Washington, DC: American Enterprise Institute for Public Policy Research, 1980), pp. 123–124.

CHAPTER 5

The Federal Reserve Board and Monetary Policy

In the preceding chapter we have seen how the continuing large deficits of the 1980s and 1990s have reduced the ability of policymakers to employ fiscal policy to manage the macroeconomy, a situation we will consider in more detail in Chapter 11. In this chapter we discuss a macroeconomic policy tool that has retained its potency, the regulation of the money supply, or **monetary policy**.

According to mainstream economic thinking, the influence of monetary policy on the macroeconomy occurs via interest rates. All things being equal, an increase in the money supply should make it easier to borrow money (i.e., should lead to lower interest rates), which in turn should stimulate economic activity. Much as with a fiscal stimulus, the benefits of a monetary stimulus depend on whether the economy is at or below the full employment level. If the economy is below full employment (as it is during a recession), increases in the money supply may stimulate the economy with little effect on prices. However, if the economy is near the full employment level, a monetary stimulus may have a greater effect on prices, leading to an increase in inflation. Thus, monetary policy influences both growth in the economy and price stability, potentially affecting both unemployment and inflation.

Over the last thirty years, an alternative theory of the macroeconomy, **monetarism**, has argued that growth in the monetary supply is the principal determinant of economic performance, although for different reasons

114   than the mainstream view.[1] Modern monetarism was developed by Milton Friedman and is primarily associated with the University of Chicago. Essentially, the monetarist argument is that only the supply of money influences changes in prices and the quantity of goods produced (i.e., GDP). Even here, attempts to "fine tune" the economy by manipulating the money supply will only affect prices in the short run, leading to price instability. Monetarists argue that growth in the money supply should be relatively constant (about 3–4 percent each year), which will accommodate growth in the economy but not lead to price instability. In effect, the monetarist prescription is that monetary "policy" should be to produce a constant, inflexible outcome, which monetarists believe should lead to a steady growth in the GDP and price stability.

As we have noted in earlier chapters, control over this important policy area rests mainly in the hands of a body not directly answerable to the voters, the Federal Reserve System. Thus, much of our discussion of monetary policy in this chapter will focus on the composition and activities of the Fed. We begin our discussion by describing monetary policy before the creation of the Fed, which occurred in 1913. Following this, we describe the structure and policymaking activities of the Fed. We close the chapter by considering the extent to which monetary policy is a political, rather than purely technical, process.

EARLY MONETARY POLICY

The Hamiltonian Beginnings

Under Article I, Section 8, of the Constitution, Congress was given the power "to coin money [and] regulate the value thereof"; elsewhere the states were prohibited from coining money or issuing bills of credit or to "make anything but gold and silver coin a tender in payment of debts." Armed with this authority, the secretary of the treasury in the Washington administration, Alexander Hamilton, devised a program to foster commercial enterprise and to establish the new Republic on a sound economic footing.[2] Although not based on a theory of the macroeconomy like Keynesianism or monetarism, Hamilton's intention was to use the government's ability to alter the money supply to promote economic development.

In January 1790, Hamilton submitted to Congress a *Report on the Public Credit*, which estimated the national debt (from borrowing to finance the Revolutionary War) to be $76 million. He recommended that the federal debts be fully honored in order to secure the credit of the national government, and he also proposed that the debts of state govern-

ments ($25 million of the total) be paid off by the federal government. **115**
These "funding" and "assumption" bills were enacted by Congress.

But the far-reaching objective of Hamilton's economic program reflected his belief that a "monetized" national debt (i.e., one in which the government's obligations could be used as money by those owed money by the government) would create a money supply not based entirely on specie (gold and silver). "It is a well-known fact," Hamilton argued, "that in countries in which the national debt is properly funded, and an object of established confidence, it answers most of the purposes of money."[3] The genius of Hamilton's plan was his conception of creating a "sinking fund" composed of surplus federal revenues plus new loan money from European bankers. This fund would be used to buy government securities, though not to immediately retire the national debt. The sinking fund would maintain the face value of government securities, thereby preventing any speculation and assuring the integrity of public credit.

By this method the national debt was "monetized," because since government securities held their face value they could be exchanged like currency. Banks made loans based on government securities as collateral, and the federal government issued paper money backed by the national debt. Under Hamilton's plan the government-owned First Bank of the United States (1791–1811) began to function as a central banking institution, and it used the sinking fund to "peg the market" for government securities. (This procedure anticipated latter-day operations of the Federal Reserve Board. Today fully 100 percent of the monetary base, or money supply, of the United States is based on the Fed's holdings of the federal debt.)

Monetary Policy in the Nineteenth Century

The creation of the First Bank of the United States opened a political dispute between the Federalists united behind Hamilton, who favored the development of strong national institutions, and the Anti-Federalists led by Thomas Jefferson, who opposed them. The election of Jefferson to the White House in 1800 ended Federalist rule and began a new era in American politics. The federal charter of the Bank of the United States expired in 1811, but in 1816 President James Madison and Congress granted a new charter for a Second Bank of the United States (1816–1836). Madison, though a Jefferson supporter (and his successor as president), was a pragmatist who viewed the bank as necessary for sound finances. Shortly afterwards the constitutionality of the Bank was upheld by the Supreme Court in McCulloch v. Maryland (1819).[4]

116   Under Nicholas Biddle, its director, the Second Bank of the United States began to operate like a central bank. A **central bank** is generally a government-owned banking institution that controls the money supply and often regulates privately owned banks. In most industrialized countries the majority of currency in circulation consists of bank notes (e.g., the U.S. ten dollar bill) issued by the nation's central bank.

Under Biddle, the Bank limited the circulation of state bank notes (notes issued by state-chartered banks) by requiring that they be redeemed in specie (gold or silver) or in bank notes of the national government. As a result, state banks had to keep more reserves on hand, which restricted their lending activities. This limitation on credit angered the agrarian interests who wanted "cheap money" and their spokesman, President Andrew Jackson. The Jacksonian Democrats in Congress were opposed by the Whigs, who, in the presidential election year of 1832, passed a bill rechartering the Second Bank of the United States.

On July 10 Jackson vetoed that bill and, following his reelection victory, began his "war" against the Bank. Like most farmers, Jackson was a "hard-money" advocate who distrusted banks and believed that paper money fed speculation, inflated the currency, and hurt the working class, because bank notes often were worth less than their face value. Relations between Jackson and Biddle worsened to the point where the president ordered that federal money be withdrawn from the Bank and deposited in state banks controlled by his supporters.

In the end Biddle had to liquidate the assets of the Second Bank of the U.S. to satisfy its creditors, but the most important legacy of Jackson's "bank war" was the start of an era of "free banking"—a period of limited government regulation of the economy (and virtually no federal activity)—which lasted until the Civil War. The number of state banks mushroomed from 329 in 1829 to 1,500 in 1860,[5] and on the eve of the Civil War there were more than 9,000 different types of bank notes in circulation.[6] There was no uniform currency across the entire nation, with the result that only gold and silver held their value.

In 1863 and 1864 Congress enacted the National Banking Acts to facilitate the sale of government bonds to finance the Civil War. The combined deficit for the war years (1861–1865) was nearly $2.6 billion (compared to $48 million during 1857–1860), and to service a debt of that magnitude required new departures in public finance. The 1863 act chartered national banks to issue government bonds, thus adding national bank notes as a component of the money supply, and imposed a tax on the face value of state bank notes to discourage their use. The purpose of these reforms was to regularize the banking system and to create a stable currency.

However, the 1863 and 1864 statutes were *not* viewed in terms of **117** modern-day monetary policy, where the money supply is increased or decreased in order to influence the growth rate of GNP, prices, and the flow of credit for consumption and investment. Like the Keynesian view of fiscal policy, the idea of consciously using monetary policy to achieve specific macroeconomic goals is a product of the twentieth century. Also like Keynesian theory, the development of modern views on monetary policy originated in part as a reaction to severe economic problems. The development of modern monetary policy in the U.S. begins with the establishment in 1913 of the Federal Reserve System.

THE FEDERAL RESERVE SYSTEM

Seven major depressions (severe economic downturns) rocked the country in the nineteenth century (1837, 1847, 1857, 1864, 1873, 1883, and 1893), and usually they were preceded by financial "panics" that involved widespread bank failures and business bankruptcies. After the Panic of 1907, Congress created the National Monetary Commission to make recommendations. The principal result of this activity was the Federal Reserve Act of 1913, creating the Federal Reserve System. The Fed was born in controversy; farmers and small business wanted a government-managed banking system to counter the power of Eastern bankers, but the major national financial interests (then centered in New York and popularly known as "Wall Street") feared that a politicized central bank would allow cheap money.

Most countries have one central bank; the Bank of England, the Bank of France, and the Bank of Canada are illustrations. In each of these countries, this single, government-owned bank is responsible for regulating the nation's money supply, credit system, and financial system (especially commercial banks).[7] While the Federal Reserve System is often called our central bank, the legislative compromises of 1913 allowed a more complex organization to evolve (see Figure 5.1). Its principal components are the Board of Governors of the Federal Reserve Board, the Federal Open Market Committee (FOMC), and the 12 Federal Reserve Banks.[8]

The **Federal Reserve System** is an independent agency of the federal government that reports to Congress, although its operations are not funded by congressional appropriations. Technically, the twelve regional banks are owned by the privately-owned banks within their regions that have joined the Federal Reserve System. Expenses are paid from revenues derived from interest earned on its securities holdings and fees charged for services provided to member institutions. About 95 percent of the Reserve

Figure 5.1   Organization of the Federal Reserve System

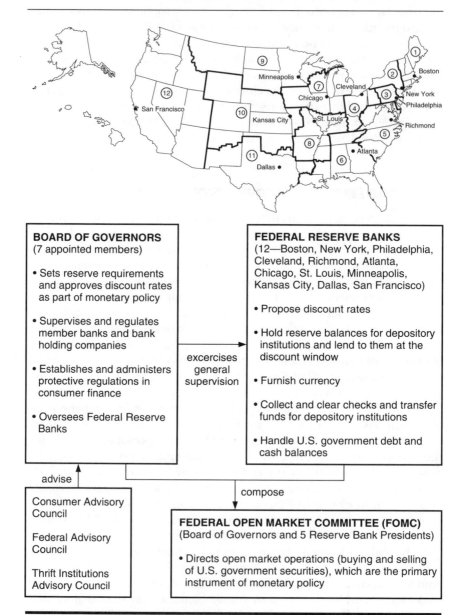

Source: Board of Governors of the Federal Reserve System, *The Federal Reserve System: Purposes and Functions* (Washington, DC: Board of Governors of the Federal Reserve System, 1984), p. 5.

Banks' net earnings (which amounted to $19.2 billion in 1991) are re-   **119**
turned to the Treasury each year.

Approximately one-third of the nation's commercial banks are members of the Federal Reserve System, but they represent about 70 percent of all commercial bank reserves and two-fifths of the deposits in all depository institutions (commercial banks, savings banks, savings and loan associations, and credit unions).[9] National banks chartered by the comptroller of the currency must, by law, be members; banks chartered by state governments can voluntarily become members if they meet Fed guidelines. The Depository Institutions Deregulation and Monetary Control Act of 1980 now subjects *all* depository institutions to the reserve requirements of the Fed; by 1983 about 33,300 nonmember institutions were brought under its control.[10] Reserves have to be maintained by banks and savings institutions against transaction-type accounts, nonpersonal time deposits, and loans from banking offices abroad.

Despite the nominal ownership of the regional banks by the member banks, real control of the Federal Reserve System rests with the Board of Governors and one of the System's committees, the Federal Open Market Committee. The seven-member **Board of Governors**, appointed by the president and confirmed by the Senate, serve fourteen-year terms, arranged so that one term expires in every even-numbered year. No member can be reappointed after serving a full term. Its chairman and vice chairman, designated from the board's membership, are confirmed by the Senate and serve four-year terms in those positions. The chair and vice chair may be reappointed, so long as their full terms have not expired.

The seven board members also sit on the **Federal Open Market Committee (FOMC)**, along with five Reserve Bank presidents, one of whom is always the president of the Federal Reserve Bank of New York. (The other Reserve Bank presidents serve one-year terms on a rotating basis.) By tradition, the chairman of the Board of Governors acts as chairman of the FOMC, while the president of the Federal Reserve Bank of New York is its vice chairman. Within their districts, the Federal Reserve Banks in New York and eleven other major cities operate the payments mechanism, distribute coin and currency, perform bank examinations, and act as fiscal agents for the Department of the Treasury.

MONETARY POLICYMAKING

The original purposes of the Federal Reserve System were to create an elastic currency, supervise the banking system, and allow for "discounted" commercial credits. In effect, the Fed was created to prevent

120   the waves of bank failures associated with previous panics and depressions by serving as a lender of last resort to banks during these periods, thereby maintaining the liquidity of the banking system. In the years since its inception, its purpose has evolved so that the Fed is now expected to take a leadership role in achieving broader macroeconomic goals.[11] Specifically, it is supposed to permit enough long-term growth in the money supply and credit to accommodate economic growth with relative price stability. In the short term, the Fed utilizes monetary policy to avoid the deflationary and inflationary pressures associated with the business cycle. The Fed exercises control over three instruments of monetary policy: reserve requirements, the discount rate, and, most importantly, open market operations.

Reserve Requirements

Since 1980, by law all depository institutions in the United States (commercial banks, savings and loan associations, savings banks, credit unions, branches of foreign banks, U.S. agencies, and specified others) must meet the **reserve requirements** of the Federal Reserve Board. Reserves are either cash on hand at those institutions (vault cash) or on deposit at a Federal Reserve Bank (reserve balance), and they must equal specific fractions of the total amounts of their deposits. The lion's share of required reserves are held against transaction deposits, deposits that permit unlimited checking privileges. Under Title I of the Depository Institutions Deregulation and Monetary Control Act of 1980 (known as the Monetary Control Act of 1980) Congress set reserve requirements for almost all depository institutions at 3 percent on the first $25 million and 12 percent on transactions above that amount. (The law provides that this threshold be adjusted upward annually.) The Federal Reserve System was given authority to alter this 12 percent requirement as it sees fit.

The Fed uses four monetary aggregates to monitor the money supply and the flow of credit. What common usage terms "the money supply" is technically defined as M1 by the Fed. It consists of currency, travelers checks, demand deposits (checking accounts), and other interest-bearing accounts with unlimited checking privileges. These M1 assets are routinely used to carry out financial transactions, whereas the three other monetary aggregates (M2, M3, and L) are ranked lower in order of their liquidity. (The term **liquidity** simply refers to the ease with which the asset can be converted into cash.) Since about ninety percent of the total monetary base is currency in circulation, reserve requirements are the optimal policy instrument to influence the M1 money supply.

The 12 percent reserve requirement in the 1980 act means, in effect, that a bank must have $12 on reserve for every $100 in deposits. If that reserve ratio is lowered to 10 percent, then $10 on reserve would support the same $100 in deposits. Since "excess reserves" can be used to make loans to borrowers, a decline in the reserve requirements provides depository institutions with more excess reserves for expanding deposits and bank credit, with the consequence that interest rates will fall.[12] A rise in the reserve requirements cuts the volume of deposits supported by a given level of reserves and curbs the supply of credit, thereby forcing up interest rates.

However, reserve requirements are not appropriate for making short-term or day-to-day corrections in monetary policy; severe fluctuations in the reserve ratios would disrupt the financial planning of depository institutions. Reserve requirements are a more significant policy instrument for their "announcement effect" to show the Fed's determination to pursue fundamental changes in the direction of monetary policy.

The Discount Rate

The Fed can lend its reserve funds through the "discount window" to depository institutions. Originally this power was expected to be the most important policy instrument of the Federal Reserve Board. As the "lender of last resort," the Fed provides credit to depository institutions facing liquidity crises for whatever reason, for example during seasonal periods (like Christmas) of heightened commercial activity.

Previously, only member banks of the Federal Reserve System had regular borrowing privileges, but the Monetary Control Act of 1980, which extended reserve requirements to nonmember depository institutions, also granted them equal access to the discount window. As a result, about 15,000 banks and 24,000 thrift institutions (savings and loans, savings banks, and credit unions) now have regular access to the Fed's reserve funds.[13]

The interest rate charged by the Federal Reserve Banks on loans to member and nonmember institutions is called the **discount rate**. The Federal Reserve Act of 1913 envisioned that the discount rate of each Reserve Bank would vary according to the credit conditions in each District, but the development of an integrated national financial market has produced one uniform discount rate across the entire nation. A higher discount rate discourages borrowing and contracts the flow of credit, because the depository institutions will have to charge yet higher interest rates on their loans to customers to maintain their profitability margin. Lower discount rates encourage lending institutions to borrow reserves from the Fed, enabling them to reduce interest rates on their loans and thus expand the money supply.

Open Market Operations

Where the reserve ratios set an upper limit on the quantity of deposits that the reserve base may support, the other two monetary policy instruments—the discount window and the **open market operations**—determine how large the volume of reserves available to depository institutions will be. The operations of the Federal Open Market Committee is the most powerful and flexible monetary policy instrument, particularly when reinforced by the use of discount rates.

The Federal Open Market Committee (FOMC) operates through the Federal Reserve Bank of New York to purchase and sell U.S. government securities on the open market. The choice of U.S. government securities is dictated by a technical need. Since the Fed must regularly buy and sell securities worth billions of dollars in order to have a measurable effect of the (huge) overall supply of reserves in the banking system, U.S. government securities are the obvious vehicle, given that the outstanding marketable federal debt rose to over $3 trillion by the early 1990s. The buying and selling of government securities are handled "over the counter" by specialized dealers located mainly in New York City. These transactions by the FOMC change the reserve base of the entire depository system.

A purchase of U.S. government securities means that the Fed issues a check to the seller, who then deposits that check in a commercial bank, which returns the check to the Fed for payment. All banks have reserve balances or accounts with a Federal Reserve Bank, and, when that transaction occurs, the reserve account of the seller's commercial bank is increased by that amount. But because the reserve account of the seller's bank is increased with no offsetting decrease of reserves at another commercial bank, the total reserves of the banking system are increased. Conversely, whenever the Fed sells U.S. government securities, the total reserves of the banking system are reduced. Thus, to increase the money supply, the Fed buys government securities, while to decrease the money supply, the Fed sells these securities. The buying and selling of government securities, therefore, has a direct and immediate impact on the size of the reserve base of the banking system. Another, but indirect, method to affect the reserve base is to charge depository institutions a fee whenever they borrow reserve funds from the Federal Reserve Banks.

Economic Indicators

Changes in reserve requirements, open market operations, and discount rates are intended to affect the supply of reserves in the banking system. An indicator that shows the effect of changes in these monetary policy instruments is the **federal funds rate** at which depository institutions borrow from one another.[14] Sometimes banks are "loaned up" and lack the funds to meet current demand, in which case they borrow money from other depository institutions with excess reserves. For these borrowings they pay a particular rate, lower or higher depending upon the degree of "ease" or "tautness" in the money market and the underlying reserve conditions of the banking system.

Any dramatic shift in monetary policy, especially changes in the discount rate, is closely watched by the financial community and the political leadership to signal whether the Fed is going to tighten or loosen the money supply. The implications of a change in the discount rate therefore depend on overall economic conditions. The Fed monitors various economic indicators to judge future trends. The specific indicators watched most closely at any particular time depend on economic conditions and perceptions of what problems are most pressing. Thus, during the late 1980s, when neither unemployment nor inflation seemed severe but great concern was expressed over the trade deficit, trade reports were closely watched. A few years later, during the recession of 1990–91, unemployment and GDP figures were much more closely monitored.

Each month the U.S. Department of Commerce publishes a series of economic indicators that are widely publicized by mass media (Table 5.1). Its Bureau of Economic Analysis tracks hundreds of economic time series to determine which best reflect the business cycle and signal turning points in economic activity.[15]

The most important indicators used to assess economic conditions are divided into three categories. The best known are such **leading indicators** as new housing starts and new orders for plant and equipment; they are termed *leading* because they anticipate future economic performance. The coincident and lagging indicators are less well known to the public. The **coincident indicators** describe the current status of the economy by tracking aggregate economic activity in employment, real income, production, and real sales; these are employed to identify and date peaks and troughs in the business cycle. The **lagging indicators** confirm that a downturn or an upturn in the economy has, in fact, occurred. For example, during a recession, bank interest rates, unit labor costs, and outstanding debt do not change as the economy "bottoms out," but instead change only after producers, workers, and consumers recognize that demand has begun to rise.

The Leading Indicators Composite Index is most important to forecasting changes in economic performance. A decline in this index over several months usually signals a recession; a rise means that a recovery is on the horizon. These signals are generally on target. One study found

124   **TABLE 5.1**   Indicators of Macroeconomic Performance

Leading Indicators
- Average length of work week
- Number of initial claims for unemployment
- Amount of new manufacturing orders
- Percentage of companies receiving slower deliveries
- Amount of new business formation
- Orders for new plants and equipment
- Number of new home building permits issued
- Change in amount of business inventories
- Change in sensitive materials prices
- Change in stock prices
- Change in M2 money supply
- Amount of outstanding business and consumer credit

Coincident Indicators
- Nonagricultural employment
- Total personal income (minus transfer payments)
- Index of industrial production
- Total manufacturing and trade sales

Lagging Indicators
- Average length of unemployment
- Ratio of business inventories to sales
- Change in labor costs
- Prime interest rate
- Amount of outstanding commercial and industrial credit
- Ratio of consumer credit to personal income

Source: U.S. Department of Commerce, Bureau of Economic Analysis, *Handbook of Cyclical Indicators* (1984).

that the Leading Indicators Index has forecasted every downturn and "growth recession" (when there is positive economic growth but nonetheless an increase in the unemployment rate) since 1948.[16]

Because of its concern with fighting inflation, the Federal Reserve Board also watches closely the **Consumer Price Index (CPI)**, the Producer Price Index (or PPI, previously called the wholesale price index), and productivity measures in order to gauge inflationary pressures. The CPI gives the actual cost to consumers of buying a given "market basket" of goods and services, while the PPI is basically a leading indicator of price movements. Because it reflects the costs of raw materials and labor used in the production process, increases in the PPI signal *future* rises in the CPI. But the relationship between the PPI and the CPI is not one-for-one, since only about one-third of total GNP is reflected in the Producer Price Index.

Does Monetary Policy Actually Work?

Our discussion up to this point would seem to imply that the Fed is, in fact, able to influence the macroeconomy through such tools as reserve requirements, the discount rate, and open market transactions. It may be worth considering this point somewhat more explicitly. The first thing to note is that it is easier for the Fed to achieve its original purpose of maintaining the liquidity of the banking system than the more ambitious macroeconomic goals of stimulating employment and limiting inflation. The Fed's very existence, in effect, achieves much of the first goal, while the latter objectives require the Fed to operate indirectly through the private banking system.[17]

The direct object of most Fed policy is the total amount of bank reserves in the banking system. Changes in this (and changes in the cost of obtaining additional funds through the discount window) are supposed to raise or lower the cost of borrowing, and thereby stimulate or deflate economic activity. However, these effects are dependent on two other sets of actors: the privately held banks and other governmental actors, particularly those directing fiscal policy. If, for whatever reason, private bankers do not respond to changes in available reserves in the predicted way, the effect of Fed policy will be blunted. For example, despite repeated cuts in the discount rate between 1989 and 1992, several classes of interest rates, such as long-term interest rates (which are closely related to housing purchases), remained at high levels long after other rates, like the prime rate and short-term rates, had fallen substantially. This was attributed to investors' fears of long-term inflation brought on by persistent, high federal budget deficits.[18] On the other hand, an expansionary Fed policy or (as is more likely) a Fed policy designed to fight inflation may be counteracted by fiscal policies in the opposite direction. Of course, in this latter instance, Fed policy may still have an effect, but the effect may not be as substantial as the Fed intended—Fed policy may lower inflation below what it would have been although inflation may remain high.

Another problem is that it may be difficult to technically control objects of Fed policy such as the money supply. Despite a clear desire to keep monetary growth within a fixed set of boundaries during the monetarist experiment of 1979–1982, the actual growth of M1 often fell outside of these bounds. This suggests that it may be even more difficult to "fine tune" the rate of monetary growth over shorter periods, such as one or two months.

126   Keeping in mind these qualifications, it does appear that the Fed is reasonably able to respond to economic conditions. A number of studies have demonstrated a reasonable fit between monetary policies and/or monetary growth and macroeconomic leading indicators related to price stability, employment level, and international economic conditions.[19] The economic indicators are related to the policy and outcome measures in what is known as a "reaction function" model, whereby the policy outcomes over time are seen to be a reaction to leading indicators, exactly what we would expect if the Fed is utilizing leading indicators in an attempt to avoid looming macroeconomic problems.

Finally, while the monetarist experiment of 1979–1982 was not an unqualified success, the basic rate of inflation dropped during this period from 9 percent to 4 percent. While other factors certainly contributed to this decline, the persistent high levels of inflation seen throughout the 1970s have yet to return to the U.S. economy. By nearly all accounts, a major share of the credit for this outcome should go to the Fed and, particularly, to Paul Volcker, the Fed chairman at that time, who continued to target inflation in the early 1980s, even as the nation settled into its worst recession since the 1930s. Although not without costs, the Fed's efforts are believed to have broken the back of inflationary pressures that had afflicted the U.S. economy since the late 1960s.

THE POLITICS OF MONETARY POLICY

Within weeks of George Bush's inauguration, Fed Chairman Alan Greenspan pointed to the 4.4 percent inflation rate seen in 1988 and a rising Producer Price Index as worrisome trends. Greenspan suggested that higher discount rates might be necessary to maintain price stability, a prospect opposed by President Bush, who preferred robust economic growth during 1989 to generate the federal revenues needed to cut the deficit. This initial disagreement was hardly their last. As the economy slipped into a recession in the summer of 1990, the tension between fighting inflation and increasing employment remained an active source of disagreement between the Fed and the Bush administration.

In fact, over the next three years the Fed reduced the discount rate repeatedly, from 7 percent in 1989 down to 3 percent by July 1992. However, while these cuts were generally welcomed (and sometimes called for) by administration officials, they also appeared to be a function of macroeconomic conditions. For example, the final cut from 3.5 percent to 3 percent on July 2 was preceded on June 24 by an unusually strong public call by President Bush for such action:

I'd like to see another lowering of interest rates. . . . I think there's room   **127**
to do that. I can understand people worrying about inflation. But I don't
think that's the big problem now.[20]

The Fed, however, did not respond to the president's call. Instead, the
reduction in the discount rate followed a rise in the unemployment rate
reported eight days later. The Fed announcement, in fact, came only min-
utes after the unemployment figures were publicly released,[21] a coincidence
that undoubtedly was an attempt by the Fed to link the discount rate
reduction to economic conditions rather than to White House calls for
such action.

Leadership Over Monetary Policy

In his dealing with Fed Chairman Greenspan, President Bush
understood the power the Fed chairman now exercises over monetary policymaking, but that decisive role had to be established by previous chairs
who were alert to the need to delicately balance their hold over monetary
policy in terms of the political needs motivating the legislative and executive branches. The political leadership exercised by the Fed chairman
is the key variable that explains how and why the Fed has evolved to
become a macroeconomic decision maker.[22] Of great importance for this
development were the tenures of four strong-willed individuals who held
that office: Marriner Eccles (1934–1948), William McChesney Martin
(1951–1970), Arthur Burns (1970–1978), and Paul Volcker (1979–1987).

After its creation in 1913 the Fed struggled to define its mission, with
the consequence that, by 1933, the agency was in peril. Observes Donald
Kettl: "It did not know what it ought to do, why it ought to do it, and
just as important, who ought to direct policy."[23] The election of Franklin
D. Roosevelt gave the Fed a new opportunity to assert monetary leadership, and that task fell upon Chairman Eccles. Eccles urged that the Fed
play an activist role in economic management, that authority be shifted
from the Reserve Banks to its Board of Governors, and that monetary
policymaking be integrated with fiscal policy. The most serious political
challenge Eccles faced, however, was to gain Fed independence from the
Treasury Department. The Federal Reserve Board had agreed to buy government bonds to peg interest rates low and thus assure the Treasury a
steady supply of low cost funds to pay for increased spending during the
Great Depression and World War II. The Treasury wanted to hold down
the cost of government borrowing, but that single-minded objective prevented the Fed from using monetary policy for broader countercyclical
goals. As Kettl explains,

128

the Fed risked having its hands tied permanently, for the Treasury might well never find it convenient to pay more for the money it borrowed. If the Fed were right [about inflation] but immobilized because of the peg, it risked losing its central, sacred mission, safeguarding the currency. No matter how strong the arguments, the Fed could not buck the Treasury and the president on its own. Yet without the freedom to tackle inflation, the Fed might well lose the reason for its existence.[24]

This policy disagreement was aggravated when the government started borrowing heavily to finance the Korean War, so in 1951 President Truman organized an interagency committee including the CEA, Treasury, the Fed, and the Office of Defense Mobilization to find a resolution to the dispute. As the Treasury Secretary was hospitalized at the time, his role in these negotiations was filled by Assistant Secretary of the Treasury William McChesney Martin. The outcome of these meetings was the famous Federal Reserve–Treasury Accord of 1951, which stated: "The Treasury and the Federal Reserve System have reached full accord with respect to debt management and monetary policies to be pursued in furthering their common purpose to assure the successful financing of the Government's requirements and, at the same time, to minimize monetization of the public debt."[25] Translated into clearer terms, the accord meant that the Fed was no longer formally obliged to maintain stable interest rates to assist Treasury's debt management.

The appointment to the Fed chairmanship of William McChesney Martin by President Truman (also during 1951) marked the beginning of a new era for the central bank. The Fed became an independent force in economic policymaking, and Martin's outlook quickly became known. As he told Congress in 1956: "Our purpose is to lean against the winds of deflation or inflation, whichever way they are blowing."[26] Those words suggested that the money supply would be expanded when recession loomed but contracted as inflationary pressures arose. To many people, however, Martin personified the hard-money philosophy that monetary policy be fundamentally concerned with combating inflation.

According to John Woolley, the "basic factor producing conflict between the president and the Federal Reserve seems to be their differential responses to the economic conditions experienced in the late phases of economic upswings and downswings. That is, the Federal Reserve is typically faster to switch to a restrictive policy and slower to move to an expansionary policy than the president."[27] Luckily for Martin, during the 1950s the White House was occupied by a moderate Republican who preferred not to become embroiled in a policy debate with the Fed.

However, a Democratic administration in the 1960s held different views of the Fed's role, and CEA Chairman Walter Heller warned President Kennedy that Martin's "foot is poised nervously above the anti-inflationary brake pedal."[28] To prevent that from happening, the Kennedy administration made more frequent use of the informal quadriad meetings among the chairmen of the CEA and the Fed, the budget bureau director, and the secretary of the treasury that had been initiated by Eisenhower. These consultations smoothed Fed–White House relations, and President Kennedy reappointed Martin as Fed chairman after he cooperated in implementing the administration's "Operation Twist" policy to correct our balance-of-payments problem (by raising short-term interest above long-term rates; see Chapter 6).

When Lyndon Johnson succeeded to the White House and secured enactment of the tax cut proposed by President Kennedy, the prospect of an economic boom worried Martin so much that, on June 1, 1965, he warned the country about the threat of another depression. His concerns were hardly mollified by the Vietnam War buildup, and Martin began to signal his intentions to tighten the money supply. The CEA chairman and the treasury secretary argued that monetary restraint was not yet necessary, but on December 5, 1965, the Fed voted to raise the discount rate from 4 percent to 4.5 percent, and its policy of tight money continued through mid-1966.

By the end of the year everybody understood the need to restrain aggregate demand, and President Johnson announced cuts in federal spending and suspension of corporate tax incentives. In his 1967 State of the Union Address, Johnson also called for enactment of a 10 percent tax surcharge. His public statements caused the Fed to ease off the monetary brake to allow Congress time to act on the tax increase proposal. However, when it became apparent that the surcharge would be too little and too late, the Fed again moved to tighten money. This episode is one of the best-known examples of open conflict between the president and the Fed chairman, but Martin survived. Kettl notes that the "Fed's tightening in 1966, ease in 1967 through 1968, and renewed tightening in 1969 were thus the product of an elaborate political minuet in which Martin struggled to accommodate the Fed to a turbulent environment."[29] The upshot was that Johnson in 1967 reappointed Martin to a fifth term as chairman.

In 1970 Martin was succeeded by Arthur Burns, who had been President Eisenhower's CEA chairman and was serving as President Nixon's economic counselor at the time of his appointment. Though an unabashed partisan who continued to work closely with the Nixon White House, Burns was also independent of the president. Nixon, in fact, angrily viewed Burns's strong advocacy of an "incomes policy" as an act of personal disloyalty. Eventually, though, Nixon accepted the imposition of wage-price controls, and Burns was reappointed Fed chairman in 1974. Burns's influ-

130   ence increased during the Ford presidency,[30] when the White House did not attempt to interfere with the Fed, and its tight money policy won quiet applause from the president.

However a new, more serious challenge to the Fed's independence and Burns's leadership erupted, not from the usual sources of conflict in the executive branch, but from the legislative branch. The preamble to the Federal Reserve Act of 1913 charged the agency "to furnish an elastic currency" but did not precisely explain what Congress had in mind. The Fed consequently enjoyed wide discretion in monetary policymaking, with the Congress normally a passive observer until complaints were heard about overly high interest rates. The economic stagflation that threatened the nation during the 1970s prompted the Congress to look into how the Fed set monetary targets, and its inquiries culminated in new oversight legislation.

In 1975 both chambers enacted House Concurrent Resolution 133 in an attempt to influence Fed policymaking and increase its accountability to Congress. Two years later the Federal Reserve Reform Act of 1977 was signed into law by President Carter. In addition to requiring Senate confirmation of the president's designations of the Fed chairman and vice chairman, this law (PL 95-188) added this key amendment to the 1913 act:

> The Board of Governors of the Federal Reserve System and the Federal Open Market Committee shall maintain long-run growth of the monetary and credit aggregates commensurate with the economy's long-run potential to increase production, so as to promote effectively the goals of maximum employment, stable prices, and moderate long-term interest rates. The Board of Governors shall consult with Congress at semiannual hearings before the Committee on Banking, Housing and Urban Affairs of the Senate and the Committee on Banking, Finance and Urban Affairs of the House of Representatives about the Board of Governors' and the Federal Open Market Committee's objectives and plans with respect to the ranges of growth or diminution of monetary and credit aggregates for the upcoming twelve months, taking account of past and prospective developments in production, employment and prices. Nothing in this Act shall be interpreted to require that such ranges of growth or diminution be achieved if the Board of Governors and the Federal Open Market Committee determine that they cannot or should not be achieved because of changing conditions.

The last sentence essentially allows the Fed *not* to follow this monetary game plan, while other wording portrays a masterful ambiguity, as Robert Weintraub explains: "In short, Congress, though willing to legislate monetary policy goals and basic long-run guidelines for its conduct, is not willing to pick the aggregate for carrying them out. The choice of **131** the target M [whether M1, M2, or M3] of open market and other day-to-day monetary policy operations is viewed as a technical, not a legislative matter."[31]

The next year Congress enacted the Full Employment and Balanced Growth Act of 1978 (the Humphrey-Hawkins Act discussed in Chapter 2), which added oversight mechanisms. This act requires the Fed to give Congress its monetary policy goals within 30 days after receipt of the *Economic Report of the President* and explain their relationship to the president's short-term economic objectives. In its semiannual reports to the Congress, the Fed must also include the "consensus" projections by the FOMC of GNP, inflation, and unemployment for the coming year.

For the first time in its history Fed policymaking is subject to regular oversight by the Congress to ascertain its economic impacts and its relationship to fiscal policy. The fact that more punitive legislation was not enacted is clearly a tribute to Burn's adroit leadership. According to Kettl,

> Burns developed defensive maneuvers to blunt the most threatening congressional tactics. He deployed shields like multiple measures of money, with broad ranges for each, and technical jargon, like velocity and M1 and M2, that befuddled most members of Congress. His constant battles diluted the reforms that [Congressman] Reuss [D-WI] and [Senator] Proxmire [D-WI] originally had in mind. Congress gained more information and the right to subject the chairman to regular harangues on the Fed's mistakes, but Burns protected the Fed from the most serious attacks. . . .[32]

Despite his successes with Congress, Burns would not survive a Carter administration worried about his independent streak and anti-inflation stridency. In 1978 President Carter replaced him with G. William Miller, whose financial connections were supposed to establish confidence among the Wall Street bankers. However, inflation roared back, and Miller's willingness to follow the White House lead by voting against a discount rate increase (which the Fed approved in late 1978) caused *Fortune* magazine to label him "a fainthearted inflation fighter."[33] With inflation hitting double digits, President Carter retreated to Camp David in July 1979 to conduct a full-scale assessment of his administration. Afterwards he fired Treasury Secretary Blumenthal and asked G. William Miller to take that post, but this maneuver did not improve Carter's weak image. The deteriorating financial and political situation had to be contained, and to repair the damage, President Carter appointed the president of the Federal Reserve Bank of New York, Paul Volcker, to the Fed chairmanship.

Volcker had a reputation as an advocate of strenuous efforts to combat inflation, and his appointment was generally hailed by the financial com-

132   munity. On October 6, 1979, he acted boldly by announcing three new policy moves. The Federal Reserve Banks would be allowed to increase their discount rates from 11 percent to 12 percent; new reserve requirements would be established to curb the growth of bank credit; and open-market operations now would be used to regulate the supply of bank reserves instead of influencing the rate of interest. The latter represented a fundamental realignment in FOMC operations, one that echoed the long-standing criticisms of Fed policy by the monetarist economists. Indeed, Samuelson and Nordhaus describe Fed policy from October 1979 through the fall of 1982 as "a monetarist experiment," in which the Fed attempted to keep monetary growth relatively constant, without regard to short-term fluctuations in economic activity or interest rates.[34]

These policy changes also made clear Volcker's determination to beat inflation, without much regard for its impact on economic growth or joblessness. These policy initiatives did not immediately bring down inflation, which actually got worse during 1980. The Reagan administration initially encouraged the Fed to maintain stable growth in the money supply, but in mid-1981 some administration officials openly engaged in criticism of the Fed. Despite interest rates at the 20 percent level, inflation was falling only slightly, while unemployment rose to nearly 10 percent at the height of the 1981–82 recession. At this juncture, Volcker faced a policy dilemma.

Should the Fed ease monetary restraint and possibly refuel inflation, or should the Fed continue its anti-inflation policy and likely aggravate the deepest recession since the 1930s? What Volcker did was to announce that the Fed would temporarily stop, for technical reasons, basing its decisions on the narrow monetary aggregate of M1. It also agreed in late 1982 to a slight reduction in the discount rate (from 10 percent to 9.5 percent). Thus Volcker gave the nation mixed signals about his intentions, which bought him some time and, in effect, allowed him to hold his policy course.

Volcker's decisive role during this trying period, argues Kettl, meant that "for the first time in the Fed's history, its chairman controlled the agenda for macroeconomic policy. He had in 1979 pushed control of inflation to the keystone of economic policymaking. He followed that by developing a strategy to break inflation, and he succeeded in winning political support for it."[35] A steadfast monetary policy was crucial for the success of Reaganomics, and Volcker generally enjoyed the good will of President Reagan. Although such powerful voices as House Majority Leader Jim Wright (D-TX) and supply-side Congressman Jack Kemp (R-NY) had called for his resignation, in 1983 he was reappointed Fed Chairman by President Reagan with the resounding support of Wall Street.

Is There a Political Monetary Cycle?

To what extent does monetary policy accommodate the economic and political needs of the White House? The president can try to influence Fed decision making through his appointment powers, but the long, staggered terms of its Board of Governors assure that no president can make wholesale personnel changes during one four-year term. Or maybe White House pressure is more subtle insofar as the Fed chairman, a politically astute leader, shapes monetary policy to anticipate the political needs of the administration.

One specific concern that has been the object of much research over the last fifteen years is whether Fed policy falls into a pattern that might be called a **political monetary cycle**. This term is a variant of a broader idea, the political business cycle, which will be discussed in detail in Chapter 7. Briefly, it is argued that political leaders use governmental policies, especially fiscal policy, to stimulate the economy immediately before national elections. It is predicted to be particularly apparent when presidents are running for reelection.[36] The monetary version of this suggests that monetary policy will be eased more than is warranted by economic conditions during election years in an attempt to stimulate the economy and garner votes for incumbents running for reelection. Since the Fed is considered to be more responsive to the president than Congress, the effect should be tied to presidential electoral concerns, rather than congressional ones.

The question of whether this actually occurs has been studied by several scholars, most recently in a very careful and thorough study by Nathaniel Beck.[37] Beck found no evidence that the Fed engages in this sort of behavior, which he attributes to the Fed's fear of being detected in such activity, thereby risking losing an independence that is buttressed by a reputation for nonpartisan technical competence. There is, in fact, a surge in the M1 money supply associated with approaching presidential elections, but Beck demonstrates that this is due to expansive fiscal policies during election years—which are not under the Fed's control—rather than to monetary policy. Beck concludes:

> The Fed does not alter its policymaking to aid presidential reelection. Monetary policy before an election responds to roughly the same forces as at other times. On the other hand, the Fed does not take special action to offset cycles in M1 that are not caused by the Fed. It passively responds, instead, to fiscal policy, whether electorally inspired or not.[38]

Other research has sought to determine whether Fed policy has changed over time and whether changes in Fed policy are related to such

134   factors as presidential partisanship or turnover in Fed leadership. A study by Robert Weintraub tracked the growth in M1 from 1951 to 1977 and found that significant monetary policy "thrusts" occurred in 1953, 1961, 1969, 1971, 1974, and 1977,[39] which, with the exception of 1971, each represent a year of turnover in the White House. Other statistical patterns were consistent with qualitative evidence about monetary policymaking in each administration since the Treasury-Fed Accord, as Weintraub concludes, "that in each administration monetary policy fitted harmoniously with the president's economic and financial objectives and plans."[40]

Later studies of the impact of economic and political variables on monetary policy by Nathaniel Beck and John Woolley show important differences based on presidential party, presidential administration, and turnover in the Fed chairmanship.[41] Because Democratic presidents typically want lower unemployment even at the cost of higher inflation, it is assumed that they would prefer a relatively loose monetary policy (i.e., one with more growth in the money supply). These studies indicate that Fed policy is generally tighter under Republicans than under Democrats, although there is important variation from administration to administration. Monetary policy was conservative under Eisenhower, Kennedy, Ford, and Reagan, but liberal under Johnson, Nixon, and Carter. At the same time, Beck also notes that "knowing who is chair of the Fed helps explain Fed policy; this holds even if we know who is president."[42] Monetary policy, for example, was tight under Paul Volcker, but easier under Arthur Burns.

Beck also examined the relationship between monetary and fiscal policy and found that "by the 1970s easy fiscal policy was often associated with tight monetary policy."[43] While seemingly a contradictory policy strategy, it may reflect a political logic that results from the inability of Congress and the president to contain inflationary pressures through the budget process. This bifurcated approach would allow the popular branches to focus their attention on the unemployment problem and let the Fed worry about inflation. If interest rates should go too high, then both Congress and the White House can resort to "bashing" the Fed as a political scapegoat.

In the end, though, it should be remembered that Fed policy is primarily driven by the Fed's response to macroeconomic conditions such as the overall level of M1, the unemployment rate, and the rate of inflation. All of the studies that examine political control begin by relating Fed policy actions and outcomes to these economic indicators and then assess the extent to which political variables appear to interfere with this basic relationship. To be sure, the Fed may alter its main macroeconomic target over time, sometimes concerned with employment and other times focusing on price stability. During the monetarist experiment of 1979–82, the Fed even adopted a different theoretical understanding of what the Fed can and should be doing to regulate the macroeconomy. However, to a degree seldom seen in other economic policy arenas, the Fed's activities in the area of monetary policy are much less likely to respond to changes in public opinion and much more likely to be a function of technocratic assessments of what is necessary in order to promote higher levels of employment and, even more consistently, lower rates of inflation.

KEY TERMS

monetary policy, monetarism, central bank, Federal Reserve system, Board of Governors [of the Fed], Federal Open Market Committee (FOMC), reserve requirements, liquidity, discount rate, open market operations, federal funds rate, leading indicators, coincident indicators, lagging indicators, Consumer Price Index (CPI), political monetary cycle

ADDITIONAL READING

Bach, George L. *Making Monetary and Fiscal Policy*. Washington, DC: The Brookings Institution, 1971. Analyzes fiscal and monetary policy during the pre-1952 era, the Eisenhower terms, and the Kennedy-Johnson years in terms of coordinating policy instruments to achieve macroeconomic goals.

Board of Governors of the Federal Reserve System. *The Federal Reserve System: Purposes & Functions*. 7th ed. Washington, DC: Board of Governors of the Federal Reserve System, 1984. Excellent summary of the Fed organization, monetary policy instruments, Federal Open Market Committee operations, and international effects.

Friedman, Milton and Walter W. Heller. *Monetary vs. Fiscal Policy*. New York: W. W. Norton, 1969. A celebrated debate between the foremost exponent of monetarism and the liberal CEA Chairman under President Kennedy.

Greider, William. *Secrets of the Temple: How the Federal Reserve Runs the Country*. New York: Simon & Schuster, 1988. A populist account of the Fed from its beginnings to 1987.

Kettl, Donald F. *Leadership at the Fed*. New Haven: Yale University Press, 1986. Excellent account of the leadership styles of four influential Fed Chairmen: Marriner Eccles, William McChesney Martin, Arthur Burns, and Paul Volcker.

Maisel, Sherman J. *Managing the Dollar*. New York: W. W. Norton, 1973. A member of the Fed's Board of Governors during 1965–1972 gives an insider's view of the workings of monetary policy.

136   Timberlake, Richard H., Jr. *The Origins of Central Banking in the United States.* Cambridge, MA: Harvard University Press, 1978. An intellectual history of central banking and monetary policy before the Fed was created, including the First and Second Banks of the U.S. and the early role of the Treasury Department.

Woolley, John T. *Monetary Politics: The Federal Reserve and The Politics of Monetary Policy.* Cambridge, England: Cambridge University Press, 1984. A study of how the Fed operates, the background of its members, and its relations with the president and Congress.

NOTES

1.   A clear exposition of the differences between mainstream economic theory and monetarism is found in Paul A. Samuelson and William D. Nordhaus, *Economics*, 14th ed. (New York: McGraw-Hill, 1992), "Chapter 35: Issues in Economic Stabilization." Our discussion of the mainstream and monetarist views on monetary policy are drawn from this source. This chapter also describes a more contemporary challenge to mainstream views, rational-expectations theory. The latter shares monetarism's views that private markets should prevail and that monetary policy should aim for fixed, long-term targets, although the theoretical underpinnings of these prescriptions differ from those of monetarism.

2.   See discussion of Hamilton's program in Forrest McDonald, *Alexander Hamilton: A Biography* (New York: W. W. Norton, 1979), Chapters 8 and 9.

3.   Quoted in McDonald, *Alexander Hamilton*, p. 166.

4.   17 U.S. (4 Wheat.) 316.

5.   Paul Studenski and Herman E. Krooss, *Financial History of the United States* (New York: McGraw-Hill, 1963), p. 104.

6.   Robert C. Puth, *American Economic History* (Chicago: Dryden Press, 1982), p. 175.

7.   Samuelson and Nordhaus, *Economics*, p. 731.

8.   This discussion is based on *The Federal Reserve System: Purposes & Functions* (Washington, DC: Board of Governors of the Federal Reserve System, 1984), Chapter 1. See also Michael D. Reagan, "The Political Structure of the Federal Reserve System," *American Political Science Review* 55 (March 1961), pp. 64–76.

9.   *The Federal Reserve System*, p. 9.

10.   Ibid., p. 10.

11.   See Reagan, "The Political Structure of the Federal Reserve System."

12.   This assumes that the demand for loans stays the same. If demand increases, interest rates may actually stay the same or even rise. Whatever the specific effect on interest rates, the overall effect is stimulative, by making credit more available.

13.   *The Federal Reserve System*, p. 58.

14. The federal funds rate is considered to be so much a function of Fed activities that studies by Beck and Woolley employed this as a measure of Fed policy activity. See Nathaniel Beck, "Elections and the Fed: Is There a Political Monetary Cycle?" *American Journal of Political Science* 31 (February 1987), pp. 194–216; and John T. Woolley, "Partisan Manipulations of the Economy: Another Look at Monetary Policy with Moving Regression," *Journal of Politics* 50 (May 1988), pp. 335–360.

15. This discussion is based on Ronald A. Ratti, "A Descriptive Analysis of Economic Indicators," in Edwin Mansfield, ed., *Managerial Economics and Operations Research* (New York: W. W. Norton, 1987), pp. 316–330.

16. Cited in Ratti, "A Descriptive Analysis of Economic Indicators," p. 328.

17. See Samuelson and Nordhaus, *Economics*, "Chapter 29: Central Banking and Monetary Supply."

18. By 1992, long-term rates began to fall sharply, reaching twenty-year lows in early 1993.

19. See, for example, Nathaniel Beck, "Domestic Political Sources of American Monetary Policy: 1955–1982," *Journal of Politics* 46 (August 1984), pp. 786–817.

20. "Bush Urges Fed to Cut Interest Rates," *Chicago Tribune*, June 24, 1992, 1:4.

21. "Unemployment Up Sharply, Prompting Federal Reserve to Cut Its Key Lending Rate," *New York Times*, July 3, 1992, A:1.

22. See S. Maisel, *Managing the Dollar* (New York: Norton, 1973).

23. Donald F. Kettl, *Leadership at the Fed* (New Haven: Yale University Press, 1986), p. 42. Our account of the chairman's role in Fed policymaking during the tenures of Eccles, Martin, Burns, and Volcker is based on this detailed case study.

24. Kettl, *Leadership at the Fed*, p. 66.

25. Board of Governors, *Thirty-eighth Annual Report* (Washington, DC: Board of Governors, 1951), p. 4. Cited in ibid., p. 74.

26. U.S. Senate, Committee on Banking and Currency, *Nomination of William McChesney Martin, Jr.*, Hearings, 84th Cong., 2d Sess., 1956, p. 5. Quoted in Ibid., p. 83.

27. John T. Woolley, *Monetary Politics: The Federal Reserve and The Politics of Monetary Policy* (London: Cambridge University Press, 1984), p. 119.

28. Cited in Kettl, *Leadership at the Fed*, p. 93.

29. Ibid., p. 109.

30. James E. Anderson, "The President and Economic Policy: A Comparative View of Advisory Arrangements," paper presented at the 1991 annual meeting of the American Political Science Association, p. 11.

31. Robert E. Weintraub, "Congressional Supervision of Monetary Policy," *Journal of Monetary Economics* 4 (April 1978), p. 347.

32. Kettl, *Leadership at the Fed*, p. 150.

138   33.   *Fortune* (December 31, 1978), p. 40. Cited in Kettl, *Leadership at the Fed*, p. 170.

34.   Samuelson and Nordhaus, *Economics*, p. 645.

35.   Kettl, *Leadership at the Fed*, p. 185.

36.   These arguments are developed more fully in William Nordhaus, "The Political Business Cycle," *Review of Economic Studies* 42 (1975), pp. 169–190; and Edward Tufte, *Political Control of the Economy* (Princeton: Princeton University Press, 1978).

37.   Nathaniel Beck, "Elections and the Fed: Is There a Political Monetary Cycle?" This article includes a concise, but thorough, review of previous work on this question.

38.   Ibid., p. 214.

39.   Weintraub, "Congressional Supervision of Monetary Policy," p. 349.

40.   Ibid., p. 350.

41.   Nathaniel Beck, "Domestic Political Sources of American Monetary Policy: 1955–1982"; and John T. Woolley, "Partisan Manipulation of the Economy: Another Look at Monetary Policy with Moving Regression."

42.   Nathaniel Beck, "Domestic Political Sources of American Monetary Policy: 1955–1982," p. 806.

43.   Ibid., pp. 810–812.

CHAPTER 6

International Economic Policy

While the United States never had an entirely "closed" economic system, not too many years ago the U.S. domestic society was much less tied to the workings of the international economy than it is today. At the close of World War II the U.S. was more than a military power; it was an economic giant. The European nations and Japan lay prostrate from extensive fighting on their soil, and they were so weak economically that American policymakers feared the onslaught of communism across the entire continent. To prevent that from happening, Congress, at the urging of President Truman, enacted the Marshall Plan, which provided massive aid for the European nations to rebuild their economies.

That was five decades ago. By the 1990s the United States had achieved a new, though more dubious, economic record—the world's largest debtor nation. The 1992 Democratic party platform declared, "Restoring America's global economic leadership must become a central element of our national security policies. . . . At stake are American jobs, our standard of living and the quality of life for ourselves and our children."[1] As the trade deficits of the 1980s continue into the 1990s, a key aspect of international economic relations, trade policy, continues to be a major issue of U.S. national politic. Things have clearly changed.

At a basic level, what has changed is that the economy of the United States has become more interdependent with the world economy. This does not mean that the rest of the world has prospered at the expense of the U.S. or that the U.S. has become economically weak, but rather that

140   the U.S. economy is increasingly part of a global market for raw materials, manufactured goods, services, and finance.

The consequences of this change for the U.S. economy are mixed, neither wholly bad nor wholly good. On the one hand, increased exports of manufactured goods since 1985 have led to a resurgence in many areas of the U.S. manufacturing sector. On the other hand, heightened imports in particular industries (e.g., automobiles) have created serious economic and social dislocations and contributed to the outflow of national wealth represented by the deficit in the nation's balance of payments. More important, though, increasing global interdependence means that the management of U.S. economic fortunes is less firmly in the hands of U.S. policymakers, since the lines of economic cause-and-effect flow across national borders. One significant impact of international economics, therefore, is to further complicate the achievement of the fundamental macroeconomic goal of economic growth without inflation.

In this chapter we consider both the mechanics and politics of international economic policymaking in the United States. We begin by discussing the changing place of the U.S. in the world economy. Next, we describe the goals of U.S. policymakers in the international economic arena since World War II, including how these have changed to confront these new realities. We then identify the key institutional actors in this policy area. Unlike the other areas of economic policy we have considered, these includes significant actors from outside of the United States, such as the World Bank, the International Monetary Fund, and the GATT. Finally, we end the chapter by considering two major issues in contemporary international economic policy, international trade and the position of the U.S. dollar in global currency markets.

UNITED STATES IN THE WORLD ECONOMY

The United States and Global Interdependence

On September 14, 1992, major U.S. newspapers carried front-page stories describing a decision by the Bundesbank, Germany's central bank, to cut German interest rates. Aside from its implications for the German and European economies, this policy decision by an agency of a foreign government was seen as having direct implications for the U.S. economy. The dollar had recently fallen to postwar lows against the German mark,[2] and it was feared that the prospect of the dollar's continuing fall against this and other currencies might lead to a drop in foreign investment in the U.S. Since foreign investment is an important source of credit in the U.S.—including credit for a federal budget deficit that ap-

proached $300 billion in FY92—a drop in this investment could have **141**
serious negative consequences, including a decrease in available credit for
private investment vital to economic growth. In addition, while a falling
dollar stimulates the export economy (by making U.S. exports cheaper for
foreign consumers), it also makes foreign imports more costly, which has
the negative consequence of leading to higher inflation. For all of these
reasons, the Bundesbank decision was important news for U.S. newspaper
readers.

Two summary indicators of the increasing interdependence of the
U.S. and global economies are the changes in the importance of exports
and imports to the overall U.S. economy. As Figure 6.1 shows, both have
doubled relative to the overall size of the economy over the last three
decades, each rising from under 5 percent to over 10 percent of the GDP.
In dollar terms, the increases in exports and imports have been even more
spectacular: even measured in constant (1987) dollars, the yearly volume

Figure 6.1 U.S. Exports and Imports as a
Percentage of GDP, 1959–1992

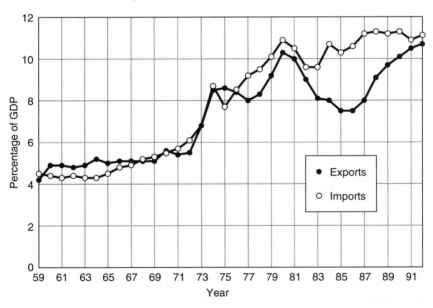

Source: Calculated by the authors from data reported in *Economic Report of the President,
January 1993*, Table B-1: Gross Domestic Product, 1959–92. Data for 1992 are for first three
quarters of 1992.

of both has risen from under $100 billion in 1960 to over $500 billion by 1990. These numbers indicate that trade is steadily becoming more important to the overall performance of the U.S. economy. Even a 10 percent drop in exports, for example, would translate into a 1 percent drop in the GDP, with a corresponding loss of employment and national income.

Although we discuss trade more extensively later in the chapter, we should point out that Figure 6.1 also illustrates what many see as one of the basic problems facing the U.S. with regard to international economics: a persistent trade deficit. The **balance of trade** is the net value of exports over imports. A positive balance, or **trade surplus**, means that the U.S. is exporting more than it is importing, while a negative balance, or **trade deficit**, means that imports exceed exports. As we noted in Chapter 1, trade represents only one component of the broader measure of international financial transactions, the balance on current account. But as the largest component, and the one most persistently showing a deficit, it is closely watched.

Although the figure indicates that the U.S. has had nearly continual trade deficits since the early 1970s,[3] there is not a general pattern of declining exports matched with rising imports. Rather, both have grown substantially, and the large gap of the mid-1980s was substantially reduced by the early 1990s. The linked increases in both exports and imports highlight a policy dilemma discussed later in the chapter. Any broad policy attempt to reduce imports risks foreign retaliation that will damage exports; given the crucial role of exports in the contemporary U.S. economy, such action may damage the economy as much as it helps it.

The increasing export- and import-dependence of the United States is part of a broader pattern of global interdependence. Simply put, the world more closely resembles a single market for goods, services, and capital than ever before. Both the volume of trade and the importance of trade for various nations' economies have increased dramatically over the last several decades. Although the data in Figure 6.1 demonstrate this is true for the U.S. economy, the United States is still much less trade dependent than most other industrialized nations. Figure 6.2 presents comparative data on the relative size of exports in the economies of several nations. It should be noted that the bases for export calculations in Figures 6.1 and 6.2 differ somewhat, so the 1990 percentages for the U.S. are similar, but not precisely the same, in the two figures. Also, although this figure reports export-dependence, imports also represent a measure of economic interdependence, and a figure based on imports would be slightly different. (Japan would be the least import-dependent, while the U.S. would remain lower than the other five countries.)

Figure 6.2 Exports as a Percentage of GDP for
Selected Countries, 1990

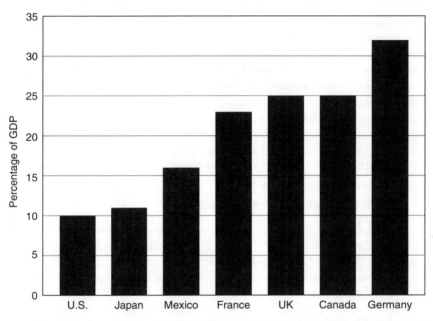

Source: *World Development Report 1992* (Washington, DC: The World Bank, 1991). German data are for Federal Republic of Germany before unification.

The data on export dependence show that the United States remains less interdependent with the rest of the global economy (in the aggregate) than other countries. Significantly, the two major economies with the lowest export dependence (and import dependence, for that matter) are those of Japan and the United States—which are also the two largest national economies in the world. Not surprisingly, these two large economies are more self-sufficient than other national economies. The European nations all have a substantially higher degree of involvement with international trade, which is also to be expected given their participation in the European Community. Thus, while trade data indicate that U.S. involvement in the global economy has grown substantially over the last three decades, in the aggregate, trade is still less important to the U.S. economy than it is to most other high-income, industrialized countries.

Our interpretation of these two figures has deliberately employed terms like *overall* and *in the aggregate* because there is substantial variability

144   in patterns of trade across the various sectors of the U.S. economy. In some areas, such as the use of crude oil, the U.S. exports little but is highly dependent upon imports, importing about half of the oil consumed in the U.S. during the 1990s. On the other hand, historically the United States has imported relatively small percentages of agricultural products, while exporting substantial amounts. The substantial variations across sectors of the economy mean that in some areas—including some essential areas like energy—U.S. interdependence with the global economy is such that a serious disruption of international transactions would have substantial effects upon the U.S. economy. As a result, governmental management of the relationship between the U.S. and global economies has varied dimensions, some relating to the overall performance of the macroeconomy, some relating to specific sectors of the economy, and some relating to both.

Is the United States in Decline?

During the 1980s, a substantial debate in both the academic and popular presses arose over the question of whether the United States is a nation in decline. Although this issue had been raised earlier, the 1980s debate was triggered by historian Paul Kennedy's best-selling book *The Rise and Fall of the Great Powers*.[4] Essentially, Kennedy argued that the United States was falling victim to "imperial overstretch," a condition he noted had led to earlier declines of global superpowers such as the Dutch and British. He traced these declines to excessive military burdens borne by superpowers, leading to insufficient economic investment and gradually faltering economies. On the face of it, the relative decline of the United States as an economic superpower since the end of the Second World War would seem to support this view.

This argument, however, has been challenged, most notably by Joseph Nye.[5] Nye has pointed out that assessments of U.S. decline rest heavily upon the baseline against which current statistics are compared. He argues that the immediate postwar period was an artificial period of U.S. dominance, since only the U.S. economy was strengthened rather than weakened by World War II. In fact, the current U.S. share of the gross world product is about the same as it was shortly before the war. Moreover, the best measure of dominance is the ability to control outcomes, and here the United States continues to fare well, both militarily and economically. Finally, the collapse of the Soviet Union has lessened the need for large conventional U.S. military forces, freeing it from some of the "imperial" military obligations Kennedy described.

Perhaps a more relevant issue that follows from this discussion is whether the United States will be able to successfully compete in the modern global system of trading states, a system where competition among major actors is more economic than military.⁶ This raises other questions for policymakers: Does the United States need to reform its educational system to prepare its labor forces to compete successfully in the global economy? How can the U.S. increase its rates of savings and investment to compete with economic competitors like Japan, Germany, and the "Asian Tigers" (South Korea, Taiwan, Hong Kong, and Singapore)? Finally, does the United States need to consciously develop a national industrial policy—a centrally organized strategic plan for investment and economic development—as some of its competitors, notably Japan, are said to have done?

THE GOALS OF U.S. INTERNATIONAL ECONOMIC POLICY

Influencing the Global Economy

In dealing with international economic affairs, U.S. policymakers have both an inward focus and an outward focus. The outward focus is on the global economy itself. Here, U.S. policymakers have one primary goal, to promote stability in the global economy—stability in trade relations, in the currency markets, and in the supply of important goods and raw materials. This pursuit of stability in economic relations is part of a general goal of promoting stability that includes noneconomic relations as well. Since the close of World War II, the United States has served as a world leader, and this leadership has been as much in the economic sphere as in military affairs. Thus the United States has played a prominent role in the normalizing of trade negotiations through the General Agreement on Tariffs and Trade (GATT) and has acted in concert with other major industrialized nations to stabilize the international currency markets.

A secondary goal of U.S. policymakers relative to the global economy is to promote economic growth in other national economies. Some of the reasons for this are related to the desire to promote general stability and growth in poorer nations, but efforts in this area are also related to self-interest: growing economies outside United States generally produce a greater demand for goods and services, some of which are supplied through increased U.S. exports. During the early 1990s, for example, U.S. policymakers urged European central banks to lower key interest rates in hopes of stimulating European economies out of the economic downturn that affected many of these economies (as well as the U.S. economy). This desire to stimulate European economies has been frankly related to a desire to expand U.S. exports to these nations.⁷

146   This last point is thus also related to the inward focus of U.S. policymakers, by which we mean their efforts to manage international economic interactions in ways that are clearly beneficial for the U.S. economy. From a practical political perspective, these domestic concerns are
probably more important to U.S. decision makers than the outward-look-
ing goals described above. There are three basic goals of U.S. policymaking
in this area: reducing barriers to trade (or promoting **free trade**), promoting
U.S. exports, and regulating the value of the U.S. dollar in world currency
markets.

Free Trade

The first goal, reducing barriers to international trade, has been
one of the basic elements of international economic policy since World
War II, although it has been increasingly questioned during the last twenty
years.[8] Between 1900 and 1930, a number of **protectionist** bills were enacted by the U.S. Congress, culminating in the infamous Smoot-Hawley
Act of 1930. These bills generally raised **tariffs** (taxes on imported goods),
often in order to protect U.S. industries from lower-priced goods produced
abroad. The general effect of increased tariffs is to provoke similar tariff
increases from the nations affected by them. When this occurred worldwide in response to the Smoot-Hawley Act, the effects were disastrous:
international trade declined enormously (by 67 percent in just three
years), further deepening the worldwide economic downturn we know as
the Great Depression.[9]

U.S. policymakers recognized this mistake fairly quickly, and they began to reverse the trend toward protectionism with the Trade Act of 1934,
which contained a crucial provision in which Congress delegated to the
president the authority to negotiate reciprocal tariff-cut agreements with
other nations. This shifting of power over trade policy from Congress to
the president was of fundamental importance, since Congress, with its
greater connection to local economic interests, had long used tariff legislation to promote protectionist policies. Once authority shifted to the
president, a number of reciprocal trade agreements were concluded.

Near the end of World War II, the victorious allies began planning
for a set of new global arrangements that would both stimulate recovery
from the war and prevent future difficulties. These world leaders shared a
general belief that economic nationalism—manifested by rising tariffs and
uncoordinated monetary policies—had contributed to both the economic
and political breakdowns of the 1930s. In the United States, a general
consensus toward free trade came to dominate national trade policy.[10]

While this general consensus toward free trade has been somewhat eroded, the U.S. government, since World War II, has pursued a fairly consistent policy encouraging the reduction of both tariff and **nontariff barriers (NTBs)** to trade. Tariffs have, in fact, been substantially reduced over this time period (falling from 40 percent to 5 percent of the value of goods traded); today, the major barriers to trade are the NTBs, which include such things as quotas, voluntary export restraints, and differing national product standards.[11] Under prodding from Democratic critics of Republican presidential policies over the Reagan-Bush years,[12] a shift in emphasis—from free trade toward **fair trade**—has occurred. Although the United States still supports general efforts toward lower trade barriers, it has begun to much more aggressively protest what it sees as unfair actions by other nations to limit foreign imports.

Nevertheless, U.S. policy remains essentially supportive of free trade for three reasons. First, policymakers believe that increased world trade leads to general prosperity, a belief strongly supported by the negative experiences from the late 1920s. Second, although free trade opens up U.S. markets to foreign imports, it also opens up foreign markets for U.S. exports. Third, U.S. policymakers generally believe that free trade brings direct, tangible benefits to U.S. consumers: first, lower priced, higher quality products that might be produced abroad and, second, competition that may stimulate domestic producers to produce better products at lower prices. Some evidence in support of this view comes from the U.S. auto industry, which, under assault from foreign automakers, has responded since 1980 by significantly improving the quality of U.S.–made automobiles.

Export Promotion

Another goal related to free trade is promotion of U.S. exports. Of course, a concern for export promotion is part of the general support for free trade, but export promotion extends beyond this. U.S. export promotion activities are not as prominent as the efforts of some other countries, such as the European Community's agricultural export subsidy programs. However, the U.S. government has undertaken a number of policies designed to stimulate and subsidize exports, such as establishing the Export-Import Bank (which provides loans to facilitate exports), providing some export subsidies for specific agricultural products, and facilitating foreign sales of U.S.–made weapons systems—efforts aimed at stimulating growth in the U.S. economy through increased sales of exported goods.

148   The recent emphasis on fair trade, particularly with Japan and the European Community, is also designed to stimulate exports and narrow the deficit in the balance of payments. Although such deficits are not always bad—the U.S. deliberately sought such deficits in the immediate postwar period in order to foster economic recovery in Europe and Japan—in the long run they represent a transfer of wealth from the United States to trading partners who have a trade surplus with the U.S.

The **balance of payments** records all financial transactions between the U.S. and other countries. Its two major components are the current account and the capital account. The latter records the capital movements (e.g., loans) from private citizens and governments into and out of the United States. The much larger **balance on current account** consists of the **merchandise trade balance** (exports and imports of goods), plus what are known as the "invisibles," items such as income from services and investments.[13] In sum, the balance on current account includes the trade balance plus the net flow of investment income, military transactions, travel and service receipts, and any unilateral transfers by individuals and the U.S. government (e.g., foreign aid). The various elements of the current account do not change in tandem: since 1946, the U.S. has always had surpluses in services and investment income and deficits in an item called unilateral transfers (related to military assistance programs). On the other hand, the merchandise trade balance has varied substantially, with both balances and deficits; however, since 1976 the trade balance has always been negative. Between 1946 and 1991 the U.S. had a current account surplus in most years, but this has deteriorated markedly since 1970. From 1946 to 1970 the U.S. had a current account deficit only three times, but between 1971 and 1991 there were deficits in fifteen of twenty-one years, including ten straight deficits beginning in 1982.

Stabilizing the Dollar

A final international economic goal of U.S. policymakers is to influence the value of the U.S. dollar in international currency markets. Prior to the early 1970s world currency markets were governed by a system of fixed exchange rates known as the **Bretton Woods system.** Since that time the value of the dollar has "floated" against other currencies.[14] As a rule, policymakers seek to maintain a stable rate of exchange of the dollar against other major currencies, such as the German mark, the Japanese yen, and the British pound. At times, however, policymakers will seek to increase (revalue) or decrease (devalue) the dollar against other currencies in pursuit of specific economic outcomes. In 1971–72, for example, the Nixon administration sought to devalue the dollar in order to stimulate exports and retard imports, a policy that succeeded (see Figure 6.1), if only **149** in the short run.

KEY ACTORS IN INTERNATIONAL ECONOMIC POLICYMAKING

International Organizations

In the international area, unlike economic policymaking within the United States, important policymakers include actors outside the country. The most important of these are three international organizations: the International Monetary Fund, the International Bank for Reconstruction and Development (better known as the World Bank), and the General Agreement on Tariffs and Trade. The first two were created as part of the postwar Bretton Woods system for managing international economic affairs (although the World Bank has evolved over time as an agency directed at Third World economic development), while the GATT deals with multilateral trade issues.[15]

The International Monetary and Financial Conference of the United and Associated Nationals was held at Bretton Woods, New Hampshire, in July 1944. The articles of agreement signed by forty-four nations created both the **International Monetary Fund (IMF)** and the **World Bank.** This Bretton Woods Agreement specified a fixed **exchange rate** at which central banks would buy and sell U.S. dollars in world financial markets and thus created the international monetary system governing relations among nations. As a result, from 1946 until 1973 most currencies had fixed exchange rates with respect to the U.S. dollar.

The role of the IMF was to serve as a "buffer" for this system. With IMF approval, each nation was supposed to establish a value for its currency and agree to maintain its fixed exchange rate within one percent of that value. At the time only the United States could settle international transactions (deficits or surpluses) by buying and selling gold (the so-called "open gold window") at the rate of $35.00 per ounce to assure the stability of the U.S.–dollar exchange rate. Other nations would buy or sell dollars to maintain the fixed rate of exchange for their currencies. Any nation with a balance-of-payments deficit could borrow gold or currency from IMF reserves (created by contributions by the member nations) according to a quota based on the size of its economy in the world.

Until about 1960, the United States played the central role in maintaining the Bretton Woods system. After 1960, decision making became more multilateral (although with U.S. leadership), and the IMF became more prominent as a lender to finance payments deficits.[16] The IMF has

150   continued in importance even after the breakdown of the Bretton Woods
system into the contemporary era of floating exchange rates.

Although today the World Bank functions essentially as a lender for
less-developed countries seeking loans to finance development projects,
its original function was to finance the recovery of the economies shattered
by World War II. At the close of the war Europeans had to import huge
amounts of American goods, since their industrial plants had been destroyed during the war, but they lacked the U.S. dollars to pay for them.
Economists talked about a "dollar shortage" in Europe, so the United
States financed loans from the World Bank to provide dollars to the European economies; within a few years this was supplemented with billions
of dollars in assistance through programs like the Marshall Plan.

The U.S. also encouraged European nations and Japan to build up
their reserves of gold and U.S. dollars in order to reestablish their economies. The economic dependency of European nations—even seven years
after World War II—is reflected in their small 1952 shares of international
reserves. **International reserves** consist of gold, special drawing rights and
other reserves in the International Monetary Fund, and whatever foreign
exchange (currencies) are held by a nation's monetary authorities. In 1952
the United States held 50 percent of all international reserves, while none
of the other nations held as much as 5 percent. Just twenty years later the
U.S. share had dropped to only 8.2 percent, less than the shares of both
West Germany (14.9 percent) and Japan (11.5 percent). By the early
1990s the U.S. once again held the largest share of reserves, although the
overall picture was one of essential parity among the major national economies—yet another indication of the growing interdependence of the
global economy.

The third major international organization of significance for international economic policy is the **General Agreement on Tariffs and Trade
(GATT).**[17] The GATT is exactly what it sounds like, an agreement
among many nations (twenty-three when it originated in 1947, but nearly
four times as many by the 1980s) aimed at liberalizing trade, i.e., reducing
tariffs and NTBs. The GATT includes a 300-person Secretariat based in
Geneva, Switzerland, designed to mediate trade disputes, but the major
activity of the GATT takes place in massive, multilateral trade negotiations (called rounds) lasting several years. There have been eight rounds
since 1947; the current Uruguay Round, begun in 1986, is still in session
as we go to press, stalled over the issue of agricultural subsidies.

The basic and most important principle that governs trade under the
GATT is the principle of nondiscrimination, which has two elements.[18]
The first is the **most favored nation provision**, which states that any ben-
eficial treatment accorded the trade with a nation's "most favored" trading

partner must be granted to all other members of the GATT.[19] The second nondiscrimination provision is that each nation must treat imports the same as domestically produced goods (e.g., with respect to taxation) once they enter the country.

The GATT does not eliminate the authority of U.S. policymakers to negotiate trade agreements with other nations, but it does limit the scope of what they can negotiate. The GATT, for example, prohibits the U.S. from entering into a bilateral agreement with Japan in which the two nations would grant special treatment exclusively to each other's trade. At the same time, though, the GATT provides a forum and mechanism for resolving trade disputes, even bilateral ones. It also creates a structure for supplying a collective good of liberalized trade relations, which would be difficult to attain through a series of bilateral negotiations.

Multilateral Groupings

In addition to the more formal international organizations (IOs), the U.S. has also participated in more informal multilateral groups, which meet to discuss economic concerns and plan joint economic actions. The most significant is what is currently known as the Group of Seven (or the **G7 nations**), consisting of the U.S., Japan, Germany, United Kingdom, France, Italy, and Canada. This group currently holds annual summit meetings attended by either chief executives, finance ministers, or the heads of central banks, although emergency meetings may also be called. One major concern of these G7 meetings is the world currency market. Thus, in September 1985, the predecessor Group of Five (the G7 minus Italy and Canada), meeting in New York, concluded the Plaza Agreement to devalue the dollar. A year and a half later, the expanded G7 met in Paris to conclude the Louvre Agreement—this time to attempt to stabilize the dollar following its steady fall since 1985. In making these agreements, the G7 nations typically agree to coordinate their central bank actions and fiscal policies to achieve a common aim, although at times the meetings have resulted in the creation of joint gold or currency pools to be used to support a specific goal.

In recent years, the G7 talks have also dealt with establishing a joint economic policy for dealing with global changes in the wake of the collapse of the Soviet Union and the changes in Eastern Europe, sometimes in connection with the actions of the IOs. Thus, for example, when the G7 chief executives met in Munich in July 1992, the major topics of discussion were the stalled Uruguay Round of the GATT, the feasibility of greater economic linkages with Eastern Europe and the Third World, and the economic problems of the former Soviet Union. Little was accom-

152   plished on the first two points, but the G7 nations agreed to provide further economic assistance to the Russian government, and they successfully pressured the IMF to approve a Russian economic stabilization plan and begin the delivery of a $24 billion aid plan to that nation.[20] At the April 1993 G7 meeting, the economic and political turmoil in Russia was again a major item for discussion.

U.S. Policymakers

The list of the important policymakers for international economic policy consists, to a large degree, of the same actors who are important for domestic economic policymaking, with one important addition in the area of trade. The Federal Reserve Board remains of paramount importance for monetary policy; interest rates, which have an important influence on the value of the dollar, represent a policy area controlled by the Fed, although subject to pressures from Congress and the White House. Similarly, Congress, the president, and important executive branch officials such as the secretaries of the treasury and commerce play an important role in policy development and execution. Because this area involves international dealings, the secretary of state and the State Department are, of course, also involved.

The important addition to the list of economic policymakers is the **United States trade representative** (USTR), a position created in 1963[21] as a staff assistant to the president, but which is now considered a cabinet-level position and has a staff of 155. The USTR is the government official who exercises the responsibility for negotiating trade agreements first delegated to the president by Congress in the 1934 Trade Act. This official is the primary U.S. negotiator at the GATT and is also generally given the responsibility for resolving trade disputes with other nations, including the recommendation of U.S. sanctions against nations believed to be engaging in unfair trade practices, such as "dumping" goods in U.S. markets (i.e., selling them for less than their prices in the domestic markets where they are produced).

Since tariffs represented a major source of Federal government revenue in the eighteenth and nineteenth centuries, control over tariffs and trade traditionally rested with the Congress. Since 1934 this responsibility has shifted to a considerable degree to the president, although Congress still plays an important role in this area through the passage of periodic trade bills and through the ratification of trade treaties. In recent years, there has been heightened tension between the president and Congress over trade as declines in selected industries have spurred calls for greater protection of domestic producers. However, there has been no clear movement to shift power back to Congress. On the one hand, a new "fast-track" provision for approval of trade treaties has been created; this requires Congress to either ratify or reject a proposed treaty without amendments, although the president must incorporate congressional suggestions into the treaty before it is signed. On the other hand, there have been repeated calls to reorganize the policymaking system for trade policy, including the creation of a Congressional Trade Office similar to the CBO, a reorganization of the congressional committee structure with respect to trade (23 committees participated in the creation of the 1988 Trade Act), and a reorganization of the executive-branch agencies responsible for trade, including a diminution of the USTR position back to its 1963 status. The most ambitious of the executive branch reorganization proposals was an effort by Senator William Roth (R-DE) to create a Trade Department, which would combine a number of existing offices, including USTR, the Export-Import Bank, and the Department of Commerce's International Trade Administration (which includes area specialists and others responsible for administering U.S. trade law).[22]

CONTEMPORARY ISSUES IN INTERNATIONAL ECONOMIC POLICY

The preceding sections describe the general position of the United States in the global economy in statistical terms and the institutional actors with influence over this policy area. The meaning of these statistics and the roles of these actors are revealed more fully in the events connected with actual policy problems and the actions taken to address these problems. In this section we describe a series of events related to the two basic problem areas in the international economic sphere: currency fluctuations and trade policy. Up to now we have discussed these two areas as though they are separate, but they are in fact linked. One of the principal underlying causes of fluctuations of the dollar in the postwar period has been trade imbalances; the interconnection of trade and currency values is thus a continuing theme in our first set of case studies. Following this we turn to a discussion of what is for many the most pressing contemporary set of international economic concerns: fair trade, U.S. competitiveness in world markets, and the persistent U.S. trade deficit of recent years.

Balance of Payments and the Value of the Dollar

Beginning with the creation of the Bretton Woods system, a major concern for U.S. policymakers has been the maintenance of a stable

154   international currency market. Up until 1960 the U.S. served as the basic protector of this system, but since then the U.S., while still a major actor in this area, has itself induced instability in financial markets, often because of a worsening in the U.S. balance of payments. Since 1965 this balance of payments problem has, on three occasions, reached a climax and forced extraordinary presidential action: in 1967–1968 under Lyndon Johnson, in 1971 with Nixon's New Economic Policy, and in 1985 when the Reagan administration moved to weaken the U.S. dollar overseas.

By the end of the 1950s the reserve position of European nations had improved markedly, resulting in an international "dollar glut" as foreign banks accumulated U.S. dollars and gold. The IMF began to refer to U.S. balance of payments as a problem, and both the CEA and the Fed counseled the need for correction action. Because foreign governments were redeeming their dollars for gold bullion, U.S. gold reserves fell steadily until 1968, when the Johnson administration took decisive actions to stem the outward flow of capital.

Earlier, President Kennedy pursued the kind of ad hoc defensive strategy used by President Eisenhower.[23] In its first year the Kennedy administration used a novel "Operation Twist" policy in its monetary affairs. By keeping short-term interest rates higher while exerting downward pressures on long-term interest rates, the objective was to encourage domestic investment and curb capital outflows to other nations. In July 1963, President Kennedy announced a more comprehensive plan, which included linking our foreign aid to aid recipients' purchases of U.S. exports, reducing the costs of stationing military abroad, asking for $500 million in standby credit from the IMF, and proposing a temporary tax on purchases of foreign securities by Americans. These proposals were continued by Lyndon Johnson when he succeeded to the White House in November 1963.

During the 1960s U.S. balance-of-payments policy generally muddled along as economists debated whether the problem was all that serious. But things worsened, as reflected in the international statistics (Table 6.1). The balance on current account shrank steadily from 1966 to 1969, President Nixon's first year in office. The chief cause of the serious deterioration was a strong increase in imports, while exports remained stable.

A contributing cause was the Vietnam War, but the Johnson administration could not readily admit that the Vietnam War was harming the balance of payments. As Kaufman observes,

> By sloughing off the economic impact of the Vietnam War in this way and by concluding that the international monetary system was structurally stable, the administration was ignoring the additional stresses and

TABLE 6.1 U.S. International Transactions, 1966–68, 1970–72, 1984–86

	1966	1967	1968	1970	1971	1972	1984	1985	1986
Exports	+29,310	+30,666	+33,626	+42,469	+43,319	+49,381	+219,926	+215,915	+223,344
Imports	−25,493	−26,866	−32,991	−39,866	−45,579	−55,797	−332,418	−338,088	−368,425
Net Merchandise	+3,817	+3,800	+635	−2,603	−2,260	−6,416	−112,492	−122,173	−145,081
Receipts	+7,528	+8,020	+9,368	+11,747	+12,707	+14,764	+100,415	+91,110	+88,998
Payments	−2,481	−2,747	−3.378	−5,516	−5,436	−6,572	−69,572	−67,875	−73,620
Net Investment Income	+5,047	+5,273	+5,990	+6,231	+7,271	+8,192	+30,843	+23,235	+15,378
Net Military Transactions	−2,935	−3,226	−3,143	−3,354	−2,893	−3,420	−2,547	−4,390	−5,181
Net Travel and Transportation Receipts	−1,331	−1,750	−1,548	−2,038	−2,345	−3,063	−8,293	−9,709	−7,324
Net Other Services	+1,496	+1,742	+1,759	+2,329	+2,649	+2,965	+30,843	+23,235	+15,378
Balance on Goods and Services	+6,095	+5,838	+3,693	+5,773	+2,423	+1,742	−78,212	−98,771	−123,354
Remittances/Pensions/Other Unilateral Transfers	−3,064	−3,255	−3,082	−3,443	−3,856	−4,052	−20,612	−22,950	−24,176
Balance on Current Account	+3,031	+2,583	+611	+2,331	−1,433	−5,795	−98,824	−121,721	−147,529

*Credits (+) and debits (−) in $ millions.

Source: *Economic Report of the President, 1993* (Washington, DC: U.S. Government Printing Office, January 1993).

strains that the war was placing on the nation's balance of payments. As a result, the dollar was further weakened in international money markets, and the world's entire monetary structure was placed in jeopardy.[24]

There was a need for radical reforms, but the day of serious reckoning was postponed until the Nixon administration.

After 1965 events moved rapidly. In June 1965 President Johnson established two study groups to consider a reserve currency other than the U.S. dollar. Their joint recommendation was that an international conference be held to consider a new reserve asset in the IMF based on a system of special drawing rights (SDRs), to be used like gold to purchase foreign exchange and to settle deficits on the current account ledgers, but without utilizing the reserves of the IMF as such. However, a "Group of Ten" European nations were reluctant to agree because, as one participant observed, "the Continentals are not going to be easily budged from their determination to hitch the new unit to gold and to keep it in a secondary position to gold."[25] The result was deadlock, which continued until April 1967, when the United States allowed the European nations a veto over how much new reserve currency (SDRs) would be created.

However, the new system was not in place fast enough to deal with a round of financial speculation against the British pound, which ended when the British government devalued the pound from $2.80 (in U.S. dollars) to $2.40, a 14 percent profit for speculators. Since the same thing could happen to the U.S. dollar, on New Year's Day 1968, President Johnson delivered a message to the American people, saying "The dollar will remain convertible into gold as $35 an ounce, and our full gold stock will back that commitment."[26] The Johnson administration hardly had a choice in this matter. There was upward pressure on gold prices (although the official price was $35.00 per ounce), and to allow the price of gold to increase on the financial markets would have the effect of devaluing the dollar.

A devalued dollar meant that the Vietnam War costs would rise, that imports would be more expensive, and ultimately that inflationary pressures would be aggravated. To meet this immediate crisis, President Johnson used his New Year's Day address to outline new restrictions on private investments abroad, limits by the Fed on foreign lending by U.S. banks, curbs on government spending and travel overseas, and efforts to help U.S. exports. More importantly, two weeks later in his State of the Union Message Johnson asked Congress to remove the 25 percent gold cover requirement on Federal Reserve Notes, which required the Federal Reserve Board to keep enough gold bullion on hand to equal the value of one-fourth the currency it issued. By lifting this statutory obligation, a substantial amount of monetized gold was available as additional reserves to **157** settle international accounts.

A final policy change under President Johnson was the creation of a two-tier price of gold, the official price and a second price as determined by the financial markets. However, only gold bought or sold at the official price could be used to settle international claims against the United States. This proposal was implemented after a new round of gold speculation began in early March 1968. Americans were prohibited from buying gold on the open markets, and during March 11–14 the "gold pool" established by the U.S. and its allies had to sell almost $1 billion worth of gold to defend the dollar.[27] After an emergency meeting of the U.S. and its allies, the central banks also agreed not to purchase gold in the private markets in the expectation that speculators would have to unload their gold stocks at close to the official price.

As a result of this joint action, the Johnson administration survived a major financial challenge to its balance-of-payments policy; as the president later observed: "The world's leading bankers were telling the speculators that henceforth the banks would be looking to the new international currency [SDRs], not to gold, to enlarge monetary reserves. They were committed to building the international economy on the basis of intensive partnership."[28] These monetary reforms bought the United States some time, but not very much.

When President Nixon took office in 1969, economist Milton Friedman urged him to "close the gold window" by ending the policy of converting U.S. dollars held by foreigners into gold. At first his advice was opposed by Arthur Burns and Paul Volcker, and Nixon was persuaded by Burns's arguments, but the issue was then forced because the international statistics were changing. From having large trade surpluses, the U.S. first experienced declining surpluses and then a trade deficit during April–June 1970. The $2.3 billion balance on current account *surplus* of 1970 became a $1.4 billion *deficit* in 1971, which widened to $5.8 billion in 1972. U.S. exports grew by less than a billion dollars between 1970 and 1971 but imports rose by nearly $6 billion, and in 1972 imports outpaced the growth in exports by another $4 billion. The unfavorable balance of payments prompted official concern that the U.S. did not have enough gold reserves to convert those foreign-held U.S. dollars to gold should that action be demanded by foreign creditors.

This situation reached a climax when CEA Chairman Paul Mc-Cracken advised President Nixon in late July 1971 to stop converting U.S. dollars into gold.[29] On August 6 the Joint Economic Committee of Congress recommended both an "incomes policy" to halt inflation and the devaluation of the U.S. dollar. On August 13, Paul Volcker contacted

158   Treasury Secretary John Connally at his Texas ranch, apprising him of the impending international monetary crisis. Connally returned to Washington and persuaded Richard Nixon to move on a variety of economic fronts.

On the evening of August 13 at Camp David, President Nixon met with McCracken, George Shultz, Paul Volcker, Connally, Herbert Stein, Arthur Burns, and various White House staffers. Two days later Nixon announced his multifaceted New Economic Policy to the American people over radio and television. While most people immediately understood the meaning of his ninety-day wage and price freeze, fewer Americans appreciated the long-term implications of Nixon's decision to abandon the international monetary system (the Bretton Woods system), which had existed since World War II.

When the United States "closed the gold window" in August 1971, it ceased to refund foreign claims against the dollar in gold. This began the process of gradually devaluing the dollar in currency markets. Over the period 1971–73 the dollar was allowed to fall in value by 20 percent, to the new exchange rate price of $42.00 per ounce of gold. The final stage in the evolution to a flexible exchange rate occurred in March 1973 (at the start of Nixon's second term), when the United States no longer officially pegged the U.S. dollar to gold at a fixed exchange rate, thereby allowing the value of the dollar to "float" against other currencies.

Nixon's devaluation of the dollar had an immediate impact on consumers here and abroad. Imported goods were priced higher in the U.S., while U.S. exports could be purchased more cheaply outside of the U.S. By this action President Nixon wanted to encourage greater exports while cutting imports in order to reduce the balance on current account deficit, and that strategy worked, at least for a while. The current account balance shifted from a $5.8 billion deficit in 1972 to a $7.1 billion surplus in 1973, and surpluses continued the next three years. But Nixon's policy did not achieve a long-term solution; over time, the balance of payments problem worsened. Beginning in 1977 there were current account deficits fourteen times over the terms of Presidents Carter, Reagan, and Bush.

In the first thirty-five years of the postwar era, the largest current account deficit was $15.1 billion in 1978 (compared to the mere $1.4 billion deficit in 1971, the year Nixon closed the gold window). There were surpluses during the six years of 1973–76 and 1980–81, but afterwards there was a marked deterioration. Deficits grew nearly fourfold, from $11 billion in 1982 to $43 billion in 1983, then more than doubled to $98 billion in 1984. In real (constant) dollars the deficits on current account during the Reagan first term were roughly double the accumulated deficit over the previous thirty-three years. This situation—while bad—actually worsened in 1985, the year of decision for the Reagan administration.

The problem area indicated in Table 6.1 was the growing merchandise trade imbalance. Between 1984 and 1986 exports grew by $3.4 billion, whereas imports increased by $36 billion. The primary reason was that a strong U.S. dollar made American goods less competitive in foreign markets, while imports were priced cheaper for domestic consumption. Ordinarily excess imports would weaken the dollar in world financial markets, but high interest rates in the U.S. (maintained in order to fight domestic inflation) bolstered the value of the U.S. dollar abroad.

The Reagan administration developed a two-prong attack on the trade deficit. The first began in September 1985, when Treasury Secretary James Baker met with four trading partners—Great Britain, West Germany, Japan, and France—in New York City. In the Plaza Agreement, this Group of Five agreed to work together to depreciate the value of the U.S. dollar relative to their currencies. A cheaper dollar would discourage Americans from buying imported goods while making U.S. products more competitive in European markets. This strategy involved manipulating the foreign exchange rates to depreciate the U.S. dollar in financial markets. Since 1967 the U.S. dollar generally lost value relative to the West German and Japanese currencies but gained ground against the weaker French franc and English pound.

The second prong required that the other nations, mainly West Germany and Japan, expand their domestic economies, and thus stimulate foreign demand for American exports. Following the Plaza Agreement, Treasury Secretary Baker, in March 1986, put pressure on Great Britain, West Germany, Japan, and France to cut their central bank rates, and a month later a second round of discount rate cuts was agreed to by everybody except West Germany.[30]

The dollar did, in fact, actually begin a steady decline after 1985, although this prolonged decline itself prompted concern among the U.S.'s allies. In February 1987, the expanded Group of Seven (now including Italy and Canada) met in Paris and drafted the Louvre Accord, agreeing to cooperate in order to stabilize the value of the dollar, a policy desired more by the other G7 members than by the U.S. European central banks agreed to make purchases of U.S. dollars on the exchange markets to support its value in the face of downward pressures. However, the dollar's slide continued through 1992, and, as a consequence, the U.S. trade deficit narrowed considerably.

Trade Policy: Where International and Domestic Concerns Intersect

One of the reasons why the Reagan administration sought to address the trade deficits by weakening the dollar was to diffuse growing

160   protectionist sentiment in Congress. One area that has become a frequent object of Congress' protests is the U.S. trade relationship with Japan, because the U.S.–Japan trade imbalance is particularly severe (Table 6.2). The United States has trade deficits with many nations, but Japan accounts for more than one-third of the total. From 1984 to 1986, while exports from the U.S. to Japan rose about $3 billion, imports from Japan to the U.S. grew by $20 billion, worsening the trade deficit by $17 billion.

Many legislators have argued that Japan is unfairly discriminating against U.S. products in its markets, particularly through the use of NTBs and collusion among major Japanese firms and the Japanese government. Some have even urged the use of quotas and tariffs to combat this perceived trade discrimination by Japan. At times the president has agreed, as when President Reagan imposed a 100 percent tariff on certain Japanese-made computers, television sets, and power tools in April 1987.[31] However, these items accounted for only $300 million of the export trade in Japanese electronics products (which totaled $23 billion in 1986), and Congress was not appeased. Later that month the House narrowly passed (218–214) a tough bill calling for retaliatory actions against unfair trade practices in countries like Japan with excessive trade surpluses. It was sponsored by Congressman Richard A. Gephardt (D-MO) who, the following year, exploited themes of economic nationalism to win the Iowa caucuses in his unsuccessful bid for the 1988 Democratic presidential nomination.

The calls for more aggressive action to combat perceived barriers to U.S. exports in foreign markets did not end with Gephardt's unsuccessful 1988 race. Partly to forestall this as a political issue, the Bush administration began the Structural Impediments Initiative (SII) talks with Japan in 1989, designed to remove NTBs and informal barriers to trade with Japan. However, by 1992, the SII had yielded only an agreement to continue the talks for a fourth year, while the U.S. trade deficit rose steadily between 1990 and 1992—reaching $44 billion in 1991 and running 10 percent higher during the first half of 1992.[32] Meanwhile, the Democratic convention held during the summer of 1992 featured a chorus of calls to "put America first," not only in federal spending priorities, but in U.S. economic relations with both Japan and the countries of the European Community.

The early days of the Clinton administration suggest that conflict with Japan over trade will continue. On Clinton's second full day in office, Japan released trade figures indicating that the Japanese trade surplus with the United States had increased 14 percent over the previous year.[33] Even before then, Clinton had named as CEA chair Laura D'Andrea Tyson, a

TABLE 6.2 Net U.S. Trade, 1984–1992 (billions of dollars)

	1984	1985	1986	1987	1988	1989	1990	1991	1992
Japan	−37.0	−43.5	−54.4	−56.9	−52.6	−49.7	−41.7	−44.3	−46.8
Canada	−14.6	−14.8	−13.2	−11.6	−10.3	−9.3	−10.2	−8.0	−9.8
Western Europe	−15.2	−21.4	−28.6	−27.5	−16.2	−4.0	+2.2	+14.9	+6.3
All Countries	−112.5	−122.1	−145.1	−159.6	−127.0	−115.7	−108.9	−73.4	−91.1
Japan Trade Deficit as % of Total Trade Deficit	32.9%	35.6%	37.5%	35.7%	41.4%	43.0%	38.4%	60.4%	51.4%

Source: *Economic Report of the President, 1993* (Washington, DC: U.S. Government Printing Office, January 1993). Figures for 1992 are for first three quarters calculated at an annual rate. A trade surplus (+) or deficit (−) is indicated.

162   proponent of tougher policies designed to force the removal by Japan and other trading partners of nontariff barriers viewed as limiting fair trade.

Although trade issues have become increasingly entangled in partisan politics over the last decade—a situation not seen since the battles of the 1930s and 1940s—regardless of whichever party controls the government through the rest of the decade, U.S. policymakers will face at least three urgent issues relating to trade. The first, and perhaps most difficult, issue is deciding how to balance the benefits of free trade with the resulting dislocations to the domestic economy (what economists term "adjustment costs"). Even where the overall benefits of a policy clearly outweigh the costs, these costs are still real. For example, an analysis of the **North American Free Trade Agreement (NAFTA)** negotiated in 1992 linking the U.S., Mexico, and Canada estimates that it will lead to a net gain in U.S. employment of 175,000 jobs over the first five years. However, this net increase will come from a decrease of 150,000 jobs concentrated in a few industries (like farming and textiles) and an increase of 325,000 jobs spread over a broader group of industries (including processed foods, plastics, and pharmaceuticals).[34] Not only will these job losses provoke opposition to the treaty by members of Congress representing affected economic interests, but the social dislocations of this generally beneficial policy represent legitimate problems the government must address. President Clinton supported NAFTA; in August of 1993, his administration negotiated a set of supplemental agreements with Canada and Mexico designed to address environmental and labor concerns over the treaty provisions, particularly regarding lax Mexican enforcement of existing laws in these areas. It passed Congress, despite union opposition, after a key House vote on which President Clinton's lobbying won over 132 Republicans and 102 (mainly southern) Democrats. The treaty takes effect January 1, 1994.[35]

A second issue that will continue to engage policymakers is how to foster competitiveness of U.S. economic interests in a marketplace that is increasingly global. This question has many dimensions, many of which extend into areas not traditionally considered related to international concerns, such as the quality of American education, the underlying theory governing U.S. antitrust law, and the role of organized labor in the U.S. economy. These concerns do not necessarily have clear answers, and their discussion will not (and should not) be limited to concerns over international competitiveness. However, it is a part of the new economic reality that an international dimension has entered many areas traditionally seen as purely domestic issues.

A third question that will face policymakers is whether to target some particular areas for greater cooperation in trade and other economic interactions. The creation of a single European market in 1992—and the **163** possibility of even greater European economic cooperation to come—has heightened the urgency of this question for U.S. policymakers. One permissible exception to the GATT principle of nondiscrimination is the creation of customs unions such as the European Community, and a primary impulse behind the U.S.–Canada free trade agreement of 1989 and the more recent NAFTA agreement is the desire to counter the new economic power of a single European market (with a GDP greater than that of either the U.S. or Japan—or NAFTA, for that matter) with a closer relationship among the major North American economies. Beyond this policy initiative, policymakers will have to consider what sort of economic relationships the U.S. will develop with the nations of the former Soviet bloc and with the major economies of the Pacific Rim, including, of course, the subject of much of the recent domestic political discussion—Japan.

KEY TERMS

balance of trade, trade surplus, trade deficit, free trade, protectionist, tariffs, nontariff barriers (NTBs), fair trade, balance of payments, balance on current account, merchandise trade balance, Bretton Woods system, International Monetary Fund, World Bank, exchange rate, international reserves, General Agreement on Tariffs and Trade (GATT), most favored nation provision, G7 nations, U.S. trade representative, North American Free Trade Agreement (NAFTA)

ADDITIONAL READING

Bergsten, Fred C. *The Dilemmas of the Dollar: The Economics and Politics of the United States International Monetary Policy*. New York: New York University Press, 1975. Scholarly analysis of the economic and political costs and benefits of alternative international monetary policy arrangements.

Cohen, Benjamin J. *Organizing the World's Money: The Political Economy of International Monetary Relations*. New York: Basic Books, 1977. Focuses on the international organizations and framework of monetary policymaking.

Dester, I. M. *Making Foreign Economic Policy*. Washington, DC: The Brookings Institution, 1980. Case studies of trade laws, Soviet grain sales, and food aid argue that economic policymaking must include domestic and international considerations.

Gilpin, Robert. *The Political Economy of International Relations*. Princeton: Princeton University Press, 1987. Uses liberal, Marxist, and nationalist

164 perspectives to analyze such topics as monetary and trade policy, multinational corporations, and finance to characterize the global political economy.

Gowa, Joanne. *Closing the Gold Window*. Ithaca: Cornell University Press, 1983. Case study of Nixon's decision to stop converting U.S. dollars into gold, thus ending the international monetary system based upon the Bretton Woods Agreement.

Kaufman, Burton I. *Trade and Aid: Eisenhower's Foreign Economic Policy, 1953–1961*. Baltimore: Johns Hopkins University Press, 1982. Case study of the political process surrounding trade policy and foreign aid during the 1950s.

Kennedy, Paul. *The Rise and Fall of the Great Powers: Economic Change and Military Conflict from 1500 to 2000*. New York: Random House, 1987. Argues that the rise and fall of great powers is linked to military spending and economic performance, popularizing the idea that the United States is now in a period of decline.

Mayer, Martin. *The Fate of the Dollar*. New York: Times Books, 1980. A journalistic account of international monetary policy from Eisenhower through Carter.

Nye, Joseph S., Jr. *Bound to Lead: The Changing Nature of American Power*. New York: Basic Books, 1990. This book takes issue with the Paul Kennedy thesis that the U.S. is in a period of economic decline, arguing that in the post–Cold War era, the United States can direct more resources into the economy.

Pastor, Robert A. *Congress and the Politics of U.S. Foreign Economic Policy, 1929–1976*. Berkeley: University of California Press, 1980. Historical overview of how congressional politics affects U.S. economic policy towards other nations.

Solomon, Robert. *The International Monetary System, 1945–1981*. New York: Harper and Row, 1982. An "insider" account of the Bretton Woods system and international monetary relations between the United States and European nations.

NOTES

1. Democratic party of the United States, "1992 Platform: 'A New Covenant with the American People,' " mimeo, p. 15.

2. A currency rises against another currency when the first currency is worth more of the second currency, whereas it falls when it is worth less of the second currency. For example, between September 1991 and September 1992 the dollar fell against the German mark from 1.67 German marks/dollar to 1.42 German marks/dollar. This means that someone wishing to exchange 100 dollars for marks would have obtained 167 German marks in September 1991, but only 142 German marks a year later.

3. Trade deficits do not necessarily mean deficits in the overall balance of payments. Because of surpluses in other components of the current account, until 1977 the balance of payments normally showed a surplus.

4. Paul Kennedy, *The Rise and Fall of the Great Powers: Economic Change and Military Conflict from 1500 to 2000* (New York: Random House, 1987).

5. See, for example, Joseph S. Nye, Jr., *Bound to Lead: The Changing Nature of American Power* (New York: Basic Books, 1990).

6. See Richard Rosecrance, *The Rise of the Trading State: Commerce and Conquest in the Modern World* (New York: Basic Books, 1986).

7. Steven Greenhouse, "Bundesbank Gives In," *New York Times*, September 14, 1992: C2.

8. *Trade: U.S. Policy Since 1945* (Washington, DC: Congressional Quarterly Inc., 1984).

9. This discussion and the discussion of subsequent trade liberalization is based upon *Trade: U.S. Policy Since 1945*, pp. 29–59.

10. This was not universal, however. The Republican-controlled 80th Congress (1947–48) urged caution in pursuing trade liberalization. Republican members of Congress had also opposed the Trade Act of 1934 and other moves to reduce protectionism. However, one measure of the change in elite attitudes is that, while the Republican leaders of the 80th Congress favored slower movement toward free trade, they did not resist this movement in general.

11. See Stanley D. Metzger, *Lowering Nontariff Barriers: U.S. Law, Practice, and Negotiating Standards* (Washington, DC: Brookings, 1974); and David Greenaway, *Trade Policy and the New Protectionism* (New York: St. Martin's Press, 1983). We are grateful to our colleague Vince Mahler for his advice and suggestions concerning our discussion of trade issues, including giving us access to his work-in-progress dealing with international political economy.

12. Bruce Stokes, "The Democrats Find a Hot Topic," *National Journal*, October 19, 1991, p. 2571.

13. Samuelson and Nordhaus, *Economics*, 14th ed. (New York: McGraw-Hill, 1992), p. 672.

14. The creation and collapse of the Bretton Woods system is described in Joan Edelman Spero, *The Politics of International Economic Relations*, 4th ed. (New York: St. Martin's Press, 1990), pp. 31–66.

15. The term *multilateral* refers to interactions involving more than two nations, as opposed to bilateral relations, which involve interactions between two nations (e.g., a nation-to-nation trade agreement).

16. Spero, *The Politics of International Economic Relations*, pp. 35–41.

17. Much of this information on the GATT can be found in *Trade: U.S. Policy Since 1945*.

18. See Spero, *The Politics of International Economic Relations*, pp. 70–73.

19. Kenneth W. Dam, *The GATT: Law and International Organization* (Chicago: University of Chicago Press, 1974), p. 392.

166

20. "Bumbling in Bavaria," *The Economist*, July 11–17, 1992, p. 44.

21. The position was authorized by the Trade Expansion Act of 1962 and was established in the EOP by Executive Order 11075, issued by President Kennedy on January 15, 1963. See I. M. Destler, *American Trade Politics: System Under Stress* (Washington, DC: Institute for International Economics, 1986), pp. 87–91.

22. Bruce Stokes, "Trading Places," *National Journal*, April 18, 1992, pp. 934–936.

23. This discussion of the Kennedy-Johnson years is based on the interpretation by Burton I. Kaufman, "Foreign Aid and the Balance-of-Payments Problem: Vietnam and Johnson's Foreign Economic Policy," in Robert A. Divine, ed., *The Johnson Years, Volume Two: Vietnam, the Environment, and Science* (Lawrence, KS: University Press of Kansas, 1987), pp. 79–109.

24. Kaufman, "Foreign Aid and the Balance-of-Payments Problem," p. 91.

25. Cited in Kaufman, "Foreign Aid and the Balance-of-Payments Problem," p. 92.

26. Cited in Martin Mayer, *The Fate of the Dollar* (New York: Times Books, 1980), p. 150.

27. Kaufman, "Foreign Aid and the Balance-of-Payments Problem," p. 95.

28. Lyndon Baines Johnson, *The Vantage Point: Perspectives of the Presidency, 1963–1969* (New York: Holt, Rinehart & Winston, 1971), p. 319.

29. This discussion is based on the detailed case study by Joanne Gowa, *Closing the Gold Window: Domestic Politics and the End of Bretton Woods* (Ithaca, NY: Cornell University Press, 1983).

30. See Leonard Silk, "Jim Baker's Cagey Global Gamble," *New York Times* (February 1, 1987), Section 3, pp. 1, 8.

31. Gerald M. Boyd, "President Imposes Tariff on Imports Against Japanese," *New York Times* (April 18, 1987), pp. 1, 20.

32. Bruce Stokes, "Losing Steam," *National Journal*, June 27, 1992, pp. 1518–1520.

33. Andrew Pollack, "Japan's Trade Surplus Leaps, Putting Pressure on Clinton," *New York Times* (January 23, 1993), A1.

34. This analysis is by Gary Huffbauer and Jeffrey Schott of the Institute for International Economics, cited in "America Builds a Trade Block," *The Economist*, August 15–21, 1992, pp. 53–54.

35. "Viva NAFTA," *The Economist* (August 21–27, 1993), pp. 21–22.

PART III

The Politics of
Economic Policy

CHAPTER 7

Business Cycles and Postwar Macroeconomic Policy

We begin this chapter by discussing the concept of the **business cycle**, the idea that general economic activity periodically rises and falls according to a cyclical pattern. Following this, we devote the bulk of this chapter to surveys of economic conditions and policy initiatives during the presidencies of each of the postwar presidents. We conclude with a brief summary of the experiences of these nine presidents.

THE BUSINESS CYCLE

For over a century, observers have noted that modern economies show variations over time with regard to such things as levels of production, income, employment, and trade. During the 1930s, economists working at the National Bureau of Economic Research (NBER)[1] formalized this in the concept of the business cycle, described in a recent publication as, "sequences of expansion and contraction in various economic processes that show up as major fluctuations in aggregate economic activity."[2] In 1946, two NBER economists, Arthur Burns and Wesley Mitchell, published *Measuring Business Cycles*, which defined the basic NBER methodology for identifying the starting and ending points for each historical cycle.[3]

The essential idea of the business cycle is that the rise and fall of economic activity, if graphed over time, will resemble a wave. The high point of each cycle—the point at which economic activity ceases to rise and begins to turn down—is called a **business peak**, while the low point— the point at which conditions begin to improve—is called a **business trough**. However, "while recurrent and pervasive, business cycles of historical experience have been definitely nonperiodic and have varied greatly in duration and intensity, reflecting changes in economic systems, conditions, policies, and outside disturbances."[4] In other words, no two cycles are the same, with the cycles varying in the heights reached by the peaks, the depths reached by the troughs, and the elapsed time between adjacent peaks and troughs.

Table 7.1 gives the dates of the peak and the trough of each business cycle since 1854. Of particular interest are the periods of contraction and expansion. A contraction is the downturn following a peak in the cycle, while an expansion is the upturn following a trough in the cycle. During the period 1854–1991 the United States experienced 569 months of contraction and 1084 months of expansion. For the period ending in 1945 there were 454 months of contraction (41.7 percent) and 636 months of expansion (58.3 percent), but since 1945 there have been (through March 1993) 97 months of contraction (17.1 percent) compared to 470 months of expansion (82.9 percent).

These data indicate that the relative occurrence of contraction and expansion in the U.S. economy has shifted markedly toward expansion since World War II. In fact, the two longest periods of expansion since 1854 have both occurred since 1960, each encompassing nearly a decade (the 1960s and the 1980s). While no policy solutions have prevented business cycles from occurring, the use of **countercyclical strategies** (and perhaps some luck) has reduced the frequency and severity of recessions in the postwar era. Countercyclical, or economic stabilization, policy (discussed in detail in the next chapter) means that fiscal policy (taxes and spending) and monetary policy (interest rates and the flow of credit) are manipulated in order to moderate the upswings and downswings of the business cycle.

Of course, some troughs have been deeper than others. The most severe downturn of the twentieth century was the Great Depression of the 1930s, and the seriousness of that collapse led economists to debate the proposition that "secular stagnation" would be the nation's overriding economic problem in the future. The stagnation thesis was first articulated by Alvin Hansen in his presidential address to the 1938 annual meeting

TABLE 7.1 Business Cycle Expansions and Contractions in the U.S.,
1854–1991

Business Cycle Reference Dates		Duration in Months			
		Contraction	Expansion	Cycle	
		Trough from Previous Peak	Trough to next Peak	Trough from Previous Trough	Peak from Previous Peak
Peak	**Trough**				
December 1854	June 1857	—	30	—	—
December 1858	October 1860	18	22	48	40
June 1861	April 1865	8	46	30	54
December 1867	June 1869	32	18	78	50
December 1870	October 1873	18	34	36	52
March 1879	March 1882	65	36	99	101
May 1885	March 1887	38	22	74	60
April 1888	July 1890	13	27	35	40
May 1891	January 1893	10	20	37	30
June 1894	December 1895	17	18	37	35
June 1897	June 1899	18	24	36	42
December 1900	September 1902	18	21	42	39
August 1904	May 1907	23	33	44	56
June 1908	January 1910	13	19	46	32
January 1912	January 1913	24	12	43	36
December 1914	August 1918	23	44	35	67
March 1919	January 1920	7	10	51	17
July 1921	May 1923	18	22	28	40
July 1924	October 1926	14	27	36	41
November 1927	August 1929	13	21	40	34
March 1933	May 1937	43	50	64	93
June 1938	February 1945	13	80	63	93
October 1945	November 1948	8	37	88	45
October 1949	July 1953	11	45	48	56
May 1954	August 1957	10	39	55	49

TABLE 7.1 Continued

Business Cycle Reference Dates		Duration in Months			
		Contraction	Expansion	Cycle	
		Trough from Previous Peak	Trough to next Peak	Trough from Previous Trough	Peak from Previous Peak
Peak	Trough				
April 1958	April 1960	8	24	47	32
February 1961	December 1969	10	106	34	116
November 1970	November 1973	11	36	117	47
March 1975	January 1980	16	58	52	74
July 1980	July 1981	6	12	64	18
November 1982	July 1990	16	92	28	108
March 1991		9	—	100	—

Source: National Bureau of Economic Research, Inc., as published in U.S. Department of Commerce, Bureau of Economic Development, *Business Conditions Digest* 30 (January 1990), p. 104. March 1991 trough reported in *New York Times*, December 23, 1992.

of the American Economic Association.[5] He argued that the closing of the frontier, a slowed population growth rate, and less technological innovation would lead to greatly reduced investment by business. These developments would therefore require a massive and continuous injection of federal spending through deficit financing to sustain economic growth.

Due to World War II, this dire scenario did not materialize. Unemployment fell dramatically, since 12 million persons were under arms by 1945, and the remaining population was busy producing armaments. Federal expenditures grew rapidly during the wartime period, and this spending was largely deficit financed. As a consequence there was a huge increase in private holdings of government securities as well as bank accounts, wealth that could be quickly converted into spending once the war ended. Because of wartime restrictions, there was a huge backlog of demand for consumption and investment goods by the end of the war.

By 1945 the stagnation thesis was replaced by renewed worries about the business cycle, and this concern was embodied in the 1946 Employment Act. Economists now assumed that continued economic growth would occur without massive infusions of deficit spending, indicating that short-term countercyclical policy should focus on ensuring that no recession degenerates into a depression.

While the performance of the macroeconomy has improved since **173** 1945, the cyclical pattern of economic activity has continued, which has often translated into political difficulties for the occupant of the White House during contractions. Although the NBER uses dozens of economic indicators to identify the peaks and troughs of the business cycle, there is a reasonable match between the broader aggregate measures of the NBER and the level of employment—which, as we know, is a closely watched measure of substantial political importance. Figure 7.1 shows the percentage of the civilian labor force employed over the postwar period; the NBER-defined peaks and troughs are also indicated. It should be noted that the employment rate in this figure (which is equal to 100 minus the unemployment rate) is a yearly rate, while the peaks and troughs are actually located at a particular month within these years.

As Figure 7.1 shows, the peaks and troughs of postwar business cycles correspond fairly well to high and low points of employment (and con-

Figure 7.1   Percent of Civilian Labor Force Employed, 1946–1992

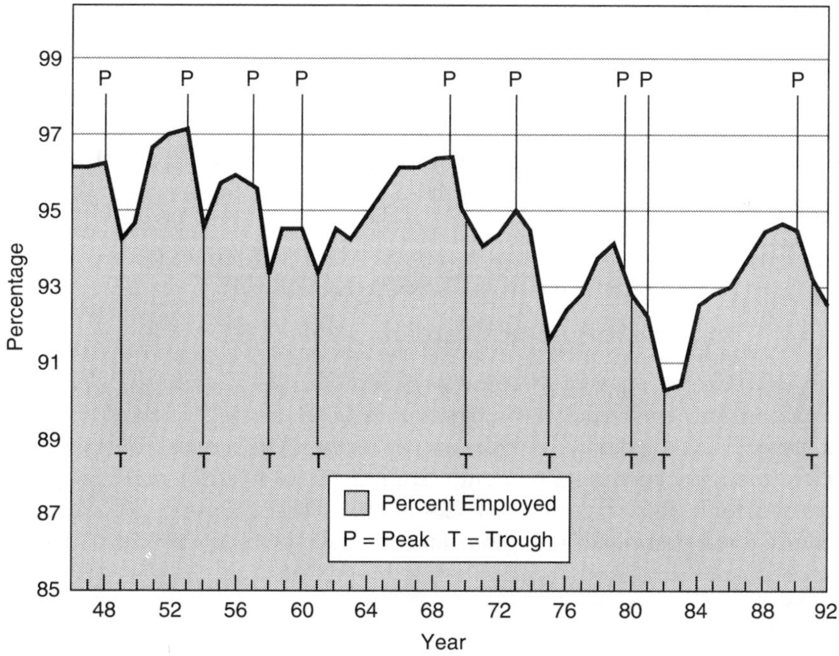

Source: Department of Labor, Bureau of Labor Statistics.

174   versely, to low and high points of unemployment). The one apparent anomaly in the figure is the concentration of two peaks and one trough in 1980–81, but this is actually an artifact of our use of yearly unemployment data in this figure. As the data in Table 7.1 indicate, these peaks and troughs are associated with the shortest of the postwar cycles, which began with a peak in January 1980 (when the unemployment rate was closer to the 5.8 percent yearly average for 1979 than the 7.1 percent yearly average for 1980), followed by a trough only six months later in July 1980 (when the unemployment rate was higher than the 7.1 percent yearly average), and a brief expansion to a July 1981 peak. In effect what occurred was a brief period of expansion that interrupted a broader pattern of economic contraction that culminated in the 1981–82 recession—the deepest economic trough since the Great Depression.

The increases and declines in employment shown in Figure 7.1 provide a powerful visual image of the political challenges created by the business cycle. Of course, as we noted in Chapter 1, stimulating employment (or reducing unemployment) represents only one of the goals faced by U.S. presidents in their role as managers of prosperity. In the surveys of each presidential term that follow, we focus on what are probably the two principal macroeconomic challenges—unemployment and inflation—that presidents face (particularly in a political sense). In each survey we track these two key macroeconomic indicators (plus additional indicators, where relevant) by presidential term and explain the economic problems that confronted each administration and the countercyclical policies that were taken. The forty-six year period we cover spans the terms of nine presidents, from Harry Truman through George Bush.

POSTWAR MACROECONOMIC POLICY

The Truman Administration, 1945–1952

Harry Truman became president in 1945 upon the death of Franklin Roosevelt and won reelection in 1948. During much of his presidency, Truman operated within an atmosphere of intense political conflict. A highly partisan Democrat, Truman faced a resurgent Republican party, which gained control of Congress in 1946. During his dramatic come-from-behind 1948 presidential campaign, he characterized Congress as a "do nothing" body controlled by his political opponents and determined to undo the political and economic policies of the previous sixteen years.

Truman's tenure included the transition from a wartime to a peacetime economy, and this included some significant economic dislocation after

World War II, given the steep cutback in military expenditures. From a **175**
high of $93 billion in 1945, federal spending fell to $30 billion in 1948,
but revenues did not fall as rapidly, so the national government shifted
from deficit financing during 1945–1946 to surpluses the next three years.

A peak of economic activity in November 1948 was followed by a
downward trend until the trough was reached in October 1949, whereupon
the economy moved through another expansionary phase (until July
1953). Unemployment was rising during this transition period and grew
worse as recession hit. The jobless rate averaged 4.4 percent during Truman's second term but peaked at 5.9 percent in the recession year of 1949
(see Figure 7.2). Because of the removal of wartime price controls, inflation
was severe during the 1946–1948 period, but during Truman's second term
the CPI rose at a 2.5 percent average annual rate, with the only spate of
inflation coming in 1951 during the Korean War buildup. Between 1949
and 1952 real GNP grew by 5.7 percent and productivity rose by 4.3
percent, a four-year record never matched since.

Figure 7.2   Unemployment and Inflation During the Truman
Presidency, 1946–1952

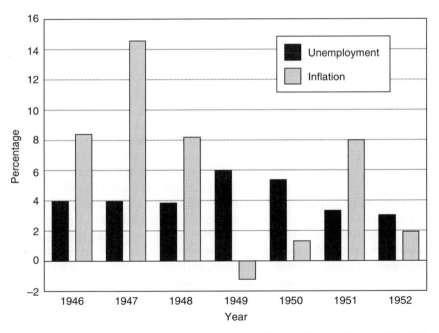

Source: Department of Labor, Bureau of Labor Statistics.

Inflation preoccupied the administration as late as July 27, 1948, when President Truman called a special session of Congress to consider his anti-inflation program. In January 1949 Truman requested new taxes to fund his Fair Deal domestic programs and the unexpected defense buildup arising from U.S.–Soviet tensions over Berlin. A tax increase made no economic sense given the impending recession of 1949, but other considerations guided macroeconomic policymaking, as Wilfred Lewis explains,

> ... fiscal prudence (the respect for balanced budgets) undoubtedly exerted a constraining influence ... the competing tenets of Keynesian compensatory fiscal policy were less widely held in 1949 than later. Then, too, there was a lag of statistics behind events and of policy behind statistics. ... And the extraordinary political attention given the inflation problem just prior to the 1949 recession make reversal even more difficult. ...[6]

A subtle change of policy followed Truman's 1949 Budget Message. His advisers wanted to bring about some price deflation, but without causing a recession. They hedged their bets, and not until July 1949 did President Truman acknowledge that a "moderate downward trend characterized most phases of economic activity in the first half of 1949."[7] He then canceled his request for a tax increase; this decision indicated Truman's acceptance of deficit financing as necessary to support an ailing economy. But Congress did not agree and in 1949 rushed headlong into economy measures to cut federal spending. As economist A. E. Holmans observed: "The significant point is not that these extreme and obscurantist views were to be heard, but that they were heard so often and the contrary argument so rarely."[8]

The Korean War began in June 1950, but the economy rebounded even before then. On the advice of the CEA, President Truman moved ahead with plans to achieve both spending cuts and tax increases, which shows again, as Lewis concludes, that "deliberate counterrecession actions [by the federal government] played an insignificant role in the [1950] recovery."[9] More important were the so-called **automatic stabilizers**, which sustain personal income during economic contractions.

Unemployment compensation is the best-known example of an automatic stabilizer. When people are thrown out of work from a recession, they receive payments through this federal-state program, which enables them to continue to spend money on consumption goods. The infusion of unemployment compensation benefits therefore sustains aggregate demand at a level higher than what might happen were the unemployed to be without any governmental assistance. The automatic stabilizers thereby act to soften the reduction in aggregate demand accompanying a recession,

and, since they trigger more governmental spending while tax revenues **177**
are declining, they result in spending deficits. From October–December
1948 to April–June 1949 the federal budget moved from a $3.8 billion
surplus to a $3.9 billion deficit; this shift of $7.7 billion helped cushion
the drop in GNP due to the recession.

Eisenhower's First Term, 1953–1956

Dwight D. Eisenhower was elected president in 1952 and 1956.
Well known as the supreme allied commander in World War II, his im-
mense popularity was symbolized by the phrase "I like Ike." His first term
in office was characterized by less of the intense partisan division seen in
the Truman's administration. Although a Republican-controlled Congress
was elected with him in 1952, the Democrats regained control of Congress
in 1954; except for Republican control of the Senate from 1980 to 1986,
the Democrats have controlled both houses of Congress ever since. As a
result, after 1954 Eisenhower—like all of his Republican successors (except for Reagan to some degree)—was forced to deal with a legislative
branch controlled by the opposition party.

Eisenhower's mandate was to proceed slowly, consolidate the reforms
of past decades, and assure domestic and world stability after the turmoil
of warfare. He expressed support for the Employment Act of 1946 but did
not aggressively utilize countercyclical fiscal or monetary policies. Particularly in the first of his two terms, unemployment was much more of a
problem than inflation (Figure 7.3). The expansion that began in October
1949 peaked in July 1953, and was followed by a contraction that lasted
until May 1954. Following this trough there was economic growth until
August 1957 (after Eisenhower's reelection campaign). The recession year
of 1954, therefore, showed the highest jobless rate, declines in real GNP
and real per capita disposable personal income, and lower growth in productivity. The fact that the three Eisenhower era recessions—1953–54,
1957–58, and 1960–61—did not become depressions was due primarily to
the automatic stabilizers.

Eisenhower could point to relative price stability, as the CPI increased
by an average annual percentage rate of 1.3 percent during 1953–1956.
His administration's approach to the inflation threat was to curb federal
spending, and budget surpluses were recorded in three years.

The Eisenhower administration was mainly concerned with inflation,
and its critics charged that the failure of macroeconomic policymaking
during the 1950s was reflected in sluggish economic growth and overly
high levels of unemployment. In his first term, real GNP grew by an annual
rate of 2.5 percent—less than half the rate during Truman's terms—and

Figure 7.3   Unemployment and Inflation During the Eisenhower
Presidency, 1953–1960

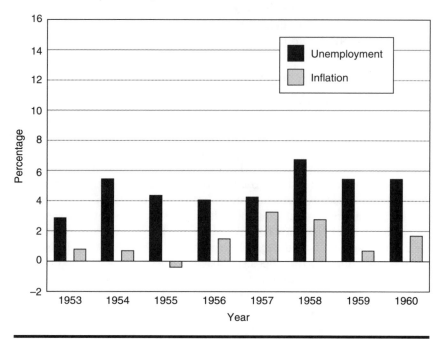

Source: Department of Labor, Bureau of Labor Statistics.

real per capita disposable personal income increased by a meager 1.3 percent. During the 1950s and 1960s economists used a 4 percent jobless rate
to indicate full employment—and that rate was exceeded every year after
1953.

Eisenhower's Second Term, 1957–1960

The business cycle was not kind to the second Eisenhower administration (see Figure 7.1). The first recession, short but sharp, began
in August 1957 and ended in April 1958. It was followed by a second,
which extended from April 1960 through February 1961 (into Kennedy's
term). These recessions were accompanied by a rise in both the inflation
and unemployment rates (Figure 7.3), the first time this happened in the
postwar era, and this unique occurrence prompted much discussion among

economists about a new "cost-push" (rather than "demand-pull") infla- **179**
tion.[10]

This cost-push theory already had some credence within the economics profession, but now it gained popular attention. Policymakers also
learned that when two recessions come back-to-back the second may be
prolonged because the short interval between them does not allow the
economy enough time to recover (a circumstance repeated more than
twenty years later in 1980–1982). Consequently, macroeconomic indicators performed much worse during Eisenhower's second term. The inflation
rate was higher, real GNP grew at a slower rate, and real per capita disposable personal income increased by less than 1 percent annually during
1957–1960.

Liberal economists criticized the relaxed Eisenhower view of countercyclical policy, and in 1958 John Kenneth Galbraith wrote his influential
book *The Affluent Society*. In it, he pointedly observed: "Nothing in our
economic policy is so deeply ingrained, and so little reckoned with by
economists, as our tendency to wait and see if things do not improve by
themselves."[11] The second recession bottomed out in April 1958, and by
June there was agreement that recovery was underway, but this economic
upswing cannot be attributed to macroeconomic policies, according to
Wilfred Lewis.

> The discretionary antirecession actions made their peak contribution in
> the last quarter of 1958—well after the cyclical trough in the first quarter
> of 1958—but had not been completely turned off in the second quarter
> of 1959. More important during the recovery than deliberate counter-
> recession actions were those taken for other reasons [for example, the
> Sputnik-inspired defense spending]. . . .[12]

The short-lived recovery did not prevent the federal government from
recording a record peacetime deficit (at that time) of $12.8 billion in 1959.
Congressional Democrats blamed President Eisenhower for the red ink,
and he resolved to balance the next budget. Weeks before sending his
FY60 budget to Congress, Ike took the unusual step of announcing his
intention to balance that budget at a level $2 billion under the original
estimate for FY59 spending. The actual spending was $92.1 billion in FY59
and $92.2 in FY60, and this retrenchment is cited by economists as one
reason why the economy slipped back into recession during 1960–61. The
experiences of the late 1950s show that, even though the administration
did not countermand the countercyclical impact of the automatic stabilizers, as economist Richard Froyen also points out, "*discretionary* fiscal
policy actions were only timidly countercyclical in the 1958 recession and
were restrictive in 1959–60."[13]

180   The Kennedy-Johnson Administration, 1961–1964

Vice President Richard Nixon waged his 1960 campaign for the White House in the midst of a new recession, and John F. Kennedy emerged the victor by only 100,000 votes. Kennedy promised to "get the country moving again," and the record shows that he and Lyndon Johnson were able to take the credit for a vastly improved economy. The recession inherited from the Eisenhower years bottomed out in February 1961, and a period of economic expansion unsurpassed in the postwar era lasted through December 1969.

During 1961–1964 unemployment averaged 5.8 percent but ranged from a 6.7 percent high in the 1961 recession year to a 5.2 percent low in 1964 (see Figure 7.4). Over the four-year period, the CPI grew at an average annual percentage rate of 1.2 percent, while real GNP increased by 4.3 percent annually. The current account balance showed a surplus every year, and the yearly rise of 3.9 percent in productivity was the best

Figure 7.4   Unemployment and Inflation During the Kennedy-Johnson Presidencies, 1961–1968

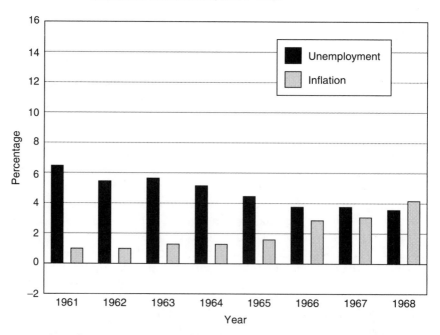

Source: Department of Labor, Bureau of Labor Statistics.

showing since Truman. The result was that per capita real disposable personal income increased as well; its annual rate of 2.7 percent was exceeded only by the 1965–68 period that followed. With the exception of unemployment (which was higher than during the 1950s), good times were back and the outlook was upbeat.

The Kennedy CEA embraced the Keynesian "new economics" and favored an aggressive countercyclical policy because they feared that the country faced serious economic stagnation, not merely a temporary downturn. Kennedy asked Congress for tax credits to stimulate business investment; however, like before, the federal budget response to the 1960–61 contraction was triggered mainly by automatic stabilizers.[14]

The significant departure from previous economic orthodoxy was the decision by President Kennedy to recommend tax cuts and deficit financing to *anticipate* and thereby *prevent* a future recession. He laid the groundwork in speeches and meetings during early 1962. As Theodore C. Sorensen explains: "[Kennedy's] political judgment told him that a period of gradual reeducation would be required before the country and Congress, accustomed to nearly sixteen years of White House homilies on the wickedness of government deficits, would approve of an administration deliberately and severely unbalancing the Budget."[15] His request for an income tax cut was made in the 1963 State of the Union Message, but Congress was not impressed, and no tax cut was enacted before Kennedy's assassination in November.

President Johnson declared in his first address to the Congress on November 27:

> No act of ours could more fittingly continue the work of President Kennedy than the early passage of the tax bill for which he fought all this long year. This is a bill designed to increase our national income and federal revenues, and to provide insurance against recession.[16]

In a meeting with his advisers LBJ opposed any FY65 budget exceeding $100 billion, explaining: "We won't even get it [tax cut] to the Senate floor unless we tell Congress that the new budget will be about one hundred billion dollars."[17] After Johnson unveiled his proposed FY65 budget of $97.9 billion, the Senate Finance Committee reported a tax bill on January 28. House-Senate differences were ironed out by February 26, and the bill was signed into law. Fourteen months had passed before Congress approved the Kennedy tax cut, but that measure is credited with bolstering the economy and heading off any recession.

The Johnson Administration, 1965–1968

President Johnson's full term in office was a picture in contrasts. Elected in a landslide in 1964, he declined to run for reelection four years

182   later in the face of strong opposition within his own party. His term was marked by an explosion of legislation to address social problems, yet his administration was ultimately undone by the unpopular Vietnam War.

President Johnson presided over an economy that showed its best overall performance since the 1940s. After his 1964 landslide election, good economic news coupled with his enormous popularity allowed Johnson to promote his Great Society programs to extend social welfare, fight racial discrimination, and uplift the poor. The share of human services spending going to the poor grew from 4.7 percent in 1961 to 7.9 percent in 1969.[18] However, even more costly, though not realized at the time, were middle-class **entitlement programs** such as Social Security and Medicare. These are called entitlements because the laws creating them require the federal government to spend as much money as is required to cover the costs of providing benefits to all people who qualify. Qualifying persons are "entitled" to benefits and cannot be denied them—regardless of whether Congress wishes to fund them. As a result, spending for these programs is today considered "uncontrollable."

In 1965 Johnson also began the massive military buildup that would eventually lead to the sending of 500,000 troops into South Vietnam to oppose a communist takeover. This protracted conflict led to social unrest at home, cost more than 58,000 American deaths (and a far greater loss of life among Southeast Asians), and expended billions from the Treasury. Defense expenditures rose from $49.5 billion in 1965 to $81.2 billion in 1969 (Nixon's first year in office) before falling[19]; since no new taxes were levied, deficits were incurred, and the national debt grew.

Real GNP grew substantially over Johnson's term, and as a consequence, real per capita disposable personal income increased by more than during both Eisenhower terms. The 2.8 percent annual rate of increase in productivity was also an improvement over the 1950s. The jobless rate was driven down from 4.5 percent in 1965 to an average of 3.9 percent over the four-year term, a rate not achieved since the Korean War. A worrisome sign, however, was seen in the balance on current account; the total 1965–68 surplus was one-half the amount generated during the 1961–64 period, largely because the military spent billions of dollars overseas to purchase supplies and war materiel closer to the field of battle in Vietnam.

The major impact of the deficit spending was upward pressure on consumer prices. The yearly change in the CPI grew steadily each year, reaching 4.2 percent in 1968, indicating that the serious inflationary pressures endemic to the national economy during the 1970s had already begun by the end of Johnson's term. For reasons we discuss in detail in the next chapter, Johnson was reluctant to ask the Congress to enact an income tax surcharge. When he finally did in August 1967 (which Congress did not approve until June 1968), his action was too little and came too **183** late. This period was not characterized by tough-minded fiscal policymaking. As one economist remarked: "It would be difficult to find a more perfect example of irresponsible government action that inevitably would have serious inflationary consequences."[20] The serious problem of dealing with inflation was left to Johnson's Republican successor.

The First Nixon Term, 1969–1972

After President Johnson declined to seek reelection, Vice President Hubert Humphrey waged the 1968 presidential campaign against Richard Nixon. In a three-way race (with Alabama's former governor, George C. Wallace, running on a third-party ticket), Republican Richard Nixon narrowly emerged as winner. Later, a victorious Nixon declared that an assault on rising prices would be the cornerstone of his economic program. His advisers saw the problem as "demand-pull" inflation resulting from the massive defense buildup and domestic expenditures, as well as the delayed 1968 income tax surcharge. However, they discounted the government's ability to "fine tune" the economy, feeling that the impact of fiscal policy was "probably slower and smaller than commonly assumed and probably also difficult to predict."[21] These views reflected in part the monetarist critique of Keynesianism that gained credence at that time.

The nearly decade-long economic expansion of the Kennedy-Johnson years ended in December 1969, and a contraction held sway until November 1970. Unemployment averaged 5.0 percent over Nixon's first term but reached 5.9 percent in 1971, and the CPI rose along with the jobless rate during 1969 and 1970 (Figure 7.5). The average annual change in the CPI was only 4.7 percent, however, a result of the wage-price controls Nixon imposed in mid-1971. (The ultimate failure of this policy, however, is discussed in the next chapter.) The average rate of increase in real GNP was 2.5 percent, and growth in productivity was at the low rate of 1.8 percent yearly; real per capita disposable personal income increased at an annual rate of only 1.7 percent. This was not a stellar performance for the macroeconomy.

Unlike Kennedy, Nixon was not intrigued with macroeconomic policy, but like JFK he was not rigid when dealing with economic problems. As his CEA chairman observed: "Nixon was predisposed toward using the market to make most economic decisions, and toward maintaining a free-market economy. Mixed with this philosophy, he had a pragmatic turn of mind that tended to keep him free of confinement by any ideology."[22] At first the Nixon team adopted a gradualist strategy based on fiscal and monetary policy, but in 1970 some advisers expressed the view that "cost-push"

184   **Figure 7.5**   Unemployment and Inflation During the Nixon-Ford
Presidencies, 1969–1976

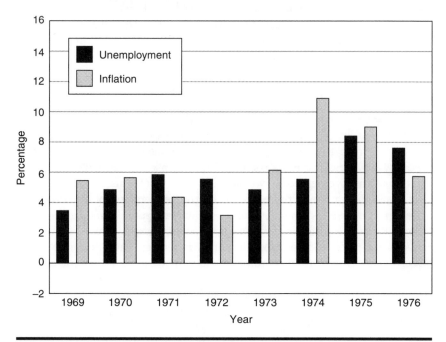

Source: Department of Labor, Bureau of Labor Statistics.

inflation (from increased costs of production) was the fundamental problem, not excessive consumer demand. Such inflation was thought to be
immune from countercyclical policy, thus implying that direct controls
over prices might be needed.

The Democrats decided to force Nixon's hand, and in 1970 Congress
enacted the Economic Stabilization Act to arm the president with standby
authority to freeze wages, prices, and rents. A decisive turning point came
when Nixon appointed John Connally to be secretary of the treasury in
1970; according to Reichley, "Nixon looked to Connally to give leadership
in finding a way out of the economic quagmire in which the nation seemed
to be descending, while the president planned epochal foreign policy
moves."[23] In late summer of 1971 John Connally convinced Nixon that
wage-price controls were the only answer, a view that was widely supported
by that time. As George Shultz, Secretary of Labor, quipped: "In the end,
the only people opposed to controls were Richard Nixon, Milton Friedman

[the University of Chicago economist], and myself."[24] On August 15, 1971,   **185**
Nixon announced his New Economic Policy, which included a 90-day
wage-price freeze, in direct response to a serious erosion in the nation's
international balance of payments (discussed earlier in Chapter 6).

The Nixon-Ford Term, 1973–1976

The economy was not a critical issue in the 1972 presidential
election; more important were the personality and policies of Nixon's opponent, George McGovern. President Nixon won by a landslide, but two
years later had to resign in the face of impeachment proceedings arising
from the Watergate scandals. The rest of his term was completed by Gerald
Ford; unfortunately for Ford, the economy did not improve very much by
the time of his reelection bid in 1976.

The economic expansion beginning in November 1970 peaked in
November 1973, after which a new recession began that extended through
March 1975. The March 1975 trough gave way to economic growth
through January 1980. But the long and deep contraction of 1973–75—
the worst up to that time in the postwar era (see Figure 7.1)—guaranteed
that the macroeconomic indicators would be bleak. Unemployment averaged 6.7 percent during the Nixon-Ford term, with a high of 8.5 percent
in the recession year of 1975. But prices did not fall. The average yearly
rate of increase in the CPI was 8.0 percent, and the high reached 11.0
percent in 1974 (Figure 7.5). During 1974 and 1975 there had been declines in both real GNP and real per capita disposable personal income.
Only the balance on current account was encouraging; surpluses were recorded every year.

The experiment with an "incomes policy" was generally viewed a
failure. In 1972 the CPI rose 3.3 percent, less than during the preceding
three years, but then it rose by 6.2 percent in 1973, 11.0 percent in 1974,
and 9.1 percent in 1975 before falling to 5.8 percent as recession took
hold. This experience with wage and price controls "raised serious doubts
about their potential effectiveness under political democracy, except in
times of national emergency, and it went a long way, at least among conservatives, toward enhancing the prestige of the market as the best available means for allocating resources, establishing incentives, and making
most economic decisions."[25]

One conservative who learned this lesson was President Ford, who
refused to abandon his economic game plan as the 1976 presidential campaign approached (which may have cost him the election). Ford devised
an Economic Policy Board to allow a fuller consideration of macroeconomic policies. His major concern was inflation, which he believed was

186   caused by too much federal spending and the mounting costs of entitlement programs enacted during the 1960s and early 1970s. In late 1974
Ford held an economic summit conference to obtain advice from a diverse
group of economists, after which he announced a variety of strategies to
hold down prices, including his wearing a WIN button to symbolize the
"Whip Inflation Now" campaign (a ploy quickly ridiculed by his detrac-
tors).

As the recession got worse, Ford's 1975 State of the Union Message
abandoned the tax surcharge in favor of a $16 billion tax cut, a moratorium
on new programs except energy, and a ceiling on domestic spending.[26] But
Congress approved a larger tax cut and more expenditures than the president wanted, leading to an executive-legislative confrontation. To hold
down federal spending Ford wielded his veto frequently against bills passed
by the Democratic-controlled Congress; relative to his time in office Ford
vetoed more bills than all but three other presidents.[27]

President Ford remained committed to fiscal integrity, and in 1976 he
rejected the advice of some aides that he "pump up" the economy to assist
his reelection. He felt that added federal spending would rekindle inflation
without significantly reducing the jobless rate, so he took a political risk
that the economy would improve by election time. As things worked out,
the economy could not have performed worse.

The jobless rate reached 8 percent in November 1976 as voters went
to the polls. Ford gambled with fiscal austerity and lost. However his immediate legacy was a much stronger economy. In 1976 the CPI rose at a
lesser rate; both real GNP and real per capita disposable personal income
scored impressive gains compared to declines the previous year; and even
the jobless rate fell slightly. But unemployment was the sore point; the 7.7
percent unemployment rate of 1976 was (except for 1975) a postwar high.

The Carter Presidency, 1977–1980

In 1976 Jimmy Carter campaigned as an outsider with no ties to
the Washington establishment. He cultivated the anti-Watergate feelings
of the time and an image that stressed his personal integrity, moral and
religious values, and centrist politics. To reassure liberal groups that he
was a real Democrat, Carter detailed a far-reaching domestic agenda during
the campaign. He pledged to "achieve an unemployment level of 4 percent
or less by the end of my first term"[28] and endorsed countercyclical fiscal
policy, expansionary monetary policy, more funds for public works jobs
and training, and the Humphrey-Hawkins "Full Employment" Bill pending before the Congress.

During 1977 and 1978 President Carter promoted a liberal agenda to **187**
redeem his campaign pledges, including economic stimulus to bring down
the jobless rate. But in 1979 and 1980 he had to confront double-digit
inflation (Figure 7.6), brought on at least in part by rapidly rising oil prices
(a factor beyond the president's control). The president now recognized
that more people were worried about rising prices than unemployment. In
his 1980 *Economic Report of the President* Carter declared inflation to be
"the Nation's number one economic problem," and thereby reversed his
economic priorities. What caused Carter so much political damage, however, was his refusal to use the correctives preferred by the liberal wing of
his Democratic party. A cry for direct wage-price controls was raised by
Senator Edward Kennedy (D-MA), who challenged the president in the
1980 primaries. Instead Carter turned to a standard Republican recipe for
dealing with inflation. He wanted to reduce domestic spending, balance
the budget, and implicitly allow the jobless rate to ease upwards. But that

Figure 7.6   Unemployment and Inflation During the Carter
Presidency, 1977–1980

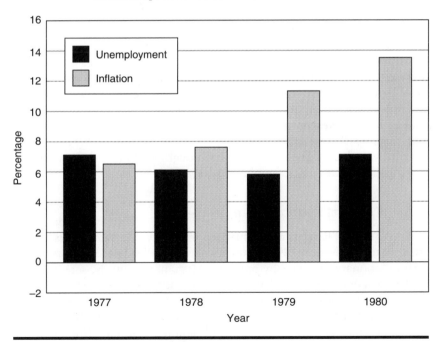

Source: Department of Labor, Bureau of Labor Statistics.

188   strategy did not work fast enough, and Carter only managed to alienate voters within the Democratic party without attracting much support from the GOP or conservatives.

During the 1970s economists were concerned about **stagflation**, the combination of rising and high unemployment, sluggish economic growth, and a loss of productivity. These conditions were reflected in the macroeconomic indicators during the Carter term (Figure 7.6). The recession that bottomed out in March 1975 yielded an expansion lasting through January 1980. The timing of this business cycle was not fortuitous for President Carter, because the peak was followed by a quick contraction that lasted until July 1980—only four months before the presidential election. The Carter administration began and ended with short recessions, but the major economic problem to beset Jimmy Carter was inflation—caused primarily by a rapid escalation in oil prices and the short-term shortages that were created. The average rate of increase in the CPI over Carter's term was 9.8 percent, but it moved into the double-digit range during 1979 (11.3 percent) and 1980 (13.5 percent).

Nor was Carter able to bring down the jobless rate, although a large number of new jobs were created during his administration.[29] Unemployment averaged 6.5 percent overall but was increased by the two recessions to 7.1 percent in both 1977 and 1980. The balance on current account showed deficits in three years, and even more serious was the paltry annual increase of less than 0.3 percent in the rate of productivity. Despite these negatives, real GNP managed to grow at an annual average rate of 3.1 percent and the yearly growth in per capita disposable personal income was 2.0 percent. The voters, however, apparently focused on inflation and unemployment when, during the 1980 presidential election, Carter's opponent Ronald Reagan asked them: "Are you better off than you were four years ago?" The majority answered *no* in November 1980. Ronald Reagan was elected president, and he brought to Washington a radical new perspective on macroeconomic policy.

The First Reagan Term, 1981–1984

Ronald Reagan was influenced by supply-side economists, a new breed in the profession. Where Keynesian demand-side economists would curb inflationary pressures by reducing consumer spending, supply siders (as they came to be known) wanted to attack rising prices by increasing the supply of goods and services. The linchpin of supply-side theory was the argument that high marginal income taxes undermine productivity by discouraging work, personal savings, and capital investment. (Marginal tax rates are the rates paid on the last dollar a taxpayer earns.) This thinking

was reflected in the Kemp-Roth bill, which Reagan endorsed, to cut federal **189**
taxes by 30 percent. In 1980 Jimmy Carter called that legislation irresponsible, and even Reagan's then-opponent for the Republican nomination, George Bush, called supply-side tax cuts "voodoo economics." Although many mainstream economists doubted supply-side theory,
politically it was the right message delivered at the right time.

The economic expansion that started in July 1980 came to a halt in
July 1981, and a new recession began that did not reach its trough until
November 1982. This was a sixteen-month contraction that, at the trough,
posted the highest unemployment rate since the Great Depression. A period of economic growth then began that lasted through the second Reagan term. However, the macroeconomy performed very unevenly during
1981–84.

The jobless rate averaged 8.6 percent but exceeded 9 percent in 1982
and 1983 (Figure 7.7). The CPI showed marked improvement, falling from

Figure 7.7   Unemployment and Inflation During the Reagan-Bush
Presidencies, 1981–1992

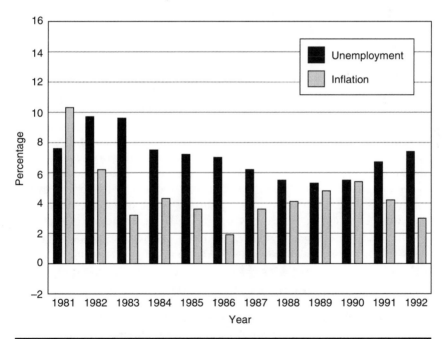

Source: Department of Labor, Bureau of Labor Statistics.

10.4 percent in 1981 to 3.2 percent in 1983 before rising slightly to 4.3 percent in 1984. The average annual increase in prices over Reagan's first term was 6.0 percent. The severe recession caused real GNP to fall in 1982 by 2.5 percent from its 1981 level, and per capita disposable personal income also declined during 1982, as did the balance on current account.

Reagan's Second Term, 1985–1988

Reagan's entire second term was part of the second-longest expansion in the U.S. economy since 1854. As a result, the macroeconomy showed marked improved over its 1981–84 performance. The unemployment rate declined steadily over the four years, with the result that the 1985–88 average was approximately the jobless rate experienced during Carter's term. The economy also experienced more real growth, as shown by a four-year average that exceeded 3 percent. Of greatest significance, the inflationary cycle was broken; the four-year average rate of change in the CPI during 1985–88 (3.3 percent) was almost half what it was during Reagan's first term.

In other areas, though, the macroeconomy did not perform as well. The increase in productivity for 1985–88 was hardly much improvement over what happened during the 1981–84 period. The most serious negative, however, was the balance on current account; the postwar record four-year deficit recorded during the first Reagan term more than *tripled* in real terms from 1985 through 1988.

Following November 1982, when the severe recession bottomed out, there were 92 months of economic growth (until July 1990). Since 1854, this expansionary period was exceeded only by the Kennedy-Johnson prosperity, which spanned 106 months from the trough of the business cycle in February 1961 until the expansion peaked in December of 1969. One point of similarity with the 1980s is that the prosperity of the 1960s was also an economic byproduct of deficit spending by the federal government. However, unlike the 1980s, the 1960s expansion was fueled in part by the Vietnam War. (The Reagan years did witness massive increases in defense spending, although the country was at peace.) The economic growth during the last six years under Reagan (and into President Bush's second year), therefore, represents a *peacetime* record for economic expansion.

The Bush Presidency, 1989–1992

In the midst of this long period of economic expansion and with America at peace, Vice President George Bush became the first sitting vice president to win the presidential election in over 150 years. For the first eighteen months of the Bush presidency it seemed as if the economic expansion would go on forever. Some commentators (though not economists) began to speculate that the economy had entered a new phase in which the business cycle—so long a staple of American economic life—might be fading away. Unfortunately, this was not to be the case. During 1990 the long expansion began to slow, finally reaching its turning point (peak) in July 1990—just as Iraqi leader Saddam Hussein prepared to invade Kuwait.

The juxtaposition of the end of the long Reagan recovery and the invasion of Kuwait nicely summarizes Bush's presidency. From a distance, this was a tumultuous period in world affairs: the collapse of the Soviet Union, the reunification of Germany, the wave of liberalization followed by repression in China, the end of the Cold War, the Gulf War—all of these took place during this four-year period. President Bush's expertise in foreign affairs, culminating in the creation of a multinational force that successfully prosecuted the Gulf War, raised his presidential approval ratings to the highest levels recorded in the history of polling.[30] Less than one year later, the lingering downturn in the economy had caused his approval ratings to drop by half.

The Bush term began well, with the yearly unemployment rate reaching its lowest point (5.3 percent) since 1973 (see Figure 7.7). Inflation, however, began to edge upward, rising to 6.1 percent in 1990, its highest level in eight years. The downturn that began in July 1990 led to real declines in the GNP in the last quarter of 1990 and the first quarter of 1991, technically qualifying this contraction as a recession. By the second quarter of 1991 the GNP again began to grow, although the recovery was anemic, with drops actually being recorded in real per capita disposable income in two successive quarters between the second and fourth quarters of 1991—*after* the recovery was supposedly underway. Bush's own assessment of the critical year of 1991 states:

> The recession, which began in the third quarter of 1990 . . . continued into 1991. The high oil prices and the uncertainty occasioned by events in the Persian Gulf were quickly resolved with the successful completion of Operation Desert Storm early in the year. Most analysts expected a sustained recovery to follow. Indeed, signs of a moderate expansion began to appear in the spring. . . . By the late summer, however, the economy flattened out and was sluggish through the rest of the year.[31]

In fact, although President Bush went on in the same *Economic Report* to state, "As we move into 1992, the fundamental conditions to generate economic growth are falling into place,"[32] as the election approached in November 1992, the looked-for recovery had still not arrived. Although

192   the NBER's Business Cycle Dating Committee would finally announce on December 22, 1992, that the contraction had ended in March of 1991, the signs of economic recovery were mixed through much of the year. The unemployment rate averaged 7.4 percent—reaching a peak of 7.8 percent in June—fully 2 percent higher than the year Bush took office. Although inflation had declined, dropping to only 3 percent for 1992, the high unemployment and declines in personal income seemed to convert the 1992 election into a referendum on Bush's management of the macroeconomy, particularly his response to the rising unemployment.

BUSINESS CYCLES AND POSTWAR MACROECONOMIC POLICY

Surveying the collective experiences in managing the macroeconomy of the nine postwar U.S. presidents, five points stand out. First, whatever the cause, the business cycle appears to be an intrinsic element of the modern U.S. economy. Although sustained periods of either expansion or contraction sometimes seem to usher in new economic eras, eventually the level of economic activity has always changed. For the foreseeable future, U.S. presidents can expect to continue to have to deal with the business cycle and the macroeconomic conditions it spawns, particularly alternating periods of unemployment and inflation.

Second, over time there has been a change in perceptions over what constitutes problematic macroeconomic performance. With regard to employment, for example, from 1946 through 1974 the yearly unemployment rate exceeded 6 percent only twice (in the recession years of 1958 and 1961). In the 18 years that followed, the only sustained period below this level was during the last three years of the 1980s expansion. Even more dramatic are the changes in perception of "acceptable" inflation. During the 1950s, annual rates of inflation over 2 percent were considered a serious failure in macroeconomic policymaking. For most Americans living in the 1990s, though, sustained inflation rates below 3 percent are simply not part of their adult memories.

Third, the techniques and perceived importance of macroeconomic management have significantly evolved since the end of World War II. Until the 1960s, attempts at macroeconomic management—despite legislative pronouncements like the Employment Act of 1946—were tentative, at best. As our surveys of these years indicate, most countercyclical efforts during this period were due to automatic stabilizers rather than discretionary actions. Since 1961 this has changed. From the Keynesian "new economics" of the Kennedy era, to the pragmatic eclecticism of

Nixon, to the bold (some would say reckless) supply-side theory of the   **193**
Reagan years, presidents have been more extensively involved in trying
to affect the performance of the economy.

Fourth, economic policymaking is perhaps the most closely scrutinized
and publicly reported area in which policymakers operate.[33] Despite the
fact that the president and other policymakers have little direct control
over much of the economy, the public is bombarded with economic statistics that, in a sense, are measuring how well the president is performing
as manager of prosperity. This continual process of measurement creates
substantial pressure for the president to take decisive action to correct
what are often real economic problems. However, some problems are actually self-correcting through market adjustments, and the correct "action"
is to do nothing. Inaction, however, is almost never politically popular, as
President Bush found during 1992.

Finally, not all policy efforts are successful, or, perhaps what is more
important in a political sense, not all policy efforts are both economically
effective and politically acceptable. This has been particularly the case
since the macroeconomy began to be afflicted by stagflation around 1970.
Some presidents, such as Ford, Carter, and Bush, stuck to policies they
deemed correct for the economy and suffered politically as a result. Others,
such as Nixon when he imposed wage and price controls in 1971, adopted
politically popular approaches that were ultimately failures from the stand-
point of improving the economy. (Many wonder whether the large cuts
in marginal tax rates engineered by President Reagan in 1981 may be
another case of a popular but ill-conceived policy.) In the next two chapters we will continue to examine this issue of whether good policies and
popular policies are the same thing—first, in Chapter 8, from the perspective of the policymakers and then, in Chapter 9, from the view of the
public.

KEY TERMS

business cycle, business peak, business trough, countercyclical
strategies, automatic stabilizers, entitlement programs, stagflation

ADDITIONAL READING

Economic Report of the President. Washington, DC: U.S. Government Printing
Office. This volume is published each February and contains the Annual Report
of the Council of Economic Advisers. Submitted to Congress by the president,
it discusses economic problems, policy initiatives, and the outlook for the

194   future. One section includes a comprehensive set of statistical tables on the economy.

Federal Reserve Board of Governors. *Federal Reserve Bulletin*. Published each month, this volume has statistical data on monetary, financial, and interest rate matters, coverage of foreign exchange/international trade statistics, reports of the Federal Open Market Committee, and articles of current interest.

Feldstein, Martin, ed. *The American Economy in Transition*. Chicago: University of Chicago Press, 1980. This book marks the 60th anniversary of the National Bureau of Economic Research by detailing changes in the U.S. economy during the postwar era.

Lewis, Wilfred, Jr. *Federal Fiscal Policy in the Postwar Recessions*. Washington, DC: The Brookings Institution, 1962. Analysis of the role of fiscal policy, especially automatic stabilizers and countercyclical policy, in responding to economic downturns in the Truman and Eisenhower administrations.

Sommers, Albert T. *The U.S. Economy Demystified (What the Major Economic Statistics Mean and Their Significance for Business)*. Lexington, MA: Lexington Books, 1985. Discusses the major statistical series published by various federal agencies, explaining their meaning and derivation and how they may be used to assess national trends. Appendices list other available series, their publication cycles, and sources.

Stein, Herbert. *Presidential Economics: The Making of Economic Policy from Roosevelt to Reagan and Beyond*. New York: Simon and Schuster, 1984. Discusses fiscal policymaking by modern presidents, through the early Reagan administration.

U.S. Department of Commerce, Bureau of Economic Analysis. *Historical Statistics of the United States, Colonial Times to 1970*. Washington, DC: U.S. Government Printing Office. Includes collections of economic statistics dating back to colonial times.

U.S. Department of Commerce, Bureau of Economic Analysis. *The Survey of Current Business*. Washington, DC: U.S. Government Printing Office. This monthly serial includes a section with statistical series on national income, prices, foreign trade, etc., and articles on macroeconomic and data-related issues.

U.S. Department of Commerce, Bureau of Economic Analysis. *Business Statistics*. Washington, DC: U.S. Government Printing Office. This biennial volume has summary tables for all the statistical series found in *The Survey of Current Business* for a period back to either 1929 or 1947.

NOTES

1.   Despite its official-sounding name, the NBER is not a governmental agency, but a private, nonpartisan institute whose mission is to collect economic data, to interpret information relating to the economy, and to increase public

knowledge of economic statistics and economic theory. It has, however, achieved a sort of semi-official status, with many of its analyses being incorporated into official U.S. government publications, such as *Business Conditions Digest* (a compendium of economic data published from 1960 to 1990) and the *Survey of Current Business* (which continued publishing NBER data after 1990), both published by the U.S. Department of Commerce.

2.   "Cyclical Indicators," *Business Conditions Digest* 29 (December 1989), p. 1.

3.   Arthur F. Burns and Wesley C. Mitchell, *Measuring Business Cycles* (New York: National Bureau of Economic Research, 1946). For a recent discussion of alternative methods of identifying business cycles, see George R. Green and Barry A. Beckman, "The Composite Index of Coincident Indicators and Alternative Coincident Indexes," *Survey of Current Business* 72 (June 1992), pp. 42–45.

4.   "Cyclical Indicators," p. 1.

5.   Alvin H. Hansen, "Economic Progress and Declining Population Growth," *American Economic Review* 29 (March 1939), 1–15.

6.   Wilfred Lewis, Jr., *Federal Fiscal Policy in the Postwar Recessions* (Washington, DC: The Brookings Institution, 1962), pp. 105–106.

7.   *Midyear Economic Report of the President* (July 1949), p. 3.

8.   A. E. Holmans, *United States Fiscal Policy 1945–1959* (New York: Oxford University Press, 1961), p. 117.

9.   Lewis, *Federal Fiscal Policy in the Postwar Recessions*, p. 124.

10.   See Gardner Ackley, *Macroeconomics: Theory and Policy* (New York: Macmillan, 1978), pp. 434–437.

11.   John Kenneth Galbraith, *The Affluent Society* (Boston: Houghton Mifflin, 1958), p. 207.

12.   Lewis, *Federal Fiscal Policy in the Postwar Recessions*, p. 233.

13.   Richard T. Froyen, *Macroeconomics: Theories and Policies* (New York: Macmillan, 1983), p. 540.

14.   Lewis, *Federal Fiscal Policy in the Postwar Recessions*, p. 274.

15.   Theodore J. Sorensen, *Kennedy* (New York: Harper and Row, 1965), p. 413.

16.   Quoted in Herbert Stein, *The Fiscal Revolution in America* (Chicago: The University of Chicago Press, 1969), p. 452.

17.   Reported in Rowland Evans and Robert Novak, *Lyndon B. Johnson: The Exercise of Power* (New York: The New American Library, 1966), p. 371.

18.   Reported in Henry J. Aaron, *Politics and the Professors: The Great Society in Perspective* (Washington, DC: The Brookings Institution, 1978), pp. 11–12, Tables 1-A1 and 1-A3.

19.   U.S. Department of Commerce, Bureau of the Census, *Historical Statistics of the United States, Colonial Times to 1970* (Washington, DC: U.S. Government Printing Office, 1975), p. 1116.

196   20.   Wallace C. Peterson, *Income, Employment, and Economic Growth*, 5th ed. (New York: W. W. Norton, 1984), p. 532.

21.   Quoted in Neil de Marchi, "The First Nixon Administration: Prelude to Controls," in Craufurd D. Goodwin, ed., *Exhortation and Controls: The Search for a Wage-Price Policy 1945–1971* (Washington, DC: The Brookings Institution, 1975), p. 298.

22.   Quoted in A. James Reichley, *Conservatives in an Age of Change: The Nixon and Ford Administrations* (Washington, DC: The Brookings Institution, 1981), p. 206.

23.   Ibid., p. 218.

24.   Quoted in ibid., p. 222.

25.   Ibid., p. 231.

26.   Ibid., p. 392.

27.   Ibid., pp. 323–325. Only Cleveland, FDR, and Truman cast more vetoes relative to their tenure in office. Of the 66 vetoes cast by Ford, 39 affected the federal budget.

28.   Reported in Jeff Fishel, *Presidents and Promises: From Campaign Pledge to Presidential Performance* (Washington, DC: CQ Press, 1985), p. 100.

29.   This seeming paradox is because the overall job pool grew rapidly during Carter's four years in office due to the entry into the labor force of large numbers of "baby boomers" and women (who had not previously entered the labor force to the same degree). As a result, while the number of employed persons increased substantially—with average yearly increases greater than during the four-year expansion of the second Reagan term (1985–88)—the percentage of those seeking jobs who were employed did not change to the same degree.

30.   In the Gallup poll conducted February 28–March 3, 1991, immediately following the end of the Gulf War, Bush received an approval rating of 89 percent, exceeding the previous of 87 percent received by President Truman at the end of World War II.

31.   *Economic Report of the President 1992* (Washington, DC: Government Printing Office, February 1992), p. 3.

32.   Ibid., p. 3.

33.   We are grateful to John Sloan for raising this point.

CHAPTER 8

The Politics of Countercyclical Policy

One of the legacies of the rise of Keynesian theory is the widespread expectation that government will take some corrective action in response to fluctuations in the business cycle. This type of government action is known as countercyclical policy, since its purpose is to work against deviations from high employment and low inflation, i.e., smooth out fluctuations in the economy, stimulating employment during recessions and reducing inflation when the inflation rate is too high. Countercyclical policy frequently requires making a choice among competing goals, since the key macroeconomic goals are not always compatible or easily obtained. Trade-offs are clearly involved when trying to achieve economic growth, full employment, price stability, high productivity, and a positive balance of trade. Perhaps the most familiar of these trade-offs is the tension between high levels of employment and low levels of inflation.

When economic problems are multifaceted and expert opinion is contradictory or uncertain, there are political risks involved in formulating any kind of policy response. Politics is sometimes called the art of the possible, and in these situations creating an optimal macroeconomic policy involves presidential statecraft of a high order. The bulk of this chapter will be spent analyzing three modern episodes involving presidential efforts at countercyclical policy. Two show how presidents can fail this challenge of economic leadership, while the third describes a president who sought to "do the right thing," but lost the presidency in the process. In each of

198   these episodes, the president found it difficult to fashion a policy that would effectively fight inflation. This was an especially difficult policy problem during the 1970s, when stagflation—the simultaneous appearance of high inflation and high unemployment—was a persistent occurrence. During the postwar era presidents have found it much easier to fashion a policy response to unemployment than to inflation. Before turning to our three case studies, we will discuss why this is the case.

FIGHTING INFLATION VERSUS FIGHTING UNEMPLOYMENT

Fighting Unemployment

When unemployment begins to rise, it is usually not long before cries are heard to do something. In fact, for this policy problem policy-makers have a fairly good idea of what to do—and, normally, it is also politically popular to do it. The general consensus among economists is that a common cause of increasing unemployment is exactly what Keynes said it was—insufficient aggregate demand for goods and service. The standard prescription for this is either a cut in taxes or an increase in spending (or both), which will increase demand and stimulate employment. Tax cuts are always popular, while spending increases provoke a number of responses, depending upon what kind of spending is contemplated and how severe the public assessment of unemployment. During periods of stagflation, for example, some levels of unemployment may not seem worth attacking with spending increases if this may lead to higher inflation rates.

Supply-side economists, who were so important in the development of economic policies during the Reagan and Bush administrations, also favor tax cuts as a remedy for unemployment, although for different reasons than those argued by Keynes. By cutting taxes, they believe, the incentives to work and produce are increased, which should lead to heightened production and employment and consequently, demand for the newly produced goods. According to supply-side theory, increased government spending should have no direct effect on employment, although it may indirectly harm the economy if it leads to increased governmental borrowing, which takes money away from private borrowers.

Thus, tax cuts, and to a lesser degree, spending increases, are both prescribed by economic theory and welcomed by the population. As a result, the government normally responds with countercyclical stimulative policies when the economy appears to be falling short of the full-employment level. This condition is also sometimes called a GNP gap, by which is meant that there is a gap between what the economy could produce if all resources were productively employed and what it is actually producing.

In fact, our economy today has certain policies—unemployment compensation, food stamps, and other elements of the "safety net"—that automatically increase government spending when unemployment rises. These policies are known as automatic stabilizers, since they lead to an upsurge in spending without any new action by the government (and a decrease in spending when unemployment drops). The presence of such stabilizers is believed to be one reason why the difference between the peaks and troughs of the business cycle have decreased since the Great Depression; automatic stabilizers are, in effect, dampening down fluctuations in the business cycle.

A Policy Dilemma: The Phillips Curve

Over time, policymakers and others have come to recognize that attempts to reduce unemployment and reduce inflation work at cross-purposes. Put somewhat differently, there is a trade-off between inflation and employment. This trade-off is sometimes described as a **Phillips curve**, after A. W. Phillips. the economist who first sought to quantify this relationship.[1] Although during the initial development of the Phillips curve in the 1960s economists and policymakers thought there was a fairly simple relationship between these two outcomes, the contemporary view is that the trade-off is more complex.

In the short-run, there seems to be a clear trade-off: attempts to lower unemployment through stimulating the economy will lead to more price inflation as the economy approaches the full-employment level. Conversely, price inflation can be reduced, but at the cost of higher unemployment. However, in the long run, the relationship is more complex. The key reason is that inflation has a strong inertial component. Inflation tends to continue at a certain level until it is jolted upward or downward by events, such as a sudden rise in oil prices or a large increase in unemployment. Thus, low unemployment is not necessarily associated with high inflation but with *increasing* rates of inflation. More importantly, high unemployment is associated with downward pressure on the inflation rate, but not with low inflation; if the inertial level of inflation is high, high unemployment may still be associated with high levels of inflation (although the short-run movement in inflation may be downward).

Even with this qualification, though, the Phillips curve captures a basic dilemma for policymakers, particularly when the inertial rate of inflation is higher than the public's "comfort level." During most of the 1950s and 1960s and since 1982, inflation has been relatively mild—gen-

200 erally below 5 percent (actually below 2 percent for much of the pre-1965 period), and policymakers have been relatively free to respond to unemployment with stimulative policies. During the period 1965–1980, however, higher rates of inertial inflation made macroeconomic policymaking a more difficult enterprise. Each of the three episodes described in this chapter date from this period. However, these should not be read as simply accounts of economic history. The threat of renewed inflation remains a powerful element of contemporary economic policy discussions, and the problems faced by Presidents Johnson, Nixon, and Carter may once again confront the managers of our prosperity.

THE POLITICS OF COUNTERCYCLICAL POLICY: THREE MODERN EPISODES

Johnson's Income Tax Surcharge

In 1965 the Council of Economic Advisers was pleased that the GNP gap had been closed during the early 1960s. It declared that "in the last four years the main challenge to U.S. policy has been to stimulate a massive growth in total demand, sufficient not merely to *keep up* but to *catch up* with the growth of productive capacity. During the past four years, fiscal policy has been dominated by this purpose."[2] The CEA believed that price stability would extend through 1965. A year later President Johnson remained upbeat about the outlook for 1966, saying that we "will have demonstrated that a free economy can both maintain full employment and avoid inflation—and do so without arbitrary controls."[3]

By this time (January 1966), many economists inside and outside the government viewed the ongoing economic expansion as jeopardizing price stability, but no official action was taken until 1967. To contain inflation, both Presidents Kennedy and Johnson used wage-price "guideposts" to jawbone industry and unions into rejecting unreasonable price or wage increases.[4] The Johnson administration also endorsed a 3.2 percent target as the standard of acceptable wage-price settlements based upon the 5-year annual average increase of output per man-hour (i.e., the increase in productivity).

During 1965 several industries abided by the 3.2 percent standard. But when inflationary trends in 1966 promoted administration economists to recalculate the acceptable level of wage-price increases at 3.6 percent, LBJ's advisers disagreed over whether the guidepost strategy should be kept, changed, or abandoned. In the end Johnson stood by the original 3.2 percent figure, despite economic realities. However, the unions and industry ceased to comply with that target; even Congress, in 1966, raised the minimum wage and federal salaries above that limit. The final blow to the wage-price guideposts came when a prolonged and costly strike by the International Association of Machinists against the airline industry resulted in a contract granting wage increases of 4.9 percent, a flagrant violation of Johnson's leadership. Though not openly acknowledged, by January 1967 the Johnson administration abandoned its 3.2 percent wage guidepost, and President Johnson had to consider using fiscal policy to wage the fight against inflation.

That month the CEA noted that, while the jobless rate fell to its lowest level since 1953, prices were also rising faster than any time since 1957. The December-to-December climb in the CPI was 1.9 percent in 1965, but jumped to 3.4 percent in 1966, 3.0 percent in 1967, and 4.7 percent in 1968. These numbers do not seem large by today's standards, but what then concerned policymakers was that the inflation rate had doubled since 1965. Moreover, the Johnson administration was proposing substantial increases in federal spending at a time when the U.S. economy was approaching the full-employment level. This raised the prospect that increased demand in an economy near the full-employment level would cause prices to rise.

The basic problem facing President Johnson is revealed in Figures 8.1 and 8.2. As Figure 8.1 shows, by the mid-1960s the unemployment rate was approaching a ten-year low, a level indicating that the economy was operating at or very near the full-employment level. During this same period, the U.S. was escalating its involvement in the Vietnam War, a policy leading to a substantial increase in spending for defense over the next several years (Figure 8.2). Unfortunately, President Johnson was conducting a simultaneous War on Poverty, a policy that resulted in substantial increases in nondefense spending over the same period. Thus, at a time when the economy was already at the full-employment level, the president was proposing substantial increases in federal spending, increases that would likely overstimulate aggregate demand and increase inflation. The appropriate fiscal response, Johnson was told by most of his economic advisors, was to increase taxes, which would both avoid deficit spending and reduce aggregate demand, thereby diminishing the possibility of increasing inflation. Proposing a tax increase was politically risky, however, particularly since the president believed he needed to spend his political capital on other policies, such as prosecuting the Vietnam War, promoting the War on Poverty, and enacting civil rights legislation.

What Johnson did (after some delay) was recommend a modest surcharge on corporate and personal income taxes (exempting the lowest income earners) and the accelerated collection of corporate tax receipts. His decision was made in August 1967, but deadlock in Congress pre-

Figure 8.1   Civilian Unemployment Rate, 1955–1969

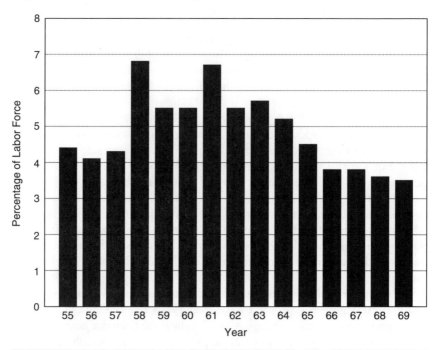

Source: Department of Labor, Bureau of Labor Statistics.

vented action until June 1968, when the Revenue and Expenditure Control Act was enacted. It authorized a 10 percent income tax surcharge on personal income retroactive to April 1, 1968, and on corporate income retroactive to January 1, 1968. This levy remained at 10 percent through 1969, dropped to 5 percent in 1970, and ended on June 30, 1970.

The verdict by most economists is that Johnson's surcharge was too little and came too late. This episode called into question the liberal faith, expressed by Kennedy's CEA, that decision makers could (or would) fine-tune the economy using stabilization policy. In the opinion of two economists,

> the experience of 1968–69 should be sobering but not stunning. Fine tuning is difficult—perhaps even impossible—given our present state of knowledge. Any stabilization move so subtle as to seek to alter the unemployment rate by a single point or less runs the risk of being nullified

Figure 8.2   Changes in Federal Spending, FY62–FY69, Measured in Constant (FY82) Dollars

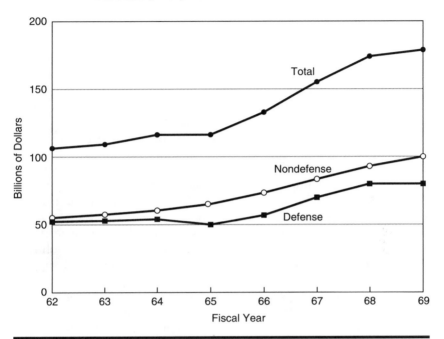

Source: *Budget of the U.S. Government 1992*, Part VII, Historical Tables, Table 3.1.

by unpredictable (or at least unpredicted) shifts in the strength of private (or public) demand. . . .[5]

The CPI rose much faster in 1969 (5.4 percent) and 1970 (5.9 percent) despite the surcharge. This inflationary trend was not arrested until the recession of 1969–70 took hold, after which the CPI grew at 4.3 percent during 1971.

The same economic logic that guided Kennedy's proposed 1963 tax cut underlay Johnson's 1968 surcharge, but Johnson's objective was to reduce aggregate demand by cutting disposable income of consumers and businesses. Arthur Okun, who chaired the CEA in 1968, agrees that its impact was less than anticipated:

It was hoped and expected that this legislative victory would usher in a period of gradual disinflation. . . . A real growth rate of about 2 percent between mid-1968 and mid-1969 was expected to push the unemployment rate up slightly above 4 percent from its 3½ percent level of the time. . . . Actual developments did not follow the flight plan. The slow-down was not nearly so pronounced as had been anticipated. Still, economic activity did change pace.[6]

One miscalculation by the CEA was its $6.7 billion underestimation of consumption spending. Econometric models developed later by Okun determined that the surcharge softened demand for nondurable goods and services but had little effect on durable goods, especially automobiles.[7] Nor did the surcharge have much effect on business investment or housing construction. Okun concludes that the 1968 surcharge was the correct action, but inadequate to the problem then faced.

A more important question is, why was enactment of the surcharge so late in coming? In December 1965, Gardner Ackley (who replaced Walter Heller as CEA Chairman) warned that a tax increase was necessary given the size of the upcoming FY67 budget (beginning July 1, 1966). President Johnson did not accept that advice. The failure to raise taxes in 1966 Okun viewed as "the first defeat of the new economics by the old politics."[8] Johnson's decision was partly based upon his assessment that a tax increase would not pass Congress in 1966.[9] It seems likely that Johnson was also afraid that an income tax increase would weaken public support for the Vietnam War and jeopardize his Great Society as well.

It has also been alleged that LBJ was not entirely to blame, given that his economic advisers offered conflicting advice during this period.[10] President Johnson sought advice from many people, including Congressman Wilbur Mills, who chaired the Ways and Means Committee and unalterably opposed any tax increase. However, Gardner Ackley claims Johnson's decision against raising taxes "was against the unanimous advice of his presumably principal advisers in this area: the Treasury, Council, and Budget Bureau."[11]

Nobody can force a president to accept the advice of the CEA (or anyone else), and here Johnson was asked to consider a policy with negative political overtones. How likely would it have been for Congress to approve an income tax surcharge in 1966, an election year? Ackley concluded, "when he recommended it [a tax hike] . . . and didn't get it till July 1968, and this under circumstances in which the evidence as to what was happening was obvious to everyone, convinces me that his political judgment was absolutely right: he couldn't have gotten a tax increase [in 1966]."[12]

It may be that no macroeconomic policy could have relieved the inflationary pressures fueled by massive Vietnam War expenditures. Some critics would argue that the surcharge, even coming earlier, would have had little effect unless coupled with deep cuts in domestic spending. Although President Johnson was alerted to the inflation problem in Decem-

ber 1965, his request for a surcharge was not transmitted to Congress until **205**
August 3, 1967, and final legislative action took until June 28, 1968. This
was more than two years after the CEA first recognized the need for fiscal
restraint. This episode illustrates the *internal lags* accompanying fiscal policy. There is always a delay between the recognition of an economic problem and the ability of decision makers to formulate a policy response. In
addition, it shows that "fine tuning" remains a political decision, whatever
its technical possibilities.

Nixon's Incomes Policy

The year 1968 was not a good one for the Democratic party.
President Johnson bowed to popular pressures that he not seek reelection.
The Vietnam War was dragging on; there were riots in America's big cities;
and the Democrats nominated Hubert Humphrey amidst antiwar dem-
onstrations in the streets of Chicago. From the political right, Alabama's
Governor George Wallace campaigned for the White House as the American Independent party candidate, and many conservatives of both major
parties joined in attacking Johnson's Great Society domestic programs. It
was in this era of political turmoil that Richard Nixon, defeated eight
years earlier by John F. Kennedy, won his first of two terms as president.

As the 1970s approached, inflation displaced unemployment as the
most important economic problem. To ease inflationary pressures, the
Nixon administration adopted a gradualist approach using fiscal and monetary policy that became known as its economic "game plan." Excluded
initially was any consideration of **wage-price controls**, limits on increases
in prices and wages established and enforced by the government. Nixon
had worked in the Office of Price Administration during World War II,
and that experience led him to conclude that wage-price controls "can
never be administered equitably and are not compatible with a free economy."[13] His view was not supported by every economist in the administration, however.

Among the dissenters was Murray Weidenbaum, assistant secretary of
the treasury, who in March 1970 sent memoranda to Paul Volcker, then
undersecretary for monetary affairs, arguing that price rises were the result
of **cost-push inflation**—i.e., were due to the increased costs of production,
not excessive demand. Since cost-push inflation is largely immune from
fiscal and monetary restraints, he urged evaluation of alternative policies,
including wage-price controls.[14]

The first public challenge to the gradualist game plan came from Arthur Burns, newly appointed chairman of the Federal Reserve Board. In a
speech on April 29, 1970, Burns said that "we have moved from demand-

206   pull inflation to a transitional phase in which cost-push adjustments are prevalent." And on May 18 he added that "there may be a useful—albeit a very modest—role for a prices and incomes policy to play."[15] Paul McCracken, who was Nixon's CEA chairman, reacted by restating the administration's opposition to any wage-price controls.

This debate increased when George Shultz was appointed director of the newly created Office of Management and Budget. Shultz also was opposed to wage-price controls (or any other guidelines policy), and he hoped that increased productivity would make individual markets more efficient and thereby dampen inflationary pressures. Three anti-inflation steps Shultz did support were announced by President Nixon on June 17, 1970: a National Commission on Productivity, a Regulations and Purchasing Review Board, and a series of "inflation alerts" by the CEA to draw attention to excessive wage or price increases. These actions were mainly symbolic and represented no shift in macroeconomic policy by McCracken and Shultz, who were then Nixon's key advisers. Three "inflation alerts" were issued by the CEA (on August 7, 1970; December 1, 1970; and April 13, 1971), but as De Marchi observed, "There was a sharp distinction drawn between turning the spotlight on significant wage or price increases and actual intervention to secure more moderate behavior in particular industries."[16]

Inflation eased during the first nine months of 1970, only to rebound during the fourth quarter. The result was that *both* inflation and unemployment were higher in 1970 compared to the previous year, something the CEA did not anticipate.[17] Sensing that Nixon was politically vulnerable, the Democrats in Congress forced passage of the Economic Stabilization Act of 1970 (as an amendment to the Defense Production Act of 1950), which armed the president with standby authority to freeze salaries, wages, prices, and rents. Nixon reluctantly signed that bill, but affirmed his personal opposition to controls.

Political pressures mounted on President Nixon to utilize his new wage-price authority. The Business Council and the Committee for Economic Development (CED) called for more activist federal policies, and Fed chairman Arthur Burns joined forces with those critics. In a speech on December 7, 1970, Burns said, "It would be desirable to supplement our monetary and fiscal policies with a prices and incomes policy," and added, "We are dealing, practically speaking, with a new problem— namely, persistent inflation in the face of substantial unemployment—and that the classical remedies may not work well enough or fast enough in this case."[18] One week later Nixon moved to confront the economic problems by reshaping his advisory team, appointing John Connally as his new secretary of the treasury.

Then a conservative Democrat and former three-term governor of Texas, Connally was a shrewd political operative with ties to Texas oilmen. At first he had no firm views on wage-price controls, but shortly he became sympathetic to the arguments of Weidenbaum and Volcker that standby wage-price controls should at least be considered. During the spring of 1971 the jobless rate continued upwards and passed the 6 percent mark without any reduction in the inflation rate. At a meeting in June at Camp David, McCracken recommended economic stimulation to hold down unemployment, and Connally agreed, but President Nixon sided with the opposing view of Shultz that no action be taken.

Connally was now the administration's chief economic spokesman and, after that meeting, he told a press conference that the administration contemplated no tax cut, no added federal spending, no wage-price review board, and no controls. Within one month of this unambiguous statement, official policy had shifted to wage-price controls. A major development was the series of inflationary wage settlements that were negotiated in 1971, the last being a thirty percent wage increase over three years won by the United Steel Workers in August. Republicans in Congress also made known their concerns that a deteriorating economy would jeopardize their party's chances in the 1972 elections.

During late July and early August, Connally apparently persuaded President Nixon that wage-price controls were the only alternative, and on August 2 and 9 details of what became known as the New Economic Policy were ironed out in meetings between Connally and OMB director Shultz. At first, Nixon wanted to delay the implementation of wage-price controls, but his hand was forced by events. A badly eroding balance-of-payments situation had brought on an international monetary crisis (discussed in Chapter 6). On August 13 Paul Volcker contacted Connally at his Texas ranch to apprise him of the deteriorating international economic situation, and Connally returned to Washington and persuaded President Nixon to take decisive action on various economic fronts.

On the evening of August 13 Nixon met with McCracken, Shultz, Volcker, Connally, Herbert Stein, Arthur Burns, and other economic advisers at Camp David. "By the time the meeting assembled," recalls McCracken, "the decision to go to wage and price controls had already been made."[19] Now not even George Shultz expressed opposition. On Sunday, August 15, 1971, President Nixon announced his new economic policy to the American people over radio and television. This dramatic about-face by the president was a political success. The new economic policy showed decisive executive action in the face of an economic crisis, undermined the Democratic party's ability to exploit that issue, and

208 proved to be immensely popular. A Gallup poll taken one week later found 73 percent supporting his decision.[20]

Nixon's new economic policy began with a ninety-day freeze on wages and prices. The conversion of U.S. dollars into gold was suspended by the United States, and a 10 percent surcharge was levied on all imports. There would be a reduction in federal spending, a tax credit for new capital investment by business, and repeal of the excise tax on automobiles. In addition, a scheduled January 1973 increase in the personal income tax exemption would be moved up to January 1972. Thus ended the gradualist economic game plan that had guided the Nixon administration during its first thirty months; in its place, the first *peacetime* use of mandatory wage-price controls in the nation's history began.

The Nixon **prices and incomes policy** evolved through four stages. The immediate ninety-day freeze on all wages and prices became known as *Phase I*. It was very popular because most Americans believed that drastic action was called for and that everybody was asked to sacrifice equally for the common good. A freeze sounded obvious enough, a stopgap measure to allow the government enough time to develop its Phase II program, but its implementation was anything but simple. As explained by Douglas Greer,

> No less than four government agencies got their fingers in the enforcement stew—Internal Revenue Service, Office of Emergency Preparedness, Agricultural Stabilization and Conservation Service, and Cost of Living Council, the last of which was specially created to oversee the controls program. In the short span of 90 days, these agencies had to answer no fewer than 800,000 inquiries at field office level, 2435 special exemption requests, 400 executive-level questions, and 75 key policy issues. . . .[21]

Phase I decelerated wage and price increases. During these ninety days (from August to November 1971) the CPI rose at an annual rate of 1.0 percent compared to the 4.5 percent registered during the preceding six-month period.[22]

Phase II lasted fourteen months, from mid-November 1971 until January 1973. The Cost of Living Council held overall authority, but prices were monitored by a Price Commission, and a Pay Board reviewed wages and salaries. Since the Pay Board and the Price Commission relied on only about 1,700 IRS agents, they focused their energies on big corporations and unions, the assumption being that greater competition in other sectors of the economy would hold down wages and prices there. (In contrast, during World War II about 60,000 agents supported by virtually every household in America monitored wages and prices.)

The Price Commission grouped companies according to size and used different enforcement strategies. The objective under Phase II was to allow price increases to cover any increases in production costs, which varied according to business. This approach required case-by-case reviews and permitted exemptions to the guidelines, which were set at 5.5 percent for wage increases and 2.5 percent for increases in prices. In terms of wages, the government softened where strong unions were involved: the average rate of approved increases in union contracts during 1972 was 7.0 percent, whereas smaller approved increases for nonunion workers caused their wages to rise by only 5.6 percent. A general assessment of Phase II is that "*if* there was any effect at all, prices were restrained more than wages."[23]

Phase III began on January 11, 1973. The prenotification and reporting requirements were ended, so Phase III relied on self-administration by companies and unions to comply with the wage-price guidelines. Both the Pay Board and the Price Commission were abolished. Since most people viewed Phase III as the beginning of the end of controls, prices began to creep upwards. During the next six months the CPI rose by an 8.0 percent annual rate, mainly because food and energy were exempted from controls; food prices rose 20 percent and energy prices increased 19 percent during the first six months of 1973. These steep increases also caused the prices of nonfood commodities and services to rise, by 4.8 percent and 4.3 percent respectively, which were above the guidelines.[24]

This renewed inflation prompted demands from members of Congress and the news media that wage-price controls be restored. Bowing to political pressure at a time when the Watergate scandals were reaching a climax, President Nixon ignored the advice of his CEA and, in June 1973, reimposed a price freeze. In response to CEA Chairman Herbert Stein's remark, "You know, Mr. President, you can't walk on water twice," Nixon retorted, "Maybe you can if it's frozen."[25] But Stein correctly foresaw that the result of this new price freeze would be "a total disaster. There were all the visible symptoms of a price control system gone wild. Cattle were being withheld from market, chickens were being drowned, and the food store shelves were being emptied."[26] This second price freeze, lasting from mid-June to mid-August, was followed by Phase IV.

Phase IV eased into a period of decontrol that ended on April 30, 1974, the termination date of the Economic Stabilization Act. Congress refused to extend its life, and by now almost everyone—economists, labor leaders, business executives—sensed the limitations of wage-price controls. To prevent inflationary pressures from beginning again, the Cost of Living Council attempted to decontrol the economy sector-by-sector and thus allow gradual wage and price increases. But since America's economy is so interdependent, wage-price rises in one sector would inevitably affect

210   others, so increases in the Consumer Price Index were experienced as each
sector of the economy was freed from controls. The CPI rose three times
faster toward the end of Phase IV than it had before Phase I began.

   This experiment with a prices and incomes policy was a policy failure,
though not a political failure. Phase I was very popular with the American
people, and surveys find that many Americans continue to support wage-
price controls as an anti-inflation strategy. Unfortunately, wage and price
controls appear to have done little to restrain inflation. In each of the two
six-month periods preceding the onset of Phase 1 in August 1971, the
inflation rate was 4.5 percent. Over the 33-month period encompassed by
the four phases, prices rose over 19 percent, for an annual rate of 7 percent.
To be sure, price increases moderated significantly during Phase 1, and to
a lesser extent in Phase 2 (Figure 8.3), but price increases did not significantly moderate until the onset of a recession in 1976, when the inflation

Figure 8.3   Annual Rate of Inflation Before, During, and After
Imposition of Nixon Administration Prices and Incomes
Policy

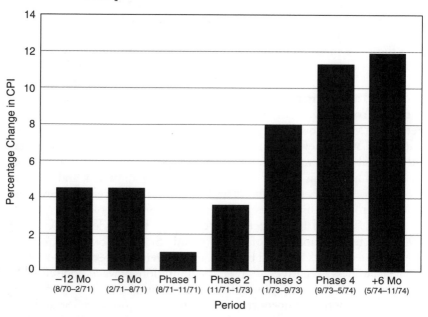

Source: Calculated from CPI-U data provided by Bureau of Labor Statistics.

rate fell to 5.8 percent (more than one percentage point higher than the "unacceptably high" rate that brought on the prices and incomes policy).

Though Richard Nixon was renowned as a conservative, his use of wage-price controls showed that his policies were guided as much by political opportunities as by ideology. At the same time, his was the first administration to face a period of intense stagflation. This was something that neither the original Keynesian theory nor its 1960s "new economics" version had a clear solution for, which rendered it difficult to develop a policy that was both effective and politically acceptable. This would not be the last time that a president would be forced to decide between giving the country what it needs and what it wants, all the while guided by conflicting technical advice.

Carter's Reversal on Inflation

As a moderate Democrat, Jimmy Carter was faced with having to reassure the party's liberal activists that he would not abandon traditional Democratic concerns. This he accomplished by spelling out an ambitious domestic agenda (including national health insurance) and by espousing a liberal economic program. He committed himself to cutting the unemployment rate to 4 percent by the end of his term and endorsed the Humphrey-Hawkins full-employment bill pending before the Congress. To fulfill his employment pledge, President Carter recommended to Congress a two-year, $31 billion economic stimulation package. Included was a one-time income tax rebate of $50 on 1976 returns, a change in the standard personal deduction, investment tax credits for business, a doubling of the jobs funded under CETA (Comprehensive Employment and Training Act) and other training programs, and more money for revenue-sharing (a grant of relatively unrestricted funds to states and localities).

In April 1977—suddenly and without warning—Carter withdrew his backing for the $50 tax rebate and the investment tax credit, a move that left his congressional allies dismayed. The reason for this policy reversal was a surge in consumer spending during the first quarter of 1977, though that reasoning was not accepted by all his advisers. CEA chairman Schultze favored the tax rebate to sustain the economic momentum, but OMB director Bert Lance and Fed chairman Arthur Burns joined in opposition on the grounds that added stimulation might rekindle inflation.[27] Fear of inflation was President Carter's overriding concern, as he later acknowledged:

> The [tax rebate] bill passed the House quite rapidly but was delayed in the Senate. To Budget Director Bert Lance, Treasury Secretary Mike

Blumenthal, and me, this rebate now seemed not only unnecessary but likely to spur inflation. . . . My other advisers were convinced that we should go ahead with it, either because they believed it was necessary or because my reputation for consistency would be damaged if I reversed our earlier decision. In April, I decided to bite the bullet, notify the key members of Congress, and cancel my request for the quick tax reduction.[28]

In May 1977 Congress approved a scaled-down version of the Tax Reduction and Simplification Act, as well as public works, public service jobs, and employment/training programs.

Carter presided over an economic expansion through 1977 and 1978, but his CEA believed nonetheless that a "GNP gap" existed, reflected in an unemployment rate that was too high. The 1977 jobless rate was 7.1 percent, barely lower than the 7.7 percent figure of 1976, so the 1978 *Economic Report* recommended to Congress more tax cuts (amounting to $25 billion) and other reforms, effective at the start of the next fiscal year. However, in May President Carter again changed his mind, reducing the tax cut request to $20 billion. This revision also was triggered by White House fears that inflation would be higher than predicted. Congress eventually approved $18.9 billion of new stimulation in the Revenue Act of 1978.

The CEA may have overestimated the degree of slack in the economy, because in 1978 the macroeconomic indicators performed better than the CEA had earlier predicted. Carter's economic advisers came to the realization that the jobless rate was falling too quickly (from 7.1 percent in 1977 to 6.1 percent in 1978) and that there was not very much excess capacity in the economy. Looking back upon this period of economic uncertainty, Charles Schultze characterized the policy problem in this way:

> . . . it became clear to us by the end of 1978, which made it too late, that not so much the *level* of unemployment but the *speed* with which it had come down was a problem . . . we pretty much reached the conclusion that one of the problems in late 1978 . . . was that we had pulled the rate of unemployment down too fast.[29]

Given inflationary pressures, the Carter administration reluctantly concluded that the unemployment rate probably could not be cut much below 6 percent, but this understanding could not be acknowledged publicly. Liberals in the Democratic party and organized labor would have balked at the idea.

The stage was set for the key economic reversal, which came in the 1979 *Economic Report*. The task now, President Carter said, was "to manage an economy operating close to its capacity," so that "reducing inflation must be our top economic priority."[30] Scant reference was made to unemployment, although this problem had been high on the legislative agenda of the Congress during 1978.

In 1978 Congress passed the Humphrey-Hawkins Bill, named after Democratic co-sponsors Senator Hubert Humphrey (D-MN) and Congressman Augustus Hawkins (D-CA). Both men were upset with the Nixon administration's emphasis on fighting inflation, and this legislation was supported by organized labor, civil rights groups, and liberals. But its immediate political effect was to embarrass President Carter, who had to disclaim its full-employment objectives shortly thereafter.

As enacted, the Humphrey-Hawkins Act mandated that the first *Economic Report* pursuant to the law (the 1979 *Report*) establish the goals of a 4 percent unemployment rate and a 3 percent increase in the CPI for the year 1983. But a loophole in the statute allowed the president to alter the timetable for reaching those goals, beginning with the 1980 *Economic Report*. Should he do so, the president had to declare the year in which he expected to attain the unemployment target. President Carter invoked this exception, as the 1980 *Economic Report* reveals.

> Reduction of the unemployment rate to 4 percent by 1983 ... would require an extraordinary high economic growth rate. Efforts to stimulate the economy to achieve so high a growth rate would be counterproductive. The immediate result would be extremely strong upward pressure on wage rates, costs, and prices. . . .[31]

President Carter reminded the country that the short-term Phillips curve exacts a heavy cost in terms of inflation should the jobless rate be driven down below its natural rate. While the natural unemployment rate was judged to be about 4 percent in the 1950s and 1960s, by the 1970s most economists believed that it had risen to approximately the 6–7 percent range, a change due partly to the large numbers of women then entering the work force. Cutting inflation from the 1978 rate of 9.0 percent to the 1983 goal of 3 percent was, declared Carter, an "equally unrealistic expectation. Recent experience indicates that the momentum of inflation built up over the past 15 years is extremely strong. A practical goal for reducing inflation must take this fact into account."[32]

President Carter extended the timetable for achieving the Humphrey-Hawkins economic goals. The 4 percent unemployment rate target was pushed back to 1985 and the 3 percent inflation goal was set for 1988. Thus, just two years after the Democratic majority in Congress passed Humphrey-Hawkins, a fellow Democrat in the White House explained how unreasonable its macroeconomic agenda was. But the liberals and organized labor had always thought that Carter's support for the bill was lukewarm, at best, and this action by the White House confirmed their worst suspicions.

The difficulties between Carter and liberal Democrats aligned with organized labor worsened when reports circulated about his forthcoming FY80 budget. When the Democratic party held a mini-convention in Memphis during the fall of 1978, Senator Edward Kennedy (D-MA) received thunderous applause when he declared:

> I support the fight against inflation. But no such fight can be effective or successful unless the fight is fair. The party that tore itself apart over Vietnam in the 1960s cannot afford to tear itself apart today over budget cuts in basic social programs. . . . There could be few more divisive issues for America and for our party than a Democratic policy for drastic slashes in the federal budget at the expense of the elderly, the poor, the black, the sick, the cities and the unemployed.[33]

A year later Kennedy announced his candidacy for the Democratic presidential nomination, but within five months his challenge had been beaten back by Carter. Kennedy refused to accept his defeat in the primaries and carried his challenge to Carter's renomination to the party convention, where his supporters forced President Carter to accept minority planks on unemployment in the party's platform. One asked for a $12 billion antirecession package; another pledged "no fiscal action, no monetary action, no budgetary action" causing "significant" increases in unemployment; and a third advocated a program to guarantee "a job for every American who is able to work as our single highest domestic priority."[34] Though Kennedy could not win, his challenge severely handicapped the efforts by Jimmy Carter to reshape his economic program in time for the 1980 election.

Having temporarily contained the liberal wing of his own party, Jimmy Carter turned to bolstering his faltering popularity with the electorate. In January 1980 the CEA had revised federal spending for FY80 upwards by $32 billion from the figure proposed one year earlier by the president. The early signs that the deficit for FY80 would be larger than predicted undermined the image of fiscal austerity Carter had tried to portray. The problem was compounded when Carter submitted his budget for FY81 to Congress. While real defense spending was to be increased, total expenditures adjusted for inflation would remain constant, and President Carter anticipated cutting the deficit to $16 billion in FY81. But there was a credibility gap in these statistics given the fact of increasing federal expenditures during FY80.

The business community reacted accordingly. The announcement of the FY81 budget was followed by a sharp decline in long-term bond prices

as the prime interest rate hit 21 percent. Because the president failed again **215**
to balance the budget, Wall Street expressed a strong vote of no confidence in Carter's economic program. To save this situation, the president
announced in February 1980 that he was meeting with the Democratic
leadership in Congress to revise his FY81 budget. After a series of meetings
lasting eleven days, at the end of March the White House recommended
added cuts of $3 billion in the ongoing FY80 budget and $17 billion in
the revised FY81 budget.

But a bad economy during 1980 worsened the budgetary outlook for
the year. The original budget deficit of $29 billion assumed that real ec-
onomic growth during 1980 would be 3.25 percent, that the inflation rate
would be 6.25 percent, and that unemployment would increase to no more
than 6.25 percent. On all three counts the economy did much worse.
When the FY80 budget ended on September 30, 1980, little more than a
month before election day, the estimated deficit was nearly double the
amount that the Carter administration had predicted. The recession bot-
tomed-out later than anticipated and at exactly the wrong political time.
From the January 1980 peak to the July 1981 peak the business cycle lasted
only 18 months, but the trough came in July of 1980—four months before
election day.

The economy was only one factor working against Carter's reelection.
The Soviets had invaded Afghanistan, and religious fundamentalists in
Iran seized the U.S. embassy and held Americans hostage for 444 days.
Carter was unable to persuade independent voters that his anti-inflation
program was real, and Republicans were rallying behind the promises of
supply-side economics, championed by their candidate, Ronald Reagan.
Within the Democratic party, liberals also abandoned Carter's candidacy;
the Americans for Democratic Action declared that "Carter's failure to
adhere to the basic tenets of the Democratic platform on which he ran
. . . have eroded the vital differences between the two major parties and
suggest that party principle and platform matter little to him."[35] In the
end, Carter satisfied nobody, and opinion polls showed conclusively that
the majority voted *against* Carter rather than *for* Ronald Reagan in 1980.[36]

FINAL OBSERVATIONS

The Johnson income tax surcharge and Nixon's wage-price controls failed to stop inflationary pressures, which continued to worsen under
Carter until he had little alternative but to reverse his economic game
plan. Given the public perception of the president as the manager of
prosperity, it is not surprising that each of these presidents, especially

216   Carter, has been blamed for the various economic woes that afflicted the
U.S. economy during this period. Perhaps a more balanced view is that
there is plenty of blame to be passed around.

Sharing the blame begins within the president's immediate circle: the
presidential economic advisors. During the period from which these episodes are drawn, the dominant macroeconomic theory, Keynesianism,
struggled to explain how an economy could simultaneously experience
both inflation and high unemployment. At the same time, economists
discovered the limits of their own art—the sheer difficulty of accurately
tracking and forecasting the performance of the economy and the technical problems associated with fine-tuning such a complex social system.

Then, too, some of the blame for these failed policies should be laid
at the steps of Congress. While President Johnson can be faulted for not
promoting the surcharge earlier, no doubt he correctly sensed that Congress would not approve a tax hike before the 1966 midterm elections.
The Democrats in Congress who enacted wage-price controls did so precisely to embarrass President Nixon, who then felt pressured by events to
consider a prices and incomes policy, something he had long opposed.
And Carter might have been better off had the Congress been under the
control of the Republican party during his term. Not only did the Democrats force his hand by enacting Humphrey-Hawkins, but they opposed
Carter's economic policies and resisted the popular demand that inflation
be brought under control.

A third party for sharing the blame is the public itself—or, more precisely, the voting public. While we desire low inflation and high employment, quality services and low taxes, our own short-term and highly personal perspectives on economic performance reward political leaders who
offer benefits (e.g., lower taxes or increased Social Security payments) and
ignore or defer the costs. This is particularly evident in the first two episodes, where Johnson resisted imposing the tax increase that was needed[37]
because of fear over the public response, and Nixon chose the popular
action of a prices and incomes policy rather than a more long-term assault
on inflation through fiscal and monetary policy.

A final perspective is that no blame is really necessary, because the
performance of the U.S. economy and of economic policy during this
period was actually relatively strong. The rate of inflation grew steadily
over the period 1965–81, exceeding 10 percent in four years (1974, 1979,
1980, and 1981), a barrier exceeded only one other time (1947) during
the entire postwar period.[38] However, during the same period the U.S.
economy was subjected to a pair of "oil shocks" (1973–74 and 1979),
during each of which the price of imported oil quadrupled over its previous
price level. (The rate of price inflation in the energy sector exceeded 25

percent during three of the four high inflation years, for example.) These significant inflationary events were essentially beyond the control of any U.S. political leader, including Presidents Nixon and Carter.

The record on employment is even more positive in retrospect. It is true that unemployment during the 1970s (and much of the 1980s as well) remained nearly twice as high as the very low levels of the mid- to late 1960s, but the number of people entering the work force also swelled during the same period. Because of both the arrival of the baby boom demographic cohort and the larger number of women participating in the work force, the number of people seeking employment increased greatly, particularly after about 1975. As a result, even though the unemployment rate did not fall appreciably during the late 1970s, the employment performance of the economy was quite strong. For example, while the unemployment rate was 7.1 percent in both 1977 and 1980, the number of employed civilian workers actually grew from 92 million to 99 million. In fact, although the popular perception of the Carter presidency is one of economic disarray, the number of new jobs created during the Carter years (10.5 million) exceeded the number created in either the first or second Reagan administrations (5.7 million and 10.0 million, respectively). The average annual increase in jobs during the Carter years (2.6 million) is more than a third larger than the comparable figure for the eight Reagan years. Although during these years both inflation and unemployment rates very clearly departed from a set of ideal goals like the Humphrey-Hawkins goals, as in all such evaluations, an overall assessment of the efficacy of government economic policy depends upon which aspects of the economy the analyst feels deserve the greatest emphasis.

KEY TERMS

Phillips curve, wage-price controls, cost-push inflation, prices and incomes policy

ADDITIONAL READING

Anderson, James E. and Jared E. Hazleton. *Managing Macroeconomic Policy: The Johnson Presidency.* Austin: University of Texas Press, 1986. Drawing heavily on Johnson's presidential papers, two political scientists analyze decision making as applied to fiscal and monetary policy, wage-price controls, and foreign economic policy.

218 Baumer, Donald C. and Carl E. Van Horn. *The Politics of Unemployment.* Washington, DC: CQ Press, 1985. An overview of federal jobs programs with special attention to CETA under both Jimmy Carter and Ronald Reagan.

Goodwin, Craufurd D., ed. *Exhortation and Controls: The Search for a Wage-Price Policy 1945–1971.* Washington, DC: The Brookings Institution, 1975. A collection of scholarly articles on the use of "jawboning" to curb wage-price increases from Truman through the early Nixon administration.

Meyer, Jack A. *Wage-Price Standards and Economic Policy.* Washington, DC: American Enterprise Institute for Public Policy Research, 1982. Studies the U.S. Council on Wage and Price Stability during 1974–1980, giving primary attention to its implementation of wage-price standards under President Carter.

Pierce, Lawrence. *The Politics of Fiscal Policy Formation.* Pacific Palisades, CA: Goodyear, 1971. A solid examination of the political process underlying fiscal policymaking, with special attention to the 1968 income tax surcharge decision.

Silk, Leonard. *Nixonomics.* New York: Praeger, 1973. Well-written popularized account of macroeconomic policymaking during President Nixon's first term.

Weber, Arnold R. *In Pursuit of Price Stability: The Wage-Price Freeze of 1971.* Washington, DC: The Brookings Institution, 1973. The director of the Cost of Living Council discusses how Phase I of President Nixon's wage-price freeze was formulated and implemented.

NOTES

1. This brief discussion of the Phillips curve is based on a more detailed treatment in Paul A. Samuelson and William D. Nordhaus, *Economics*, 14th ed. (New York: McGraw-Hill, 1992), pp. 606–612.

2. *Annual Report of the Council of Economic Advisers*, 1965 (Washington, DC: U.S. Government Printing Office, 1965), p. 62.

3. *Economic Report of the President*, 1966 (Washington, DC: U.S. Government Printing Office, 1966), p. 13.

4. James L. Cochrane, "The Johnson Administration: Moral Suasion Goes to War," in Craufurd D. Goodwin, ed., *Exhortation and Controls: The Search for a Wage-Price Policy 1945–1971* (Washington, DC: The Brookings Institution, 1975), p. 203. Our discussion of wage-price controls is based upon this excellent article.

5. Alan S. Blinder and Robert M. Solow, "Analytical Foundations of Fiscal Policy," in Alan S. Blinder, Robert M. Solow, George F. Break, Peter O. Steiner, and Dick Netzer, *The Economics of Public Finance* (Washington, DC: The Brookings Institution, 1974), p. 115.

6. Arthur M. Okun, *The Political Economy of Prosperity* (Washington, DC: The Brookings Institution, 1970), pp. 91–92.

7.   Arthur M. Okun, "The Personal Tax Surcharge and Consumer Demand **219** 1968–1970," *Brookings Papers on Economic Activity*, No. 1 (1971), pp. 167–211.

8.   Okun, *The Political Economy of Prosperity*, p. 71.

9.   Charles E. McLure, Jr., "Fiscal Failure: Lessons of the Sixties," in *Economic Policy and Inflation in the Sixties* (Washington, DC: American Enterprise Institute for Public Policy Research, 1972), p. 11.

10.   John W. Sloan, "President Johnson, The Council of Economic Advisers, and the Failure to Raise Taxes in 1966 and 1967," *Presidential Studies Quarterly* 15 (Winter 1985), pp. 89–98.

11.   Erwin C. Hargrove and Samuel A. Morley, eds., *The President and the Council of Economic Advisers: Interviews with CEA Chairmen* (Boulder, CO: Westview Press, 1984), p. 251.

12.   Ibid., pp. 254–255.

13.   Quoted in A. James Reichley, *Conservatives in an Age of Change: The Nixon and Ford Administrations* (Washington, DC: The Brookings Institution, 1981), p. 205.

14.   Neil de Marchi, "The First Nixon Administration: Prelude to Controls," in Goodwin, ed., *Exhortation and Controls: The Search for a Wage-Price Policy 1945–1971*, p. 315.

15.   Ibid., p. 316.

16.   Ibid., p. 322.

17.   *Economic Report of the President, 1971* (Washington, DC: U.S. Government Printing Office, 1971), p. 60.

18.   Quoted in Reichley, *Conservatives in an Age of Change*, p. 217.

19.   Quoted in ibid., p. 224.

20.   Quoted in ibid., p. 225.

21.   Douglas F. Greer, *Industrial Organization and Public Policy* (New York: Macmillan Publishing Co., 1980), p. 556.

22.   Calculated by the authors. The actual CPI-U figures are as follows (1982–84 = 100): February 1971 = 39.9; August 1971 = 40.8; November 1971 = 40.9.

23.   Greer, *Industrial Organization and Public Policy*, p. 562–563.

24.   George P. Shultz and Kenneth W. Dam, *Economic Policy Behind the Headlines* (New York: W. W. Norton, 1977), p. 74. Also see their discussion of Nixon's prices and incomes policy on pp. 67–85.

25.   Ibid., p. 74.

26.   Herbert Stein, *Presidential Economics: The Making of Economic Policy from Roosevelt to Reagan and Beyond* (New York: Simon and Schuster, 1984), p. 186.

27.   "Such Friendly Quarrels," *The Economist* (August 6, 1977), p.22.

28.   Jimmy Carter, *Keeping Faith: Memoirs of a President* (New York: Bantam Books, 1982), p. 77.

220   29.   Hargrove and Morley, eds., *The President and the Council of Economic Advisers*, p. 482.

30.   *Economic Report of the President*, 1979 (Washington, DC: U.S. Government Printing Office, 1979), p. 3.

31.   *Economic Report of the President*, 1980 (Washington, DC: U.S. Government Printing Office, 1980), p. 9.

32.   Ibid., pp. 9–10.

33.   Reported in W. Bowman Cutter, "The Presidency and Economic Policy: A Tale of Two Budgets," in Michael Nelson, ed., *The Presidency and the Political System* (Washington, DC: CQ Press, 1984), p. 481.

34.   Jeff Fishel, *Presidents and Promises: From Campaign Pledge to Presidential Performance* (Washington, DC: CQ Press, 1985), p. 111.

35.   Reported in ibid., p. 86.

36.   See Kathleen A. Frankovic, "Public Opinion Trends," in Gerald M. Pomper, ed., *The Election of 1980* (Chatham, NJ: Chatham House Publishers, 1981). On p. 97 she concludes that "disapproval and dislike of the incumbent outweighed any other single explanation for supporting Ronald Reagan on Election Day." The same conclusion is reached in Paul R. Abramson, John H. Aldrich, and David W. Rohde, *Change and Continuity in the 1980 Elections*, Revised Edition (Washington, DC: CQ Press, 1983).

37.   This view that a tax increase was necessary is predicated first on the assumption that Johnson would not relent in his desire to simultaneously fight the Vietnam War and the War on Poverty, and second on the general Keynesian belief that fiscal policy affects economic performance by influencing aggregate demand. While the latter was widely accepted at the time that Johnson dealt with this question, later economic critics, such as supply-side economists, would question this assumption.

38.   The source for this discussion of prices and employment is the 1992 *Annual Report of the Council of Economic Advisors* (Washington, DC: Government Printing Office, February 1992), especially Table B-60, "Changes in Consumer Price Indexes, Commodities, and Services, 1929–91," and Table B-32, "Civilian Employment by Demographic Characteristics, 1954–91."

CHAPTER 9

Public Opinion and Economic Policy

The values Americans hold toward government and economics shape the fundamental character of the U.S. political economy. This is not to say that people have a well defined ideology about the political economy (they do not) or that they are knowledgeable about macroeconomic theory (they are not). Most citizens lack the time, energy, and inclination to become fully informed about such matters, although this does not stop them from expressing opinions about the political economy. But often what people believe carries more political significance than economic reality. An astute president will seek to mobilize public opinion to exert leadership over public policy, but the attitudes held by Americans are also a political constraint, limiting how macroeconomic goals are defined and what policy instruments may be used.

In this chapter we summarize the themes that characterize public opinion towards the political economy and then proceed to evaluate existing research that tries to determine what impact the public has on the conduct of macroeconomic policymaking. The questions we address include:

- What is the nature of U.S. public opinion with regard to the economy and to economic policy?

- To what extent does economic performance influence the voters' evaluations of political leaders?

- Have presidents deliberately manipulated macroeconomic policies to cultivate support among the voters?

222
- Do elections indicate with any precision the collective preference for macroeconomic policy?

GENERAL ATTITUDES TOWARDS ECONOMICS AND POLITICS

Capitalism

In the United States, macroeconomic policy operates through a capitalist economic framework, and Americans intertwine economics and politics so closely that capitalism is almost synonymous with democracy in many people's minds. One consequence is that "socialism" is deemed an illegitimate goal of public policy; government ownership of the means of production has never been advocated by any president (not even FDR in the depths of the Great Depression) or by either major political party.[1] Commenting on this history, Richard Hofstadter observes, "The major political traditions [in the United States] have shared a belief in the rights of property, the philosophy of economic individualism, the values of competition; they have accepted the economic virtues of capitalist culture as necessary qualities of man."[2]

The capitalist heritage flows from particular socioeconomic developments. One development was that—with the possible exception of the antebellum South, where race and class divided people into a caste system—the United States did not have a feudal tradition. Says Louis Hartz, "Where the aristocracies, peasantries, and proletariats of Europe are missing, where virtually everyone . . . has the mentality of an independent entrepreneur, two national impulses are bound to make themselves felt: the impulse towards democracy and the impulse towards capitalism."[3]

Historians also point to the vast undeveloped territories of the American West, which allowed the alienated to escape the East in search of greater economic opportunities. This "safety valve" function of the frontier moderated class tensions in America, unlike the situation in Europe, where most land was owned by the aristocracy. The U.S. also differed from Europe in that it experienced few radical political movements (with substantial influence) seeking to overthrow capitalism. In the United States, many socialists advocated government regulation of private property rather than class warfare, and when the working class organized into labor unions, they fought for limited goals, such as the right to collective bargaining, higher wages, and humane working conditions.[4]

The Constitution of 1789 did not mandate a laissez faire economy, but similar views of economic man and political man guided the framers who wrote that document. One was the belief that humankind was motivated not by altruism or reason but by self-gratification ("passions") and self-interest. The framers understood the dangers of economic conflict, and James Madison wrote in *Federalist* 10 that "the most common and durable source of factions has been the various and unequal distribution of property. Those who hold and those who are without property have ever formed distinct interests in society." Madison viewed society as being divided not into two classes (as did Karl Marx half a century later), but into a multitude of economic interests. To preserve liberty, Madison proposed governmental structures that made it difficult for the diverse social groups to unite into a tyrannical majority.

Both Federalists and Anti-Federalists accepted the view (propounded by Locke) that government cannot deprive people of their natural rights without their consent. This sentiment had been expressed clearly by Thomas Jefferson in the Declaration of Independence and was later embodied in the Bill of Rights. One natural right secured by the Fifth Amendment was private property, which the framers viewed as a bulwark against governmental tyranny.

Capitalism was not preordained by the Constitution, but shortly after its ratification the national government and capitalism became inextricably intertwined. What transformed this nation into a capitalist economy was the financial program of Alexander Hamilton, the first secretary of the treasury. Hamilton funded the national debt incurred during the Revolutionary War and persuaded Congress to assume payment of the states' debts as well. He sought to encourage commerce and industry, in contrast to Jefferson's ideal of an agricultural society, and raised a protective tariff to generate revenues and to insulate American industry from foreign competition. Hamilton also established the first Bank of the United States to assure the credit of the new nation. All these programs, as Forrest McDonald explains, underscored Hamilton's desire to engineer a new economic order based on laissez faire principles.

> [Hamilton proposed to use the public debt] to establish a system in which the value of all things would be set in the marketplace and measured in money—and in so doing, to erect a social order in which success, status, and power would derive from merit and industry rather than, as in the existing scheme of things, from inherited wealth or social position. . . .[5]

Elite Attitudes Towards the Economic Order

Even today, when people speak of capitalism they generally think in terms of those Hamiltonian ideals. It is synonymous with private

224   property, private enterprise, the profit motive, economic competition, and the marketplace. Like the framers, many Americans believe that individuals are guided by their self-interest and will be rewarded for their hard work, self-reliance, and thrift by enjoying the fruits of their labors. Scholarship on how elite and mass public opinion understand capitalism shows the persistence of these ideals in American political thought, though in many ways the reality of economic life in the United States departs from the mythology of capitalism.

Since the business community directly benefits from the popular beliefs underlying a capitalist system, corporate leaders should be very supportive of those economic values. A classic study published in the 1950s, *The American Business Creed*,[6] tried to determine whether any ideology characterized the thinking of business elites. The values of economic self-interest, profits, personal achievement, competition, and the marketplace were highly significant for all business elites but this research also uncovered two divergent strains in the business creed.

One was the "classical" outlook which "centers around the model of a decentralized, private, competitive capitalism in which the forces of supply and demand, operating through the price mechanism, regulate the economy."[7] Those holding this view were more committed to laissez faire economics; in contrast, the "managerial" viewpoint tried to accommodate the reality of big government, big labor, and big business in the modern industrial society. This "classical" versus "managerial" distinction separates small businesses from larger corporations. Small entrepreneurs feel that they suffer disadvantages from the costs of government regulations, labor unions, and unfair business practices by corporations, with the result that owners of small businesses are generally more conservative and antigovernment than corporate leaders.[8]

In the early 1970s research on nearly 500 elites from various sectors of the economy found "a clear consensus for capitalism among American leaders, but for a capitalism modified by Keynesian antidepression policies, direct wage and price controls against inflation, and government action against poverty and unemployment.[9] American elites, whether they represent business, labor, government, or academia, do not want laissez faire economics; they want a governmental role in the economy. However, there is also a negative consensus against radical alternatives, such as socialism.[10] The only subgroup to harbor socialist instincts are a few intellectuals, which underscores the staying power of capitalist values or the failure of academics to sway public opinion (or perhaps both). Intellectuals have been a much less potent force in American history than the business community.[11]

Moreover, what "leading intellectuals" think about capitalism may **225** not represent the values of the broadly defined U.S. intelligentsia. When more than 4,000 college faculty were surveyed in 1977, they expressed strong support for the capitalist ethos, although they were more liberal than the general public.[12] Eighty-one percent agreed that "the private business system in the United States, for all its flaws, works better than any other system devised for advanced industrial society," and 69 percent agreed that "the growth of government in the U.S. now poses a threat to the freedom and opportunity for individual initiative of the citizenry."

A recent study by McClosky and Zaller compared the values of elites and masses toward democracy and capitalism.[13] This study found that the "vast majority of Americans consistently uphold such key capitalist notions as private property, the profit system, economic competition, and the general fairness of the private enterprise system. In addition, they overwhelmingly reject every suggestion that communism or socialism might prove desirable alternatives to American capitalism."[14] These authors also uncovered differences of opinion (analogous to what *The American Business Creed* had found) that reflect a nineteenth century "laissez faire capitalism" versus a twentieth century "welfare capitalism." People who understand the modern form of welfare capitalism more readily accept social legislation and government regulation, but within the context of free enterprise.

Economic Crisis and Support for the System

The support Americans display for the existing system of economic organization is not only widespread, it is relatively deep. Although business contractions might act to undermine popular support for capitalism—as disillusionment causes people to seek out economic alternatives—this has not proven to be the case in the United States. The severest economic crisis to face the U.S. in modern times was the Great Depression, when at least 25 percent of the work force was unemployed, but even in the face of this sustained, severe economic downturn, relatively few people rejected the basic structure and promise of the American political economy. A 1938 Roper poll asked if "the great age of economic opportunity and expansion in the U.S. is over or [whether] American industry can create a comparable expansion and opportunity in the future?" Only 13 percent chose the pessimistic response, whereas 72 percent saw hope in America's future. Even more significantly, only 5 percent of those polled believed that "the systems of private capitalism and democracy are breaking down, and we might as well accept the fact that sooner or later we shall have to have a new form of government."[15]

226   Since the 1930s the country has enjoyed relative prosperity (though subject to the ongoing business cycle), but the nation's resolve was tested again during the 1970s when stagflation was experienced. In 1975 the United States suffered its worst recession (up to that time) since the 1930s, but one study "showed an overwhelming majority of Americans still remain faithful to our economic system: 64 percent said they felt free enterprise was the best economic system . . . only 10 percent thought socialism was a better economic system."[16]

An even more severe recession followed during 1981–83, and its effect on support for the system was evaluated by an ABC News/*Washington Post* survey statement propounded several times during the recession: "It is true in this country that if you work hard, eventually you will get ahead." The results showed a slight relationship between short-term economic conditions and support for the existing economic system, but the changes in opinion were not very large: 63 percent agreed with that statement in 1981, before the economic downturn hit, declining to 58 percent by the end of 1982 (when unemployment was at record levels), then rising to 66 percent in November 1983, after the long period of economic expansion had begun.[17]

Attitudes Towards Government

During the Revolutionary period government was decried as an oppressive force, and the American colonists rebelled against "taxation without representation." This strain of antigovernment thinking has not dissipated, as politicians continue to run for office by running against big government. In his 1971 State of the Union Message President Nixon departed from his prepared text to add: "Let's face it. Most Americans today are simply fed up with government at all levels." Ten years later, attacks on government spending, federal waste, and high taxes were a mainstay of Ronald Reagan's political rhetoric—even after he was elected to head the national government.

Until 1981 the Gallup organization regularly asked, "Which of the following do you think will be a bigger threat to the country in the future—big business, big labor, or big government?" For over two decades, through both Republican and Democratic presidential administrations, most people usually picked government as the biggest threat. The popular image is of a government staffed by overpaid and underworked bureaucrats who spend too much money and bury the country under red tape. Compared to private sector employees, a 1977 Gallup poll found that most Americans believed that federal employees are paid more and get more fringe benefits but do not work as hard. In addition, 67 percent thought there were too many federal employees.[18]

How much tax money do people think is wasted by government? Research by the University of Michigan found that the percentage saying that "a lot" of money is wasted grew steadily from 47 percent in 1964 to 78 percent in 1980 before dropping to two-thirds in 1982.[19] A similar question by Gallup asks "of every tax dollar that goes to the federal government in Washington, D.C., how many cents of each dollar would you say are wasted?" In 1978, 1979, and 1981 the average estimate was that 48 cents of each federal dollar was wasted, a much higher figure than the estimates given for state or local governments.[20] Ten years later (in 1990), this assessment remained the same: the public again estimated waste at 48 cents of each federal dollar, compared to 40 cents and 35 cents for states and localities, respectively.[21]

Level of Economic Knowledge

A study commissioned by the Hearst Corporation during the 1980s concluded that a "large segment of the American public is sadly deficient in its knowledge of basic business and economic facts of life."[22] Fifty-five percent said they felt "uncomfortable most of the time" by their lack of knowledge about economics, and the majority had *not* been exposed to economics, business and finance, accounting, or statistics in high school or college. Most people relied on the mass media, mainly TV and newspapers, for information about the economy.

The poor prior exposure to these subjects was reflected in a substantial lack of knowledge about either the derivation of the most commonly discussed economic statistics or the current values of these statistics. Even on a question pertaining to the Federal Reserve Board that was answered *correctly* by the public as a whole, 46 percent gave incorrect responses, even though the Fed is regularly cited in news coverage. In addition, 61 percent did not know how unemployment is derived, and 62 percent could not accurately select the current unemployment rate from a list of widely spaced alternatives, although this is perhaps the most widely publicized economic statistic in the United States. Only 35 percent knew roughly what the projected deficit for FY84 would be, and only 40 percent correctly understood that GNP is not the value of goods and services purchased by government.

Two questions measured the public awareness of spending trends. Although other surveys reveal that most people believed that domestic programs are generally underfunded (see Table 9.2), in the Hearst study 50 percent of the public overestimated military spending, while 75 percent

228   underestimated expenditures for social programs. Of course, these responses may be understandable; based on personal observation people may draw the conclusion that too little money is spent on a certain program regardless of how large a share of the budget it represents. Nevertheless, these findings indicate that Americans have no real sense for how federal expenditures are allocated between "guns and butter," although this is a major source of political contention between conservatives and liberals in Congress and in broader public debate.

ATTITUDES REGARDING PARTICULAR ECONOMIC POLICY ISSUES

The general attitudes held by the U.S. public restrain leaders to a certain degree as they formulate economic policy. The broad support for the basic American political economy—a capitalist order of limited government—means that much of the American economic policy debate takes place within a fairly narrow range of options, considered from a global perspective. For example, the contemporary debate in the U.S. over a national health-care policy does not, for all practical purposes, include as an option a reliance upon a government health service run by the national government. Even though similar programs exist in many other Western industrialized nations, this option is considered inconsistent with the antigovernment, pro–private enterprise features of American political culture.

Beyond these rather broadly drawn limitations, policymakers are also guided by the public's attitudes toward specific policy problems and proposals. Much of the recent debate over deficit reduction, for example, has been constrained by leaders' perceptions that the public would punish electorally any officials who sought to raise taxes. In addition, the public plays an important role in elevating certain issues to prominence, i.e., in agenda setting.

Setting the Economic Policy Agenda

The public is alert to economic conditions, as changes in the inflation or unemployment rates are given front page coverage and exposure on the evening news and are used by the opposition party to embarrass the White House. The effect of these interactions between media elites, political leaders, and the public is that a degree of consensus is established about what the key economic problem is. Opinion polls are one source of information about what troubles Americans, and since 1935

the Gallup poll has asked people, "What do you think is the most impor- **229**
tant problem in this country today?" The trend during 1935–1992 (Table
9.1) shows that the American public's perception of the "most important
problem" closely follows the key events and social trauma over those years.

In general, economic concerns dominate this list, supplanted or supplemented by international concerns during wartime and other crises. During the Great Depression unemployment was the primary concern. Joblessness was less important with the coming of World War II, after which
economic issues again surfaced as Americans worried about a postwar recession. Foreign affairs dominated the agenda until the early 1960s, after
which Vietnam occupied the public's attention. The "high cost of living"
was cited as second "most important" in 1967 (the year when President
Johnson pondered his tax surcharge) and again in 1971 when President
Nixon announced his New Economic Program. Inflation continued to be
the primary concern in 1973, which no doubt influenced Nixon to reim-
pose a price freeze.

Over the years Gallup polls show that public concern about economics
grows during periods of recession, for example in 1954, 1958, and 1960–
1961. After Vietnam, however, the "high cost of living" was named most
frequently from 1973 until 1981 (during a sustained bout of relatively high
inflation), with unemployment being ranked second most years. However,
joblessness again surfaced as the key concern beginning in 1982, when the
nation experienced the highest unemployment rate since the 1930s. After
slipping to second-most-important by the late 1980s, unemployment again
reached the top of the list during the economic contraction of the early
1990s.

One analysis of these trends from 1946 through 1976 revealed that
inflation is cited most often as the primary economic concern, almost twice
as often as unemployment.[23] One reason may be that inflation affects
nearly everyone, while unemployment directly affects only a fraction of
the population. While higher prices were a less paramount concern before
1961, inflation has grown in political significance since then. Concerns
about inflation also correlate with stages in the business cycle as researcher
Tom W. Smith notes:

> Low points [in our concern for inflation] occurred in 1949, 1954, 1958,
> and 1961, during postwar recessions, and similar drops appeared during
> the 1970–71 slowdown and the 1975 recession. Peaks appeared in 1966
> and 1974. The 1966 point in part reflects the beginning of the 1966–
> 1975 inflationary spiral, but in part appears to reflect the relative absence
> of unemployment. . . . The 1974 crest, on the other hand, probably re-
> flects the double-digit inflation that crested that year. . . .[24]

230 TABLE 9.1 Gallup Poll Trends on "Most Important Problem"

1935	unemployment	1968	Vietnam
1936	unemployment	1969	Vietnam
1937	unemployment	1970	Vietnam
1938	keeping out of war	1971	Vietnam/high cost of living
1939	keeping out of war	1972	Vietnam
1940	keeping out of war	1973	high cost of living/Watergate
1941	keeping out of war/winning war	1974	high cost of living/Watergate/ energy crisis
1942	winning war	1975	high cost of living/unemployment
1943	winning war	1976	high cost of living/unemployment
1944	winning war	1977	high cost of living/unemployment
1945	winning war	1978	high cost of living/unemployment
1946	high cost of living	1979	high cost of living/unemployment
1947	high cost of living/labor unrest	1980	high cost of living/unemployment
1948	keeping peace	1981	high cost of living/unemployment
1949	labor unrest	1982	unemployment/international tensions
1950	labor unrest	1983	unemployment/international tensions
1951	Korean War	1984	unemployment/international tensions
1952	Korean War	1985	international tensions/ unemployment
1953	keeping peace	1986	international tensions/ unemployment
1954	keeping peace	1987	international tensions/ unemployment
1955	keeping peace	1988	(no data)
1956	keeping peace	1989	drug abuse/economy
1957	race relations/keeping peace	1990	federal deficit
1958	unemployment/keeping peace	1991	unemployment
1959	keeping peace	1992	unemployment
1960	keeping peace		
1961	keeping peace		
1962	keeping peace		
1963	keeping peace/race relations		
1964	Vietnam/race relations		
1965	Vietnam/race relations		
1966	Vietnam		
1967	Vietnam/high cost of living		

*The question asked was: "What do you think is the most important problem facing the country today?"

Source: *The Gallup Report,* No. 219 (December 1983), p. 5. Updates in No. 226 (July 1984), No. 235 (April 1985), No. 252 (September 1986), No. 260 (May 1987), No. 302 (November 1990), No. 304 (November 1991), No. 308 (May 1992). These findings were derived from multiple polls for the years 1986, 1987, 1989, and 1990.

Balancing the Budget

Americans traditionally express the belief that the federal budget should be balanced. In 1936, in the midst of depression, a Gallup poll asked whether it was "necessary at this time to balance the budget and start reducing the national debt?" Seventy percent agreed.[25] A heightened awareness of government spending during the 1970s led the Gallup poll to ask: "How important do you think it is to balance the federal budget—very important, fairly important, or not so important?" Even though Keynesian theory had come to dominate macroeconomic policy discussions, the number saying "very important" was 60 percent in 1973.[26] By 1990, this percentage had grown to 70 percent—the same figure recorded over fifty years earlier during the Great Depression.[27]

Public opinion seems to have hardened to where there is now overwhelming support for a constitutional amendment to achieve a balanced budget. When asked whether they would "favor or oppose a constitutional amendment that would require Congress to balance the federal budget each year—that is, keep taxes and expenditures in balance?" between 78 percent and 81 percent of the respondents in the late 1970s answered affirmatively.[28] In September 1982, 75 percent again responded to the simple statement "I favor/oppose a constitutional amendment to balance the federal budget" in the affirmative.[29] A later poll, however, suggests that support for this amendment, while still strong, may be eroding; in 1989 only 59 percent of the public supported such an amendment.[30]

As long as pollsters have surveyed public opinion on this subject, the majority has voiced support for a balanced budget. But federal budgets routinely show an excess of expenditures over revenues, and even President Reagan, a self-proclaimed champion of government frugality, oversaw deficits in excess of $100 billion. This record might lead one to conclude that America's historic devotion to balanced budgets is either dead or empty rhetoric. This is precisely the argument by Buchanan and Wagner, who argue that the Keynesian new economics undermined the "fiscal constitution" that once existed in the United States: "Once democratically elected politicians, and behind them their constituents in the voting public, were finally convinced that budget balance carried little or no weight, what was there left to restrain the ever-present spending pressures."[31]

Spending Priorities

There is a paradox in our attitudes toward government. When public opinion deals with abstract propositions, Americans express anti-government sentiments, but when public opinion is focused on specific

232   programs, then a very different picture emerges. This paradox has been documented by Free and Cantril, who classify most Americans as **ideological conservatives** but **operational liberals**.[32] Public opinion is conservative on fiscal policy (spending and taxing) but liberal on domestic programs that benefit individuals.

The National Opinion Research Center (NORC) asks respondents to the General Social Surveys to judge how much to spend on various programs. As Table 9.2 shows, with few exceptions the public wants spending for most domestic programs continued at the same rate or increased. In the five surveys from the GSS series shown in the table, a majority believed that the U.S. is spending too little money on the environment, health, crime, drug addiction, and education. Only three areas—space exploration, welfare, and foreign aid—found substantial numbers of Americans saying that too much money is spent. The most dramatic shift in priorities affected defense spending. Between 1973 and 1978 support for military spending increased, but by 1983 this trend was reversed. By 1990, support for higher defense spending had completely evaporated, returning to the low levels of the early 1970s. It is obvious from these data that most people do *not* want sharp cuts in most domestic programs. On the contrary, they claim, in increasing numbers, to want more spending. Between 1986 and 1990, for example, there were noticeable increases in support for increased spending across an array of domestic policy areas—the environment, health, urban problems, crime, and drugs—despite the fact that the federal budget was registering historically high deficits.

During 1981–84 President Reagan's budget ax fell largely on poverty programs, but his second term began with an assault on middle-class entitlement programs that constitute an even larger share of federal expenditures. During this period several news organizations polled the American people on that shift in federal spending priorities.[33] They found that the majority supported retrenchment in two programs but refused to cut back on eight others, including veterans care, food stamps, and Aid to Families with Dependent Children. Interestingly, the public reacted strongly against cutting farm subsidies (71 percent opposed) and the Small Business Administration (81 percent opposed), even though the vast majority of Americans do not benefit directly from them. This finding would imply tremendous resistance to expenditure cuts, even for programs that advantage the middle class.

This was further illustrated by a January 1985 ABC News/*Washington Post* survey. Ninety-five percent responded in the negative when asked, "Do you think the government should cut Social Security benefits substantially to reduce the budget deficit, or not?" In the same survey, 89 percent were opposed to cutting Medicare. Yet, at the same time, other

TABLE 9.2   Public Attitudes Towards Government Spending, Selected Years 1973–1990

	1973		1978		1983		1986		1990	
	too much	too little	too much	too little	too much	too little	too much	too little	too much	too little
Space exploration	61%	8%	50%	12%	40%	14%	41%	11%	39%	11%
Environment	8%	65%	10%	55%	8%	54%	5%	59%	5%	71%
Health	5%	63%	7%	56%	5%	57%	4%	58%	3%	72%
Problems of big cities	14%	55%	22%	44%	15%	41%	16%	43%	10%	50%
Rising crime rate	5%	69%	6%	67%	5%	66%	5%	63%	4%	70%
Drug addiction	6%	70%	9%	58%	5%	59%	6%	58%	7%	64%
Education	9%	51%	11%	54%	6%	60%	4%	60%	3%	71%
Condition of blacks	23%	35%	27%	26%	18%	29%	16%	33%	15%	37%
Military/armaments and defense	40%	12%	24%	29%	32%	24%	40%	16%	42%	10%
Foreign aid	74%	4%	71%	4%	73%	4%	70%	6%	66%	5%
Welfare	54%	21%	61%	14%	47%	21%	40%	22%	38%	22%

Source: National Opinion Research Center (NORC), General Social Survey, 1973, 1978, 1983, 1986, and 1990. Percentages derived from raw data. The question asked was: "We are faced with many problems in this country, none of which can be solved easily or inexpensively. I am going to name some of these problems, and for each one I'd like you to tell me whether you think we're spending too much money on it, too little money, or the right amount." Beginning in 1984, NORC added the categories highways and bridges, social security, mass transportation, and parks and recreation, but these were excluded here due to lack of comparability across time.

234   surveys revealed that most Americans wanted federal spending trimmed. When a February 1984 Gallup poll asked, "In general, do you feel that the size of the administration's budget for 1985 is too large, too small, or about the right amount?" 77 percent responded that the Reagan FY85 budget was too large!

Taxes

Where public opinion agreed with Ronald Reagan was in his opposition to higher taxes, although that sentiment is hardly new. However, the U.S. faces a dilemma on taxes because, despite antitax feelings, revenues are necessary to fund all the programs the public apparently wants.

Surveys indicate that people feel that taxes are too high, and they are specifically unhappy about federal income taxes. Almost identical questions by Gallup and NORC asked if the respondents considered their amount of federal income tax too high, about right, or too low. The responses showed that the majority almost always responded that its federal income tax burden was too high.

That sentiment was echoed in Harris surveys showing that between 1969 and 1980 the number of people who believed that they had "reached the breaking point on the amount of taxes" ranged from 57 percent to 72 percent.[34] Polls commissioned by the Advisory Commission on Intergovernmental Relations allowed respondents to evaluate the federal income tax relative to other kinds of taxes, and since 1979 most people have given the federal income tax the dubious honor of being "the worst tax, that is, the least fair."[35] Similar public reactions were documented by a 1978 CBS News poll reporting that only 13 percent cited the federal income tax as "most fair,"[36] and by repeated Harris surveys that found that about two-thirds of the samples complained that the federal income tax was "too high" as compared to state income taxes, property taxes, or sales taxes.[37]

Despite public discontent, no sustained outcry has mobilized the electorate on this issue. One study of election issues during 1960–1980 found that no more than 3.1 percent (in 1964) cited taxes as "the most important problem facing the country." Polls from 1991 and 1992 showed comparable figures of 3 percent and 6 percent, respectively.[38] However the number of people indicating that they would vote against a party or a candidate based upon the tax issue rose appreciably from 7.0 percent in 1976 to 14.8 percent in 1980.[39] The increased political salience of this issue reached a climax because, as Jack Citrin observed, "by late 1978 the confluence of anxiety over future economic conditions, anger about high taxes, and skep-

ticism about the performance of government had created a climate of
opinion that strongly favors cuts in public expenditures."[40]

Widespread concern over taxes undoubtedly encouraged Ronald Reagan, in his 1980 presidential campaign, to formally pledge that as president
he would work to cut federal income taxes by 30 percent. Much to the
surprise of his political opponents, once elected, Ronald Reagan proceeded
to vigorously (and successfully) push through Congress a bill to cut marginal federal income tax rates by 25 percent. Although this was a very
popular move, it dramatically reduced projected revenues, directly leading
to the large deficits that have plagued the federal budget since 1981. As
a result, during the 1984 presidential election, Reagan's Democratic opponent, Walter Mondale, declared that he would raise taxes to close the
budget deficit, while Reagan reiterated his opposition to tax increases.
Mondale's declaration is believed to have contributed to his overwhelming
defeat, and Democratic leaders have avoided taking similar stands ever
since.

During the 1988 presidential campaign, George Bush once again reiterated the position embraced by Reagan, dramatically declaring, "Read
my lips. No new taxes." In 1990 Bush broke this pledge by agreeing to a
bipartisan budget compromise that involved both tax increases and spending cuts. Although it is not clear what effect this action had on Bush's
overall popularity, his reversal on taxes caused him severe difficulties
among conservative members of his own party, including a 1992 primary
challenge from conservative Pat Buchanan.[41] By 1992, the public had
begun to name the Democratic party as the party most trusted to hold
down taxes, an historic reversal brought on in part by pledges by several
Democratic presidential primary candidates to support tax cuts.[42]

Regardless of which party or candidate reaps temporary advantages
from the tax issue, the public's attitude toward taxes clearly complicates
the resolution of the ongoing deficit crisis. The public simultaneously desires balanced budgets, increased spending in a variety of areas, and lower
taxes.[43] They cannot have all three, and since 1981, the lowest priority
for elected officials is the policy option that is least tangible to the voters,
whatever their responses to survey questions—a balanced federal budget.
In 1993, a newly elected President Clinton proposed a deficit reduction
program that combined increased taxes with spending cuts. The initial
public response was favorable; eight months later Congress passed a version of Clinton's proposal by the narrowest of margins—two votes in the
House and Vice-President Gore's tie-breaking vote in the Senate. The
closeness of the margin reflected, in part, the difficulty of enacting a policy
that addresses the contradictory desires of the American public.

236   THE ECONOMY AND PRESIDENTIAL APPROVAL

The president is the only political leader, says Theodore J. Lowi, that the electorate holds personally responsible for providing government services and safeguarding the nation's well-being.[44] Politicians had always assumed that bad economic times hurt incumbent presidents and their parties, and recently this relationship has been given systematic attention by scholars. To measure presidential popularity, researchers use a Gallup poll question that has been asked at least once each month since the 1940s: "Do you approve or disapprove of the way —— is handling his job as president?" The percentage indicating approval is known as the president's **approval rating**.

Because of the regularity with which this question has been asked, the presidential approval rating has become a closely watched and regularly reported political statistic—in effect, a sort of running scorecard of how the president is doing politically. The regularity of its collection also makes it ideal for scholars wishing to understand the relationship between changing economic conditions and the public's evaluation of the "manager of prosperity." Research in this area has sought to answer two basic questions: First, do economic conditions have a positive and/or negative impact on presidential popularity? Second, which economic conditions are the most important?

Bad Times Hurt

Bad economic conditions hurt the president much more than a good economy helps him, which implies that public opinion expects prosperity, or at least the absence of recession, to be the norm. The debate over this question was begun by Kramer's 1971 analysis of congressional elections from 1896 to 1964, which showed that "a 10 percent decrease in per capita real personal income would cost the incumbent administration 4 to 5 percent of the congressional vote, other things being equal."[45] A later study by Tufte for the period 1938–1970 found comparable results,[46] although other research has doubted the validity of Kramer's findings.[47]

One methodological deficiency was Kramer's failure to distinguish between economic downturns and upturns. This aspect was studied by Bloom and Price who examined the congressional vote from 1896 to 1970 to determine the impact of changes in real per capita income on the normal political party vote. Their model verified an asymmetrical version of Kramer's "throw the rascals out" thesis insofar as "economic downturns reduce the vote for the party of the incumbent President, but economic upturns have no corresponding effect."[48] Both Republicans and Democrats were affected by this phenomenon. Later work by Erikson[49] and Markus[50] again documented a clear connection between economic conditions—especially changes in disposable personal income—and success of the incumbent party's presidential candidate.

During an economic downturn, most people suffer, but not equally, so one can hypothesize that working-class voters would react more negatively to recession than the middle class. This relationship was found in a study of the 1958 and 1960 recessions, which concluded: "In the face of worsening national economic conditions, working-class citizens are more likely to deviate from their expected vote than are middle-class ones, for the simple reasons that the impacts of macroeconomic cycles are unevenly distributed through the class structures."[51] In both years the GOP was hurt because working-class voters suffered disproportionately from those recessions and consequently deserted the Republicans.

The most recent scholarly study of this question offers yet a different view of the effect of economic events upon presidential approval. In a provocative article, MacKuen, Erikson, and Stimson argue that it is the expectations of future economic conditions, rather than economic conditions themselves, that lead to changes in presidential approval.[52] Of course, actual economic conditions are not irrelevant—it is events that form the basis for individuals' assessments concerning future economic conditions. However, the most significant feature of the MacKuen, Erikson, and Stimson view is that the public is forward looking, or prospective, in its evaluations, rather than backward looking, or retrospective.

Inflation vs. Unemployment

Inflation seems to be a stronger influence on presidential popularity than unemployment, which suggests that, while increases in the jobless rate may have a great impact on segments of the population, rising prices adversely affect many more people. Not all research is conclusive on this point,[53] but an important study by Kernell found that unemployment rates were not a key determinant of presidential popularity but that price levels had some effect on two of five executives he studied (Kennedy and Nixon).[54] Using another methodology, Kristen Monroe found that prolonged inflation will hurt a president's approval ratings:

> While there is some immediate response to inflation, the major response is a cumulative one. This suggests that the public does not blame the president for brief periods of inflation but will hold him responsible for sustained inflation. The lagged impact suggests the public has a long memory. The public is not easily distracted by sudden declines in inflation which immediately precede an election. . . .[55]

Other research by Monroe found no such impact by unemployment on presidential popularity,[56] while inflation was affirmed as being the more important factor in another study by MacKuen.[57]

But unemployment can undermine presidential popularity among blue-collar workers in particular, according to a study of the 1961–1979 period, which found that blue-collar workers were more sensitive to changes in unemployment, whereas white-collar employees and retirees were more alert to inflation-rate fluctuations. A more significant finding was a partisan difference: "The political approval indices for Democrats and Independents were far more responsive to movements in unemployment and the real income growth rate, and less responsive to movements in the inflation rate, than is the approval index of Republican partisans."[58]

Presidential Approval and the Economy: The Case of George Bush

No recent president better illustrates the perils of an economic downturn for presidential popularity than George Bush. As we have noted already, his 89 percent approval rating of early March 1991 was the highest rating on record. From these heights, however, his fall was dramatic (Figure 9.1). In less than a year, the record approval rating was cut in half. The culprit, it would appear, was bad economic conditions, in this case, unemployment.

As the trend line in Figure 9.1 indicates, during the first year of his presidency Bush's approval was generally high, although there were short-term fluctuations. During the second year, his ratings began to fall— roughly at the time when economists indicate that the economy was approaching the peak of the long 1980s expansion. This decline was arrested in August 1990 by the foreign policy crisis brought on by the Iraqi invasion of Kuwait. Following another sharp decline, Bush's popularity again rose sharply in January 1991 as war approached and then broke out. Shortly after the battlefield victory, however, the approval ratings began a long, steady decline that continued into the fall presidential election campaign.

Although the relationship between the rising unemployment level and the falling approval ratings is not perfect, it is clearly evident, particularly after March of 1991. Even before then, however, the basic outline of the decline in Bush's popularity is apparent. Looked at over the course of the Bush presidency, the long-term trend from January 1990 is downward, being interrupted only in the short run by the events in Kuwait and the normal tendency of presidential popularity to rise during periods of international crises.

Figure 9.1   Monthly Unemployment Rate and Presidential Approval
Ratings, Jan. 1989–Nov. 1992

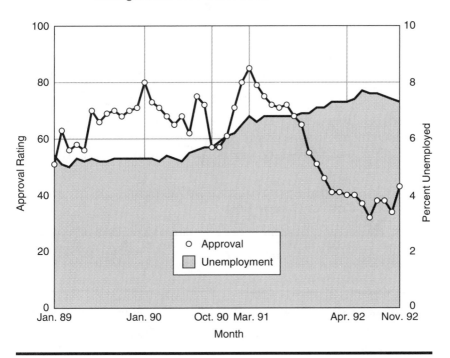

ELECTIONS AND THE ECONOMY

Historically, when the economy has surfaced as a political issue
the Democrats have enjoyed an advantage over the Republicans. Since
1951 Gallup has asked: "Looking ahead for the next few years, which
political party—the Republican or the Democratic—do you think will do
the better job of keeping the country prosperous?" The data in Figure 9.2
show that most people generally believe that the Democrats will do a
better job with the economy.

The GOP's image was positive during 1955–57, but dropped with the
1958 Eisenhower recession. Its next high point came in 1968 (the last
year of President Johnson's tenure) and again during the 1972 recovery,
but afterwards the Democrats regained their advantage. The stagflation
under President Carter greatly harmed his party's image with the electorate

Figure 9.2   Gallup Poll Trend on Political Party Better for Prosperity

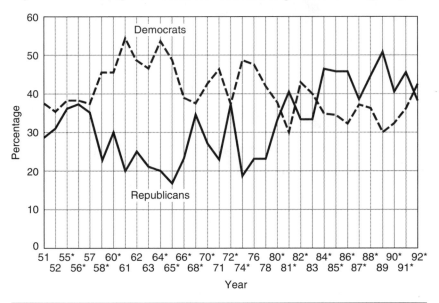

Source: *The Gallup Report*, Number 277 (October 1988), p. 5 as updated in No. 286 (July 1989) and No. 317 (February 1992). The asterisk (*) indicates an average percentage based on multiple surveys. The question was: "Looking ahead for the next few years, which political party—the Republican or the Democratic—do you think will do the better job of keeping the country prosperous?"

and paved the way for Ronald Reagan's 1980 victory—due in large measure to adverse economic conditions. However, the lingering downturn in the latter half of the Bush administration led to the Democrats reclaiming their historic position as the "party of prosperity," with their first preelection edge in four elections.[59]

The general image of the Democrats as the party of prosperity has some basis in events. The normal rhetoric of Republicans seeking the White House focuses more on government frugality, the national debt, and inflation, rather than on trying to achieve full employment. Moreover, since World War II recessions have occurred more often under Republican presidents (1954, 1958, 1970, 1975, 1982, 1990) than Democratic ones (1949, 1961, 1980). Economist Paul Samuelson relates this pattern to the differing voter groups within each party.

> The difference between the Democrats and the Republicans is the difference in their constituencies. It's a class difference . . . the Democrats

constitute the people, by and large, who are around median incomes or below. These are the ones whom the Republicans want to pay the price and burden of fighting inflation. The Democrats [are] willing to run with some inflation [to increase employment]; the Republicans are not.[60]

Samuelson raises a plausible argument that macroeconomic policy is guided by political considerations. Since blue-collar workers, minorities, and the poor are more vulnerable during economic contractions (and may suffer unemployment even during eras of prosperity), Democrats express more concern about full employment. Because the GOP is a middle-class party whose constituents view job security as a lesser threat than the erosion of real income due to inflation, Republicans focus on price stability as their key concern. A study of the period 1948–1972 concluded that a difference of 2.36 percent in the jobless rate depended upon whether a Democrat (lower rate) or a Republican (higher rate) occupied the White House.[61]

Perhaps Democrats are perceived to be better guardians of the nation's prosperity because, in the past at least, so many Americans were working class and thus vulnerable to layoffs during recessions. The decline in manufacturing jobs and union membership, coupled with expanding services and high-technology employment, may be eroding the significance of class in American politics. This argument is made by Charles Prysby who found that, while different occupations may defend their economic self-interests, no generalized class conflict seemed to shape their views towards economic issues.[62] The arrival of a postindustrial economy and the perception that inflation is the more serious economic problem may, therefore, serve to bolster the Republican party's image. If so, then the political calculus affecting the trade-off between inflation and unemployment may have changed since the 1950s and the 1960s.

According to survey data for the 1971–76 period, blue-collar groups were found to be more sensitive to unemployment than white-collar employees, who were more concerned about inflation. But during recessions all occupation groups were more alert to the jobless rate, whereas they became more intolerant of inflation whenever prices began to rise. What was unexpected, however, was the finding that people were willing to tolerate high unemployment rates so long as inflation was not excessive.[63] This outlook would cripple efforts to drive down unemployment much below its natural rate during a period of inflationary pressures, which again implies that Republicans might enjoy a political advantage.

The growing intolerance towards inflation during the 1970s may be related to the fact that America has enjoyed remarkable price stability since World War II. What happened to prices during the Nixon and (especially) the Carter years was unprecedented, a shock to most people.

242   Except during exceptional times, such as the end of wartime price controls in 1946–47, the U.S. had never seen double-digit inflation rates and price increases that exceeded increases in real personal income.

In the 1980s the business cycle dragged the nation into a new recession, and joblessness again dominated the political agenda. This experience reminds us that public opinion will not accept excessive unemployment any more than spiraling prices. One view is that the Reagan administration allowed unemployment to rise in order to bring down double-digit inflation rates. If so, this strategy was politically costly in the short term. Reagan suffered the steepest decline in his approval ratings of any postwar executive, and this repudiation of his leadership is attributed to the deep recession.[64] Unemployment reached ten percent, a post-depression high. As a result the Democrats gained 26 House seats in the 1982 midterm congressional elections, and Congress proceeded to enact a public works program to assist the unemployed.

During the rest of the decade, however, the economy favored the Republicans, although they only reaped an advantage from this at the presidential level. Despite presidential victories in both 1984 and 1988, the Republicans lost control of the Senate in 1986, and they have not seriously threatened Democratic control of either the House or the Senate since. President Bush's defeat by Democrat Bill Clinton in the 1992 election was viewed by most observers—including the candidates themselves—as attributable to the economic woes that afflicted Bush's administration from mid-1990 until the election.

Is There a Political Business Cycle?

The question of whether the president is driven by reelection incentives to manipulate the economy to bolster his ability to retain office has received a great deal of scholarly attention in recent years. This idea was first advanced by economist William Nordhaus in 1975, based upon an econometric model he developed for nine Western democracies. The United States showed marked support for his hypothesis that unemployment falls prior to a presidential election but rises thereafter.[65] This idea was further advanced by Tufte, who documented that U.S. politicians tend to increase benefits to constituents before elections and delay tax increases until afterwards—precisely the kind of behavior that would be expected if political leaders were seeking to manipulate the economy for electoral gain.[66] This thesis became known as the **political business cycle**, since the suggestion was that the economy was being manipulated by political leaders in such a way as to peak right before U.S. national elections.

It certainly seems to be the case that the economy and election results **243**
are interrelated. In 1948, 1956, 1964, 1972, and 1984 the presidential
election came during the expansionary phase of the business cycle. In
every case the incumbent party won. Three more presidents were defeated
(in 1976, 1980, and 1992), even though the cycle had bottomed out and
recovery had begun. President Carter faced the voters only four months
after a short recession had reached its trough, while 20 months was not
long enough to rebuild the economy (along with President Ford's reputation) after one of the deepest recessions (1975) in the postwar era. In
the final case (1992), the recovery was sufficiently weak that economists
were not able to identify that an expansion was underway after the election.

In four other elections, incumbents did not seek reelection. In 1952
and 1968 their parties' nominees were beaten despite prosperity, but in
these elections political considerations were more important than the
economy. In 1960 Vice President Richard Nixon waged his presidential
campaign during a recession and lost, whereas the "peace and prosperity"
of the Reagan years greatly helped Vice President George Bush win the
1988 election.

The historical record seems to point to a connection between the
economy and presidential victories, but the question is whether the condition of the economy or the presidential election is the independent
variable—i.e., which causes which?[67] Nearly all researchers who have systematically analyzed this question since Tufte fail to find evidence in support of the Nordhaus-Tufte political business cycle hypothesis.[68] A detailed
examination of the logic underlying the political business cycle thesis led
Alt and Chrystal to argue that the weight of scholarly evidence is strongly
against that interpretation:

> No one could read the political business cycle literature without being
> struck by the lack of supporting evidence. There must be cases where
> politicians have undertaken electorally motivated interventions. It is
> difficult to imagine politicians not exploiting some extra information or
> other resources. But while this clearly happens, and happens particularly
> clearly in some cases, such cycles may be trivial in comparison with other
> economic fluctuations.[69]

The point made by Alt and Chrystal is that politically motivated
manipulations will have only a marginal impact on the business cycle.
Thus, it might take a *massive* infusion of federal spending to guarantee a
president's election. By one estimate the deficit would have to be increased
by about $5.5 billion to raise the president's vote percentage by one per-
cent, which means that perhaps a $20 billion infusion would be necessary

244 in a tight election.[70] Although it is possible that a president, working with a supportive Congress, might be able to bring about such stimulation, the evidence suggests that this has not been the case.

PUBLIC OPINION AND ECONOMIC POLICY

Divergent attitudes towards abstract values versus specific policies is not uncommon in public opinion. It is well known that Americans universally support the principle of political liberty but stop short of tolerating groups considered to be extremist. So questions that probe vague feelings about big government find most people expressing antigovernment, antitax, and antispending opinions, but that kind of hostility evaporates when specific programmatic cutbacks are mentioned.

Public opinion sends mixed, and irreconcilable, signals to economic policymakers. A cynical view might be that Americans are hypocritical, because they want something for nothing. A less harsh interpretation of the prospending but antitax mentality is offered by Everett Ladd, who suggests that while most people wish government to provide needed services, they also actually believe "that government is highly inefficient, that they are not getting their money's worth as tax dollars are used for services, that it is possible to reduce taxes without reducing services by cutting the 'waste.' And that is exactly what they say."[71]

But is "reducing government waste" a realistic response to the modern budgetary dilemma? Is there enough waste in existing programs to markedly reduce a yearly deficit that approached $300 billion, or over 20 percent of the FY92 budget? And why fault the public when political leaders make extraordinary claims about macroeconomic management? It was President Reagan who promised to cut marginal income tax rates by 30 percent, reduce domestic expenditures while increasing defense spending, and balance the budget. In the end Reagan never did bring federal revenues and spending into balance—and he left office with the highest approval rating of any retiring president since FDR.[72]

Public opinion may effectively neutralize taxes and spending as countercyclical policies, a policy dilemma illustrated by the Reagan deficits. Despite their unprecedented size, heated debate in Congress, widespread publicity, and dire warnings from many economists, the public seemed unwilling to endorse decisive action. Gallup polls in 1983, 1984, and 1985 showed that large majorities were opposed to domestic spending cuts or to any income tax increase in order to bring down the deficit.[73] Perhaps the public mood is shifting. Asked for the best way to reduce the federal deficit in 1990, 50 percent of the public indicated that a combination of spending cuts and tax increases was necessary.[74] However, when polled shortly after Clinton's 1992 victory, a plurality of Americans (44 percent) indicated that deficit reduction should be postponed "if Clinton is forced to choose between raising taxes, cutting entitlements, or putting off action on the deficit."[75]

A balanced-budget amendment, on the other hand, would essentially repudiate the policy prescriptions of John Maynard Keynes. Not only would it prevent the deficit financing needed to counteract an economic downturn, but efforts to comply with the balancing requirement would have a procyclical impact. Specifically, expenditure reductions necessary to balance the budget that were enacted during a recession would have a deflationary effect, deepening the recession—as happened during the 1959 economic contraction. A less drastic solution, however, that might placate public opinion while also accommodating macroeconomic policy would be a law that mandates a balanced budget over the course of a business cycle. This means that surpluses generated during periods of economic growth would compensate for the deficits caused by recession.

Will the public recognize the significance of emerging problems before they reach crisis proportions, given that economic processes are very complex and many citizens lack even basic knowledge about the economy? Fixing one problem may involve economic costs elsewhere, as shown by the current debate over trade sanctions. Seventy-four percent correctly told the Hearst survey referred to earlier that import quotas "usually result in higher prices for consumers," yet other polls over the last two decades show nearly two-thirds support for import quotas.[76] Since 1934 there has been widespread support among political elites for lowering trade barriers among nations, but the current mood for protectionism, due largely to America's unfavorable balance of trade with Japan, has generated renewed political pressures.[77]

President Nixon was also guided by public opinion when he imposed a wage-price freeze in 1971. It lifted his popularity but also fueled inflationary pressures after the wage-price freeze was over. When he reimposed a sixty-day price freeze in June 1973, almost every economist called it unworkable, but a Gallup poll found that 52 percent favored a return to controls after that sixty-day period was over.[78] Most economists agree that wage-price controls distort the market, but almost every Gallup poll taken on this subject since the 1940s finds at least a plurality of Americans favoring that policy.[79] Despite the experiences of the Nixon years, wage-price controls remained popular throughout the 1970s.

In the public mind the fundamental consideration is that the nation avoid recession, certainly any repeat of the 1930s. People want employment to be high and the purchasing power of their dollars secure, and

246   while there will be political debate over whether the nation has reached full employment or how much inflation is too much, the answers to those questions are ultimately made by the electorate. When President Carter reversed his economic game plan from cutting unemployment to fighting inflation, he recognized that public opinion judged rising prices to be the more important problem. And like Carter, most politicians believe that they will be held responsible for the nation's economic well-being.

Presidential popularity declines and the president's party loses votes when unemployment rises too high or inflation becomes excessive. The notion that presidents can (and do) manipulate the economy to assure their political fortunes has been repudiated by much scholarship. The performance of the macroeconomy cannot be precisely controlled by the chief executive. But the president, nonetheless, is held strictly accountable by the body politic. The tendency for public opinion to punish an incumbent more for economic bad times and reward him less when the economy performs well can be interpreted to mean that the electorate accepts the presidential role as "manager of prosperity" quite literally. And since the business cycle has not been eliminated, public intolerance for recessions will signal political difficulties for presidents in the future as in the past.

KEY TERMS

ideological conservative, operational liberal, approval rating, political business cycle

ADDITIONAL READING

Alt, James and Alec Chrystal. *Political Economics*. Berkeley: University of California Press, 1983. A sophisticated theoretical discussion that includes a powerful critique of the political business cycle thesis.

Beard, Charles A. *An Economic Interpretation of the Constitution*. New York: Macmillan, 1913. Classic work arguing that the framers wrote the Constitution to protect their economic self-interest.

Hibbs, Douglas A., Jr. *The American Political Economy: Macroeconomics and Electoral Politics in the United States*. Cambridge, MA: Harvard University Press, 1987. A comprehensive analysis of the relationship between partisan politics and macroeconomic policy in the postwar era.

Kiewiet, D. Roderick. *Macroeconomics and Micropolitics: The Electoral Effects of Economic Issues*. Chicago: The University of Chicago Press, 1983. Concludes that voters evaluate political incumbents based on their perceptions of national economic conditions.

McCloskey, Herbert and John Zaller. *The American Ethos: Public Support for* **247**
Capitalism and Democracy. Cambridge, MA: Harvard University Press, 1985.
The definitive empirical study of how the general public and elites assess
economic and democratic values.

McDonald, Forrest. *We the People: The Economic Origins of the Constitution.*
Chicago: University of Chicago Press, 1958. This study refutes the Charles
Beard thesis by arguing that the framers did not profit economically from the
Constitution.

Peretz, Paul. *The Political Economy of Inflation in the United States.* Chicago:
University of Chicago Press, 1983. Applies pluralist, elitist, and Marxist theories
to determine which best explains the impact of inflation on public opinion and
politics.

Sutton, Francis X. and Seymour E. Harris, Carl Kaysen, James Tobin. *The
American Business Creed.* New York: Schocken Books, 1962. A classic study of
the values of American business during the 1940s and 1950s.

Tufte, Edward R. *Political Control of the Economy.* Princeton: Princeton
University Press, 1978. This book has provoked much scholarly research by
arguing that a political business cycle affects macroeconomic policymaking in
the United States.

NOTES

1. This is true as a general proposition, although government ownership has
been proposed for certain specialized programs (e.g., ownership of early telecom-
munications satellites) or when private ownership was not seen as feasible. The
principal example of the latter would be the Tennessee Valley Authority during
the 1930s.

2. Richard Hofstadter, *The American Political Tradition* (New York: Vintage,
1972), p. xxxvii.

3. Louis Hartz, *The Liberal Tradition in America* (New York: Harcourt Brace,
1955), pp. 8–9.

4. Not all unions adopted this strategy. However, as Mancur Olson demonstrates in *The Logic of Collective Action* (Cambridge, MA: Harvard University
Press, 1965), unions that focused on narrower workplace issues succeeded in the
long run, in marked contrast to the unions that adopted a more broadly defined
agenda to alter the political order within the United States. See, especially, Chapter III, "The Labor Union and Economic Freedom," pp. 66–97.

5. Forrest McDonald, "The Constitution and Hamiltonian Capitalism," in
Goldwin and Schambra, eds., *How Capitalistic Is the Constitution?* p. 68.

6. Francis X. Sutton, Seymour E. Harris, Carl Kaysen, James Tobin, *The
American Business Creed* (New York: Schocken Books, 1962).

7. Ibid., p. 68.

248

8. The views of small entrepreneurs represent the "agrarian spirit" according to John H. Bunzel, *The American Small Businessman* (New York: Knopf, 1962). See a review of this literature and similar findings in Carol Spielman, "The Political Agenda of Big and Small Business for the 1980s: A Content Analysis of Selected Publications," Unpublished M.A. thesis, Department of Political Science, Loyola University of Chicago, 1983.

9. Allen H. Barton, "Consensus and Conflict Among American Leaders, "*Public Opinion Quarterly* 38 (Winter 1974–75), 522. The questions to follow are taken from the Appendix, pp. 526–530. For this discussion, we collapsed the four responses "agree strongly," "agree with qualifications," "disagree with qualifications," and "disagree strongly" into two dichotomous categories.

10. Ibid, p. 517.

11. See Richard Hofstadter, *Anti-intellectualism in American Life* (New York: Knopf, 1963).

12. Reported in *Public Opinion* 1 (May/June, 1978), p. 37.

13. Herbert McClosky and John Zaller, *The American Ethos: Public Support for Capitalism and Democracy* (Cambridge, MA: Harvard University Press, 1985). Our account is drawn from Dennis Chong, Herbert McClosky, and John Zaller, "Patterns of Support for Democratic and Capitalistic Values in the United States," *British Journal of Political Science* 13 (October 1983), 401–440.

14. Ibid., p. 407.

15. Reported in *Public Opinion* 7 (February/March, 1984), 28.

16. David Caplovitz, "Making Ends Meet: How Families Cope with Inflation and Recession," *Public Opinion* 1 (May/June, 1978), 53.

17. NORC, General Social Surveys, July 1984, pp. 87–92.

18. American Institute of Public Opinion, *Public Opinion 1972–1977*, vol. 2 (Wilmington, DE: Scholarly Resources, Inc., 1978), pp. 1111–1114.

19. Arthur Miller, "Is Confidence Rebounding?" *Public Opinion* 6 (June/July 1983), p. 20.

20. *The Gallup Report*, No. 185 (February 1981), pp. 44–45.

21. ABC News/*Washington Post* survey, September 7–11, 1990.

22. The Hearst Corporation, *The American Public's Knowledge of Business and the Economy*, A Hearst Report (New York: Hearst Corporation, 1984).

23. Tom W. Smith, "America's Most Important Problem—A Trend Analysis, 1946–1976," *Public Opinion Quarterly* 44 (Summer 1980), pp. 164–180.

24. Ibid., pp. 169–170.

25. George H. Gallup, *The Gallup Poll: Public Opinion 1935–1971*, vol. 1 (New York: Random House, 1972), p. 12.

26. *The Gallup Report* 18 (May 1981), p. 31. Various polls on this question are reported in: Paul E. Peterson, "The New Politics of Deficits," in John E. Chubb and Paul E. Peterson, eds., *The New Direction in American Politics* (Washington, DC: The Brookings Institution, 1985), p. 387.

27. *Gallup Poll Monthly* 296 (May 1990), p. 27.   **249**

28. *The Gallup Report* 164 (March 1979), pp. 23, 25.

29. *The Gallup Report* 206 (November 1982), p. 5.

30. *Gallup Report* 281 (February 1989), p. 3.

31. James Buchanan and Richard Wagner, *Democracy in Deficit* (New York: Academic Press, 1977), p. 50.

32. Lloyd A. Free and Hadley Cantril, *The Political Beliefs of Americans* (New York: Simon and Schuster, 1968), Chapter 3.

33. These various surveys are reported in *Public Opinion* 8 (February/March, 1985), pp. 19–20.

34. Reported in Everett Carl Ladd, Jr., "The Polls: Taxing and Spending," *Public Opinion Quarterly* 43 (Spring 1979), p. 127.

35. The 1979 results are discussed in Ladd, "The Polls: Taxing and Spending," p. 23. Similar results for 1988 are reported in "Opinion Roundup," *Public Opinion* 12 (March/April 1989), p. 23.

36. Reported in Jack Citrin, "Do People Want Something for Nothing: Public Opinion on Taxes and Government Spending," *National Tax Journal* 32 (June 1979), Supplement, p. 115.

37. Reported in *Public Opinion* 1 (July/August, 1978), p. 29.

38. *The Gallup Monthly* 319(April 1992), p. 30.

39. Discussed in Susan B. Hansen, *The Politics of Taxation* (New York: Praeger Special Studies, 1983), pp. 176–177.

40. Citrin, "Do People Want Something for Nothing," p. 116.

41. See Stuart Rothenberg, "Politics '92: Taxes Are No Longer Just a GOP Issue," *The Public Perspective: A Roper Center Review of Public Opinion and Polling* 3 (March/April 1992), pp. 25–27.

42. Ibid.

43. To further complicate the picture, survey majorities also indicate that they would favor tax increases for specific purposes, such as antidrug policies or programs to extend health benefits to those who cannot afford them. See "What Americans Are Saying About Taxes," *Public Opinion* (March/April 1989), p. 21.

44. Theodore J. Lowi, *The Personal President: Power Invested, Promise Unfulfilled* (Ithaca: Cornell University Press, 1985).

45. Gerald H. Kramer, "Short-Term Fluctuations in U.S. Voting Behavior, 1896–1964," *American Political Science Review* 65 (March 1971), 131–143. Quote on p. 141.

46. Edward R. Tufte, "Determinants of the Outcomes of Midterm Congressional Elections," *American Political Science Review* 69 (September 1975), 812–826.

47. George Stigler, "Micropolitics and Macroeconomics: General Economic Conditions and National Elections," *American Economic Review* 63 (May 1973), 160–167. Also see Francisco Arcelus and Allan H. Meltzer, "The Effect of Ag-

250   gregate Economic Variables on Congressional Elections," *American Political Science Review* 69 (December 1975), 1232–1239.

48.   Howard S. Bloom and H. Douglas Price, "Voter Response to Short-Run Economic Conditions: the Asymmetric Effect of Prosperity and Recession," *American Political Science Review* 69 (December 1975), 1240–1254.

49.   Robert S. Erikson, "Economic Conditions and the Presidential Vote," *American Political Science Review* 83 (1989), pp. 567–573.

50.   See Gregory B. Markus, "The Impact of Personal and National Economic Conditions on Presidential Voting, 1956–1988," *American Journal of Political Science* 36 (1992), pp. 829–834.

51.   M. Stephen Weatherford, "Economic Conditions and Electoral Outcomes: Class Differences in the Political Response to Recession," *American Journal of Political Science* 22 (November 1978), 917–938.

52.   Michael B. MacKuen, Robert S. Erikson, and James A. Stimson, "Peasants or Bankers? The American Electorate and the U.S. Economy," *American Political Science Review* 86 (September 1992), pp. 597–611.

53.   See Henry C. Kenski, "The Impact of Economic Conditions on Presidential Popularity," *Journal of Politics* 39 (August 1977), 764–773; "The Impact of Unemployment on Presidential Popularity from Eisenhower to Nixon," *Presidential Studies Quarterly* 7 (Spring/Summer, 1977), 114–126; "Inflation and Presidential Popularity," *Public Opinion Quarterly* 41 (Spring 1977), 86–90.

54.   Samuel Kernell, "Explaining Presidential Popularity: How Ad Hoc Theorizing, Misplaced Emphasis, and Insufficient Care in Measuring One's Variables Refuted Common Sense and Led Conventional Wisdom Down the Path of Anomalies," *American Political Science Review* 72 (June 1978), 506–522.

55.   Kristen R. Monroe, "Inflation and Presidential Popularity," *Presidential Studies Quarterly* 9 (Summer 1979), 334–340. Quote on p. 339. A critique of this methodology, which assumes a "lag" structure in public opinion, is found in: Helmut Norpoth and Thom Yantek, "Macroeconomic Conditions and Fluctuations of Presidential Popularity: The Question of Lagged Effects," *American Journal of Political Science* 27 (November 1983), 785–807.

56.   Kristen R. Monroe, "Economic Influences on Presidential Popularity," *Public Opinion Quarterly* 42 (Fall 1978), 360–369.

57.   Michael B. MacKuen, "Political Drama, Economic Conditions, and the Dynamics of Presidential Popularity," *American Journal of Political Science* 27 (May 1983), 165–192. Quote on p. 191.

58.   Douglas A. Hibbs, Jr., "The Dynamics of Political Support for American Presidents Among Occupational and Partisan Groups," *American Journal of Political Science* 26 (May 1982), 312–331. Quote on p. 328.

59.   *The Gallup Monthly* (October 1992).

60.   Paul A. Samuelson, "Some Dilemmas of Economic Policy," *Challenge* 20 (March/April, 1977), 30–31.

61. Douglas A. Hibbs, Jr., "Political Parties and Macroeconomic Policy," **251**
American Political Science Review 71 (December 1977), 1467–1487.

62. Charles L. Prysby, "Mass Policy Orientations on Economic Issues in Post-Industrial America," *Journal of Politics* 41 (1979), 541–563.

63. Douglas A. Hibbs, Jr., "The Mass Public and Macroeconomic Performance: The Dynamics of Public Opinion Toward Unemployment and Inflation," *American Journal of Political Science* 23 (November 1979), 543–563.

64. See D. Roderick Kiewiet and Douglas Rivers, "The Economic Basis of Reagan's Appeal," in Chubb and Peterson, eds., *The New Direction in American Politics* (Washington, DC: The Brookings Institution, 1985), pp. 69–90.

65. William H. Nordhaus, "The Political Business Cycle," *Review of Economic Studies* 42 (April 1975), 169–189.

66. Edward R. Tufte, *Political Control of the Economy* (Princeton: Princeton University Press, 1978), Chapter 2.

67. This point is also discussed in a recent paper by William R. Keech and G. Patrick Lynch, "Business Cycles and Presidential Elections in the United States: Another Look at Key and Downs on Retrospective Voting," a paper presented at the 1992 annual meeting of the American Political Science Association, Chicago, IL, September 3–6.

68. See, for example, John T. Woolley, "Partisan Manipulation of the Economy: Another Look at Monetary Policy with Moving Regression," *Journal of Politics* 50 (May 1988), pp. 336, n 2.

69. James Alt and Alec Chrystal, *Political Economics* (Berkeley: University of California Press, 1983), p. 125.

70. David G. Golden and James M. Poterba, "The Price of Popularity: The Political Business Cycle Reexamined," *American Journal of Political Science* 24 (November 1980), 696–714.

71. Everett Carl Ladd, Jr., with Marilyn Potter, Linda Basilick, Sally Daniels, and Dana Suszkiw, "The Polls: Taxing and Spending," *Public Opinion Quarterly* 43 (Spring 1979), 133–134.

72. *The Gallup Report* 280 (January 1989), pp. 12–13.

73. But the public would cut defense spending. See *The Gallup Report* 209 (February 1983), p. 20; 229 (October 1984), p. 6; 237 (June 1985), pp. 2–7.

74. *Gallup Poll Monthly* 296 (May 1990), p. 27. Forty-three percent responded "reduce spending," and only 4 percent responded "raise taxes."

75. *The Gallup Monthly* (November 1992), p. 11.

76. Reported in Kevin Phillips, "The Politics of Protectionism," *Public Opinion* 8 (April/May, 1985), p. 42.

77. Ibid.

78. *The Gallup Opinion Index* 159 (October 1978), pp. 4–5.

79. See *The Gallup Report* 185 (February 1981), p. 19. To the question "Would you favor or oppose having the government bring back wage and price controls?" five polls taken between 1974 and 1981 showed 44–57 percent in favor.

PART IV

Economic Policy and Economic Performance

CHAPTER 10

Presidential Styles of Economic Management

How each president makes use of the CEA, Treasury, and OMB to provide economic advice depends upon his mode of decision making, organizational preferences, and political ideology. What emerges is a personalized, informal, and ad hoc style of economic management that, in most cases, is tilted towards telling the president what he prefers to hear. Although events intrude—unemployment will rise or fall regardless of the president's wishes—economic advisers are often selected because their general view of the economy accords with the president's. In macroeconomic policy, as elsewhere,[1] we can point to few examples of "multiple advocacy," where presidents deliberately engineer a structure that provides them with wide-ranging and conflicting viewpoints from different advisers. Only Gerald Ford, through his Economic Policy Board, tried to institutionalize this system,[2] and even there, key advisers like Alan Greenspan and Henry Kissinger tried to circumvent the board to avoid conflicting viewpoints.

There is scholarly disagreement over whether macroeconomic policy is nonpolitical or partisan. Those in the first camp say that national economic problems are publicized so much by the media that no president can systematically favor one group of voters over others when formulating economic policy. The counter-argument is that presidents are influenced by political ideology and party affiliation to shape macroeconomic policy in ways that benefit their supporters rather than the opposition. Whether

256   macroeconomic policy is "consensus" oriented or "class" biased is largely debated in the studies of electoral behavior and presidential popularity. But the divergent styles of economic management adopted by the various presidents support the view that the organization of economic advice generally reinforces the policy agenda of the White House.

In his typology of economic policymaking Michael Genovese classifies modern presidents according to ideology (probusiness "enterprisers" or progovernment "statists") and strategy ("traditionalists" who pursue incremental goals and "innovators" who pursue bold new economic objectives). Only Franklin Roosevelt and Ronald Reagan are considered innovators, but within the larger category of traditionalists Genovese found "the division is clearly along partisan lines, with the Democrats supporting a statist position, and the Republicans favoring an enterpriser approach."[3]

These tendencies are amply illustrated by the case studies in this chapter. The key economic players under President Eisenhower had tremendous faith in laissez faire principles and only begrudgingly resorted to countercyclical policy to moderate three recessions during the 1950s. In contrast, John Kennedy's advisers were unabashed Keynesians who believed they could fine-tune the economy using fiscal policy to achieve economic growth and full employment. In the mid-1960s Milton Friedman advanced a strong monetarist dissent to Keynesian economics. The gradualist game plan to reduce inflation under President Nixon was strongly influenced by monetarist doctrine, but was short-lived; in three years, with inflation growing worse, Nixon took the unprecedented step of imposing wage-price controls. In the 1980s, a new economic approach, supply-side economics, gained political influence. Though many economists attacked its assumptions as being unsupported by empirical research, theory, or common sense, this school of thought preached exactly what the Republican party and President Reagan wanted to hear. The commitment of Eisenhower to economic orthodoxy, the love affair between Kennedy and Keynesian economics, the rise of monetarism with the new Nixon, and the supply-side revolution under Reagan all resulted because these presidents chose key advisers whose thinking was influenced by ideology as much as by economics.

EISENHOWER AND ECONOMIC ORTHODOXY

By nominating Dwight Eisenhower in 1952 the Republican party repudiated the darling of its conservative wing, Senator Robert Taft of Ohio, in favor of a World War II hero who could win. Eisenhower's views on politics were not well known, so the country waited for early indications of how this "nonpolitician" would govern. New research plays down some of the stereotypes that Eisenhower was old-fashioned in his views and passive in his responsibilities. A major study by John Sloan concludes that Eisenhower "was the most significant player in determining his administration's macroeconomic policy" and was "constantly attentive and often assertive in this policy area." However, Eisenhower, a career military man, also "recognized his lack of expertise and experience in economic policymaking and attempted to learn from those he felt had greater knowledge."[4]

On economic matters Ike did not openly repudiate the theory behind the Employment Act of 1946. As he stated in the 1954 *Economic Report*,

> Government must use its vast power to help maintain employment and purchasing power as well as to maintain reasonably stable prices. Government must be alert and sensitive to economic developments. . . . It must be prepared to take preventive as well as remedial action; and it must be ready to cope with new situations that may arise. This is not a start-and-stop responsibility, but a continuous one.[5]

How this responsibility would be translated into policy depended upon his economic advisers. The first CEA chairman, Arthur Burns, joined an administration that believed that good government should be modeled on sound business practices. Having great faith in entrepreneurs who ran large organizations, Eisenhower recruited successful businessmen into his cabinet (described by *The New Republic* as "eight millionaires and one plumber"). These top-level advisers to the president, as one commentator put it, "shared an orthodoxy based on simple precepts that had filtered down out of the eighteenth and nineteenth centuries"[6] They believed in laissez faire principles, and the hallmarks of their political economy were balanced budgets and reduced taxes, a faith in private enterprise and the competitive marketplace, and no government planning or intrusive regulation of the economy.

Eisenhower's 1956 State of the Union Message reflected these themes, as shown by his analogy between government finances and the family budget: "Over the long term, a balanced budget is a sure index of thrifty management—in a home, in a business, or in the federal government. When achievement of a balanced budget is for long put off in a business or home, bankruptcy is the result."[7] Respect for individual achievement also curbed Ike's appetite for welfare. The federal government, as he stated in 1955, "must do its part to advance human welfare and encourage economic growth with constructive actions, but only where our people cannot take the necessary actions for themselves."[8]

258   The approach used by CEA Chairman Burns was compatible with these Republican principles. While he did not deny the theoretical contribution of Keynes, Burns saw practical difficulties in applying macroeconomic theory to fiscal policy. Burns spent much of his energy trying to counter the conservative opinions of Treasury Secretary George M. Humphrey, one of the most influential members of Eisenhower's cabinet.[9] Whatever countercyclical policy came about during these years was due largely to Burns's impact, according to Edward Flash: "The Burns Council . . . reconcile[d] Republican conservatism with the administration's countercyclical responsibilities. Through its activities, the Council achieved a . . . liberalization of administration views—not as much as a revision, but an updating to modern circumstances."[10]

However, critics judge countercyclical policy during the 1950s to have been largely inadvertent.[11] There were three recessions during Ike's tenure: 1953–54, 1957–58, and 1960–61. That they did not degenerate into major contractions was due more to automatic stabilizers than to discretionary countercyclical policy. The primary concern of the Eisenhower administration was inflation.

That concern about price stability tempered the use of fiscal policy. Sloan characterizes the president's outlook in this way:

> As is true of most conservatives, Eisenhower feared inflation more than unemployment. During his presidency, and especially in his second term, he was more willing to act—and endure the resulting political heat—to combat inflation than unemployment. He felt that infrequent, wisely selected, and well-timed governmental interventions in the economy could moderate economic fluctuations and provide for steadier growth. . . . But he rejected the notion espoused by liberal Democrats and many Keynesian economists that more public intervention to manipulate aggregate demand would improve the economy and possibly eliminate the negative consequences of the business cycle.[12]

In May 1953 Eisenhower recommended that Congress make more cuts in the FY54 budget (to begin July 1, 1953) that President Truman had formulated. He also asked for a six-month extension of the excess profits tax (levied during the Korean War and due to expire on June 30), so that the Treasury would not lose about $800 million in revenue. Federal outlays were cut each year from 1953 to 1955, and the deficit was reduced from $6.5 billion in 1953 to a $1.2 billion surplus in 1954. Economists point to this retrenchment in federal spending as one cause of the first Eisenhower recession.

From the beginning of 1953 there were signs that the economy was weakening, but Eisenhower was preoccupied with getting his administration organized. What saved the economy was a series of tax cuts already scheduled to go into effect. On December 31, 1953, the income tax increase and excess profits tax from the Korean War era ended, and Congress also acted on Ike's promise of tax relief by approving the Excise Reduction Act of 1954. Additional income tax reforms enacted in 1954 further cut revenues by $1.4 billion during FY55.[13] All told, these tax cuts, which reduced federal revenues by $6.1 billion, stimulated the economy. However, the official response was timid, according to Lewis.

> With the possible exception of excise taxes, these reductions were not put into effect primarily to counteract the recession. They had been previously scheduled, or planned earlier as part of the administration's campaign to reduce the size of the federal budget, or to reform the tax system. . . . In all likelihood, they would have taken place without a recession.[14]

Arthur Burns had studies done by the CEA and the BOB to define various antirecession programs. On his agenda were new highway construction, coaxing the Fed to ease credit, and accelerated public works spending. By the spring of 1954, however, signs appeared that the recession had bottomed out (the trough came in May 1954), so little of Burns's standby program was implemented. Defense spending was accelerated due to the upcoming 1954 midterm elections, though its impact was not felt until the first quarter of 1955. In sum, countercyclical policies "were slow to be initiated, were not all announced to the public, and were modest in scope—being limited at first to a within-year shift of government expenditures. While considered early in 1954, the general speed-up of expenditures was not actually initiated until May."[15]

In 1956 Burns resigned as CEA chairman and was succeeded by Raymond Saulnier, a CEA staffer who had been appointed by Burns. Years later Saulnier would recollect what Eisenhower told him upon taking office: "What I want is your best judgment as a professional economist; the job is economic advising, not political advising, and in any case I have too much political advice as it is."[16] During Saulnier's tenure budget surpluses were recorded in 1956 and 1957, but then back-to-back recessions clouded the remainder of the administration. The first seemed to be much worse than the 1953–54 downturn, and during the early months of 1958 a debate among Ike's advisers focused on what antirecession steps should be taken. Eisenhower's advisers recommended caution. In letters to GOP congressional leaders on March 8, 1958, Eisenhower said that the role of government "must necessarily be to stimulate private production and employment, not to substitute public spending for private spending, nor to extend public domination over private activity."[17] He listed actions being

260   undertaken: speed-up of public works projects, release of $200 million in mortgage assistance funds, targeting defense contracts to areas with labor surpluses, increased discount allowances on VA-guaranteed mortgages, and liberalized lending rules for savings and loan associations. Eisenhower also asked Congress to enact a temporary extension of jobless benefits, but no tax cut.

Arthur Burns (now an outsider) advocated an immediate tax cut to stem the recession, as he feared that the administration's wait-and-see approach might allow the economy to fall too deeply into recession. But Eisenhower was now guided by Secretary of the Treasury Robert Anderson, who was even more conservative on fiscal policy than his predecessor,[18] and Fed Chairman William McChesney Martin, and both wanted to delay any action on taxes.

There was another obstacle to more aggressive countercyclical policy during the second recession—Eisenhower himself. Sloan makes the persuasive argument that the "Eisenhower of 1958 was not as politically sensitive or as flexible as the Eisenhower of 1954. In the first recession, the president had recognized how politically sensitive a rise in the unemployment level was; in the second, he did not."[19] The president did not seek help from the Congress in 1958 because, according to Sloan, the "new Eisenhower" became rigidly moralistic during his second term, and "Eisenhower and [Treasury Secretary] Anderson no longer believed that they could negotiate reasonable compromises with the Democrats in Congress. By losing faith in the legislative process, Eisenhower surrendered a large part of the presidency's power of initiative and placed himself and his party in a very vulnerable position. The political price for this was high in 1958 and 1960."[20]

The trough in the second recession came in April 1958, and by June there was general agreement that recovery was underway; the business cycle had taken its own course without much help from the Eisenhower administration. An analysis of spending patterns during this period concludes that

> The discretionary antirecession actions made their peak contribution in the last quarter of 1958—well after the cyclical trough in the first quarter of 1958—but had not been completely turned off in the second quarter of 1959. More important during the recovery than deliberate counterrecession actions were those taken for other reasons [such as Sputnik-inspired defense spending]. . . . [21]

But the recovery was not strong enough to prevent a record peacetime deficit ($12.8 billion) in FY59, and congressional Democrats blamed Eisenhower for the red ink. The president then resolved to have no more deficits, and weeks before sending the FY60 budget to Congress Ike took **261** the unorthodox step of announcing his desire to balance that budget at $2 billion below the latest estimate for FY59 expenditures. This statement, says Lewis Kimmel, "showed conclusively that the balanced budget idea continued to be influential in shaping public policy."[22]

Actual outlays by the federal government were almost equal in FY59 and FY60, and this retrenchment is cited by economists as one reason why the economy slumped back into recession. While President Eisenhower did not countermand the automatic stabilizers, as economist Richard Froyen also points out, "*discretionary* fiscal policy actions were only timidly countercyclical in the 1958 recession and were restrictive in 1959–60."[23]

The commitment to balance the FY60 budget (which showed a $300 million surplus) is evidence against the political business cycle theory. Richard Nixon had to wage his 1960 presidential campaign in the midst of a new recession, and his narrow loss by 100,000 votes to John Kennedy can be attributed to the depressed economy. (Certainly Vice President Nixon thought so.) But Eisenhower did not sway the budget to assist partisan politics; on the contrary, he recommended frugality and a budget surplus in his last Budget Message to Congress in early 1961.

The balanced budget goal restrained countercyclical policy to the end of the Eisenhower years, although Ike was not as rigid as the Republicans who occupied the White House before the Great Depression. The 1946 Employment Act survived the 1950s, as Keynesian economics was filtered through a conservative ideology that stressed a wait-and-see approach, reliance on market forces and private capital, and minimal intervention by government. The important concession to Keynesianism was that Ike's economic advisers "argued that the budget need not be in balance every year—a break with traditional party principles—but only over the course of an entire business cycle, a period of several years."[24]

KENNEDY AND KEYNESIANISM

During the 1960 campaign John Kennedy promised to move the country to a New Frontier. At 43, Kennedy was the youngest elected president, and he recruited an energetic staff to achieve his domestic objectives and elevated the prestige and influence of economics like no previous executive. "Economics has come of age in the 1960s," said Walter Heller, who chaired the CEA during that period.[25] Kennedy consulted various economists outside government, including John Kenneth Galbraith and Seymour Harris of Harvard, Paul Samuelson of MIT, and James Tobin of Yale. All were Keynesians, which was not surprising since if

262   Kennedy "had chosen six American economists at random the odds were high that he would have obtained five with the ideas on fiscal policy that his advisors actually had, because those ideas were shared by almost all economists in 1960."[26] The policy views of these Keynesian economists, which became known as the **new economics**, may be summarized as follows:

1. Investment is the unstable element in the economic system and leads to instability in national income.

2. Of the twin problems of unemployment or inflation, unemployment is the more severe problem and must be given primacy even when inflation threatens, though the trade-off between full employment and price is also acknowledged.

3. The emphasis on policy is activist and is primarily demand-management oriented. Keynesians assume that aggregate supply will adjust accordingly.

4. Both fiscal policy and monetary policy are required to achieve full employment since the macroeconomy, if left alone, is not structured so that it would self-generate a stable condition of full employment.

5. Fiscal policy is effective in the short run, and perhaps in the long run, in effecting changes in the GNP. And fiscal policy is more effective when aided by an accommodative monetary policy.

A Cautious Beginning

Even before his inauguration Kennedy asked Walter Heller to be his CEA chairman so that work on the economic agenda could begin immediately. Like JFK, Heller was a dynamic personality, but unlike Kennedy his views were less pragmatic and driven more by a liberal ideology he inherited from his mentor, economist John Commons. Heller's objective was to cut unemployment and use educational and training programs to develop "social capital," and thus he focused on public policy rather than on theoretical economics.

Heller believed that fiscal policy could guide economic growth; as soon as he took office, the CEA wasted no time confronting the 1960–61 recession. Heller worked long hours, deluged his CEA staff with research, and turned to outside consultants. One study, "Prospects and Policies for the 1961 American Economy," done by Paul Samuelson during the transition period, argued a position that Heller championed throughout his tenure. Since the economy was not operating at its full potential,

> The goal for 1961 must be to bring the recession to an end, to reinstate a condition of expansion and recovery and to adopt measures likely to make the expansion one that will not after a year or two peter out at levels of activity far below our true potential. Indeed, policy for 1961 should be directed against the background of the whole decade ahead.[27]

Although the 1960–61 recession was the least severe of the four postwar recessions to date, it had followed the shortest period of economic expansion. This led some economists to fear that a dangerous stagnation was gripping the nation, which is why Kennedy's advisers favored a stronger dose of stimulus than that mild recession warranted.

In his 1961 State of the Union Message, President Kennedy said that the problem was not merely recession but "seven months of recession, three and one-half years of slack, seven years of diminished economic growth, and nine years of falling farm income."[28] Three days later his Economic Message to Congress recommended actions to combat recession and lay the foundation for economic growth: more federal spending, extended jobless benefits, more stimulus for housing construction, and a speed-up of urban renewal projects. Kennedy also recommended to the Fed a monetary policy that coupled low interest on long-term bonds with high interest on short-term bonds (which became known as Operation Twist), designed to encourage domestic investment and attract foreign capital while curbing the outflow of U.S. dollars abroad. Missing was any mention of a tax cut.

A tax cut at this point would have jeopardized congressional support for Kennedy's domestic programs. According to Samuelson, "whatever the economic merits of a tax cut, it seemed politically out of the question. The president had run on a platform that asked sacrifices of the American people. How then could he begin by giving them what many would regard as a 'handout'?"[29] There was also opposition to any tax cut from Treasury Secretary Douglas Dillon, who preferred tax reforms that would not unbalance the budget.

Only CEA Chairman Heller favored an immediate tax cut, on the grounds that existing tax rates were too high and thus acted as a "fiscal drag" on the economy. But Kennedy was cautious, and thus receptive to Dillon's concern about excessive deficits, with the result that the president dealt with the 1960–61 downturn using a blend of conventional antirecession spending policies. On taxes he would go no further than recommend in April that Congress enact a tax credit to stimulate business investment. Even this did not win easy approval. Not until October 1962 did the

264   Congress enact its version (a 7 percent tax credit) of the legislation Kennedy had proposed eighteen months earlier.

The trough of the recession came in February 1961, and, as with the earlier postwar recessions, the impact of federal spending on cushioning this economic downturn was largely due to the automatic stabilizers. Analysis by Lewis indicates that "no discretionary antirecession actions were in effect before the trough month; discretionary actions are therefore relevant to the speed of the recovery but not to the initiation of a turning point."[30]

World events intervened to force changes in economic policy during Kennedy's first year. The ill-fated Bay of Pigs invasion of Cuba was in April 1961; the Berlin Crisis followed in June and July. To meet the Soviet challenges President Kennedy pondered an increase in defense spending for FY62, and this renewed the debate within his administration over whether deficits should be allowed to rise or taxes increased. Walter Heller stood against any tax increase, but President Kennedy was unsure what to do. Finally, in July 1961 Kennedy requested $3.4 billion in new defense spending without a tax increase, but to placate the opposition he stated that he would submit a balanced budget for the next fiscal year.[31] While a victory for Heller, it was only a partial victory because, as Edward Flash observed, "The commitment to balance the budget was a far more important battle lost. To avoid raising taxes did nothing to the existing taxes that were stunting economic growth short of full employment."[32]

Walter Heller testified to Congress in March 1961 about the inadequacies of countercyclical policy based entirely on automatic stabilizers. While the built-in stabilizers cushion an economic downturn, he said, they also work to retard economic recovery because tax revenues are generated at the expense of consumer spending and private investment. As the economy approaches full employment, revenues would exceed expenditures by several billions (called the "fiscal dividend"), enough to fund new programs, retire some debt, and restrain inflation. But the problem, he argued, is that high existing tax rates would extract too much income from the private sector as the economy moves toward full employment. The result he called a "fiscal drag" on economic expansion, meaning the economy would be prevented from realizing its full potential. Heller wanted a tax cut to remove this obstacle to growth.

Moreover Heller criticized the balanced budget concept, saying, "The success of fiscal and budget policies cannot be measured only by whether the budget is in the black or in the red. The true test is whether the economy is in balance. Only an economy that is realizing its potential can produce the goods and create the jobs the country needs."[33] This was a reference to the gap between actual GNP and potential GNP (GNP at full employment). Another concept promoted by the Heller CEA was the "full employment surplus." Both were elaborated upon in the CEA's 1961 *Annual Report.*

In this, its first *Annual Report,* the CEA charted the actual versus potential GNP during the 1950s and early 1960s. It also plotted the unemployment rate against this **GNP gap** to show that the economy operated below its potential during the fifties, with the result that the jobless rate was too high. The council projected a trend line for potential GNP from mid-1955 (when unemployment was 4 percent and no GNP gap existed) and estimated that by 1961 potential GNP exceeded actual GNP by $40 billion. The reason that unemployment stayed above the 4 percent full-employment level, the CEA concluded, was insufficient economic growth. This problem was caused *not* by inadequate private investment or consumer demand but by the restrictive fiscal policy of the Eisenhower administration.[34]

The Kennedy Tax Cut

President Kennedy laid the groundwork for a major policy shift in speeches and meetings during the spring of 1962. He was trying to repair the political damage from his famous confrontation with the steel industry over its price increases, which was followed by a steep decline in the Dow-Jones averages as Wall Street perceived Kennedy to be antibusiness. This negative reaction by the financial community worried JFK's advisers, who feared that unemployment might rise and economic growth stagnate just about the time of the 1964 presidential election.

But this political development simply dramatized the fact that the economic outlook was not upbeat. The expansion had bogged down, with the jobless rate holding at 5.5 percent, and there were projections that the FY63 budget deficit might be as high as $4 billion. All this caused Kennedy to renounce his wage-price guidelines policy and to rethink his position on taxes. During the summer of 1962 a familiar debate was taking place within the administration, between Walter Heller and White House aides who advocated an immediate tax cut and Treasury Secretary Douglas Dillon who sought tax reforms. Those deliberations ended in August 1962, when Kennedy sided with Walter Heller but chose *not* to cut taxes until January 1963. Again political considerations were paramount.

Kennedy was aware that powerful figures in Congress and in his administration would oppose, and surely defeat, any immediate tax cut, and his much-publicized pledge to balance the FY63 budget was an additional obstacle. But his August 1962 decision to seek a tax reduction signified more than a turning point in Kennedy's economic outlook.[35] This was the

266   first time since World War II that a president recommended tax cuts as a countercyclical policy to anticipate (and prevent) a downturn in the business cycle.

From August until January, there was jockeying by White House aides to fashion a policy consensus on taxes in preparation for the next State of the Union Message. The only question was how much to cut taxes the next year. Heller wanted a large tax reduction in 1963 to stimulate the economy, with the remainder tied to subsequent tax reforms, while Dillon reversed those priorities. Since tax reform is Treasury's jurisdiction, Dillon held the political advantage, so Heller moved to influence the president by giving congressional testimony, writing articles, and making public speeches.

Kennedy's January 1963 State of the Union Message recommended cutting taxes by $13.5 billion: an $11 billion reduction in personal income taxes and a $2.5 billion lowering of corporate taxes. These would be achieved by cutting the minimum-maximum rates on income from the existing 20–91 percent rates on individuals to 14–65 percent, and the corporate rate from 52 percent to 47 percent. The major reductions would come over three years, with only $6 billion earmarked for 1963. In the Budget Message that followed, Kennedy predicted that the tax cuts would cause the budget deficit to reach $11.9 billion.

Kennedy broke his promise to strictly balance the FY63 budget, and Dillon won his battle to get the tax cuts spread across three years. However, the State of the Union Message defended the tax cuts as "the surest and the soundest way of achieving in time a balanced budget in a balanced full employment economy."[36] This allusion to a full employment surplus shows how Kennedy's thinking was influenced by those arguments about a lag in economic growth, a gap in gross national product, and a fiscal drag on private investment and consumption. "The Council [of Economic Advisers], primarily in the person of its chairman, encouraged Kennedy to develop a sophisticated economic philosophy he had not previously possessed and, in so doing, transformed an instinctive conservative into a conscious liberal."[37]

Congress was not impressed. It approved no tax cut in 1963 because the legislative debate got bogged down on the issues of reforming versus cutting taxes, the size of the budget, and the deficit. There was jockeying for partisan advantage because House Republicans wanted a tax cut linked to spending cuts, and when the economy began to rebound in April 1963, there was less pressure on Congress to act boldly. Through it all, as economist Herbert Stein notes, "with respect to the modern economics of fiscal and monetary policy, the Congressional debates show more skepticism and indifference than conviction and conversion."[38]

Senator Harry Byrd (D-VA), who chaired the Finance Committee and strongly advocated government economy, refused to hurry consideration of the tax bill before the year was over. On November 22, 1963, President Kennedy was killed by an assassin's bullet, and Vice President Lyndon Johnson succeeded to the highest office, where he had the task of prodding Byrd and the Congress to act. Johnson won over the opposition by promising to keep the FY65 budget under $100 billion and, as a result, tax legislation was finally readied for his signature on February 26, 1964.

The Revenue Act of 1964, along with the Excise Tax Reduction Act of 1965, cut taxes both years by an estimated $11 billion for individuals and $3 billion for business.[39] They would stimulate the economy, and the logic underlying this strategy was discussed by the CEA in its 1963 *Annual Report*. The key to the economic expansion was the Keynesian **multiplier effect**.

In the short term, tax cuts would increase personal disposable (after-tax) income of households and corporate profits (which also increase household income through higher dividend payments). Most of this increase in personal disposable income would be spent on consumption, and the cuts in corporate taxes would foster capital investment by businesses. Over the long term the multiplier would then take hold.

> Tax reduction will start a process of cumulative expansion throughout the economy. . . . The initial increases in spending will stimulate production and employment, generating additional incomes . . . as inventories are depleted, retailers will quickly expand orders. As manufacturers' sales rise in response and their own inventories of finished goods decline, they will activate idle production lines, hire additional workers, place orders for materials and components. Thus the expansion will spread to other industries, leading to further expansion of production, employment, and orders.[40]

After the first infusion of money from the immediate tax cut, the problem was to estimate how much additional spending would be generated by the rise in GNP, because not all income generated by this multiplier effect is spent on consumption. Corporate profits increase as GNP rises, so businesses pay more taxes, and other taxes are taken from household income by state, local, and federal governments. After deducting these "leakages" the CEA estimated that about 7 percent would be diverted into personal savings, but 93 percent would be spent on consumption. The Council of Economic Advisers, therefore, estimated that the multiplier effect would be two—the initial tax cut would be doubled in its cumulative economic impact.

The evidence shows that those effects were probably achieved by the Kennedy tax cut.[41] The GNP gap was narrowed from a peak of $50 billion

268   annually in the first quarter of 1961 to an annualized rate of $10 billion in the first quarter of 1965. The unemployment rate dropped from 5.2 percent in 1964 to 4.5 percent in 1965 and even further in 1966. In 1963 real GNP had risen by only 4 percent, compared to 5.5 percent increases in both 1964 and 1965. Finally, federal revenues increased from 1964 to 1965 *despite* the tax cut, supporting the CEA's view that economic stimulation caused by tax reduction would yield more government revenues in the future. (Supply-side economists who persuaded President Reagan to severely cut income taxes in 1981 recalled the Kennedy experience to make the same argument.)

This era of prosperity allowed President Johnson to take political risks, leading him to simultaneously fight the Vietnam War and attempt to create the Great Society. Due to escalating defense and social expenditures the economy achieved full employment. The unemployment rate dropped from 3.8 percent in 1966 and 1967 to 3.6 percent in 1968 and 3.5 percent in 1969, the lowest levels since the Korean War. But since these increased expenditures were financed without additional taxes, the growing deficits generated inflationary pressures. Where the CPI had risen 4.6 percent over 1961–64, during 1965–68 it rose by 11.7 percent. To counter rising prices, Keynesian economics prescribes that spending be reduced or taxes raised, but for political reasons President Johnson was reluctant to do either. He delayed making his request to Congress for an income tax surcharge, with the result that inflation became an acute problem his successor had to deal with.

NIXON AND MONETARISM

The Monetarist Critique

Richard Nixon's advisers believed that the fundamental economic problem they faced was demand-pull inflation caused by Great Society and Vietnam War spending and aggravated by the delayed enactment of the 1968 tax surcharge. They also felt that the impact of fiscal policy alone was "probably slower and smaller than commonly assumed and probably also difficult to predict."[42] The Nixon CEA thus discounted government's ability to fine-tune the economy using spending and taxes and, for this reason, was sympathetic to the arguments being raised by a new breed of economist—the monetarists.

The monetarist school of thought was founded by Milton Friedman, then of the University of Chicago, who was awarded the Nobel Prize in Economics in 1976 for his theoretical contributions to economics. But the beginnings of the monetarist critique was a 1950 study by Clark Warburton,[43] which concluded that changes in the money supply *preceded* turning points (contraction or expansion) in the business cycle. Warburton hinted that a stable money supply was associated with economic stability and, most importantly, that fluctuations in the money supply were related to changes in government policy. The implication was that government policy exacerbates (perhaps even causes) business fluctuations.

The next round in this intellectual debate came in 1956 when Friedman published his seminal work, *Studies in the Quantity Theory of Money,* which offered a new understanding of the role of money in the macroeconomy.[44] Friedman argued that the money supply affects *both* prices and output. The empirical test he devised to validate these relationships was *A Monetary History of the United States, 1867–1960,* co-authored with Anna Schwartz in 1963.[45] These publications established **monetarism** and represented a direct attack on Keynesianism. Looking at twenty business cycles, Friedman and Schwartz confirmed that changes in the money supply *preceded* changes in national income during expansions and contractions and, furthermore, that policy decisions by government usually led to these changes in the money supply. Friedman and Schwartz concluded that stable economic growth requires a money supply that grows at a steady rate rather than one that fluctuates in order to fine-tune monetary policy.

In his 1967 presidential address to the American Economics Association, "The Role of Monetary Policy,"[46] Friedman talked about public expectations and the fluctuations of prices and wages by drawing on some ideas developed the year before by Edmund Phelps. From this evolved what is known as the Friedman-Phelps argument, or expectations-augmented Phillips curve.[47] A new concept—the **natural-rate hypothesis**—was added to the vocabulary of economics, and it posed fundamental questions about the desirability of an activist fiscal policy based upon Keynesian precepts.

To begin, Friedman assumes that there exists a *short-term* **Phillips curve** that correctly depicts a trade-off between employment and inflation (Figure 10.1). As unemployment rises, inflation falls; as the jobless rate falls, inflation rises. A comparison of pre-1965 and post-1965 trends in inflation and unemployment illustrates the short-term Phillips curve. During 1961–65 the jobless rate averaged 5.8 percent and the inflation rate averaged 1.2 percent; during 1965–68 the unemployment rate was lower, averaging 3.9 percent, while the inflation rate increased to an average of 3.3 percent. In the *long term,* however, Friedman and Phelps argue that the Phillips curve is vertical at the natural rate of unemployment, which is the rate at which the labor market is in equilibrium at any real wage given the institutional factors that prevail. (The real wage measures one's

Figure 10.1   Short-Term Phillips Curve

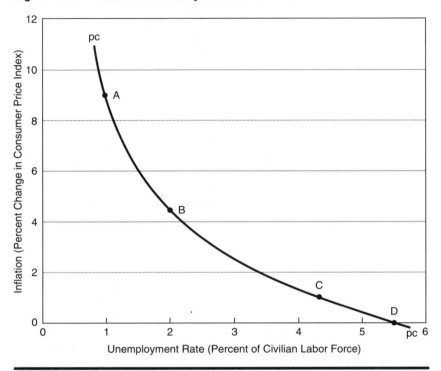

purchasing power and is simply the nominal wage divided by the price level, for example the CPI.)

There is no guarantee that the natural unemployment rate will be satisfactory to the public. And if it is too high, say 6 percent, the way to generate a lower jobless rate, according to Keynesian economics, is to use fiscal and monetary stimulus to increase aggregate demand and move the economy towards less unemployment. However, Friedman believed that fiscal stimulus would only increase prices. (This is what a vertical Phillips curve indicates.) Under this scenario, the economic impact is more inflation but at the same unemployment level as existed before the process began.

Should this cycle be repeated, with more doses of fiscal and monetary policy and higher inflation resulting, then an entirely new dimension takes effect. Eventually workers become aware that their anticipated real wage increases did not materialize, since prices had risen so much more than

their wages and salaries. The rational thing would be for workers to negotiate wage and salary increases above the *expected* inflation rate so that,
by the end of their next contract, they will have achieved a real wage
increase despite inflation.

Given this kind of "inflation psychology" a new Phillips curve has
been created, one with a higher expected rate of inflation (which yields
higher actual inflation as well) at every level of unemployment including
the natural rate. Things are now much worse. The economy suffers a
higher inflation rate but with no reduction in unemployment below its
natural rate. This argument neutralizes fiscal policies intended to drive the
jobless rate below its natural rate because the only thing achieved is higher
inflation.

In addition to Milton Friedman (now at Stanford University's Hoover
Institution) other prominent monetarists are Karl Brunner of the University of Rochester, Allan Metzler of Carnegie-Mellon Institute, and William
Poole of Brown University (and a CEA member under Reagan). All would
subscribe to these cardinal tenets of the monetarist school:

1. The economy has a natural rate of unemployment to which it
   will tend in the long run. Short-term policies, monetary or
   fiscal, to drive unemployment below that level will only lead
   to inflation.

2. Activist fiscal and monetary policies will not work. Adjust the
   growth rate in the money supply with the growth rate in real
   GNP and the economy will show greater stability.

3. The level of real GNP is determined by the quality and
   quantity of resources, technology, and consumer preferences for
   goods, income, money, assets, or leisure. Only changes in
   public attitudes toward thrift and increased productivity
   through technology can affect the real gross national product.

4. Changes in the supply of money lead to changes in prices and
   changes in nominal GNP.

The Nixon Economic Game Plan

The monetarist critique was a strong influence on the Nixon
administration in 1969. Although President Nixon had a greater personal
interest in foreign policy, he understood "how vital economic success was
to his efforts on other policy and political fronts. So, while no expert in
the field, and with no great interest in economics, Nixon felt compelled
to spend time—and political capital—on the economic front."[48]

272   Despite the monetarist critique, when Nixon entered office most economists remained Keynesian, and Keynesians tended to be more Democratic and liberal. (By contrast, monetarists were more conservative and likely to favor Republican policies.) Herbert Stein once recalled in jest (or chagrin) that "McCracken [CEA chairman under Nixon] used to say that the reason for their appointment to the CEA was that they were the only three Republican economists that Nixon could find."[49] (Besides Stein and McCracken the third CEA member appointed by Nixon was Hendrik Houthakker.)

To ease inflationary pressures the Nixon team adopted a "gradualist" economic game plan using both fiscal and monetary policy. In March 1969, President Nixon asked Congress to extend the 1968 income tax surcharge and announced cuts in the proposed FY70 budget (to begin July 1). Also to be delayed were scheduled reductions in excise taxes on automobiles and telephones. The next month Nixon followed with tax reforms, including repeal of the investment tax credit, limits on tax shelters, and the removal of below-poverty households from the income tax rolls. However, Congress went further by approving both a tax cut and increases in Social Security benefits—amounting to a $5 billion revenue loss. Though Nixon was upset, he signed that legislation against the advice of McCracken, Treasury Secretary David Kennedy, and Budget Director Robert Mayo.

The Fed also endorsed the gradualist approach by tightening up the money supply. The objective, Fed Chairman Martin told the Joint Economic Committee in February 1969, was "trying to disinflate without deflating."[50]

The gradualist game plan attempted to circumvent the policy dilemma of the short-term Phillips curve. In his 1970 *Economic Report* the president stated: "After 5 years of sustained unemployment followed by 5 years of sustained inflation, some have concluded that the price of finding work for the unemployed must be the hardship of inflation for all." Nixon could hardly admit to this dire scenario, and instead he offered hope that "if we apply the hard lessons learned from the sixties to the decade ahead, and add a new realism to the management of our economic policies, I believe we can attain the goal of plentiful jobs earning dollars of stable purchasing power."[51] This would not be an easy task given the economic experience of the past decade.

Nixon's advisers hoped that restrictive fiscal and monetary policies would contract aggregate demand gradually and thus allow only modest rises in unemployment which, in turn, would slow down wage and price increases. This strategy, it was hoped, would also help to break the inflationary psychology, because once people realized that inflation was coming under control, they would expect greater price stability and would soften **273** their wage demands.

But the gradualist policy did not work fast enough. The CPI grew by 11.3 percent over the two years from 1969 to 1971, compared to 11.7 percent during Johnson's entire term, and Richard Nixon faced the prospect of reelection. Politics dictated that something dramatic be done, and on August 15, 1971, Nixon announced his new economic policy, including wage-price controls. As we described in Chapter 8, while this unprecedented use of direct controls during peacetime temporarily held prices in check, inflation continued unabated after they were ended.

Not until the early 1980s was the inflationary spiral broken, but this time the Fed pursued a purer monetarist strategy, while the Reagan administration utilized an approach fundamentally at odds with gradualism. The unemployment rate was allowed to reach a post-depression high of 10 percent, after which a long gradual recovery brought the jobless rate down to its natural rate and the inflation rate dropped significantly.

REAGAN AND THE SUPPLY-SIDE REVOLUTION

Supply-Side Economics

What became known as Reaganomics was a hybrid economic program aimed at stimulating economic growth with a reduced governmental role, less social welfare spending coupled with more defense expenditures, and a restrained monetary policy. These measures were supposed to eliminate stagflation. The fundamental problem, according to Reagan, was big government. The 1982 *Economic Report* reads much like a treatise on conservatism, as shown by Reagan's summary of the problem and its solution:

> The policies of the past have failed. They failed because they did not provide the environment in which American energy, entrepreneurship, and talent can best be put to work. Instead of being a successful promoter of economic growth and individual freedom, government became the enemy of growth and an intruder on individual initiative and freedom. My program . . . seeks to create a new environment in which the strengths of America can be put to work for the benefit of us all. That environment will be an America in which honest work is no longer discouraged by ever-rising prices and tax rates, a country that looks forward to the future not with uncertainty but with the confidence that infused our forefathers.[52]

A new macroeconomic theory strongly influenced the Reagan agenda, **supply-side economics**.[53] Supply-side economics became a popular buzz-

274   word on the national scene, though as Juster observes: "Seldom has an economic experiment been put in place with less conventional credentialing by professional economists."[54] However, the theory's economic agenda was highly compatible with the political needs of the Republican party under Ronald Reagan in 1980.

What was popularized as supply-side economics is not the meaning originally given to that term by most economists. The commonly used reference to "supply siders" identifies those economists who were highly publicized during the early Reagan administration. Conventional supply-side economists, found among Keynesians, rational expectationists, and monetarists, are concerned with productivity. They study the quantity and quality of raw materials, labor services, and capital equipment, and what distinguishes these supply siders is attention to incentives, like taxes, which influence the growth of the resources of production and of GNP. Among the better-known economists in this tradition, a minority in the profession, are Martin Feldstein of Harvard University, who was Reagan's second CEA chairman, and Michael Boskin of Stanford University, Bush's CEA chairman. Conventional supply-side economists also focus on the side effects of government programs: How do unemployment compensation, food stamps, and other income-maintenance programs affect the supply of labor? How do Social Security, taxes, and transfer payments affect the savings rate? In the 1970s supply-side economics gained more prominence because of the general perception that the United States growth rate was declining.

The economists who accompanied Ronald Reagan to Washington in 1981 were a creation of the media. They were ideologues able to market a viewpoint that many economists, including Republicans like Herbert Stein and Democrats like Walter Heller,[55] repudiated. The supply-side school is often associated with Robert Mundell of Columbia University, Manuel H. Johnson, Jr., Jude Wanniski, and George Gilder, although its most famous spokesman was economist Arthur Laffer of the University of Southern California. His famous Laffer curve provided the economic rationale for the Reagan income tax cuts.

The **Laffer curve** (Figure 10.2) takes as its starting point the observation that marginal tax rates of either 0 percent or 100 percent lead to zero tax revenues. Theoretically, tax revenues should increase along with tax rates until a turning point is reached. That turning point (labeled E in Figure 10.2) is the point at which marginal tax rates are so high that they create a strong disincentive against working. Also affected is the return on savings, which determines how much money will be provided for capital investment.

Figure 10.2 The Laffer Curve

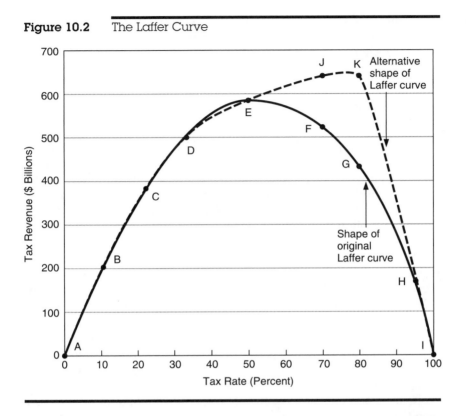

The Laffer curve thus combines two ideas, both of which the Reagan administration found very appealing. First, it argues that tax rates can be so high that they stifle productive activity and economic growth. Second, these high tax rates actually reduce tax revenues if they are "over the peak" of the Laffer curve. By assuming that tax rates are actually that high (which was an article of faith among supply-siders rather than an empirically verified observation), it could be argued that tax cuts are good for both the economy and governmental finances.

Supply-siders argued that a decrease in the marginal tax rates (e.g., from point F to point E in Figure 10.2) would stimulate more work and more savings. These increases would be so large that output would grow rapidly, and within a short period federal revenues would increase above the level where they were prior to the tax cuts. However, if tax rates are not actually beyond the peak of the Laffer curve, then the cut just described would move revenues from point J to point E—if work and savings

276   do not increase as expected, then these tax cuts (without equal reductions in government spending) give rise to even larger budget deficits. And this is exactly what happened.

Reaganomics

Although there was talk in Congress about cutting income taxes to spur economic growth long before Ronald Reagan was elected president, nothing much happened until Arthur Laffer explained his theory to Jude Wanniski, a *Wall Street Journal* editorial writer, who then publicized the idea. Wanniski brought it to the attention of Congressman Jack Kemp (R-NY),[56] who later co-sponsored with Senator William Roth (R-DE) the Kemp-Roth Bill to cut marginal income tax rates across the board by 30 percent.

In late 1977 the Republican National Committee endorsed this bill; its backers also included some prominent Democrats, like Senators Sam Nunn (D-GA) and Lloyd Bentsen (D-TX). (The latter became President Clinton's treasury secretary.) Outside Congress, supply-side economics was promoted by Irving Kristol, editor of *The Public Interest*, and Paul Craig Roberts, associate editor of the *Wall Street Journal* (later assistant secretary of the treasury for economic policy in the Reagan administration.)

In the 1980 presidential campaign Reagan strongly endorsed the Kemp-Roth Bill, which President Carter branded irresponsible. George Bush, also a contender for the Republican nomination, went even further than Carter, calling supply-side tax cuts "voodoo economics." After Reagan was nominated, however, he picked Bush to be his running mate, and together they joined the chorus for an immediate tax cut. Within months of Reagan's decisive victory over Carter, it was enacted into law. Supply-side economics was an idea whose time had come, but its appeal was essentially political.

Keynesian economics had been embraced by the Democrats and their working-class constituency following the Great Depression. Now supply-side economics gave the GOP a program consistent with its middle-class voter base, but one with appeal to independents and Democrats. It was better than simply exploiting antitax sentiments because supply-side offered an economic rationale for cutting income taxes. Its message was simple: high marginal tax rates hurt productivity because they discourage work, personal savings, and capital investment. The policy prescriptions of supply-side economics reinforced Reagan's personal conservatism and the Republican antigovernment philosophy and served the political needs of its new constituency in the Sunbelt.

Supply-side economics also offered a less painful solution to the inflation problem. Where Keynesian demand-side theory requires that inflation be curbed through tax increases and cuts in government spending, the supply-siders argued that inflation could be reduced by increasing the supply of goods and services on the market.

Data gathered by the University of Michigan Institute for Social Research showed major changes in public attitudes toward inflation during the 1970s. After World War II Americans were upbeat and optimistic, but comparable surveys taken in the 1970s found the public lacking confidence and trust and uncertain about the future.[57] Inflation was now viewed as the major economic worry. When faced with rising prices in the 1950s and 1960s, moreover, Americans generally saved their money until prices stabilized in the future. But during the 1970s people rushed to spend their money, and even buy on credit, thinking that things would only get worse in the future. What was now "rational" economic behavior was the expectation that prices would continue to rise and that government would be unable to halt that trend.

To arrest this kind of inflation psychology a fundamentally new kind of macroeconomic policy was required. As the Reagan CEA explained in its 1982 *Annual Report,*

> Repeated attempts to use fiscal and monetary policy to stimulate output, all the while assuring the public that inflation would be slowed later, left a residue of higher inflation. . . . The entrenchment of expectations of further inflation induced policymakers to respond with another episode of restraint, thereby creating another recession, followed by another attempt at stimulus. . . . So long as economic policy had a short-run perspective, this alternating cycle of restriction and stimulus persisted. Meanwhile, the trend in the rate of inflation moved steadily upward.[58]

The greatest economic achievement of the Reagan administration was a significant lowering of the inflation rate. The CPI jumped by 39 percent over Carter's term compared to a 24 percent rise during 1981–84, and relative price stability has continued into the 1990s. What broke the back of inflation in the short-term was a severe recession; unlike his predecessors, President Reagan was willing to drive down inflation by exploiting the trade-off in the short-term Phillips curve.

This was primarily accomplished by the Federal Reserve Board under Chairman Paul Volcker, who took a determined stand to keep monetary policy tight despite the recessionary conditions. But the administration seemed to have underestimated the adverse economic impact of this "cold turkey" approach,[59] because White House staffers and Treasury Secretary Donald Regan began a "Fed bashing" campaign, fearing that a deep recession might endanger President Reagan's reelection in 1984.

278   The trough of the recession in November 1982 brought unemployment to the 10 percent rate, but afterwards the nation began a period of sustained economic growth. The reasons for this expansion are in dispute. Liberal economists would argue that the 1980s recovery was a classic Keynesian demand-led expansion, affected little by supply-side calculations. Reducing personal income taxes by 23 percent, coupled with federal budget deficits totaling $550 billion over Reagan's first term, was bound to increase aggregate demand. This is exactly what Keynesians would prescribe.

Supply-side economics had argued that long-term economic growth results from greater incentives to work, save, and invest. Because that cannot happen overnight, a supply-side-generated recovery takes longer than demand-led stimulation. The best evidence against the supply-side interpretation is that there was no dramatic increase in savings or investment during the 1981–84 period. In fact savings rates remain at historically low levels.

The lost revenue following the 1981 income tax cut (the shift from point "J" to point "E" on Figure 10.2) also suggests that the incentive to work and save was not being undermined by the existing marginal tax rates. This experience implies that the shape of the Laffer curve was different than what the Reagan supply-siders had assumed—closer to the alternate shape in Figure 10.2.

The political bickering over the Reagan deficits gave way to a crisis mentality in Congress when the Gramm-Rudman-Hollings reforms were enacted in 1985. But there was no improvement in the financial outlook, and Wall Street seemed unconvinced that the two branches would ever come to grips with a deficit problem that threatened to undermine the nation's balance of payments situation. More than anything, the unprecedented red ink under President Reagan destroyed the credibility of supply-side economics.

George Bush and the Legacy of Reaganomics

The longest peacetime economic expansion in the postwar era could not go on forever. Happily for Reagan, the previous recession came during the first two years of his term; sadly for Bush, the next contraction occurred during the last two years of his term. And worse, although this contraction reached its trough in March of 1991, the economic rebound was not dramatic: consumer confidence continued to decline, and the jobless rate rose to 7.7 percent during June of 1992—nearly a point higher than at the recession's trough. The 1977–75 and 1981–82 recessions were far deeper—reaching higher levels of unemployment than the 1990–91 contraction—but both those episodes were followed by periods of robust recovery.

Bush, who looked to be unbeatable one year earlier, trailed Arkansas Governor Bill Clinton badly in the polls after the Republican party national convention in August, and he was ultimately defeated in November. Why did the Bush administration fail to anticipate this recession and do so little to confront it? The failure to act decisively only confirmed the widespread perception that the president was preoccupied with foreign affairs and had no "vision" regarding domestic policy. A June 1992 *New York Times*/CBS News Poll found that only 16 percent approved of how President Bush was handling the economy, lower than even the worst rating given to President Carter.[60]

In fact President Bush, an economics major during his undergraduate days at Yale, held deep-seated views of how the economy should work. John Sununu, who was Bush's chief-of-staff through the end of 1991, described his mindset in this way: "The president feels very strongly that the free-market system operates best when it does not have its hands tied by government, is not shackled by a system that erroneously thinks it can improve it by command and control."[61] For this reason Bush was opposed to the demands from some Democrats for a "new industrial policy" based on planning by government and industry. "I don't think we ought to have industrial planning," Mr. Bush responded to an interviewer. "I do not want to see the government pick winners and losers."[62]

Upon taking office, the Bush administration favored trying to move the economy through a period of slow growth to allow a cooling down from the over-heated economy of the 1980s without causing a recession. But after months of stagnation the economy fell into recession in the summer of 1990. Because the executive and legislative branches were deadlocked over how to reduce the deficit from the start of 1989 through mid-1990, the Federal Reserve Board kept interest rates high as a hedge against inflationary pressures, despite protests from the Bush administration.

The only notable economic initiative that Bush advocated over his term was a proposal to reduce the capital-gains tax. It was never enacted because Democrats charged it was a windfall for wealthy Americans. Numerous studies had indicated a widening income gap between rich and poor Americans during the 1980s, which many Democrats attributed to Reaganomics. Thus, the congressional Democrats wanted to raise taxes on the rich, a proposal President Bush ardently opposed. But eventually, in what conservative Republicans believe was his biggest political blunder, the president reneged on his August 18, 1988, pledge to the Republican National Convention: "Read my lips: no new taxes." In June 1990 Bush

280   intimated that he would accept tax increases as part of a broad budget agreement to break the deadlock with Congress and reduce the deficit. The plan he later signed into law raised the tax rate from 28 percent to 31 percent on adjusted gross incomes over $80,000, phased out personal exemptions for income over $100,000, extended the income base for payroll taxes for Medicare from the first $54,000 of earnings to over $125,000, raised the gasoline tax by five cents, and added taxes on alcohol, tobacco, and luxury items.

The about-face on taxes destroyed Bush's credibility among Republican supply-siders and fueled the 1992 primary challenge by conservative columnist Patrick Buchanan, who ran TV ads in the New Hampshire primary that repeated over and over President Bush saying "Read my lips. No new taxes." Exit polls in the Republican primaries indicated that a sizable number felt betrayed by Bush's policy reversal.

Conservative Republicans blamed the budget deal on Treasury Secretary Nicholas Brady and OMB Director Richard Darman. Brady and Darman persuaded President Bush to compromise with the congressional Democrats to obtain strict limits on spending in exchange for his agreement to accept higher taxes. They also shared a belief that the recession was not as serious as people believed and thus did not encourage the president to adopt more aggressive countercyclical policies. But there was a deeper reason why the 1990–91 contraction could not be attacked with the standard policies of cutting taxes and raising expenditures. Once the recession hit, the most potent constraint on economic policymaking was another Reagan legacy, the triple-digit deficits that grew larger over Bush's term.

The national debt increased to nearly $4 trillion over the Reagan-Bush years, even though the nation enjoyed unprecedented prosperity. But if deficits cannot be reduced during good times, they can only go higher during bad times. The deficit for FY92 approached $300 billion, which limited the ability of policymakers to utilize deficit financing through increased federal spending to stimulate the economy. "United States fiscal policy has been immobilized by the failure to deal with the budget deficit," noted Stanley Fischer of MIT,[63] since even a modest infusion of $50 billion to "pump-prime" the economy could fuel new inflationary pressures. Worry about the mounting deficit was shared by both liberal and conservative economists, and when the 1990–91 recession began there was a consensus that short-term fiscal stimulus would do substantial long-term harm to the nation.

The only recession-fighting policy instrument available to the Bush administration was the Federal Reserve Board, meaning that the key economic decision maker was Fed Chairman Alan Greenspan, called the "master of obfuscation"[64] for his lengthy and circumspect responses whenever queried about the economy. The Fed eased interest rates considerably in hopes of rallying the economy, but Greenspan remained wary of the inflation problem, which explains why the Fed moved somewhat cautiously when there were early signs of recession. The economic problem also was compounded because this latest business cycle had eluded the forecasters. The Fed and other forecasters were uncertain in 1990 whether the nation was heading into recession, and in 1992 they were constantly revising their predictions of recovery.

President Bush pegged his reelection on an imminent recovery, causing Democrats to equate his passivity to Herbert Hoover's oft-quoted comment that prosperity is "just around the corner." Although the Fed cut interest rates 23 times from mid-1989 through mid-1992, bringing the discount rate in July 1992 to 3.25 percent, the lowest level in decades, monetary policy seemed unable to rekindle the economy. Why? Pressure due to growing federal deficits kept long-term interest rates higher, which discouraged home buyers from getting mortgages. Households already burdened with consumer debt and little savings were afraid to make big-ticket purchases like automobiles. Most important, businesses were down-sizing, while states and local governments were streamlining in efforts to cut their costs.

The apparent failure of monetary policy to spur recovery led economists, who just months before were disparaging the federal deficit as the root cause of our economic troubles,[65] to begin to argue that a fiscal jolt was now needed. One hundred leading economists, including six Nobel laureates, made public a letter they wrote to the Bush administration, Congress, and the Federal Reserve Board urging the expenditure of $50 billion a year on public investments to speed economic growth.[66] Those who initiated the letter were James Tobin of Yale and Robert M. Solow of MIT. "Most of us think that for the long run, the huge budget deficit and the inability of the country to reduce it are a serious economic problem," said Solow. "What has changed is that the recession has lasted a long time and the prospect is for a very slow recovery. Economists are prepared to say that there is a chance we will do more long-range damage by letting people sit in the puddle of economic stagnation than we will do if we have high deficits temporarily."[67] However, no action was taken on this proposal during 1992.

MACROECONOMIC MANAGEMENT AND POLITICAL IDEOLOGY

Although the Bush administration declined to act upon the advice offered by the economists in their open letter, the Clinton administration proved to be a more receptive audience. Like his predecessors, President Clinton selected economic advisers whose professional advice complemented, rather than contradicted, his own political impulses. Gone were the supply-side and Chicago school economists who populated the Reagan and Bush administrations; in their place are more interventionist and neo-Keynesian economists trained principally at Harvard and MIT.[68] Consistent with the advice of liberal economists, in February 1993 President Clinton proposed an economic package that, in addition to a long-term budget-deficit reduction plan, included a short-term economic stimulus package that would increase federal spending—despite abundant historical evidence that short-term stimulus programs do little to promote recoveries from economic contractions.

As with most presidents, however, the interaction between Clinton's political impulses and the professional advice of his economic advisers is complex. This is partly because each president's economic advisers include diverse actors: in addition to the academic economists at the CEA and the Fed and in various agencies, Clinton's economic team included business people and former elected officials occupying key positions such as treasury secretary, OMB director, and national economic adviser. Beyond this, there is not always an identity between professional advice and political impulses, and many presidents have learned from their economic advisers, changing their policies over the course of their administrations. In the end, macroeconomic management is a hybrid—part science, part politics, and part intuition. Overshadowing all of this is the public's increasing insistence that the president can and will be an effective manager of prosperity.

KEY TERMS

new economics, GNP gap, multiplier effect, monetarism, natural-rate hypothesis, Phillips curve, supply-side economics, Laffer curve

ADDITIONAL READING

Anderson, James E. and Jared E. Hazleton, *Managing Macroeconomic Policy: The Johnson Presidency*. Austin: University of Texas Press, 1986. Using primary sources at the Lyndon B. Johnson Library, these political scientists analyze decision making as applied to fiscal and monetary policy, wage-price controls, and foreign economic policy.

Genovese, Michael A. *The Nixon Presidency: Power and Politics in Turbulent* **283**
Times. New York: Greenwood Press, 1990. Scholarly account of the Nixon
administration, including the evolution of Nixon's macroeconomic policies.

Goodwin, Craufurd D., ed. *Exhortation and Controls: The Search for a Wage-Price
Policy 1945–1971.* Washington, DC: The Brookings Institution, 1975. A
collection of scholarly articles on the use of "jawboning" to curb wage-price
increases from President Truman through the early Nixon administration.

Pierce, Lawrence. *The Politics of Fiscal Policy Formation.* Pacific Palisades, CA:
Goodyear, 1971. A solid examination of the political process underlying fiscal
policymaking, with special attention to the 1968 income tax surcharge decision.

Silk, Leonard. *Nixonomics.* New York: Praeger, 1973. Well-written popularized
account of macroeconomic policymaking during President Nixon's first term.

Sloan, John W. *Eisenhower and the Management of Prosperity* (Lawrence, KS:
University Press of Kansas, 1991). Definitive study of economic policymaking
during the Eisenhower administration.

Weber, Arnold R. *In Pursuit of Price Stability: The Wage-Price Freeze of 1971.*
Washington, DC: The Brookings Institution, 1973. The director of the Cost of
Living Council discusses how Phase I of President Nixon's wage-price freeze was
formulated and implemented.

NOTES

1. The best example was the use of "multiple advocacy" during the Cuban
Missile Crisis. See Alexander George, "The Case for Multiple Advocacy in Making Foreign Policy," *American Political Science Review* 66 (September 1972), pp.
751–785.

2. The variety of organizational styles by modern presidents to structure
economic policymaking are discussed by Michael A. Genovese, "The Presidency
and Styles of Economic Management," *Congress & The Presidency* 14 (Autumn
1987), 151–167.

3. Ibid., p. 164.

4. John W. Sloan, *Eisenhower and the Management of Prosperity* (Lawrence,
KS: University Press of Kansas, 1991), p. 13.

5. *Economic Report of the President* (Washington, DC: U.S. Government
Printing Office, 1954), pp. 3–4.

6. Marquis Childs, *Eisenhower: Captive Hero* (New York: Harcourt Brace,
1958), p. 163.

7. Reported in Lewis H. Kimmel, *Federal Budget and Fiscal Policy 1789–1958*
(Washington, DC: The Brookings Institution, 1958), pp. 250–251, note 56.

8. Quoted in ibid., p. 250.

284

9. Thomas Parthenakis, "George M. Humphrey, Secretary of the Treasury: Eisenhower's Strongman or Svengali?," paper presented at the Eisenhower Symposium, Gettysburg College, October 10–13, 1990.

10. Edward S. Flash, Jr., *Economic Advice and Presidential Leadership* (New York: Columbia University Press, 1965), p. 158.

11. Wallace C. Peterson, *Income, Employment, and Economic Growth*, 5th ed. (New York: W. W. Norton, 1984), p. 522.

12. Sloan, *Eisenhower and the Management of Prosperity*, pp. 18–19.

13. Kimmel, *Federal Budget and Fiscal Policy 1789–1958*, pp. 247–248.

14. Wilfred Lewis, Jr., *Federal Fiscal Policy in the Postwar Recessions* (Washington, DC: The Brookings Institution, 1962), p. 182.

15. Ibid., p. 185.

16. Raymond J. Saulnier, "On Advising the President," *Presidential Studies Quarterly* 15 (Summer 1985), p. 584.

17. Quoted in ibid., p. 208.

18. Herbert Stein, *The Fiscal Revolution in America* (Chicago: The University of Chicago Press, 1969), pp. 331–332.

19. Sloan, *Eisenhower and the Management of Prosperity*, p. 150.

20. Ibid., p. 151.

21. Lewis, *Federal Fiscal Policy in the Postwar Recessions*, p. 233.

22. Kimmel, *Federal Budget and Fiscal Policy 1789–1958*, p. 257.

23. Richard T. Froyen, *Macroeconomics: Theories and Policies* (New York: Macmillan, 1983), p. 540.

24. Richard M. Pious, *The American Presidency* (New York: Basic Books, 1979), p. 296.

25. Quoted in John W. Sloan, "The Management and Decision-Making Style of President Eisenhower," *Presidential Studies Quarterly* 20 (Spring 1990), p. 297.

26. Stein, *The Fiscal Revolution in America*, p. 379.

27. *New York Times* (January 6, 1961), p. 18.

28. Quoted in Lewis, *Federal Fiscal Policy in the Postwar Recessions*, p. 248.

29. Paul A. Samuelson, "Economic Policy for 1962," *Review of Economics and Statistics* 44 (February 1962), p. 3.

30. Lewis, *Federal Fiscal Policy in the Postwar Recessions*, p. 274.

31. Quoted in Flash, *Economic Advice and Presidential Leadership*, p. 204.

32. Ibid., p. 205.

33. U.S. Congress, Joint Economic Committee, *Hearings on January 1961 Economic Report of the President and the Economic Situation and Outlook*, 87th Congress, 1st Session, p., 361.

34. *Annual Report of the Council of Economic Advisers, 1962* (Washington, DC: U.S. Government Printing Office, 1962), p. 81.

35. Flash, *Economic Advice and Presidential Leadership*, pp. 247–248.

36.   Quoted in ibid., p. 266.

37.   Ibid., p. 271.

38.   Stein, *The Fiscal Revolution in America*, p. 448.

39.   Peterson, *Income, Employment, and Economic Growth*, p. 529.

40.   *Annual Report of the Council of Economic Advisers, 1963* (Washington, DC: Government Printing Office, 1963), pp. 47–48.

41.   Peterson, *Income, Employment, and Economic Growth*, pp. 530–532. His argument has guided our discussion.

42.   Quoted in Neil de Marchi, "The First Nixon Administration: Prelude to Controls," in Craufurd D. Goodwin, ed., *Exhortation and Controls: The Search for a Wage-Price Policy 1945–1971* (Washington, DC: The Brookings Institution, 1975), p. 298.

43.   Clark Warburton, "The Theory of Turning Points in Business Fluctuations," *Quarterly Journal of Economics* 64 (1950), p. 46.

44.   Milton Friedman, *Studies in the Quantity Theory of Money* (Chicago: The University of Chicago Press, 1956).

45.   Milton Friedman and Anna Schwartz, *A Monetary History of the United States, 1867–1960* (Princeton: Princeton University Press, 1963).

46.   His presidential address is published in: Milton Friedman, "The Role of Monetary Policy," *American Economic Review* 58 (March 1968), pp. 1–17.

47.   Edmund S. Phelps, "Phillips Curves: Expectations of Inflation and Optimal Unemployment Over Time," *Economica* (August 1967), pp. 254–281.

48.   Michael A. Genovese, *The Nixon Presidency: Power and Politics in Turbulent Times* (New York: Greenwood Press, 1990), p. 62.

49.   Herbert Stein, *Presidential Economics: The Making of Economic Policy from Roosevelt to Reagan and Beyond* (New York: Simon and Schuster, 1984), p. 139.

50.   Quoted in Marchi, "The First Nixon Administration: Prelude to Controls," p. 304.

51.   *Economic Report of the President, 1970* (Washington, DC: U.S. Government Printing Office, 1970), p. 3.

52.   *Economic Report of the President, 1982* (Washington, DC: U.S. Government Printing Office, 1982), p. 10.

53.   Reagan policies were also influenced by the rational expectations school, also known as the new classical economics, whose prominent proponents include Robert Lucas and Robert Barro of the University of Chicago. The major propositions of the rational expectations school include:

- Money markets adjust very rapidly following a shock to the economy.
- If left alone, all markets will tend toward equilibrium at full employment. (Full employment means the natural rate of unemployment.)
- Monetary policy as historically used is destabilizing to the economy, and fiscal policy is largely irrelevant.

- Money affects prices—if the money supply rises by 10 percent, so will the level of prices.

For rational expectationists, the best macroeconomic policy is passive-adaptive, meaning that government programs should be announced, adhered to, and made permanent. The Fed ought to set monetary rules and not deviate from them, and Congress should establish spending and taxing limits over a long-term period.

54. F. Thomas Juster, "The Economics and Politics of the Supply-Side View," *Economic Outlook USA* (Autumn 1981), The University of Michigan, Survey Research Center, p. 81.

55. See Stein, *Presidential Economics*, pp. 246–248; Walter Heller, "The Kemp-Roth-Laffer Free Lunch," *Wall Street Journal* (July 12, 1978). The controversies surrounding the radical supply-side economics are discussed in: "Understanding the Supply Siders," in W. C. Stubblebine and T. D. Willet, eds., *Reaganomics: A Midterm Report* (San Francisco: Institute for Contemporary Studies Press, 1983).

56. Stein, *Presidential Economics*, p. 246.

57. This discussion is based on: George Katona, "How Expectations Are Really Formed," *Challenge* (November/December, 1980), pp. 32–35.

58. *Economic Report of the President, 1982* (Washington, DC: U.S. Government Printing Office, 1982), p. 52.

59. A theoretical discussion of "cold turkey" vs. "gradualism" is found in Rudiger Dornbusch and Stanley Fischer, *Macro-Economics*, 3rd ed. (New York: McGraw-Hill, 1984), pp. 446–451.

60. Quoted in David E. Rosenbaum, "On the Economy, Bush Followed Reagan's Lead, Not His Success," *New York Times* (June 29, 1992), p. A10.

61. Ibid.

62. Ibid.

63. Quoted in Steven Greenhouse, "U.S. Limited on Economic Stimulus," *New York Times* (August 31, 1992), p. C1.

64. Steven Greenhouse, "The Fed's Master of Obfuscation," *New York Times* (April 20, 1992), p. C1.

65. Robert D. Hershey, Jr., "Why Economists Fear the Deficit," *New York Times* (May 26, 1992), pp. C1 and C3.

66. Peter Passell, "Making a Case for a Fiscal Jolt," *New York Times* (July 10, 1992), pp. C1 and C4.

67. "Quoted in Louis Uchitelle, "Economists Shifting Priorities," *New York Times* (March 31, 1992), p. C4.

68. Steven Greenhouse, "Cambridge Pushes Chicago Aside," *New York Times* (February 2, 1993): pp. C1 and C4.

CHAPTER 11

Responding to Fiscal Crisis: Gramm-Rudman-Hollings, the Balanced Budget Amendment, and Federal Deficits

No discussion of contemporary fiscal policy can avoid the topic of the persistent deficits in the federal budget. Two dimensions of this problem are illustrated in Figures 4.1 and 4.2 (see pages 93 and 94). Figure 4.1 shows the *magnitude* of this problem. After World War II—during which the government ran huge deficits in order to fight the war—the budgets were roughly in balance, sometimes in deficit and other times in surplus. Large deficits were seen primarily in recession years, such as FY53 and FY59. This situation began to deteriorate after 1970; since that time the federal government has run a deficit in every fiscal year. Bad as the 1970s were, though, the period since 1980 has been even worse, with the ten largest deficits (in real terms) since World War II. This occurred despite the longest peacetime economic expansion in U.S. history.

Figure 4.2 shows one of the principal fiscal effects of these deficits, the increase in the **national debt**. The national debt, which represents the total short- and long-term debt obligations of the federal government (other than bills for operating expenses), totaled slightly more than $4 trillion at the end of FY92 (September 30, 1992). Of this, about $1 trillion is held by other federal government accounts, principally major trust funds like the Social Security, Medicare, and federal retirement accounts. An-

288   other $300 billion is held by the Federal Reserve System, partly to facilitate its control of the monetary system through its open market operations. The remainder is held by other individuals and institutions, both in the U.S. and abroad.[1]

Figure 4.2 displays the debt in relative terms, measured as a percentage of the GDP. The critical turning point is in the early 1980s. In relative terms, the national debt had been gradually reduced over the postwar period, reaching its lowest point at the end of FY81 (of course, in both nominal and real terms the debt increased over this period). Since then, it has risen steadily, approximately doubling as a percentage of the GDP in the last decade. In these terms, the debt is now much greater than it was at the end of the Great Depression.

In this chapter, we discuss the politics of federal deficits and the national debt. This is a fiscal drama in five acts. The drama begins with the start of the Reagan administration, when the stage is set by the passage of the massive 1981 tax cut. We then turn to the opening of the great debate over deficits and the debt, which occurs as part of the consideration of the FY86 budget during 1985, and continues with the next act, the passage of the "doomsday bill"—Gramm-Rudman-Hollings. Next, we consider a series of actions that occurred (or failed to occur) during the Bush administration. Finally, we turn to a portion of the story that is still unfolding, the prospects for action during the Clinton administration.

THE ECONOMIC RECOVERY TAX ACT OF 1981

In 1980, candidate Ronald Reagan promised to cut taxes, increase defense spending, cut overall federal spending, and balance the federal deficit. In his first year in office he fulfilled the first of these pledges by strongly supporting the passage of the **Economic Recovery Tax Act of 1981** (ERTA), which cut marginal personal income tax rates a total of 23 percent over three years and indexed income tax rates to inflation (to prevent bracket creep) beginning in 1985. The effects on the federal budget were substantial; ERTA significantly eroded the revenue base of the federal government. From 1978 to 1981 federal revenues grew by about $200 billion, a 50 percent increase, whereas during the period 1981–84 the increase was only $67 billion, or about 11 percent.[2] The FY83 budget showed a deficit of $208 billion, $100 billion of it representing a cyclical deficit from the 1981–82 recession and the remainder a structural deficit. A **cyclical deficit** is an imbalance between revenues and outlays produced by contractions in the business cycle; when economic conditions improve, such deficits are eliminated (and, in fact, surpluses should result). In con-

trast, a **structural deficit** is a revenue-outlay gap that exists even under **289**
conditions of full employment; in effect, it is a deficit built into the laws
that structure expenditures and revenues. Michael Levy of the Conference
Board called the 1983 budget "the first in postwar history with a built-in
'structural deficit' that cannot be cured by successive years of economic
expansion."[3] This problem was something new.

In the past, deficits were caused by wars or recessions, and the coming
of peace or recovery usually brought about budget surpluses or much reduced deficits. While Keynesian economists advocated budget deficits to
moderate business downturns, they anticipated that federal expenditures
and revenues would be roughly balanced over the course of the business
cycle.

The modern budget dilemma is illustrated by comparing the actual
deficits and the "full employment deficits" over the first Reagan term (Table 11.1). The latter represent what the deficits would be under conditions
of full employment. The data show the budgetary impact of the gap between actual versus potential GNP by projecting the probable surplus (or
deficit) that would exist if the economy operated at its productive capacity.
In effect, full employment deficit represents the structural deficit, which,
as the table clearly shows, would persist even under conditions of full
employment.

Both branches of government shared the blame for the mounting red
ink. The administration's optimistic forecasts of economic growth, when
unrealized, had the primary effect of slowing the growth in federal revenues. Congress regularly added to domestic spending above whatever cutbacks it achieved in military expenditures. And policy changes enacted
by both branches, mainly tax cuts, were the major reason for the huge
growth in deficits in the 1980s.[4] This is obvious from the pattern of deficit
growth between FY81 and FY83, the time before and after the 1981 tax
cut.

TABLE 11.1   Actual vs. Full-Employment Deficits Under Reagan
(deficit as percent of GNP)

	1982	1983	1984	1985
Actual	4.8	5.7	4.9	4.1
Full-Employment	1.7	2.3	2.2	2.1

Source: Rudiger Dornbusch and Stanley Fischer, *Macro-Economics,* 3rd ed. (New York:
McGraw-Hill, 1984), p. 91.

290   The budget President Carter submitted to Congress for FY81 anticipated a $15.8 billion deficit. This statistic upset the financial community
so much that Carter had to revise his budget figures to anticipate a surplus
of $16.5 billion. Eventually FY81 showed a deficit five times as large as
the original Carter estimate ($79 billion). The budget for FY82 was for-
mulated by the Carter administration and transmitted to the Congress at
the time Ronald Reagan was inaugurated president. Its $27.5 billion deficit
was revised upwards to $45.0 billion due to the budget changes made under
President Reagan, but the 1981–82 recession added substantially to that
figure; FY82 ended $128 billion in the red. The deficit of $91.5 billion
that the administration predicted for FY83 more than doubled by the time
the fiscal year ended. That original estimate was approximately the
amount attributed to the economic downturn, while the remaining $100
billion structural deficit was a byproduct of the Reagan tax cut.

In FY84 and FY85 the projected deficits were closer to the actual
figures but now were firmly entrenched in the triple-digit category. A realization that revenues obviously would not grow enough to markedly
reduce the deficit forced the Congress to think about the unthinkable—
how to cut government expenditures—as they prepared the FY86 federal
budget.

THE 1985 BUDGET BATTLE

In 1984 President Reagan won reelection by a landslide, and he
proclaimed a "Second American Revolution" in his 1985 State of the
Union Message. The Budget Message that followed promised severe retrenchment; now the budget ax would fall on programs long considered
to be "sacred cows" for the middle-class and special interests. A one-year
freeze on total expenditures (except debt service) was proposed. There
would be opposition to this budget, Reagan told Congress, because every
dollar "benefits someone, and that person has a vested self-interest in seeing those benefits perpetuated and expanded." He then asked: "Where is
the political logrolling going to stop?" The answer was apparent from
Reagan's budgetary agenda. About 82 percent ($38.8 billion) of the budget
cuts fell on nonmilitary programs. He proposed a 5 percent pay cut for
civilian federal employees, a one-year elimination of the cost-of-living adjustment for civilian and military pensions, cuts in farm price supports, a
freeze on Medicaid payments to hospitals and physicians, and the abolition
of twelve domestic programs. In total, the FY86 budget represented the
largest spending cutback in the nation's history, intended to reduce the

deficit by $56 billion in 1986 and nearly $300 billion over the next three **291** years.[5]

The battle lines were drawn on May 10, when the Senate Budget Committee approved a budget resolution that reduced the FY86 budget by $56 billion and the three-year deficit by $295 billion. Included was a one-year cost-of-living freeze on Social Security, and military expenditures were increased only by the inflation rate. But there was immediate talk among Democrats in the House to resist any cut in Social Security. The House Budget Committee on May 16 adopted a budget resolution that forced a confrontation with the Senate. It wanted no Social Security freeze; domestic spending was reduced one-third less than under the Senate plan; and military expenditures were held to the FY85 level without an inflation adjustment. Eleven (of twelve) programs being eliminated by the Senate were spared.

Although President Reagan did not win the budget battle that year, on one point he emerged the victor. As one reporter noted: "The climate has changed on Capitol Hill since the first year of Mr. Reagan's term, when Democrats were outraged at his attempts to reduce taxes and restrict domestic programs. In the budget debate so far, hardly any voices from either party have challenged the president's basic demand that Congress slash the deficit."[6] The debate was confined to spending priorities.

After the House adopted its budget, President Reagan on May 25 told the National Association of Manufacturers: "It is, frankly, unacceptable— unacceptable to me and to the American people . . . the House plan fails adequately to address the fundamental problem of unbridled domestic spending." He added: "Such a further cut in defense spending would undermine our negotiating position in Geneva [summit talks] and put the defense of our nation at risk."[7] Three days later Reagan unveiled his income tax overhaul plan in a nationwide television address. He asked for public support to transform an "un-American" income tax system into one that is "clear, simple, and fair for all." Reagan proposed the elimination of the graduated rate structure in favor of only three tax brackets on individuals (15 percent, 25 percent, 35 percent) and four corporate tax rates. The goal was to streamline the tax code in a revenue neutral fashion— that is, without any tax increase.

The matter of revenue-neutral tax reform complicated the budget debate during 1985. When the House-Senate conference committee met in early June to resolve their differences, Robert Dole advised his colleagues that $50–$60 billion in additional cuts would be needed. His comment followed an updated forecast by OMB Director Stockman that projected less robust economic growth and a larger deficit. Dole and Representative William Gray (D-PA), who chaired the House Budget Committee, both hinted that new taxes might be necessary. But House Speaker O'Neill quickly interjected his opposition to any Social Security freeze and said that new taxes would have to be recommended by the president.

The conference committee deadlocked in late June, with the Senate Budget Committee chairman, Peter Domenici (R-NM), saying that "no useful purpose" would be served unless the House scaled back its Social Security increases. Domenici hoped that his action would "have a traumatic and dramatic effect on members of the House and members of the Senate and they'll begin to understand that we are playing with dynamite, all of us."[8] After Congress returned from its July 4th recess, President Reagan held a series of meetings with the congressional leadership. The upshot was his decision to side with the House Democrats. As Speaker O'Neill declared, "We agreed that Social Security, in every phase, is not on the table anymore. No COLAs slippage, no taxes on Social Security, nothing happens to Social Security."[9]

Senate Republicans felt they had been betrayed, particularly since seventeen of them faced reelection in 1986. Especially upset was Robert Dole, who said the White House was "surrendering to the deficit," and he criticized the other chamber. "Democrats and a few noisy House Republicans want to play politics. They never made a hard choice in their lives."[10] The apparent reference was to Dole's party rival Congressman Jack Kemp (R-NY), who met with White House chief-of-staff Donald Regan to arrange the deal that excluded any Social Security freeze or new taxes.

In mid-July the budget talks broke down as the conferees recessed indefinitely. To leverage the Senate, the House—voting along party lines—put its budget resolution into effect, and its Appropriations Committee began reporting money bills. In response, the Senate leadership forged a new bipartisan deficit-reduction package that increased the three-year savings to $338 billion. Included was an oil-import fee, expansion of Social Security and Medicare coverage to state and local employees, and a shift in the Social Security COLA from each year to every two years.

Once again President Reagan undercut his Senate allies. On July 9th, he announced his opposition to the oil import tax and any changes in the Social Security COLA calculation, which doomed any hope for a FY86 budget. Congressman Gray and Senator Domenici then began quiet negotiations to salvage some kind of budget resolution. The anticlimax came on August 1, 1985, when Congress passed a spending package that reduced the deficit by much less than the original proposal. Everybody understood that these figures were based on earlier, optimistic economic forecasts, so at best this budget would save $40 billion in FY86 and possibly $200 billion over the next three fiscal years. By all accounts this was not a stellar performance by the Congress.

When Congress reconvened, attention shifted to passing a continuing resolution to fund most agencies through November 14 at the current spending rate. No regular appropriations bills had been enacted as yet, and this law avoided a partial shutdown of the federal government, but a confrontation with Reagan was only postponed until later in the fall.

GRAMM-RUDMAN-HOLLINGS

Passage of the Bill

As November approached, Congress had to raise the statutory debt ceiling to allow the government to borrow enough money to pay its expenses. Senate Republicans intended to use that debt-ceiling legislation to reduce future deficits. On October 3rd, the GOP House and Senate leadership endorsed a bill known as Gramm-Rudman, named for its two Republican sponsors, Senators Phil Gramm (R-TX) and Warren Rudman (R-NH), which mandated reduced deficits until 1991, when the federal budget would be balanced. (This legislation was also co-sponsored by Democratic Senator Ernest Hollings of South Carolina and is also known as **Gramm-Rudman-Hollings**.) If a projected deficit exceeded the ceiling established in the bill, then the president was authorized to make automatic expenditure cuts in order to meet that goal. The proposal dramatized the deficit issue and showed that the Senate was prepared to take decisive action. Caught off guard by its political appeal, Speaker O'Neill appointed a task force to formulate a policy alternative.

President Reagan endorsed the bill a day later. "The United States government is not only going to pay its bills, but we're also going to take away the credit cards," he said. "From now on it'll be cash and carry."[11] The next day, Senate minority party leader Robert Byrd (D-WV) and House majority whip Thomas Foley (D-WA) both supported the balanced-budget goal, though they wanted more time to debate the question. But things moved quickly in the Senate. On October 6 the Senate held an unusual Sunday session (its fourth in twelve years) to consider the measure. Majority party leader Dole and President Reagan wanted to pressure the Congress into fast action since, very soon, the federal government would not be able to borrow more funds without an increase in the debt ceiling.

Democrats in the House complained that a fake emergency was being created to bulldoze the legislation through Congress. Their suspicions were justified when the Treasury Department borrowed $5 billion from in-house accounts to cover outstanding checks rather than repudiate outstanding

294   bills. But on October 9 the Senate voted 75–24 to approve Gramm-Rud-man-Hollings. Conservative Republicans were joined by liberal Democrats like Senator Edward Kennedy (D-MA) in a huge bipartisan coalition. Underlying this vote was a consensus that the deficit problem could not be safely ignored in 1986, an election year. Two days later House Democrats endorsed the principle but not the specifics of the bill.

The financial maneuver by Treasury gave Congress some breathing room, and in mid-October the House-Senate conferees began considering Gramm-Rudman-Hollings. Legislative deadlock ensued, prompting another fiscal crisis on November 1, 1985, when the Treasury Department announced that it would have to borrow funds from the Social Security Trust Fund to pay outstanding obligations unless Congress acted soon on the debt-ceiling increase. The new OMB director, James Miller III, warned, "If nothing is done before the 14th, and the Congress has not acted, then there would be the orderly shutting down of the entire government and stopping of checks going to almost everyone."[12] Such an action would be unprecedented.

Efforts to reach a legislative compromise were halted on October 31, when each chamber scheduled a showdown vote on its version of the deficit-reduction legislation. On November 1 the House approved the Democratic bill along strictly partisan lines; on the 5th Senate Republicans passed the Gramm-Rudman-Hollings bill. The negotiations now involved Dole, O'Neill, and Reagan. There was an obvious urgency to the deliberations since, in addition to the pending fiscal deadline, President Reagan was scheduled to meet Soviet Premier Gorbachev in Geneva in late November. To prevent government default, Congress passed two stopgap bills that President Reagan signed on November 14 to fund the government for another month. So far only four of the thirteen regular appropriations bills had been enacted.

Despite the partisan bickering in Congress there was an emerging consensus that some kind of balanced-budget law had to be enacted.[13] The conference committee impasse was broken on December 10; the next day the Senate voted 61–31, with 22 Democrats and 39 Republicans joining forces, followed by the House voting 271–154, with 153 Republican and 118 Democratic yes votes. On December 13 President Reagan signed the Balanced Budget and Emergency Deficit Control Act of 1985, along with legislation raising the debt-ceiling above $2 trillion.

The Revised Budget Process

Gramm-Rudman-Hollings mandated a five-year deficit-reduction process, with yearly deficit ceilings that would fall to zero (a balanced budget) in FY91 (amounts in billions):

FY1986	FY1987	FY1988	FY1989	FY1990	FY1991
$171.9	$144.0	$108.0	$72.0	$36.0	$0.0

The timetable was shortened during FY86 since the law was enacted three months into the fiscal year. Starting with FY87, the law mandated that in August OMB and CBO submit separate forecasts of the deficit to the General Accounting Office (GAO) for it to make its estimates. If the deficit was projected to exceed the ceiling by $10 billion or more and no recession was predicted, then the GAO would determine how much money must be trimmed to meet the statutory deficit ceiling. On September 1, one month before the new fiscal year, the president would issue a sequestering order to force spending cuts. His order would be automatic and take effect on October 15 unless a new budget was enacted or tax increases were approved to meet the existing deficit ceiling.

Half of the cuts were to be from military programs and half from domestic programs, with significant exceptions; Social Security, interest on the debt, veterans pensions, Medicaid, Infants and Children Nutrition program, AFDC, the Supplemental Security Income program, food stamps, and other programs targeted to the needy were exempted from cuts. The law also limited cutbacks in other areas; Medicare cuts were restricted to 1 percent in 1987 and 2 percent each year thereafter. In FY86, an election year, Congress prohibited the automatic spending cuts from exceeding $11.7 billion, regardless of how much the actual deficit exceeded the $171.9 billion ceiling.

President Reagan called Gramm-Rudman-Hollings a "step toward putting our fiscal house in order,"[14] but almost immediately Congressman Mike Synar (D-OK) and eleven other representatives, along with the National Treasury Employees Union, challenged its constitutionality in Federal District Court. They argued that Congress cannot abdicate its power over the purse, while the Reagan administration itself expressed reservations about the provision that authorized two congressional agencies independent of presidential control—the CBO and GAO—to estimate the deficit figure on which to base the automatic cuts.[15]

Since Congress had failed to enact an FY86 budget, the Comptroller General (head of GAO) moved to implement automatic cuts of 4.3 percent in domestic programs and 4.9 percent in military spending to effect savings of $11.7 billion on March 1, 1986. However, in February the entire process was put in jeopardy when a District Court ruled that Gramm-Rudman-Hollings violated the separation of powers by vesting "executive power in the Comptroller General, an officer removable by Congress." The automatic cuts of $11.7 billion stayed in effect pending appeal to the

Supreme Court. On July 7 the high court voted 7–2 to void that provision of the law. Chief Justice Burger, writing for the majority, held that since the Comptroller General holds office by legislation and is subject to removal, this officer is "subservient to Congress" and thus Congress "has retained control over the execution of the act and has intruded into the executive function."

Congress now had to grapple with two problems: how to maintain the $11.7 billion in automatic cuts for FY86 and how to repair Gramm-Rudman-Hollings. The first problem was resolved ten days later, when Congress enacted legislation to ratify the FY86 automatic spending cuts, but the second issue gave rise to partisan bickerings that lasted over a year. At the end of July 1986, the Republican-controlled Senate voted 63–36 to give the OMB director the authority, within limitations, to calculate the need for deficit reduction and to implement those automatic budget cuts. But Democrats balked at giving such power to the Reagan administration, and the House took no action. Not until late 1987 did Congress, with bipartisan majorities in both chambers, approve virtually the same proposal to salvage Gramm-Rudman-Hollings.

The revisions (sometimes called **Gramm-Rudman II**) that the president reluctantly agreed to on September 26, 1987, delegated the authority to order automatic spending cuts to OMB, again with half earmarked to defense spending and half to domestic programs. What irritated Reagan was its retreat from the balanced budget timetable of the original act. The revised deficit ceilings were as follows (amounts in billions):

FY1988	FY1989	FY1990	FY1991	FY1992	FY1993
$144	$136	$100	$54	$18	$0.0

These amendments postponed a balanced budget for another two years and cut the deficit for FY89, a presidential election year, by only $8 billion from the FY88 ceiling.

Gramm-Rudman-Hollings was a mixed blessing. Its enactment symbolized the budget crisis as a political issue. It is also testimony that the popularly elected branches seem unable to make hard choices on taxes and spending. During the first year of the Bush administration, the White House and Congress agreed to allow automatic spending cuts for FY90 because they were unable to reduce expenditures enough to meet the Gramm-Rudman-Hollings target. Thus the law gives the elected leadership political cover; they can protect domestic programs and blame funding cutbacks on the 1985 act. "They can be social liberals and fiscal conservatives at the same time," says economist Barry Bosworth. "It's not good public policy, but it's good politics."[16]

DEFICITS, DEBT, AND THE BUSH ADMINISTRATION   297

The 1988 Presidential Election

The 1988 presidential campaign showed an undercurrent of public anxiety about the economic future of the U.S. Democratic presidential candidate Michael Dukakis tried to exploit those fears by arguing that the economic recovery of the 1980s did not touch all Americans. The costs of a college education, health care, and home ownership had outpaced the CPI, and some middle-class families needed two income earners just to stay even.

Unprecedented borrowing by the federal government fueled the 1980s economic expansion, but the deficit did *not* surface in the opinion polls as a burning issue. Both presidential candidates were deliberately vague about how they intended to deal with the budget. George Bush opposed any new tax increase and attacked Dukakis as the governor of heavily taxed Massachusetts. A lasting image of the 1988 election was George Bush's dramatic pledge to the Republican convention: "Read my lips. No new taxes."

The Bush Deficit Agreement

In February 1990 President Bush submitted to Congress his proposed budget for FY91. Under Gramm-Rudman II, the deficit was targeted to be no more than $54 billion during FY91. But Congress refused to accept the Bush recommendations, while an economy slipping into recession caused the deficit to rise to a record $221.4 billion for FY90, with even higher deficits projected for succeeding years. To force budget cuts of Gramm-Rudman II magnitude during a recession would have a pro-cyclical effect on the economy (i.e., worsen the downturn), so President Bush and the congressional leadership held a budget summit during the summer of 1990 where they agreed to revise, once again, the deficit targets of the Gramm-Rudman-Hollings law. The resulting law, the **Budget Enforcement Act of 1990**, effectively repealed Gramm-Rudman-Hollings. Unlike the two earlier acts, the new act set no goal for achieving a zero deficit; instead it sought simply to reduce the federal deficit to $83 billion in five years, by FY95.

The bill that was passed and signed into law was the product of a compromise between President Bush and congressional Democrats.[17] In return for congressional agreement to accept firm spending limits for future fiscal years, designed to reduce projected deficits by close to $300 billion, President Bush reluctantly accepted tax increases totaling about $150 billion.

The new budget agreement divided federal expenditures into nondiscretionary (interest on the debt and entitlements) versus discretionary categories and then subdivided the latter into three types: defense expenditures, international programs, and domestic programs.[18] About a third of the spending cuts were from nondiscretionary spending and the remainder from discretionary spending, especially defense. Spending ceilings were established for each category of discretionary spending, thus preventing massive shifting of expenditures from military to domestic programs. If expenditures exceeded the ceiling in any category, then across-the-board cuts would have to be made in programs *within* that category to keep overall spending under the ceiling. However, the new law permitted the targets to be ignored if circumstances warranted—for example during recessions or national emergencies.

The 1990 budget agreement may have been a more realistic guide to deficit reduction than its predecessors, but clearly this budget agreement was a costly political strategy for President Bush. Not only did he break his no-tax promise by agreeing to taxes in exchange for expenditure ceilings, but the deficit problem grew when the economy did not quickly rebound from the 1990–91 recession. And 1992 was a presidential election year.

The Balanced Budget Amendment

At the start of 1992 the deficit issue loomed large on the political landscape as the forecasters predicted no end to the triple-digit deficits. In fact the Congressional Budget Office, whose fiscal predictions were more accurate than OMB's during the Bush presidency, released an analysis in March 1992 showing the structural deficit to be $209 billion of the total projected $368 billion federal deficit for FY92, which meant that only a $99 billion deficit could be attributed to the recessionary nature of the economy. After falling to around $180 billion in FY95, CBO predicted, the structural deficit would rise to nearly $250 billion by FY97.

Concerns about the mounting deficit in an election year when deep anti-incumbent resentment had surfaced during the primary season led some legislators to renew calls for a constitutional amendment requiring balanced budgets. By the spring of 1992 many observers believed its approval was almost inevitable, because an alliance of liberals and conservatives was behind the proposal. The version with the broadest support was authored by liberal Senator Paul Simon (D-IL) and conservative Representative Charles Stenholm (D-TX). Simon, whose proposal had fourteen Republican and sixteen Democratic co-sponsors in the Senate, said it "would make fiscal responsibility the general rule instead of the rare

exception. This is needed because the political will to reduce the deficit **299**
is absent in the White House and in Congress."[19] Congressman Stenholm,
whose bill obtained 277 House co-sponsors, was one of the conservative
Southern Democrats—known as Boll Weevils—who deserted their party
leadership to pass key pieces of Reagan's legislation, a move he later re-
gretted: "We got carried away with tax cuts in 1981, and we've paid a
high price for that mistake . . . the problems of doing nothing now about
the deficit raise far greater risks than do the problems of trying to restrain
our ability to borrow with a Constitutional amendment."[20]

This particular **balanced-budget amendment** mandated a balanced
budget unless that requirement was waived by a three-fifths vote of the
Senate and House or, in the event of war, by a majority vote in each
chamber. The president would be required to submit a balanced budget
to Congress, making both the executive and legislature accountable for
the fiscal conduct of the government.

A balanced-budget amendment had been proposed earlier by President Reagan, and when the proposal resurfaced in 1992 OMB Director
Darman made known that it also had the support of President Bush.[21] The
minority party leader in the House, Robert Michel (R-IL), agreed, saying
he backed the amendment "not because I think it's all that good, but
because I perceive a universal failure to make the tough calls."[22]

However, Governor Bill Clinton of Arkansas, the front runner in the
Democratic presidential race, did not endorse the proposal, and serious
troubles began when the Democratic leadership of the Senate balked at
the idea. The first signal that easy enactment might not come was when
the powerful chairman of the Senate Appropriations Committee, Robert
Byrd (D-WV), predicted that it would fail.[23] Beyond that, the Economic
Policy Institute made public a statement of opposition by 447 economists,
including 7 Nobel laureates. "When the private economy is in recession,"
they said, "a constitutional requirement that would force cuts in public
spending or tax increases could worsen the economic downturn, causing
greater loss of jobs, production, and income."[24]

The proposal was considered first by the House and defeated, after
which Simon withdrew his measure rather than force a confrontation that
might embarrass his Democratic party in an election year. The Stenholm
bill lost on a 280–153 roll call, with 164 Republicans and 116 Democrats
voting in favor, with 150 Democrats and only 2 Republicans opposed.[25]
(As a constitutional amendment, the measure required a two-thirds majority to pass.) In the House, opposition was led by Speaker Thomas Foley
(D-WA) and Congressman Leon Panetta (D-CA), then chairman of the
Budget Committee and later Clinton's OMB director. The vote along

300   partisan lines appeared to give the Republicans a potentially important campaign issue for the approaching 1992 elections.

In fact, this failed amendment was hardly even mentioned by the presidential candidates and was not resurrected by the GOP for campaign purposes. Given the record of debt over the Reagan-Bush years, Republicans could not easily exploit the issue, and with the economy in the doldrums and unemployment hovering around 7.6 percent, there were no political incentives for the Democrats to divert attention from the economy to the deficit. Nobody—except independent presidential contender Ross Perot—had any reason to make an issue of the mounting federal debt, and many voters seemed insensitive to a deficit problem that economists viewed with grave concern.

THE CLINTON ADMINISTRATION: CHANGE IN DIRECTION OR BUSINESS AS USUAL?

Not all voters were insensitive to the deficit, however. When the voters went to the polls in November, 19 percent of them voted for independent Ross Perot, whose principal campaign issue was the need to address the ever-increasing national debt. Although public opinion polls immediately after the election indicated a greater public concern with unemployment than with the deficit,[26] in the months after his election pressure built on the president-elect to propose a deficit reduction plan. On February 17, 1993, President Clinton unveiled a major macroeconomic policy program.

The Clinton proposal contained three basic components.[27] First, a substantial deficit reduction program combined $246 billion in new taxes over four years with $247 in spending cuts over the same period. Second, the plan proposed $169 billion in new spending on research, education, and physical infrastructure. This would offset much of the proposed spending cuts; the net savings over four years would thus be about $325 billion. Third, Clinton proposed a short-term economic stimulus package to "jump start" the economy and reduce unemployment, which still stood at 7 percent in March 1993.

The proposal to increase taxes, which represented about three-quarters of the net reduction in the deficits, had two basic parts, an increase in income taxes for wealthy taxpayers and a broad-based energy tax (called a BTU tax, because the tax would be leveled on the basis of BTUs, the unit used for measuring the energy content of various energy sources). This marked a break with pledges made by Clinton during his presidential campaign (in which he initially pledged to cut taxes on the middle class), a change he attributed to his discovery as president that conditions were much worse than he had been led to believe.

Clinton's proposals received mixed support among the public, Congress, and other policymakers. Polls generally indicated that Americans would accept tax increases if they were linked to spending cuts. The Clinton plan also drew support from Fed Chairman Alan Greenspan, who characterized the deficit as "a corrosive force that already has begun to eat away at the foundations of our economic strength."[28]

The broad outlines of Clinton's deficit reduction program were ultimately accepted by both the Senate and the House, although narrowly and in a substantially modified form. In May, different versions passed the House and Senate, with six votes to spare in the former and on the strength of Vice President Gore's tie-breaking vote in the Senate.[29] Following lengthy conference-committee negotiations, the final version was passed in early August—this time by two votes in the House and by another tie-breaking vote by Gore in the Senate. Republicans in both houses were unanimous in their opposition to both versions of the deficit reduction package, while the Democrats were split, although enough supported the measure for it to pass. Along the torturous route to passage, several key changes were made: the broad-based BTU tax was replaced by a much milder 4.3-cents-per-gallon gasoline tax; marginal tax rates on upper-income people were increased even more than originally proposed (and the tax back-dated to January 1, 1993); and some proposed increases in benefits, such as business-investment tax credits, earned-income tax credits, and spending for enterprise zones, were reduced or eliminated.

Clinton's short-term economic stimulus package fared less well, as it was opposed by a determined Republican minority in the Senate through a filibuster. After cloture votes failed in March and April, attempts were made to agree upon a compromise package that would contain a summer jobs program and increased unemployment benefits but remove a stimulus package for cities. These efforts failed, however, and the short-term stimulus package was rejected, at least for the balance of 1993. Although the failure to pass this stimulus package may have important political implications, the history of such short-term packages suggests that the effect of this failure on the timing and extent of economic recovery will turn out to be minimal.

Of far greater significance for macroeconomic policy is the deficit reduction program. Just as President Clinton unveiled his proposals, the CBO released a new projection of future deficits.[30] Barring any changes in the laws (such as those enacted in August), CBO estimated that the deficits would rise from $310 billion in FY93 to over $650 billion in FY03 (2003). Deficits of this magnitude would guarantee that the growth of the

302   national debt will continue upward—with the negative consequences that implies. Even with the newly enacted policies, the debt is still expected to increase, although more slowly.[31] Thus the stakes are high, and the debt and deficit drama will continue to unfold throughout Clinton's term of office.

THE DANGERS OF DEFICITS

During FY92 the federal government was spending $1 billion per day. By summer 1992, the debt passed the $4 trillion mark. To finance those deficits, government must borrow funds from the private sector, money that cannot be used for business investment to generate jobs or to improve the nation's productivity. Deficits now require an infusion of $200–$300 billion of funds from the credit markets each year, which puts pressure on interest rates to rise. Higher interest rates add further to the cost of financing the debt, and businesses and households are less able to borrow money when interest rates increase.[32]

The experience of the 1990–91 recession shows the impact of the federal structural deficit on countercyclical policy. The large structural deficit meant that fiscal policy was neutralized; there were few voices in Congress or the Bush administration who advocated expenditure increases or tax cuts to ameliorate the recession, given the already high levels of deficit spending. Economists and policymakers initially feared that increasing aggregate demand would rekindle inflationary pressures, and that anxiety even caused the Federal Reserve Board to act very cautiously when faced with early signs of the economic contraction.

A more fundamental problem is that the debt represents a generational transfer of resources.[33] Current consumption will have to be paid by future producers, and presently 15 percent of the federal budget is interest on the debt. This would not be all bad if current deficits were used to build the nation's infrastructure, since such projects last for years and thus would benefit future generations. But most of the deficit is allocated to paying for current consumption in the form of pensions and health care benefits, and those programs—although they may be entirely justified—do not benefit future citizens. In the long run, the next generation will have to find the money to pay for not only their current needs but also the consumption of past generations, meaning higher future taxes, possibly more inflation, and perhaps cutbacks in public programs. Whatever the scenario, unless the American economy grows much more robustly in the next century than it has in recent years, the debt burden may mean a reduced standard of living for the next generation of Americans.

KEY TERMS

national debt, Economic Recovery Tax Act of 1981 (ERTA), cyclical deficit, structural deficit, Gramm-Rudman-Hollings, Gramm-Rudman II, Budget Enforcement Act of 1990, balanced-budget amendment

ADDITIONAL READING

Buchanan, James M. and Richard E. Wagner. *Democracy in Deficit: The Political Legacy of Lord Keynes.* New York: Academic Press, 1977. Argues that Keynesian economics led policymakers to tolerate deficits with the result that previously existing social restraints on government spending were undermined.

Eisner, Robert. *How Real is the Federal Deficit?* New York: Free Press, 1986. A Keynesian economist urges the application of business accounting standards to federal finances and argues that recent apprehension about the national debt is unwarranted because, under certain conditions, the prevailing view of the magnitude of the deficit problem is erroneous.

Friedman, Benjamin. *Day of Reckoning: The Consequences of American Economic Policy Under Reagan and After.* New York: Random House, 1988. A dire economic scenario about the adverse consequences of deficits on our competitive position internationally and our domestic standard of living.

Heilbroner, Robert and Peter Bernstein. *The Debt and the Deficit: False Alarms/ Real Possibilities* (New York: W. W. Norton, 1989). Argues that the heightened concerns about federal deficits are exaggerated given the economic realities.

Kettl, Donald F. *Deficit Politics: Public Budgeting in Its Institutional and Historical Context* (New York: Macmillan, 1992). A brief and lucid examination of public budgeting practices and history in order to explain persistent budget deficits.

Lindsey, Lawrence B. *The Growth Experiment: How Tax Policy is Transforming the U.S. Economy* (New York: Basic Books, 1990). Defends the 1981 Reagan tax cut as being beneficial to the economy, but also argues that tax reform is needed.

Shuman, Howard E. *Politics and the Budget: The Struggle Between the President and Congress,* 3rd ed. (Englewood Cliffs, NJ: Prentice-Hall, 1992). Thorough treatment of modern budgetary politics, with special emphasis on budgetary policy since 1974.

NOTES

1. This discussion of the debt is based on figures and narrative contained in *Budget Baselines, Historical Data, and Alternatives for the Future* (Washington, DC: Office of Management and Budget, January 1993).

2. *Economic Report of the President, 1993,* p. 435.

304

3. Michael E. Levy, " 'Staying the Course' Won't Help the Budget," *Challenge* (May/June, 1983), p. 37. Also see his "The Budget: You Can't Get from Here to There," *Challenge* (May/June, 1982), pp. 15–20.

4. See Thomas M. Holloway and Joseph C. Wakefield, "Sources of Change in the Federal Deficit, 1970–86," *Survey of Current Business* (May 1985).

5. A summary of the 1985 budget proposals is found in Francis X. Clines, "Reagan Has His Eye on Congress and the Calendar," *New York Times* (May 12, 1985), p. E1. Also see Jonathan Fuerbringer, "Reagan to Submit Budget for 1986 to Congress Today," *New York Times* (February 4, 1985), pp. 1, 10–11.

6. Steven V. Roberts, "Budget Debate: Consensus in Congress" *New York Times* (May 18, 1985), p. 8.

7. Reported in Gerald M. Boyd, "President Assails House as Putting Defense 'At Risk,' " *New York Times* (May 25, 1985), pp. 1, 18. Quote on p. 1.

8. Reported in Jonathan Fuerbringer, "Pension Dispute Creates Impasse in Budget Talks," *New York Times* (June 26, 1985), pp. 1, 18. Quote on p. 1.

9. Reported in David Rogers and Jane Mayer, "Plan to End Social Security Rises for '86 Dropped by Reagan, Leaders of Congress," *The Wall Street Journal* (July 10, 1985), p. 2.

10. Reported in Jonathan Fuerbringer, "G.O.P. Rift Widens as Dole Criticizes Reagan and House," *New York Times* (July 13, 1985), pp. 1, 6. Quote on p. 1.

11. Reported in Jonathan Fuerbringer, "Plan to Balance U.S. Budget By '91 Delayed in Senate," *New York Times* (October 5, 1985), pp. 1, 7. Quote on p. 1.

12. Reported in Gerald M. Boyd, "Reagan Aides Prod Congress on Debt," *New York Times* (October 31, 1985), p. 16.

13. Jonathan Fuerbringer, "Like It or Not, Deficit Plan Will Pass, Lawmakers Say," *New York Times* (November 21, 1985), p. 13.

14. Reported in Francis X. Clines, "Budget-Balancing Bill Is Signed in Seclusion," *New York Times* (December 13, 1985), p. 14. A summary of this legislation is found in *New York Times* (December 12, 1985), pp. 1, 17.

15. Reported in Steven V. Roberts, "Lawmakers Challenge Scope of Budget Measure," *New York Times* (December 13, 1985), p. 13.

16. Reported in Peter T. Kilborn, "Future for Deficit-Reducing Law: A Political Balancing Act Is Required," *New York Times* (December 13, 1985), p. 13.

17. This discussion of the Budget Enforcement Act of 1990 is drawn from Howard E. Shuman, *Politics and the Budget: The Struggle Between the President and Congress*, 3rd ed. (Englewood Cliffs, NJ: Prentice-Hall, 1992), pp. 326–335.

18. See Congressional Budget Office, *The Economic and Budget Outlook: Fiscal Years 1992–1996* (Washington, DC: U.S. Government Printing Office, 1991), pp. 43–57.

19. Paul Simon, "Discipline is Overdue," *New York Times* (May 20, 1992), p. A15.

20.   Quoted in Michael deCourcy Hinds, "The Texas Congressman Behind **305** the Amendment," *New York Times* (June 12, 1992), p. A9.

21.   Clifford Krauss, "Pressure Building for an Amendment to Balanced Budget," *New York Times* (May 7, 1992), p. A1.

22.   Quoted in Adam Clymer, "House Debates Deficits and Proposed Balanced Budget Amendment," *New York Times* (June 11, 1992), p. A10.

23.   Adam Clymer, "Senator Predicts Plan to Balance Budget Will Die," *New York Times* (June 10, 1992), p. A10.

24.   Ibid., p. A12.

25.   Adam Clymer, "Balanced-Budget Amendment Fails to Gain House Approval," *New York Times* (June 12, 1992), p. A1.

26.   See "Public Hopeful Clinton Can Solve Nation's Problems," *The Gallup Poll Monthly* (November 1992), p. 11.

27.   This description is based on "Clinton's Economic Opus: A Thousand Lines of Type," *New York Times* (February 21, 1993), E3.

28.   Quoted in "Fed Chief Backs Drive to Cut 'Malignant Force'—the Deficit," *Chicago Tribune* (March 25, 1993), 3:3.

29.   This account is based on "Without Sacrifice," *The Economist* (August 7th–13th), pp. 25–26.

30.   Congressional Budget Office, *Reducing the Deficit: Spending and Revenue Options* (Washington: Government Printing Office, February 1993).

31.   Congressional Budget Office, *Federal Debt and Interest Costs* (May 1993), p. 2.

32.   Joseph E. Stiglitz, *Economics* (New York: W. W. Norton, 1993), p. 1034.

33.   Ibid., pp. 1032–1035.

CHAPTER 12

A Presidential
Economic Scorecard

In Chapter 1 we recalled Ronald Reagan's 1984 question to the electorate, "Are you better off today than you were four years ago?" With inflation running at only half the double-digit rates recorded during 1979–1980, the obvious answer for most people was "yes." That was the political answer that Reagan expected to hear, and he was reelected.

Improvements in the 1984 inflation rate compared to 1980 led people to believe that they were better off, but a more precise consideration is *how much* better was the economy under Reagan compared to under Carter; in other words, what was the *magnitude* of economic improvement? This is a question that might be asked of any president's performance. As a partial answer, we have compiled indicators on the performance of the U.S. economy over the postwar era, a sort of **presidential economic scorecard.**

THE POSTWAR PRESIDENTS AND THE ECONOMY

In 1984 Reaganomics seemed a distinct improvement over the Carter era, but the performance of the macroeconomy through Reagan's first term was not so stellar when indicators other than the inflation rate are considered. More broadly, where would Reagan stand relative to all presidents during the 1948–1992 period? Nine presidents have served during the postwar era, five Republicans and four Democrats. Are there any patterns—over time, by party, by individual president—associated with the performance of the economy?

TABLE 12.1 Presidential Economic Scorecard

	Unemployment[a]		Inflation[a]		Economic Growth[a]		Productivity[a]		Current Account Balance[a]		Overall Rank[b]
Truman (D) 1949–1952	4.4%	3	2.5%	4	5.7%	1	4.3%	1	+0.6	6	2.5
Eisenhower (R) 1953–1956	4.2%	2	0.6%	1	2.6%	6	2.3%	5	+2.0	5	4
Eisenhower (R) 1957–1960	5.5%	5	2.2%	3	2.3%	9	2.7%	4	+7.1	4	5
Kennedy/Johnson (D) 1961–1964	5.8%	6	1.2%	2	4.3%	3	3.9%	2	+18.4	2	2.5
Johnson (D) 1965–1968	3.9%	1	2.9%	5	4.6%	2	2.8%	3	+11.6	3	1
Nixon (R) 1969–1972	5.0%	4	4.7%	8	2.5%	7	1.8%	6	−4.5	7	6

President	(1) Unemployment		(2) CPI		(3) GNP		(4) Productivity		(5) Deficit		Overall Rank
Nixon/Ford (R) 1973–1976	6.7%	10	8.0%	10	2.1%	10	1.1%	9	+31.4	1	8
Carter (D) 1977–1980	6.5%	9	9.8%	11	3.1%	5	0.3%	11	−29.8	8	9.5
Reagan (R) 1981–1984	8.6%	11	6.0%	9	2.4%	8	1.5%	7	−138.1	9	9.5
Reagan (R) 1985–1988	6.5%	8	3.3%	6	3.3%	4	1.3%	8	−554.1	11	7
Bush (R) 1989–1992	6.2%	7	4.4%	7	1.0%	11	0.6%	10	−257.6	10	11

[a]Macroeconomic Indicators are: (1) four-year average unemployment rate, (2) four-year average percent change in Consumer Price Index over each year, (3) four-year average percent change in real gross national product over each year, (4) four-year average percent change in productivity (real output per hour per employee) over each year, (5) the net surplus or deficit over four years.

[b]Each macroeconomic indicator is ranked from best (1) to worst (11), and the overall rank is derived from the average of the five rankings for each president.

310

Table 12.1 presents a presidential economic scorecard based upon five macroeconomic indicators: unemployment, inflation, growth in GNP, increases in productivity, and the balance on current account. The indicators are summarized as four-year averages, that is, a single average figure has been computed for the period between two successive presidential elections. Although this does not reveal the substantial swings between highs and lows within each of these periods, it does capture the average overall performance during each president's term.

We report figures for all postwar presidential terms, beginning with the second Truman term, the first full term after the war's end. We have also ranked the eleven postwar presidential terms on each index from one (best) to eleven (worst) based on their economic performance, and the five rankings have been averaged into an overall rank-order of the eleven presidential terms. We do not mean to imply that all five indicators are equally important, since the relative importance of inflation, economic growth, or unemployment are matters of political judgment. This ranking simplifies reality. With this in mind, the scorecard is intended to characterize the economic conditions that generally prevailed during each president's tenure.

Since the postwar period includes a variety of presidents drawn from both political parties, it opens up discussion of a number of questions: Who had the best economic performance? The worst? Does political party have any relationship to macroeconomic conditions? The figures in Table 12.1 suggest that neither party has had a monopoly on good economic times. In general, the rankings indicate that the economy performed better during the first half of the postwar period than during the latter half. The best years were the 1960s, a period of generally strong growth and moderate inflation and unemployment.

Examination of Table 12.1 yields four basic conclusions. First, the economy apparently caused more grief for recent presidents than for their predecessors. The last five presidential terms rank seventh through eleventh, and Ford, Carter, and Bush all lost bids to retain their offices, due in part to adverse economic conditions. Second, Democrats have had more luck, or skill, than Republicans when dealing with the economy. The top four rankings include Truman, the Kennedy-Johnson term, and Johnson, whereas only one Democrat is among the bottom five (Carter). Third, war years have been good for economic performance, which may explain why Democrats fared better than Republicans. The Korean War occurred under Truman, and the Vietnam War was waged mainly by President Johnson, whose macroeconomic performance during 1965–68 ranked first among the eleven terms. Fourth, the rankings suggest that the common view of how the macroeconomy is working may have little relationship to reality.

The political significance of any macroeconomic indicator depends on which measure is publicized by the media and emphasized in political debate, and the overall economy may be performing differently than the most politically salient indicators.

And what of President Reagan's question in 1984? Although better in some ways, principally the rate of inflation, the years of the first Reagan term were not clearly superior to the Carter years overall. Of course, President Reagan asked the voters to specifically compare 1984 with 1980, a comparison that would have been somewhat more favorable than the comparison of each president's entire four-year term. Nevertheless, in neither of these two presidential terms did the economy perform at the levels seen one or two decades earlier.

The record shows that three indices—unemployment, real GNP, and the balance on current account—did better under President Carter, although productivity grew five times faster under Reagan, and the CPI increased at the annual rate of 6.0 percent during 1981–84 compared to 9.8 percent during 1977–80. (If we also include real per capita disposal personal income as an indicator of the standard of living, its performance was also slighter higher for the 1977–80 period.) These indices suggest that the economy overall did about the same under Jimmy Carter as during the first term of Ronald Reagan, yet most people would find that hard to believe. Of course, the economy performed much better during Reagan's second term, with an overall ranking higher than any term since 1972.

This paradox of divergent public views and economic statistics suggests that indicators like productivity and the balance on current account—and perhaps even economic growth—may not be perceived as having a direct impact on people's lives. Unemployment and inflation are more obvious problems, and people gave Reagan more credit than Carter because inflation dominated public debate on the economy in the early 1980s. During the Reagan administration the rate of inflation was, in fact, brought down to relatively low levels.

A little closer to today, how did President Bush perform as the manager of prosperity? The answer, it appears, is not very well. In several respects—productivity, economic growth, the balance of payments—the Bush years were dreadful, nearly the worst in the postwar era. Surprisingly, one of the best scores for the Bush years was for unemployment, although the unemployment rate during his term was at its worst—well over 7 percent—for much of the key political year of 1992. Given the comparative information in the table, it is little wonder that President Bush's approval ratings, and particularly his ratings for managing the economy, fell over the course of his term in office.

312   A final observation is in order. The U.S. economy did better overall in the period before the 1970s than it has since then. *Both* unemployment and inflation were higher during the 1980s than they were over the twenty years between 1948 and 1968. Perhaps this means that economic problems are more complicated today and/or that they are less amenable to easy solution based on the standard macroeconomic policies. It is a little ironic that the Republican themes of "peace and prosperity" so decisively helped George Bush win the 1988 presidential election, given that the 1985–88 period ranks seventh overall in economic performance. However, even ranked seventh this term ranked higher than the three preceding presidential terms.

But the 1950s and 1960s were a long time ago, and it is a relative and changing political standard that measures the success of macroeconomic policies and the effectiveness of presidential leadership. Herbert Hoover did not cause the Great Depression, but he was the incumbent when Wall Street crashed. And similarly, if the triple-digit deficits of Reaganomics prove to be the Achilles heel of the American economy during the decade of the 1990s, the odds are that with each passing year the public will shift more of the blame away from President Reagan and onto whomever occupies the White House at the time the economic bill for these deficits comes due.

CAN ANYONE MANAGE PROSPERITY?

This discussion of the presidential economic scorecard raises an interesting question: Can *anyone* manage prosperity in the U.S. economy? Put somewhat differently, does it make a difference who is president, or is the performance of the economy largely a function of forces beyond the president's control?

The correct answer to these questions is probably yes and no. No in the sense that much of the performance of the U.S. economy is due to structural features of the economy and to market forces that are beyond the reach of U.S. policymakers. Some of the structural features that influence economic performance include the nature of U.S. labor relations, the management styles prevalent in U.S. business, and the age of U.S. capital stock. Some of these are, of course, subject to government influence—investment decisions concerning plant modernization are affected by incentives in the tax code, for example—but these structural features remain largely under the control of private actors.

Similarly, some of the other significant influences on the U.S. economy are the result of market forces. These forces can be influenced to some degree by policymakers, particularly when the markets involved are essentially domestic, but increasingly, the U.S. economy operates within global markets. Two significant examples are the global markets for capital and oil. Although the U.S. capital market was once far more autonomous, today the cost and availability of capital is tied to world markets. In the global oil market, the U.S. is at the mercy of global prices; when major producers successfully banded together into a pricing cartel, skyrocketing oil prices contributed strongly to rising U.S. inflation rates. When the cartel collapsed in the early 1980s, inflationary pressure accordingly moderated. However, in either case, the contribution of oil prices to U.S. price stability was essentially not under control of the U.S. policymakers.

In the view of one prominent scholar, Richard Rose, changes in the electoral system and increasing global interdependence have made it increasingly difficult for U.S. presidents to govern.[1] Rose believes that the modern presidency that began with Roosevelt has evolved into a postmodern phase, one in which the global economic hegemony of the U.S. has eroded to the point that U.S. presidents can only govern effectively with the cooperation of foreign leaders. This is further complicated by the electoral demands of modern campaigning, which, in Rose's view, produce successful campaigners but not (necessarily) successful leaders.[2]

On the other hand, the question of presidential control can also be answered in the affirmative, since the president and other policymakers do play a role in some significant areas affecting the macroeconomy. The first area is in establishing the target for governmental fiscal and monetary policy. This normally involves an assessment of whether to target inflation or unemployment for reduction. Forty years of experience indicates that both fiscal policy and monetary policy *can* affect inflation and unemployment, and each president defines which will be the special target of his efforts. Examples include the decision by Lyndon Johnson in 1967 to risk a higher inflation rate in order to pursue other goals and the decision by Fed chair Paul Volcker (supported by President Reagan) to pursue an anti-inflationary monetary policy in the early 1980s, even though this risked (and in fact, contributed to) higher unemployment. In each case the subsequent performance of the economy was a direct consequence of the policies adopted.

An even clearer example of presidential control is the federal budget deficit. This looming problem is, of course, partly due to underlying social trends like the aging of the population, but at base, this is a political problem. In particular, the historically high deficits recorded since 1981 are a direct consequence of the decision of Ronald Reagan to support a large tax cut without achieving corresponding cuts in spending. At the time this was described as an economic "experiment." With hindsight, it

314 is clear that it is a supply-side experiment that failed, yet the political leaders of both major parties have yet to summon the political will to seriously address this problem.

THE U.S. ECONOMY IN THE 1990s

As we move through the 1990s, the U.S. economy faces several challenges. At the top of the list is the persistence of large and seemingly permanent budget deficits. During the 1992 presidential election this issue was like the proverbial bad penny—it kept turning up, most powerfully in the person of Ross Perot. Although Perot abandoned his presidential bid in mid-summer when it seemed he had little (if any) chance to win the presidency, he reentered the race in October, in part because he felt that neither George Bush nor Bill Clinton had laid out a clear plan for dealing with the deficit problem.

Perot, of course, was correct in this assessment, but the lack of concrete proposals was due in large measure to the candidates' assessments that any concrete proposals—either to cut spending for popular programs or to increase taxes—would invite the wrath of the voters. As we noted in Chapter 9, the voters, while concerned about ending deficits, have been even more concerned with preventing the spending cuts and tax increases necessary to accomplish that goal. As a result, the election campaign ended with the same lack of concrete solutions that it began with.

A second problem facing the U.S. economy relates to its interrelationship with the global economy. Included in this general problem are such issues as the benefits of free or fair trade, the problem of maintaining competitiveness with global competitors, and how to address the costs associated with the social and economic dislocations brought on by international trade. At a more basic level, U.S. society needs to undergo a perceptual shift, to realize that regardless of the nostalgic yearnings for the days of U.S. dominance in the 1950s, the new world economic order is already arriving.

A third problem involves the adjustment of economic policy to basic trends in U.S. society. Two related trends with tremendous implications for the U.S. economy are the aging of the population and the rapidly escalating costs for health care. Increases in health-care costs have outpaced the overall CPI every year since 1980,[3] and President Clinton has stated publicly that the fiscal crisis of budget deficits cannot be addressed effectively until health-care costs are brought under control. Budgetary trends strongly support Clinton's assertion: between FY82 and FY92 federal health-care expenditures grew by 182 percent—more than twice the

rate of growth of the total budget—with 93 percent of the increases coming in just two programs, Medicare and Medicaid.[4] To address this and
other health-care issues, one of President Clinton's first actions was to
appoint a health-care panel headed by Hillary Rodham Clinton to develop
a set of comprehensive policy proposals. These proposals were originally
due to be announced in late spring of 1993, but their announcement was
repeatedly delayed, first to the summer and later to the fall. Given the
likely cost and scope of any proposed policy changes, the debate over
health-care reform promises to be one of the most significant—and difficult—battles of the Clinton presidency. Given the closeness of the margins in the 1993 battle over the deficit-reduction package, it is unclear
whether Congress will be able to pass significant health-care reform proposals during a Clinton presidency.

Finally, a fourth basic problem facing the U.S. economy deals not
with reversing a single economic trend, but with deciding to what extent,
if any, the nation will identify desirable structural changes and take steps
to achieve them. Contrary to the myth that the U.S. economy developed
primarily through the actions of a myriad of individual actors, the national
government—from Hamilton, through Lincoln, and on to Dwight Eisenhower (in whose administration the Interstate Highway System was begun)—has always played a role in national economic development. This
has traditionally occurred in development of the national transportation
infrastructure, but at this time, the basic question concerns whether development efforts should extend beyond steel and concrete toward a re-
structuring of the economy itself.

In the 1992 presidential campaign, candidate Clinton argued that the
country was ready for a change; in November the electorate responded by
ending twelve years of Republican control of the White House. The Clinton campaign focused heavily on the economy—so much so that a sign
hung on the wall of the national campaign headquarters in Little Rock
said simply, "It's the economy, stupid," lest anyone forget. In the early
days of the Clinton administration, the new president moved swiftly to
begin addressing several economic problems, most prominently health
care, the budget deficit, and the lingering effects of the 1990–91 recession.
However, the early enthusiasm of planning, announcements, and proposal
development was followed by the reality of Washington politics—a delayed health-care proposal, a defeated short-term stimulus, and a modified
(but adopted) long-term deficit package.

In a few years, the Clinton first term will be added to the presidential
economic scorecard. Where will it rate? The lesson of this book is that
the answer will depend only partly upon the actions of President Clinton.
The economy will also respond to actions by other actors: the Fed, Con-

316   gress, foreign governments, and private actors. Overshadowing them all will be the basic rhythms of the business cycle, both in the U.S. and globally. One thing, however, is certain. Whether a second Clinton term joins the list will depend heavily upon how the public evaluates Clinton's first-term performance as the manager of our prosperity.

KEY TERM

presidential economic scorecard

ADDITIONAL READING

Bartley, Robert. *The Seven Fat Years: And How to Do It Again.* New York: Free Press, 1992. Friendly account of the Reagan economic program which selectively uses statistics to argue the success of Reaganomics and advocate its continuance.

Rose, Richard. *The Postmodern President: George Bush Meets the World*, 2nd ed. Chatham, NJ: Chatham House, 1991. Argues that increasing global interdependence and modern campaign imperatives make it more difficult for presidents to effectively address policy problems, including domestic and international economic issues.

NOTES

1.   Richard Rose, *The Postmodern President: George Bush Meets the World*, 2nd ed. (Chatham, NJ: Chatham House, 1991).

2.   A similar view of the gap between effective campaigning and effective governing is expressed in Alan Ehrenhalt, *The United States of Ambition: Politicians, Power, and the Pursuit of Office* (New York: Random House, 1991).

3.   *Economic Report of the President, 1993* (Washington, DC: Government Printing Office, January 1993), p. 416.

4.   The figures for overall health-care spending are for Function 550 (Health) and Function 570 (Medicare) in the FY82 and FY92 budgets. Budget figures are taken from the Historical Tables in Office of Management and Budget, *Budget Baselines, Historical Data, and Alternatives for the Future, January 1993* (Washington, DC: Government Printing Office, January 1993).

APPENDIX

RECRUITMENT PROFILES OF KEY ECONOMIC POLICYMAKERS

TABLE A.1   Recruitment Profiles for Chairmen, Council of Economic Advisers, 1946–1993

CEA Chairman	Service Dates	Education	Occupation	Previous Position
Nourse, Edwin G.	Aug. 9 1946– Nov. 1, 1949	Ph.D., 1915 Chicago	academic economist	vice president, The Brookings Institution, 1942–1946
Keyserling, Leon H.	May 10, 1950– Jan. 20, 1953	LL.B., 1939 Harvard	lawyer/ economist	CEA acting chairman, 1949–1950; CEA vice chairman, 1946–1949
Burns, Arthur F.	March 19, 1953– Dec. 1, 1956	Ph.D., 1925 Columbia	academic economist	director of research, National Bureau of Economic Research
Saulnier, Raymond, T.	Dec. 3, 1956– Jan. 20, 1961	Ph.D., 1938 Columbia	academic economist	CEA member
Heller, Walter W.	Jan 29, 1961– Nov. 15, 1964	Ph.D., 1941 Wisconsin	academic economist	professor of economics, University of Minnesota, 1946–1961
Ackley, H. Gardner	Nov. 16, 1964– Feb. 15, 1968	Ph.D., 1940 Michigan	academic economist	CEA member, 1962–1964
Okun, Arthur M.	Feb. 15, 1968– Jan. 20, 1969	Ph.D., 1956 Columbia	academic economist	CEA member, 1964–1968

Name	Dates	Degree	Category	Description
McCracken, Paul W.	Feb. 4, 1969– Dec. 31, 1971	Ph.D., 1948 Harvard	academic economist	professor of business policy, University of Michigan, 1948–1969; CEA member, 1956–1959
Stein, Herbert	Jan. 1, 1972– Aug. 31, 1974	Ph.D, 1958 Chicago	academic economist	CEA member, 1969–1972
Greenspan, Alan	Sept. 4, 1974– Jan. 20, 1977	M.A., 1950 New York Univ.	business economist	president, Townsend-Greenspan and Company, a New York consulting firm, 1967–1974
Schultze, Charles L.	Jan. 22, 1977– Jan. 20, 1981	Ph.D., 1960 Maryland	academic economist	professor of economics, Indiana University, senior fellow, The Brookings Institution, 1968–1976
Weidenbaum, Murray L.	Feb. 27, 1981– Aug. 25, 1982	Ph.D., 1958 Princeton	academic economist	director, Center for the Study of American Business, Washington University, 1975–1981
Feldstein, Martin	Oct. 14, 1982– July 10, 1984	D.Phil., 1967 Oxford	academic economist	president, National Bureau of Economic Research, 1977–1982
Sprinkel, Beryl	Apr. 18, 1986– Jan. 20, 1989	Ph.D., 1948 Chicago	business economist	undersecretary of the treasury for monetary affairs, 1981–1984
Boskin, Michael J.	Feb. 2, 1989– Jan. 12, 1993	Ph.D., 1971 Berkeley	academic economist	Burnet C. and Mildred Finley Wohlford Professor of Economics, Stanford University, 1970–1989
Tyson, Laura D.	Feb. 4, 1993–	Ph.D., 1974 MIT	academic economist	professor of economics, University of California Berkeley, 1977–1993

TABLE A.2 Recruitment Profiles for Secretaries of the Treasury, 1946–1993

Secretary	Service Dates	Education	Occupation	Previous Position
Snyder, John W.	June 25, 1946–Jan. 20, 1953	attended college	business executive	vice president, First National Bank of St. Louis, 1943–1945
Humphrey, George M.	Jan 21, 1953–July 29, 1957	LL.B, 1912 Michigan	business executive	chairman of the board, M. A. Hanna Co. (steel manufacturer), Cleveland, 1952–
Anderson, Robert B.	July 29, 1957–Jan 20, 1961	LL.B. Texas	business executive	president, Ventures, Ltd., of New York City and Toronto, 1955–1957
Dillon, Douglas	Jan. 21, 1961–April 1, 1965	B.A., 1931 Harvard	financier	undersecretary of state, 1959–1961; undersecretary of state for economic affairs, 1958–1959
Fowler, Henry H.	April 1, 1965–Dec. 20, 1968	J.S.D., 1932 Yale	financier	undersecretary of the treasury, 1961–1964
Barr, Joseph W.	Dec. 21, 1968–Jan. 20, 1969	M.A., 1941 Harvard	business executive	undersecretary of the treasury, 1965–1968
Kennedy, David M.	Jan 22, 1969–Feb. 1, 1971	LL.B, 1937 Geo. Wash. Univ.	banker	Continental Illinois Bank and Trust Co., 1946–1969; chairman of the board/CEO, 1958–
Connally, John B.	Feb. 11, 1971–June 12, 1972	LL.B, 1941 Texas	elected official	governor of Texas, 1963–1969

Name	Term	Education	Occupation	Other positions
Shultz, George P.	June 12, 1972– May 8, 1974	Ph.D., 1949 MIT	academic economist	director, Office of Management and Budget, 1970–1972
Simon, William E.	May 8, 1974– Jan. 20, 1977	B.A., 1952 Lafayette	financier	deputy secretary of the treasury, 1973–1974
Blumenthal, W. Michael	Jan. 23, 1977– Aug. 4, 1979	Ph.D., 1956 Princeton	business executive	chairman of the board, president, CEO, Bendix Corporation, 1972–1977
Miller, G. William	Aug. 6, 1979– Jan. 20, 1981	J.D., 1952 California	business executive	chairman, Federal Reserve Board, 1978–1979
Regan, Donald T.	Jan. 22, 1981– Feb. 2, 1985	B.A., 1940 Harvard	financier	chairman of the board, CEO, Merrill, Lynch, Pierce, Fenner, Smith, Inc., 1973–1981
Baker, James A. III	Feb. 4, 1985– Aug. 22, 1988	LL.B., 1957 Texas	lawyer	chief of staff under President Reagan, 1981–1985
Brady, Nicholas F.	Sept. 15, 1988– Dec. 20, 1993	M.B.A., 1954	financier	secretary of the treasury under President Reagan, 1988–
Bentsen, Lloyd	Dec. 20, 1993–	LL.B., 1942 Texas	politician	member, U.S. Senate (D–TX), 1970–1993; chairman, Committee on Finance

TABLE A.3 Recruitment Profiles for Director, Bureau of the Budget and Office of Management and Budget, 1946–1993

Director	Service Dates	Education	Occupation	Previous Position
Webb, John W.	July 13, 1946– Jan. 27, 1949	B.A., 1928 North Carolina	business executive	executive assistant to undersecretary of the treasury, 1946; Gardner, Morrison, and Rogers (law firm) 1945–1946
Pace, Frank Jr.	Feb. 1, 1949– April 12, 1950	LL.B., 1939 Harvard	lawyer	asst. director, bureau of the budget, 1948–1949
Lawton, Frederick J.	April 13, 1950– Jan. 21, 1953	LL.B., 1934 Georgetown	government official	asst. director, bureau of the budget, 1949
Dodge, Joseph M.	April 22, 1953– April 15, 1954	graduated high school	banker	president, The Detroit Bank, 1933–1953
Hughes, Rowland R.	April 16, 1954– April 1, 1956	Ph.D, 1917 Brown	government official	deputy director, bureau of the budget, 1953–1954
Brundage, Percival F.	April 2, 1956– March 17, 1958	B.A., 1914 Harvard	business consultant	deputy director, bureau of the budget, 1954–1956
Stans, Maurice	April 15, 1958– Jan. 21, 1961	attended college	business consultant	deputy director, bureau of the budget, 1957–1958
Bell, David E.	Jan. 22, 1961– Dec. 20, 1962	M.A., 1941 Harvard	economist	secretary, Littauer Center, Harvard Graduate School of Public Administration, 1959–1961
Gordon, Kermit	Dec. 28, 1962– June 1, 1965	B.A., 1938 Swarthmore	academic economist	member, Council of Economic Advisors, 1961–1962
Schultze, Charles L.	June 2, 1965– Jan. 28, 1968	Ph.D, 1960 Maryland	academic economist	asst. director, bureau of the budget, 1962–1965

Name	Dates	Profession	Education	Career
Zwick, Charles J.	Jan. 29, 1968– Jan. 21, 1969	banker	Ph.D., 1954 Harvard	asst. director, bureau of the budget, 1965–1968
Mayo, Robert P.	Jan. 22, 1969– June 30, 1970	economist	M.B.A., 1938 Washington	vice president, Continental Illinois Bank, Chicago, 1960–1969
Shultz, George P.	July 1, 1970– June 11, 1972	academic economist	Ph.D, 1949 MIT	secretary of labor, 1969–1970
Weinberger, Casper	June 12, 1972– Feb. 1, 1973	lawyer	LL.B., 1941 Harvard	deputy director, Office of Management and Budget, 1970–1972
Ash, Roy L.	Feb. 2, 1973– Feb. 3, 1975	business executive	M.B.A., 1947 Harvard	Litton Industries, Inc., 1953–1972; president since 1961
Lynn, James P.	Feb. 10, 1975– Jan. 20, 1977	lawyer	LL.B, 1951 Harvard	secretary of housing and urban development, 1973–1974
Lance, Thomas Bertram	Jan. 22, 1977– Sept. 23, 1977	banker	attended college	highway director, State of Georgia, 1970–1973
McIntyre, James T.	March 24, 1978– Jan. 20, 1981	lawyer	J.D., 1963 Georgia	acting director, Office of Management and Budget, 1977–1978 and deputy director, 1977
Stockman, David	Jan. 21, 1981– July 26, 1986	elected official	B.A., 1968 Michigan State	member, House of Representatives, 1977–1978; chairman, Republican Economic Policy Task Force, 1977–1981
Miller, James C. III	Oct. 8, 1986– Oct. 15, 1988	economist	Ph.D, 1969 Virginia	chairman, Federal Trade Commission, 1981–1985
Darman, Richard G.	Jan. 25, 1989– Jan. 10, 1993	investment banker	M.B.A., 1967 Harvard	deputy secretary of the treasury, 1985–1988; managing director, Shearson Lehman Brothers, 1988–
Panetta, Leon E.	Jan. 21, 1993–	elected official	J.D., 1963 Santa Clara	member, House of Representatives (D-CA), 1976–1993; chairman, Budget Committee

TABLE A.4 Recruitment Profiles for Chairmen, Federal Reserve Board, 1934–1993

Chairman	Service Dates	Education	Occupation	Previous Position
Eccles, Marriner	Nov. 15, 1934–Jan. 31, 1948	attended college	banker	asst. to the secretary of the treasury, 1934; president, First National Bank of Ogden and Ogden Savings Bank, Utah, 1920–1934
McCabe, Thomas B.	April 15, 1948–March 31, 1951	B.A., 1915 Swarthmore	banker	director, Federal Reserve Bank of Philadelphia, 1938–1948
Martin, William McChesney Jr.	April 2, 1951–Jan. 31, 1970	B.A., 1928 Yale	financier	executive director, International Bank for Reconstruction and Development, 1949–1952; board of directors, Export–Import Bank, 1945–1948
Burns, Arthur F.	Feb. 1, 1970–Jan. 31, 1978	Ph.D., 1925 Columbia	academic economist	counselor to President Richard Nixon, 1969–1970; National Bureau of Economic Research, 1974–1978
Miller, G. William	March 8, 1978–Aug. 6, 1979	J.D., 1952 California	business executive	chairman of the board, Textron, Inc., 1974–1978
Volcker, Paul A.	Aug. 6, 1979–Aug. 11, 1987	M.A., 1951 Harvard	banker	president, Federal Reserve Bank of New York, 1975–1979
Greenspan, Alan	Aug. 11, 1987–	Ph.D., 1977 New York Univ.	business economist	president, Townsend–Greenspan and Company, a New York consulting firm, 1977–

INDEX

A

Aaron, Henry J., 195n18
Abramson, Paul R., 220n36
Ackley, Gardner, 52, 74n12, 195n10, 204
Agenda setting, 46
Agricultural Adjustment Act of 1933 (AAA), 29
Aldrich, John H., 220n36
Almond, Gabriel, 26, 40n11
Alt, James, 243, 251n69
Anderson, Robert, 260
Anderson, James E., 50, 73n1n2n3, 74n8, 76n40n42n49, 137n30
Angell, Wayne D., 63–64
Antideficiency Act of 1950, 105
Appropriations legislation, 78
Appropriations committees, in Congress, 78, 79–80, 81, 82, 85, 86, 90
Approval rating, presidential, 236–238
Arcelus, Francisco, 249n47
Ash, Roy, 60, 323
Authorizing legislation, 78
Automatic stabilizers, 176

B

Bailey, Stephen K., 40n2, 41n27n33n35
Baker, James A., III, 55, 56, 159, 321
Balanced Budget and Emergency Deficit Control Act of 1985, 84, 294
    Also see Gramm-Rudman-Hollings Act
Balance of payments, 8–9, 148, 153–160
Balance of trade, 142
Balance on current account, 148

Balanced-budget amendment, 106, 245, 298–300
Banking Act of 1935, 61
Barton, Allen H., 248n9n10
Basilick, Linda, 251n71
Beck, Nathaniel, 133–134, 137n14n19, 138n37n38n41n42n43
Beckman, Barry A., 195n3
Bentsen, Lloyd, 55–56, 276, 321
Biddle, Nicholas, 116
Blinder, Alan S., 64, 218n5
Bloom, Howard S., 236, 250n48
Blumenthal, Mike, 131, 212, 321
Board of Governors, of Federal Reserve Board
    See Federal Reserve Board
Bonello, Frank, 40n8
Boskin, Michael, 55, 274, 319
Bosworth, Barry, 296
Boyd, Gerald M., 166n31, 304n7n12
Bracket creep, 94
Brady, Nicholas, 55, 56, 69, 280, 321
Break, George F., 218n5
Bretton Woods System, 148, 149, 153
Brown, E. Cary, 32, 41n23
Brunner, Karl, 271
Buchanan, James, 231, 249n31
Buchanan, Patrick, 235, 280
Budget Committees, in Congress, 84, 85
Budgets, federal
    dangers of deficits, 302–303
    deficits, 77
    deficit trends, 91–96
    reasons for growth in, 99–102
Budgetary process, 78–87
Budget Enforcement Act of 1990, 297
Bunzel, John H., 248n8

326

Bureau of Economic Analysis, 123
Bureau of the Budget (BOB), 49, 57,
58–59, 81, 82
Also see Office of Management and
Budget (OMB)
Burger, Warren, 296
Burns, Arthur F., 54, 55, 62, 64, 68,
127, 129–131, 134, 157, 169,
205–207, 211, 257–260, 324
Bush, George, 3–4, 13, 25, 55, 56, 62,
69, 89, 92, 97, 99, 106, 126, 127,
147, 158, 174, 189, 193, 195n3,
235, 240, 242, 243, 274, 276,
282, 299, 302, 310, 311, 314
economic performance under,
190–192
economic policy, 278–281
FY91 Deficit Agreement, 297–298
approval ratings, 238–239
Business cycle, 20, 169–170
Byrd, Harry, 267
Byrd, Robert, 293, 299

C

Cabinet Council on Economic Affairs
(CCEA), 69
Campbell, Colin, 76n46
Cantril, Hadley, 232, 249n32
Capitalism, 11
Caplovitz, David, 248n16
Carter, Jimmy, 38, 56, 61, 62, 67, 69,
91, 92, 95, 101, 102, 107, 130,
131, 134, 158, 193, 200, 216,
217, 219n28, 239, 241, 243, 246,
276, 279, 290, 307, 310, 311
economic performance under,
14–15, 186–188
policy reversal on inflation,
211–215
Catchings, Waddill, 30
Central bank, 116
Chandler, Lester, 40n12n15
Chicago School (of economics), 54
Childs, Marquis, 283n6
Chong, Dennis, 248n13n14

Chubb, John E., 111n43, 248n26,
251n64
Chrystal, Alec, 243, 251n69
Citrin, Jack, 234, 249n36
Classical economics, 21
Clines, Francis X., 304n5n14
Clinton, Bill, 51, 55, 56, 60, 62, 64,
70, 89, 160, 162, 235, 242, 245,
276, 279, 281–282, 299, 314–316
trade policy, 161–162
economic policy, 300–302
Clinton, Hillary Rodham, 315
Clymer, Adam, 305n22n23n24n25
Cochrane, James L., 218n4
Coincident (economic) indicators,
123
Commons, John, 262
Concurrent (budget) resolutions, 84
Congressional Budget and Impound-
ment Control Act of 1974,
83–86, 104–105
Congressional Budget Office (CBO),
84, 85, 295, 298, 301
Connally, John, 55–56, 66, 158, 184,
206–207, 320
Constitution, and origins of capital-
ism, 222–223
Consumer Price Index (CPI), 7, 124
Coolidge, Calvin, 81
Cost-push inflation, 205
Council of Economic Advisers
(CEA), 36, 47, 49–55
Countercyclical (fiscal) policy, 30,
170, 197
Cronin, Thomas, 75n25
Current services budget, 85
Currie, Lauchlin, 31
Cutter, W. Bowman, 220n33
Cyclical deficit, 288

D

Dam, Kenneth W., 165n19,
219n24n25
Daniels, Sally, 251n71
Danziger, Sheldon, 110n23

Darman, Richard, 55, 69, 280, 299, 323
Davis, James W., 109n16
Dawes, Charles G., 81
Daynes, Byron W., 73n7
Deflation, 7
de Marchi, Neil, 196n21, 206, 219n14n15n16, 285n42n50
Department of the Treasury, 50, 57, 127–128
Depository Institutions Deregulation and Monetary Control Act of 1980, 119
Destler, I.M., 166n21
Devaluation, of the dollar, 158, 159
Dewey, Thomas E., 34
Dillon, Douglas, 56, 263, 265–266, 320
Dirksen, Everett M., 101
Discount rate, of Federal Reserve Board, 121
Divine, Robert A., 166n23
Dole, Robert, 291–294
Domenici, Peter, 292
Dornbusch, Rudiger, 286n59
Dukakis, Michael, 297
Dye, Thomas, 73n1

E
Eatwell, John, 39n1
Eccles, Marriner, 31, 62, 127, 324
Economic indicators, 122–125
Economic Policy Board (EPB), 68–69, 70, 185, 255
Economic Policy Council, 69
Economic Policy Group, 69
Economic Recovery Tax Act of 1981 (ERTA), 93, 95, 96, 288
Economic scorecard, of modern presidents, 307
how presidents rank on economic performance, 308–312
Economic Stabilization Act of 1970, 184, 206, 209
Economic subpresidency, 50

Edwards, David V., 110n31
Ehrenhalt, Alan, 316n2
Eisener, Marc Allen, 76n49
Eisenhower, Dwight D., 50, 54, 56, 59, 62, 68, 82, 87, 129, 134, 154, 180, 239, 265, 315
economic performance under, 177–179
economic policymaking, 256–261
Elections, and economic conditions, 239–242
Elites, attitudes towards capitalism, 223–225
Ellwood, John W., 104, 110n34, 111n37
Employment Act of 1946, 20, 32–37, 48, 177, 192, 261
Entitlement programs, 101, 182
Erikson, Robert S., 73n5, 237, 250n49n52
Exchange rate, 148–149
Executive budget, 81
preparation of, 86–87
Evans, Rowland, 195n17
Executive Office of the President (EOP), 49, 57
Expenditure ceilings, as reform, 104

F
Fair Labor Standards Act of 1938, 29
Fair trade, 147
Fast-track, in trade policymaking, 153
Federal funds rate, of Federal Reserve System, 123
Federal Reserve Board ("Fed"), 50, 61–64, 115, 279, 280
Board of Governors, 61, 62, 63, 65, 117, 119, 127, 130
chairman of, 127–132
Federal Open Market Committee (FOMC), 61, 62, 117, 119, 122, 130, 132
Federal Reserve Act of 1913, 50, 130
Federal Reserve Reform Act of 1977, 130–131

328

Federal Reserve System, 57, 117–119, 120, 121, 288

Federal Reserve–Treasury Accord of 1951, 128

Feldstein, Martin, 54, 274, 319

Fenno, Richard F., 109n7n11

Finance Committee, of Senate, 78, 79, 80, 86

Fink, Richard, 40n8n9

First Bank of the United States, 115

Fiscal policy, 11

Fiscal year, 58, 84, 86

Fischer, Stanley, 280, 286n59

Fishel, Jeff, 196n28, 220n34n35

Fisher, Louis, 80, 102, 108n2, 109n3n4n6

Flash, Edward, 258, 264, 284n10n31n32n35

Foley, Thomas, 293, 299

Ford, Gerald, 54, 56, 62, 67, 91, 92, 95, 130, 134, 193, 243, 255, 310

    use of Economic Policy Board, 68–70

    economic policymaking, 185–186

Forecasts (budgetary), of the economy, 87–89

Foster, William T., 30

Franklin, Grace, 73n4

Frankovic, Kathleen A., 220n36

Fraser, L.M., 19

Free, Lloyd, 232, 249n32

Free trade, 146

Friedman, Milton, 51, 114, 157, 184, 256, 268–271, 285n44n45n46

Froyen, Richard T., 179, 195n13, 261, 284n23

Fuerbringer, Jonathan, 304n5n8n10n11n13

Full employment, 6

Full Employment and Balanced Growth Act of 1978, 37, 131

G

G7 nations, of international finance, 151, 159

Galbraith, John Kenneth, 179, 195n11, 261

Gallup, George H., 248n25

General Accounting Office (GAO), 295

General Agreement on Tariffs and Trade (GATT), 140, 145, 150, 163

Genovese, Michael A., 256, 283n2n3, 285n48

George, Alexander, 283n1

Gephardt, Richard A., 160

Gilder, George, 274

GNP gap, 198, 200, 212, 264–265, 267

Gold quadrangle, of economic policy goals, 5

Golden, David G., 251n70

Goodwin, Craufurd D., 74n18, 196n21, 218n4, 285n42

Gorbachev, Mikhail, 294

Gordon, Kermit, 59, 75n25, 322

Gore, Albert, 235, 301

Gournay, 21

Gowa, Joanne, 166n29

Gramm, Phil, 293

Gramm-Rudman II, 296, 297

Gramm-Rudman-Hollings Act, 85, 86, 106, 278, 288, 293

    passage of, 293–294

    deficit reduction process, 294–297

Gray, William, 291, 292

Great Depression, 19, 25, 26–27, 29, 32, 33, 90, 170, 174, 189, 225, 276, 288

Green, George R., 195n3

Greenaway, David, 165n11

Greenberg, Sanford D., 75n25

Greenhouse, Steven, 74n10n20, 165n7, 286n63n64n68

Greenspan, Alan, 54, 56, 62, 126–127, 255, 280–281, 301, 319, 324

Greer, Douglas F., 208, 219n21n23

Greider, William, 110n25

Gross domestic product (GDP), 6

Gross national product (GNP), 5

H

Hailstones, Thomas, 40n4
Hamilton, Alexander, 55, 79,
    114–115, 223, 315
Hansen, Alvin H., 30, 41n20, 170,
    195n5
Hansen, Susan B., 249n39
Harding, Warren G., 20, 81
Hargrove, Erwin C., 53, 74n15n17,
    75n28, 219n11n12, 220n29
Harris, Seymour E., 247n6, 261
Hartz, Louis, 222, 247n3
Haveman, Robert, 110n23
Hawkins, Augustus, 213
Hazelton, Jared, 74n8
Heclo, Hugh, 75n26, 109n20, 110n32
Heilbroner, Robert, 35, 41n31
Heller, Walter, 51–52, 74n11n13,
    128, 204, 261–266, 274, 318
Herren, R. Stanley, 74n18
Hershey, Robert D., Jr., 286n65
Hibbs, Douglas A., Jr., 250n58,
    251n61n63
Hinds, Michael deCourcy, 305n20
Hofstadter, Richard, 222, 247n2,
    248n11
Hollings, Ernest, 293
Holloway, Thomas M., 95, 304n4
Holmans, A.E., 176, 195n8
Hoover, Herbert, 27, 30, 81, 281, 312
Houthakker, Hendrik, 272
Huffbauer, Gary, 166n34
Humphrey, George M., 55–56, 258,
    320
Humphrey, Hubert H., 183, 205, 213
Humphrey-Hawkins Act, 37–38, 131,
    186, 211, 213, 216, 217
Hussein, Saddam, 191

I

Ideological conservatives–operational
    liberals, in public opinion, 232
Impoundments, by presidents,
    104–105
Incrementalism, as budget strategy, 90

Independent regulatory agencies,
    60–61
Inflation, 7
    effect on presidential approval
        ratings, 237–238
    as most important problem facing
        nation, 229
    versus unemployment dilemma,
        198–200
International Monetary Fund (IMF),
    140, 149, 152, 154, 156
International reserves, 150
Interstate Commerce Commission, 20,
    64

J

Jackson, Andrew, 116
Jaroslovsky, Rich, 110n29
Jefferson, Thomas, 105, 115, 223
Johnson, Alvin, 31
Johnson, Lyndon Baines, 50, 59, 62,
    68, 82, 90, 129, 134, 166n28,
    190, 216, 229, 239, 267, 268,
    310, 313
    Council of Economic Advisers un-
        der, 51–52
    balance of payments policy,
        154–157
    economic performance under,
        181–183
    income tax surcharge decision,
        200–205
Johnson, Manuel H., Jr., 63, 64, 274
Joint Economic Committee, of
    Congress, 36
Jones, Charles, 73n1
Juster, F. Thomas, 274, 286n54

K

Katona, George, 286n57
Kaufman, Burton I., 154, 166n23n27
Kaufman, Herbert, 110n30
Kaysen, Carl, 247n6
Keech, William, 76n38, 251n67
Keleher, Robert E., 40n9

330

Kemp, Jack, 132, 189, 276, 292
Kennedy, David, 272, 320
Kennedy, Edward, 187, 214, 294
Kennedy, John Fitzgerald, 50, 54, 56,
    59, 62, 68, 87, 90, 129, 134, 154,
    178, 183, 190, 192, 200, 202,
    203, 205, 237, 256, 310
  Council of Economic Advisers
    under, 51–52
  economic performance under,
    180–181
  economic policymaking, 261–268
  income tax cut decision, 265–268
Kennedy, Paul, 144, 165n4
Kenski, Henry C., 250n53
Kernell, Samuel, 237, 250n54
Kettl, Donald, 127, 129, 131–132,
    137n23n24n28n29n32, 138n35
Keynes, John Maynard, 22–24, 30–32,
    35, 41n24n32, 198, 245, 258
Keynesian (economics), 24, 33, 34,
    36–37, 51, 82, 211, 231, 272, 289
  as influence on John Kennedy, 181,
    256, 261–262
Keyserling, Leon H., 53–54
Kiewiet, D. Roderick, 251n64
Kilborn, Peter T., 75n36, 304n16
Kimmel, Lewis, 40n13n14, 41n25n26,
    261, 283n7n8, 284n13n22
Kissinger, Henry, 255
Klein, Lawrence, 40n4
Kozak, Andrew, 40n8
Kramer, Gerald H., 236, 249n45
Krauss, Clifford, 305n21
Kristol, Irving, 276
Krooss, Herman E., 136n5

L

Ladd, Everett Carl, Jr., 244,
    249n34n35, 251n71
Laffer Curve, 274–276
Laffer, Arthur, 274, 276
Lagging (economic) indicators, 123
Laissez faire economics, 20–22, 225
Lance, Bert, 211, 323

Leading (economic) indicators, 123
Legislative (or central) clearance, 59,
    82
Lehrman, John, 41n34
LeLoup, Lance, 41n34, 110n33,
    111n36
Levy, Michael E., 289, 304n3
Lewis, Wilfred, Jr., 176, 179,
    195n6n9n12n14, 259, 264,
    284n14n15n21n28n30
Lincoln, Abraham, 315
Line item veto, 105
Lippmann, Walter, 22, 40n3n16n17
Liquidity, in money supply, 120
Locke, John, 223
Lowi, Theodore J., 236, 249n44
Lynch, G. Patrick, 251n67

M

MacKuen, Michael B., 237, 238,
    250n52n57
Macroeconomics, 22–23
Madison, James, 79, 115, 223
Mainstream economic view, 25
Manager of prosperity, as presidential
    role, 13, 37
Maisel, S., 137n22
Mann, Thomas E., 110n35
Mansfield, Edwin, 137n15
Markus, Gregory B., 237, 250n50
Martin, Preston, 64
Martin, William McChesney, Jr., 62,
    127–129, 260, 272, 324
Marx, Karl, 223
Mayer, Jane, 304n9
Mayo, Robert, 272, 323
McCabe, Thomas B., 61
McCloskey, Herbert, 225, 248n13n14
McCracken, Paul, 157–158, 206–207,
    272
McCulloch v. Maryland, 115
McDonald, Forrest, 136n2n3, 223,
    247n5
McGovern, George, 185
McLure, Charles E., Jr., 219n9

Merchandise trade balance, 148
Meier, Kenneth J., 17n15, 76n49
Metzger, Stanley D., 165n11
Metzler, Allan H., 249n47, 271
Michel, Robert, 299
Milgate, Murray, 39n1
Mill, James, 25
Miller, Arthur, 248n19
Miller, G. William, 61, 131, 324
Miller, James, III, 294, 323
Mills, Wilbur, 204
Mitchell, Wesley C., 169, 195n3
Moe, Terry, 76n49
Mondale, Walter, 97, 235
Monetarism, 63, 113–114, 132, 268–271
    as influence on Richard Nixon, 183, 271–273
Monetary policy, 12, 113, 119–122, 125–127
Monroe, Kristen R., 237–238, 250n55n56
Montgomery, J.D., 75n25
Moore, W.S., 111n45
Morley, Samuel A., 53, 74n15n17, 75n28, 219n11n12, 220n29
Morris, Irwin L., 76n38
Most favored nation provision, trade policy, 150
Mufson, Steven, 76n48
Multiplier effect, 267, 269
Mundell, Robert, 274
Murray, James E., 34–35

N

Nathan, Richard, 75n27
National Banking Acts of 1863 and 1864, 116
National Bureau of Economic Research (NBER), 169, 173, 192
National debt, 287–288
National Economic Council, 70
National income, 22
National industrial policy, 9, 279
National Industrial Recovery Act of 1933 (NIRA), 29

Natural-rate hypothesis, 269–271
Nelson, Michael, 220n33
Neo-Keynesian, as economic theory, 25
Netzer, Dick, 218n5
Neustadt, Richard E., 109n9
New Deal, 19, 28, 29, 30, 32, 53, 90
New Economic Policy, under Nixon, 154, 185, 207, 229
New economics, 82, 181, 262
    Also see Keynesian economics
Newman, Peter, 39n1
Nichols, Donald, 110n23
Nixon, Richard M., 56, 58, 59, 62, 66, 68, 83, 91, 92, 95, 104, 105, 134, 148, 154, 180, 182, 193, 200, 216, 217, 226, 229, 237, 241, 243, 245, 256, 261, 268
    balance of payments policy, 157–158
    economic performance under, 183–185
    wage-price controls, 205–211
    economic policymaking, 271–273
Nontariff Barriers (NTBs), 147, 160
Nordhaus, William D., 17n8n11, 25, 40n5n10, 132, 136n1n7, 137n17, 138n34n36, 165n13, 218n1, 242–243, 251n65
Norpoth, Helmut, 250n55
North American Free Trade Agreement (NAFTA), 162–163
Norton, Hugh S., 49, 73n6
Nourse, Edwin G., 53–54, 318
Novak, Robert, 195n17
Nunn, Sam, 276
Nye, Joseph S., Jr., 144, 165n5

O

O'Neill, Tip, 292–294
Office of Management and Budget (OMB), 49–50, 57–60, 83, 87
Oil (price) shocks, 216–217
Okun, Arthur, 203–204, 218n6, 219n7n8

332

Olson, Mancur, 247n4
Open market operations, of Federal
     Reserve Board, 122
Operation Twist, as balance of pay-
     ments policy, 129, 154, 263
Ornstein, Norman J., 110n35
Orzechowski, William P., 40n9

P

Palmer, John L., 110n27
Panetta, Leon, 60, 299, 323
Parthenakis, Thomas, 284n9
Passell, Peter, 286n66
Patman, Wright, 64
Peak, of business cycle, 170, 173–174
Pear, Robert, 74n16
Penner, Rudolph G., 111n45
Perkins, Frances, 31
Perot, Ross, 300, 314
Perry, David, 17n14
Peters, B. Guy, 5, 16n3n4, 17n12
Peterson, Paul E., 106, 111n43,
     248n26, 251n64
Peterson, Wallace C., 196n20,
     284n11, 285n39n41
Phelps, Edmund S., 269, 285n47
Phillips Curve, 199, 213, 269–271,
     272, 277
Phillips, A.W., 199
Phillips, Kevin, 251n76
Pious, Richard M., 284n24
Policy adoption, 46
Policy evaluation and reformulation,
     46
Policy formation, 46
Policy goals for the economy, 5–11
Policy implementation, 46
Policy tools for the economy, 11–13
Political business cycle, 242–244
Political economy, 19
Political monetary cycle, 133–135
Political parties, as keepers of nation's
     prosperity, 240–242
Pollack, Andrew, 166n33
Pomper, Gerald M., 220n36

Poole, William, 271
Pork barrel legislation, 101
Porter, Roger, 66, 67, 68,
     76n39n41n43n44n45
Poterba, James M., 251n70
Potter, Marilyn, 251n71
Prices and incomes policy (wage-price
     controls), 157, 185, 208
     formulation of, 205–208
     implementation of, 208–211
Producer Price Index (PPI), 124, 126
Protectionism, in trade policy, 146–
     147
Proxmire, William, 131
Price, H. Douglas, 236, 250n48
Prysby, Charles L., 241, 251n62
Public opinion, and economic knowl-
     edge, 227–228
     towards balancing the budget, 231
     towards economic policy, 244–245
     towards government, 226
     towards import quotas, 245
     towards inflation, 277
     towards policy issues, 228–231
     towards spending priorities, 231–
          234
     towards taxes, 234–235
     towards wage-price controls, 208,
          245
Pump-priming theory, 30
Puth, Robert C., 136n6

Q
Quadriad, as economic advisory sys-
     tem, 50

R
Ratti, Ronald A., 137n15n16
Reagan, Michael D., 75n30,
     136n8n11
Reagan, Ronald, 13, 25, 51, 53, 56,
     58, 60, 62, 63, 64, 65–66, 69, 91,
     92, 93, 96, 97, 99, 102, 105, 106,
     132, 134, 147, 154, 158, 177,
     193, 215, 217, 226, 231, 232,

234, 235, 239, 242, 243, 244, 256, 268, 282, 289, 299, 300, 307, 311–312, 313
balance of payments policy, 159–160
budget deficits, 95–96
budget priorities, 96–97
Council of Economic Advisers under, 54–55
economic performance under, 14–15, 188–190
economic policymaking, 273–278
1985 budget battle, 290–296
Reconciliation bill, in budget process, 86
Regan, Donald, 54, 55, 277, 292, 321
Regulatory policy, 12–13
Reich, Robert, 70
Reichley, A. James, 184, 196n22n23n24n25n26n27, 219n13n18n19n20
Reserve requirements, of Federal Reserve System, 120
Reuss, Henry S., 64, 131
Revenue and Expenditure Control Act of 1968, 202
Rhoads, Steven, 74n14
Ringquist, Delbert, 109n16
Ripley, Randall, 73n4
Rivers, Douglas, 251n64
Roberts, Paul Craig, 276
Roberts, Steven V., 304n6n15
Rogers, David, 304n9
Rohde, David W., 220n36
Roosevelt, Franklin Delano (FDR), 19, 32, 34, 35, 49, 62, 81, 105, 127, 174, 244, 256, 313
    Depression policies, 27–32
Rose, Richard, 313, 316n1
Rosecrance, Richard, 165n6
Rosenbaum, David E., 286n60n61n62
Ross, Russell M., 111n41
Rossiter, Clinton, 17n16, 37, 41n36
Roth, William, 153, 189, 276
Rothenberg, Stuart, 249n41n42
Rubin, Robert, 70
Rudman, Warren, 293

S

Saddler, Jeanne, 110n29
Salamon, Lester M., 109n20, 110n32
Sale, Kirkpatrick, 17n14
Samuelson, Paul, 17n8n11, 22, 25, 40n5n10, 132, 136n1n7, 137n17, 138n34, 165n13, 218n1, 240–241, 250n60, 261, 262–263, 284n29
Saulnier, Raymond, 259, 284n16n17, 318
Sawhill, Isabel V., 110n27
Say, J.B., 25
Say's Law, 25
Schechter Poultry Corp. v. United States, 29
Schick, Allen, 41n34, 86, 87, 104, 109n12n19n20, 110n32n34n35, 111n37n38n39
Schlesinger, Arthur, M., Jr., 41n21n22
Schott, Jeffrey, 166n34
Schultze, Charles L., 51, 107, 111n45, 211, 212, 319
Schwartz, Anna, 269, 285n45
Schwengel, Fred, 111n41
Second Bank of the United States, 115–116
Secretary of the treasury, 55–57
Seger, Martha R., 64
Seidman, L. William, 67, 68
Shultz, George P., 60, 66, 158, 184, 206–207, 219n24n25, 321
Shuman, Howard E., 83, 109n8n13n14, 304n17
Silk, Leonard, 166n30
Simon, Paul, 298, 304n19
Simon, William E., 56, 321
Slichter, Sumner, 30
Sloan, John W., 54, 74n19, 219n10, 257–258, 260, 283n4, 284n12n19n20n25
Smith, Adam, 21, 25

334

Smith, Alfred E., 19
Smith, Tom W., 229, 248n23
Smithies, A., 75n25
Smoot-Hawley Act of 1930, 146
Socialism, 11, 225
Solow, Robert M., 76n47, 218n5, 281
Sorensen, Theodore C., 181, 195n15
Spero, Joan Edelman, 165n14n16n18
Spielman, Carol, 248n8
Spitzer, Robert J., 106, 111n44
Sprinkel, Beryl, 54
Stagflation, 38, 188
Stagnation theory, 170, 172
Steiner, Peter O., 218n5
Stewart, Joseph, Jr., 76n49
Stein, Herbert, 158, 195n16, 207,
    209, 219n26, 266, 272, 274,
    284n18n26, 285n38n49n55n56,
    319
Stenholm, Charles, 298
Stigler, George, 249n47
Stiglitz, Joseph E., 305n32n33
Stimson, James A., 237, 250n52
Stockman, David, 60, 96, 291, 323
Stokes, Bruce, 165n12, 166n22n32
Structural deficit, 289
Structural unemployment, 7
Stubblebine, W. Craig, 110n27,
    286n55
Studenski, Paul, 136n5
Sununu, John, 279
Supply-side economics, 25
  as influence on Ronald Reagan,
    188, 198, 273–275
Suszkiw, Dana, 251n71
Sutton, Francis X., 247n6
Swartz, Thomas, 40n8
Synar, Mike, 295

T

Taft, Robert, 256
Taft, William Howard, 80
Tariffs, 146–147
Tatalovich, Raymond, 73n7
Taylor, Zona, 76n49

Thurow, Lester, 16n5
Tobin, James, 40n7, 76n47, 247n6,
    261, 281
Trade Act of 1934, 152
Trade deficit, 142
  current trends in exports-imports,
    141–144
Trade policy, 146–148, 160–163
Trade surplus, 142
Train v. City of New York, 105
Troika, as economic advisory system,
    50, 68, 70
Trough, of business cycle, 27, 170,
    173–174
Truman, Harry, 15, 53, 54, 59, 61, 62,
    82, 128, 139, 181, 258, 310
  economic performance under, 174–
    177
Tufte, Edward, 16n2, 138n36, 236,
    242–243, 249n46, 251n66
Tugwell, Rexford G., 30, 41n18
Tyson, Laura D'Andrea, 55, 160

U

Uchitelle, Louis, 286n67
Uncontrollable expenditures, 101, 182
Unemployment rate, 6
United States Trade Representative
    (USTR), 152
United States v. Butler, 29

V

Volcker, Paul A., 62, 127, 131–132,
    134, 157–158, 205, 207, 277,
    313, 324

W

Wage-price controls, 187, 200–201,
    205
  under Nixon, 208–211
Wagner, Richard, 231, 249n31
Wakefield, Joseph C., 95, 304n4
Wallace, George C., 183, 205
Walrus, Leon, 25
Wanniski, Jude, 274, 276

Warburton, Clark, 268–269, 285n43
Washington, George, 55, 78, 114
Watkins, Alfred, 17n14
Ways and Means Committee, of
    House of Representatives, 78, 79,
    80, 86
Weatherford, M. Stephen, 250n51
Weaver, Warren J., 110n28
Webb, Sidney and Beatrice, 41n19
Weidenbaum, Murray, 51, 54, 205,
    207
Weinberger, Casper, 60, 323
Weintraub, Robert E., 130, 134,
    137n31, 138n39n40
Wildavsky, Aaron, 77, 82, 108n1,
    109n5n10, 110n21n22

Willet, Thomas D., 110n27, 286n55
Wilson, Woodrow, 80–81
Wolfe, Barbara, 110n23
Woolley, John, 63, 75n32n33n34n35,
    76n37, 128, 134, 137n14n27,
    138n41, 251n68
World Bank, 140, 149
Wright, Jim, 132

Y

Yantek, Thom, 250n55

Z

Zaller, John, 225, 248n13n14

THE MODERN PRESIDENCY AND ECONOMIC POLICY
Edited by Norm Mysliwiec
Production supervision by Kim Vander Steen
Designed by Lesiak/Crampton Design, Chicago, Illinois
Composition by Impressions, Madison, Wisconsin
Paper, Champion Pinehurst
Printed and bound by McNaughton & Gunn, Inc., Saline, Michigan